The Bible in Middle English Literature

Noli me tangere

The Bible
in Middle English
Literature

By DAVID C. FOWLER

UNIVERSITY OF WASHINGTON PRESS

Seattle and London

This book was published with the assistance of a grant from the National Endowment for the Humanities.

Library of Congress Cataloging in Publication Data

Fowler, David C., 1921–
  The Bible in Middle English literature.

  Bibliography: p.
  Includes index.
    1. English literature—Middle English, 1100–1500—History and criticism.   2. Bible in literature.   3. Bible—Influence—History.   4. Christianity in literature.
  I. Title
  PR275.B5F68   1984   820'.9'001   84-7453
  ISBN 0-295-95438-8

To the memory of
Susan Covington Fowler
1887–1981

Contents

Illustrations

Illustrations are included by permission of the
Bodleian Library, Oxford

[ix]

Introduction

THIS is the second of two studies devoted to the influence of the Bible on early English literature. The first, *The Bible in Early English Literature*, appeared in 1976 and was concerned primarily with general background and major examples of biblical influence in the Old and Middle English periods. The present study deals exclusively with the later period: the first two chapters survey the substantial categories of drama and lyric, while the next three chapters examine in some detail specific poems by major fourteenth-century authors—Chaucer's *Parliament of Fowls*, works of the *Pearl* poet, and, deliberately in climactic position, *Piers the Plowman*, the most profound example of a work written in imitation of the Bible. In a sense, all the earlier studies could be regarded as preparation for an understanding of the poem that is the subject of the final chapter.

In the first two chapters of this volume I had the difficult task of compressing into relatively small space a large amount of material, while at the same time offering a few insights into the significance of this material as a reflection of biblical influences. Chapter One seeks to settle the dust of recent controversy over the origin and development of the medieval drama, to provide some examples of how the Bible was brought to life on the medieval stage, and to offer a possible explanation of the origin of the morality play in England. As the title of Chapter Two suggests, my effort here is to examine the shorter medieval lyrics as occasional poems and to show how many of them were evidently composed to memorialize a particular feast of the Church calendar.

The final three chapters focus on particular literary works, those which in my opinion are outstanding examples of poems composed in the biblical tradition. The works of Geoffrey Chaucer offer a wide range of possibilities, but in Chapter Three I chose the *Parliament of Fowls* for two reasons: first, the theory of its structure offered here seems to resolve many of the "difficulties" pointed out by scholars; second, that poem seems to me to be the most intriguing example of biblical influence in all of Chaucer's works. Chapter Four treats the works of the *Pearl* poet, excluding *Sir Gawain and the Green Knight* but including *Saint Erkenwald*. Here my aim is to convey something of the blend of humor and seriousness so characteristic of this poet, and indicate in what interesting and varied ways he makes use of his biblical materials. The *Pearl* poet is placed here in order to provide a stark contrast with *Piers the Plowman*, the subject of Chapter Five. Whereas the poet who wrote the *Pearl* expresses throughout his works a Christian serenity, untroubled (apparently) by the turbulence of his time, *Piers the Plowman* both had an impact on and was deeply affected by events of the decades during which it was being composed. The final chapter, approaching the poem in the context of history, has an emphasis quite different from that found in most current studies, for I seek to show the importance of the A text as an ideological influence on the leadership of the Peasants' Revolt of 1381, and the significance of eschatology in the later versions of the poem (especially the B text). My hope is that future studies of *Piers* will increasingly take history into account and likewise consider the versions of the poem separately. The late G. Ernest Wright, speaking of the Bible, once referred (in conversation) to the scholar's responsibility to "walk from the biblical text out into history." This dictum applies with great force to the study of *Piers the Plowman*, a poem written in a time of riots, burnings, and assassinations. Until we learn to walk from this text out into history, we run the risk of missing the important message that this profound and troubling poem offers to twentieth-century readers.

To the acknowledgments recorded in the Introduction of the first volume, in particular to Robert B. Heilman and D. W. Robertson, let me here add my gratitude to colleagues of more recent acquaintance who have in one way or another advanced my understanding of matters discussed in these volumes: Robert Adams (eschatology), John Coldewey (drama), Richard K. Emmerson (the tradition of Antichrist), and Míceál Vaughan (drama and the liturgy). Other more explicit acknowledgments are intended by the references in the bibliographical essay at the end of the book.

I am indebted in a very practical way to the Guggenheim Foundation for financial support during my studies abroad; to the many kindnesses of officials of the Bodleian, the English Faculty Library, St. Cross, and other libraries and colleges of Oxford too numerous to mention in that hospitable town; and to my own University of Washington for many services over the years and for sabbatical leave to do the research and writing necessary to complete both of these volumes.

The Bible in Middle English Literature

CHAPTER ONE

Medieval Drama

THE anonymous authors of the late medieval English cycle plays had a remarkable ambition, namely to present on stage the entire history of the world from Creation to Doomsday. Although these dramas sometimes took several days to perform, they became very popular and were an effective means of presenting the Bible as a living book to large and impressionable audiences in Britain in the fourteenth, fifteenth, and sixteenth centuries. No doubt the texts of many of these plays have perished, but five major cycles survive, four written in English and one in the Cornish language.

Beginning with the encyclopedic work of E. K. Chambers on the medieval stage in 1903, scholars have studied the early drama intensively. But in the past quarter century a surprising new development, stimulated by the Festival of Britain and the coronation of Elizabeth II, has been the revival of the medieval drama in modern productions, particularly in such places as York, Chester, and Cornwall. These productions stimulated a new interest in the techniques of the medieval stage, and they have proved that the drama of the Middle Ages makes effective theater today.

Biblical Drama in Cornwall

In the summer of 1969 I was fortunate enough to see a performance of the Cornish *Ordinalia* in Piran Round near Perranporth, Cornwall, presented by students of the Drama Department of

Bristol University. The Cornish drama is less well known than the English, but it is deserving of our attention, and will be used here (in translation) as a general example of the medieval drama in England before we turn our attention to particular English plays.

The drama in Cornwall seems to have originated as a project undertaken by clerics in the collegiate church of Glasney in Penryn about the middle of the fourteenth century. Of the history of its production we know nothing, but the text itself, surviving in a manuscript of the early fifteenth century, allows us to make a few deductions. The action is divided into segments designed for performance on three successive days. On the first day we have the *Origo Mundi* or the Beginning of the World, which extends from the Creation through the reign of Solomon. At the conclusion of this play Solomon addresses the audience:

> The fullness of God's blessing be upon you, men and women both. The play is ended, but, in order to see the Passion which Christ suffered for us, return tomorrow in good time. And now let us all go home. Play, good musicians, in honor of the Father on high.

The second day's performance, *Passio Christi*, is much more compressed than the usual dramatizations of Christ's life. For instance, it omits the birth in Bethlehem and begins strikingly with the temptation in the desert. At the end of the *Passio*, Nicodemus helps Joseph of Arimathea with the burial of Christ's body, and then speaks the final lines to the audience:

> I ever pray that the blessing of Jesus will descend upon you and remain with you, always. Depart for your homes; the play is ended. But I ask that you return early tomorrow that you may see how Christ rose, radiant and gentle, from the grave.

The *Resurrexio Domini* starts with the arrest of Joseph and Nicodemus, proceeds through the major events leading to the Resurrection, including the Harrowing of Hell and (uniquely in the cycles) the legendary death of Pilate, and ends with Christ's Ascension into heaven. At this point the Emperor Tiberius (whose presence was required in the death of Pilate sequence) steps out of character and speaks the concluding lines:

> Good people, you have witnessed the true circumstances of Christ's resurrection: how he broke the gates of hell, leading into bliss Adam and Eve and all those who did the Father's will. Very great, surely, was the love he bore mankind.

[4]

And Jesus ascended to heaven's joy. May he ever preserve you from the Devil and his train, and may the Lord's blessing descend upon each of you present here today and go with you as you turn your steps toward home.

Now, musicians, strike up a brisk tune that we may dance.

Evidence that the Cornish plays were originally performed at Penryn (near Falmouth) can be found in the amusing, anachronistic (and dramatically effective) use of local place names by the playwright. Thus when Solomon is informed that the walls of the Temple are complete, he praises the craftsmen and adds, ". . . as a reward for your fine work, I am giving you the parish of Budock, plus Seal Rock with all its land," to which one of the masons replies: "Ah, such generosity! Many thanks, many thanks! We can really make merry over a gift like that. Now we see, comrades, that there are no true master craftsmen in this kingdom, except us masons." Of course it is absurd to imagine Solomon turning over an entire local parish as a reward to the workers, however diligent; and, on the other hand, the gift of Seal Rock, a barren, dangerous rock in the mouth of Falmouth harbor, is of no value whatsoever. A local audience would not need to have all this explained, and would immensely enjoy the ironic exclamation of the mason: "Ah, such generosity!" Indeed, Solomon ends by giving away practically all the lands surrounding Glasney College: "I give you forthwith the following: the entire field of Bohelland and all of Penryn wood, plus the whole of Gwarder, Enys, and Arwennack, Tregenver and Kergilliack."

With this telescoping of time and place the exotic king of ancient Israel finds a local habitation in the remote territory of Cornwall, which John de Grandisson, bishop of Exeter (1327–69), had described on his arrival as "the very end of the ends" of the earth. "My Diocese," he wrote, "which embraces Devon and Cornwall, is separated from all the rest of England, and except on one side only, surrounded by seas so tempestuous that they can scarcely be called navigable. The people of Cornwall speak in a tongue which is unknown to the English, and only known to Bretons."

In view of the isolation of Cornwall, it is remarkable that this remote region produced the earliest (ca. 1350–75) and one of the best constructed of the cyclical plays composed in Britain. In part this may be due to the likelihood (from its appearance) that the entire Cornish text is the work of a single author, and therefore reflects a unified conception lacking in the English plays, which

[5]

seem to be of composite authorship and often revised and re-
worked. In any case, it is worth pointing out, since we are using
a translation, that the original text of the Cornish *Ordinalia* shows
great concern for the use of varied stanza forms appropriate to
the speakers. Thus Christ, in the *Passio Christi*, delivers an opening speech of great dignity and stanzaic complexity (*PC* 1–9):

> IHC: thyvgh lauara · ow dyskyblyon
> pyseygh toythda · ol kes-colon
> dev dreys pup tra · evs a huhon
> theygh yn bys-ma · y grath danvon
> yn dyweth may feugh sylwys
> gans an eleth yw golow
> yn nef agas enefow
> neffre a tryg hep ponow
> yn ioy na vyth dywythys

> JESUS: To you, I say, · my disciples,
> Pray forthwith, · all with one heart,
> To God above all things, · who is on high,
> To you in this world · to send his grace,
> In the end that you be saved.
> With the angels who are bright
> In heaven your souls
> Ever shall dwell without troubles,
> In joy that shall not be ended.

Notice that the first four lines of the original actually function
as eight short ones of four syllables each, rhyming alternately,
followed by five lines of seven syllables each to make up a nine-
line unit rhyming *abababc dddc*: Christ's opening speech (of thirty-
four lines) continues with a repeat of the first stanza pattern in
lines 10–18. The form is then modified by the removal of one line
from the closing quatrain, thus producing the pattern *abababbc
ddc*, which occurs twice (lines 19–26, 27–34). Peter and Andrew then
respond to Jesus in a much simpler stanza (*abababab*), and Jesus
replies in that form.

Like the other Celtic peoples (Irish, Scottish, Manx, Welsh, and
Breton), the Cornish resisted foreign domination with considerable tenacity and staying power, but even at this early date the
Cornish language was in an embattled position, pressured from
above by Norman-French conquerors and from below by English
settlers. Both French and English words and phrases are scattered
throughout the text, but English of course occurs much more frequently, and is sometimes employed for dramatic purposes.

[6]

Thus God throughout speaks a relatively pure form of Middle Cornish, and in the *Origo Mundi*, in fact, it is not until we reach the temptation that we find a major break in the style. Significantly, perhaps, it is the Devil who uses the first English phrases, in attempting to persuade Eve to taste the apple (*OM* 197–200):

> torr'e yn ow feryl vy
>> heb hokye *fast have ydo*
> hag inweth gvra the'th worty
>> may tebro ef annotho.

> Pluck it at my risk,
>> Without delay *quickly have done*:
> And also make thy husband
>> Eat of it.

French is sometimes used to express the pomp and self-importance of some of the characters; while both French and English are skillfully employed for comic purposes, as in the bilingual asides assigned to Caiaphas's messenger (*PC* 335–40). The plays are indeed quite sophisticated in their use of language, both for stage business and for social satire.

Unlike most of the English plays, the Cornish text includes three diagrams designed to show the deployment of the cast of characters, and rather extensive stage directions which show that this drama was performed in a medieval theater-in-the-round. The circular stage was known as the "place," Latin *platea*, and situated along its perimeter were the scaffolds of the main characters in each of the three plays. Thus the diagram for *Origo Mundi* lists (clockwise) *celum* (heaven), *episcopus* (the bishop consecrated by Solomon), *Abraham, Rex Salamon, Rex David, Rex Pharao, infernum* (Hell-mouth), and *tortores* (the torturers for the martyrdom of Maximilla near the end of the play).

It is by no means certain that the "rounds" that survive in Cornwall were built specifically for drama. What is more likely is that the round was a much older structure adapted by the Cornish inhabitants in the fourteenth century for use as a *plen an gwary*, "playing place." The evidence of place names suggests that in medieval Cornwall there were playing places at St. Ives, Ruan Major, Ruan Minor, Landewednack, Newlyn East, St. Columba Major, Redruth, St. Hilary, Sancreed, Sithney, Kea, and Camborne; and recent archaeological excavations show that a round may have been adapted for dramatic use in the second half of the

[7]

fourteenth century at Castilly near Bodmin. Portions of a round survive at St. Just in Penwith (extreme west Cornwall), but the finest example is St. Piran's round near Perranporth, where the Cornish *Ordinalia* was performed in 1969.

The staging of the *Ordinalia* by the students from Bristol in St. Piran's round was quite effective and, in my judgment, authentic in its use of medieval theatrical techniques. An ark was built before the eyes of the spectators, and shaggy, mewing devils emerged dramatically from the smoking mouth of Hell to carry off their victims. During the week the drama was spread over three successive days (as originally intended), but on Sunday the energetic cast presented the entire *Ordinalia*, the uncut text of which has more than ten thousand lines.

Since our survey will allow only a glimpse here and there of the vivid scenes that make up this drama, we shall pay particular attention to episodes not found in the English plays discussed later in this chapter. One such incident, for example, is the dramatization of Adam's naming of the animals (Gen. 2:19–20), a curious detail dramatized in no other Creation play to my knowledge. God the Father speaks:

> Direct your attention, now, Adam, to the birds of heaven, to the animals both on land and in the sea, and to the fishes; give them their names. They will come at your command, but do not ever misuse them.
>
> ADAM: I name cow and bull, I name horse, beast without equal as a help to men; also goat, hind, stag, sheep. In brief, let each kind take its right name.
> Now I name goose and hen, which I consider peerless food-birds; duck, peacock, dove, partridge, swan, kite, crow, and eagle I name in addition.
> I will likewise give names to the fishes: salmon, porpoise, conger, ling, cod, all shall obey me. And if I worship God perfectly, not a one shall escape from before me.

There are no stage directions here, but one wonders whether this speech was accompanied by a procession of animals, real or fabricated. Adam's closing remark reminds us that fishing was an important occupation in Cornwall, but otherwise this list seems without a local emphasis. The opening reference to cow, bull, and horse is curiously apt, in that these three animals are sometimes seen peering from behind the opening initial of Genesis in medieval illuminated Bibles, but I have never been able to find a reason for the choice of these particular beasts for that purpose. In *Piers the Plowman*, which we will be considering in a later chapter, the Dreamer sees a vision of the Creation (B XI 312ff.), and, in the course of describing it, he names the animals beginning also with cow, bull, horse, and continuing with the birds, identified by their nesting and mating habits. This touches on an interesting expansion of the Creation story to which we shall return later in considering Chaucer's poem, the *Parliament of Fowls*.

After the Fall and expulsion from Paradise, Adam is shown making his first attempt to till the ground (Gen. 3:23). When he takes his spade and begins to dig, according to the Latin stage direction, "the earth cries out; and again he shall dig, and the earth cries out." Startled, Adam appeals to God for assistance, bargaining with him (as Abraham later does for different reasons in Gen. 18:23–33) until the Lord generously allows Adam to use as much of the world as he desires, cautioning him to set aside one tenth of all he produces as an acknowledgment of God's gift. This interesting scene, not found in the Bible, looks back to a golden age when "the earth was not yet *wounded* by the plow," and forward to the story of Cain and Abel which follows, and which in the drama turns on the issue of Cain's failure to offer a full and ungrudging tithe to God as Abel does.

When Cain makes his offering, God refuses it (we are not told how this is shown on stage), whereas he makes a point of accepting Abel's by calling it a "true tithe," and promising that Abel "shall have at the last the joy that never fails and in my kingdom, rest." In a fit of jealousy Cain then kills Abel, whereupon the devils issue forth gleefully from Hell's smoking mouth and carry the body of Abel into Hell.

In medieval tradition we find that malevolent creatures like Grendel in *Beowulf* were classified as the offspring of Cain. This led to some awkwardness, since the death of Abel meant that he could not be thought of as the corresponding ancestor of the people of God. This problem was solved by the selection of Seth, a younger son of Adam and Eve, as the ancestral representative of the chosen people. Seth was thus used in biblical legend as a replacement for Abel.

Alone among the cycle plays in England, the Cornish drama makes important use of the legend of Seth in a form somewhat different from that found in *Cursor Mundi*, discussed in *The Bible in Early English Literature*. Weary of his life, Adam directs his son

[9]

Seth to Paradise to learn whether God will ever send him the oil
of mercy which he promised. The angel guarding the gate does
not allow Seth to enter, but lets him peer inside. There he sees
a dead tree, in which there is coiled a serpent, with roots extending down to hell and branches up to heaven. At the top he
sees a child wrapped in swaddling clothes. This child, says the
angel, is the oil of mercy promised to Adam, through whom all
the world shall be saved. Seth returns with this comforting message to Adam, bringing with him three seeds from the apple used
in the temptation. Following the angel's instructions, when Adam
dies Seth plants these seeds under Adam's tongue. The devils
carry Adam's soul to hell.

The three seeds meanwhile grow into three shining rods, and
Moses takes them with him when Israel escapes from Egypt. Those
bitten by poisonous serpents in the desert are miraculously healed
when they kiss the rods. Before he dies, Moses plants them on
Mount Tabor, where they are later found by David and brought
to Jerusalem. The blind, the lame, and the deaf are healed by
them (Matt. 11:5), and when they are replanted, overnight they
take root, and the three stems join together into a single tree (the
Trinity). This tree is encircled with a silver band, and under it
David composes the Psalter in penance for his affair with Bath-
sheba. When Solomon orders the building of the Temple, the car-
penters cut down this sacred tree, but find that its length keeps
changing, so that it cannot be used. Impressed by the miraculous
wood, the king orders it placed with full honors in the Temple
as an object of public veneration. While services are in progress,
a girl named Maximilla sits on the wood and is burned by it.
Shocked into a prophetic state, she miraculously speaks the name
of Christ. For this heresy she is tortured to death, and the tree
is thrown in the pool of Bethsaida (A.V. Bethesda, John 5:2). When
word of miraculous cures begins to circulate, Solomon's "bishop"
orders the wood placed as a bridge over the river Cedron. No
more use is made of the wood in the drama until after the trial
of Christ, when Pilate gives orders for the Crucifixion. The torturers remember hearing of some timber lying at Cedron under
a curse and decide to let it serve for the cross of Christ.

The legend of Seth is thus employed in the Cornish drama as
a means of linking people and events of the Old Testament (Adam,
Seth, Moses, David, Solomon) with the coming Redemption, which
is itself prefigured vividly in Seth's description of the tree of Par-

adise. This is good theater. The audience is given, as it were, a physical object, the tree, distinctively marked with its silver band, to follow with their eyes as it is handed down by patriarch, prophet, and king, until it is taken up and used for the cross. The wood thus functions as an effective replacement for the messianic prophecies spoken by biblical figures in plays such as the Towneley *Processus Prophetarum*, in which Moses, David, the Sibyl, and Daniel rehearse in turn their predictions of the coming Redemption.

One other distinctive feature in the Crucifixion is the episode of the forging of nails for the cross, which is popular in legends of the Passion, but finds no place in the drama of Britain, so far as I know, except in the Cornish *Passio*. One of the torturers goes to Market Jew (either a street in Penryn or modern Marazion near Penzance) to have the nails forged. The smith evades the job by claiming that his hands are sore, but his wife scornfully takes his place and engages in sexual repartee with the torturer, who helps her by operating the bellows. The two of them exchange curses and insults until the nails are forged with a roughness designed to make crucifixion even more painful.

When I first read this episode, before having seen the play performed, I felt that the dramatist had blundered—that this scene interrupted the somber march of events leading to the Crucifixion. But I must confess that it did not have that effect in the Bristol production. It rather seemed to underscore the darkness of human iniquity which lay behind the story and had necessitated the Redemption itself. And since the circular *platea* of the medieval stage allows several incidents to take place simultaneously, the episode of the nails did not in fact interrupt the ongoing preparations of the other characters in the Calvary area, and the two actions blended into a single scene of harsh tragedy. The Crucifixion had, in fact, a greater impact than any other segment of the entire 1969 production.

Yet the third day's play, the *Resurrexio*, had its memorable moments. The events of this play are of particular interest, for once again apocryphal and biblical materials are curiously mingled in a way that may seem strange to the modern reader. The Resurrection of course adheres closely to the biblical narrative, but it is preceded by the apocryphal imprisonment of Joseph of Arimathea and Nicodemus, together with the Harrowing of Hell, and is followed by the apocryphal story of the death of Pilate, which was well established as a part of biblical tradition in *The Golden Legend*. The Ascension itself, with which the play ends, can be called biblical, but only in a special sense.

The imprisonment of Joseph and Nicodemus is skillfully used by the Cornish dramatist for comic purposes at the expense of Pilate. When the jailor has locked up the two men, he comes to Pilate and says, "Without ceremony, my lord magistrate, take personal possession of all nine keys of your jail, that there may be no fear of trickery." Pilate accepts the keys, and rewards the jailor with the customary Cornish lands and manors in the vicinity of Penryn. Then, following the Harrowing of Hell, the angel Gabriel descends to earth and sets free the prisoners without breach of wall or unlocking of doors (Isa. 61:1; Luke 4:18; Acts 5:18–23). Meanwhile the soldiers appointed to guard the tomb have slept through the Resurrection and must report to Pilate that Jesus has escaped. Pilate's initial reaction is sharp: "Shame on you, paper soldiers! What is this gossip and rumor I hear to be going the rounds in the province? If he really has been stolen from the grave, I swear by Mohammed you four will die!"

As Pilate's anger grows, one of the soldiers challenges him: "You show us Nicodemus and Joseph of Arimathea, and we'll show you the body you put in the tomb, namely, that of Jesus, son of Mary." Still in a rage, Pilate sends for the jailor and orders him to open the cell and bring out the prisoners, Joseph and Nicodemus. The jailor reminds Pilate that he has the keys himself, and, seeing his temper, persuades him to come personally and open the nine locked doors. Discovering the prisoners gone, Pilate fumes and threatens, warning all and sundry that if the prisoners are not found, "You people will need to do a lot of praying." The jailor's servant then timidly says: "Oh, sir, don't blame us. Didn't you have all the keys and aren't the doors still in one piece?"

This simple truth suddenly takes all the wind out of Pilate's sails, and he covers his confusion with sweet reasonableness: "You speak the truth, my word on it. This is surely a miracle, for the doors are perfectly intact and the walls as well. Soldiers, I find you blameless, holding that to punish you would be itself a crime." The storm is past, and Pilate persuades his men to say nothing about these miraculous occurrences by making them a present of Penryn and Helston. This is but one of several excellent scenes in the Cornish *Ordinalia* where apocryphal additions to the bibli-

cal narrative are used to depict the amusing frustration of the
pagan establishment confronted with the march of divinely ordained historical events. Men like Pilate are evil, but in the light
of eternity, evil is finally comic.

The Cornish cycle concludes with the Ascension of Christ to
heaven, an incident treated briefly in the Bible (Acts 1:9–11), but
one which was very important in the services of the medieval
church. This fact is reflected in the drama. Christ bids farewell to
his disciples and the ascension proper begins. In the 1969 production this scene was beautifully staged, with angels in white descending to meet the scarlet-robed figure of Christ ascending the
stairs to the scaffold of heaven where God stood waiting to receive his Son. During this majestic procession, a dialogue takes
place between Jesus and the angels, which I quote only in part
(approximating the verse form):

> THIRD ANGEL: Who is he that hath come from the earth,
>   Red as blood, head and shoulders,
>   Legs and feet?
> I am astonished at the one of human kind!
> So swiftly as he hath come here,
>   An angel doth never approach.
>
> FOURTH ANGEL: He from Edom hath come;
>   To a thousand devils if he caused not grief,
>   A wonder is to me;
> For I swear that this is
> That same Son who went hence;
>   He is the King of Joy.
>
> FIFTH ANGEL: Who canst thou be,
>   When thy clothing is so red,
>   In the kingdom of Heaven?
> For I know certainly, one of human kind,
> Unless through the full Godhead,
>   Stands not here.
>
> JESUS: I am a King, who have done battle
>   To bring Adam and all his seed
>   From evil plight.
> The King I am of joy,
> And the victory was gained by me
>   In arms of red.
> . . . .
> Fitting it is that red should be
> My habergeon, which was turned
>   From dark to light,

[13]

All the length of my skin scourged,
So that deep in my flesh were pierced
Many thousand holes.

Nowhere to my knowledge is the Ascension more powerfully presented than here, although the language itself is quite traditional and can be found in similar form in the Chester cycle, the fourteenth-century *Stanzaic Life of Christ*, and *The Golden Legend*. All these texts reflect the liturgical use of an important passage in Isaiah (63:1–3):

Who is this that cometh from Edom, with dyed garments from Bozrah? This that is glorious in his apparel, travelling in the greatness of his strength? I that speak in righteousness, mighty to save. Wherefore art thou red in thine apparel, and thy garments like him that treadeth in the winefat? I have trodden the winepress alone. . . .

This is a good example of what treasures were made available to dramatists and poets through the figural interpretation of Scripture. In this instance, the Christological meaning of Isaiah 63:1–3 is used effectively to characterize the Ascension. On stage, the vividly contrasting white robes of the angels and red robe of Christ are not only spectacular, they bespeak the doctrinal meaning of the Ascension, as set forth in *The Golden Legend*:

A great dignity have we gotten when our nature is lift up unto the right side of the Father. . . . And of this S. Leo saith in a sermon of the Ascension: This day the nature of our humanity hath been borne above the height of all puissances unto where as God the Father sitteth. . . .

Christ descended to earth as God; he ascends to heaven as man, symbolized by the red robe of his Passion. This concept, stripped of its theological significance, is the cornerstone of modern humanism. But to medieval worshipers such a view would be incomplete. The drama ends with a simple but deeply meaningful exchange between the Son and the Father:

JESUS: Heavenly Father enthroned, now I am come to you from the world in the likeness of a mortal. With my heart's blood, I have redeemed mankind in order that none whom we created need be lost.

GOD THE FATHER: Welcome are you in heaven, my Son, twice welcome to me. Take your place at my right hand, you who have undergone surpassing toil and in victory have delivered the souls of men from the torment of perdition.

Origins: The Drama and the Liturgy

Medieval dramas like the Cornish *Ordinalia* did not appear suddenly and fully developed, but rather they emerged in this form as a result of influences from many sources. In the early Middle Ages there was no recognized stage tradition in western Europe, since the Church had denounced the late classical drama from the start as corrupt and degenerate. Ironically, the new drama was destined to be reborn in the very institution that had sought the ruin of the theater. The reason for this is to be found in the dramatic instinct embodied at a very early date in the liturgy of the Church.

The responsorial chants of matins were particularly suited to dramatic development, constituting a kind of lyrical meditation on the prescribed text for the day. As the name implies, these were two-part recitations, the first part being taken by the precentor or leader, and the second by the choir. In the opening words of the matins responsory for the first Sunday in Advent, for example, the precentor assumes the voice of Isaiah (see Isa. 33:17): "Gazing from afar, behold, I see the power of God coming and a cloud covering the whole earth. Go to meet Him and say: Tell us whether Thou art He Who is to reign among the people Israel." The choir repeats a portion of this opening, and then there follows a kind of incremental repetition and progression of key ideas and texts associated with Advent (and pulled together from widely separated books of the Bible) which almost becomes a dialogue between precentor and choir:

PRECENTOR: Thou Who rulest Israel, turn to us. Thou Who leadest Joseph like a sheep! Who sittest upon the Cherubim!

CHOIR: Tell us whether Thou art He Who is to reign among the people Israel.

PRECENTOR: Open your gates, O princes, and ye eternal portals, be lifted up, and He will enter.

CHOIR: Who is to reign among the people Israel.

It should be stressed that the text just quoted is a part of the liturgy, and there is no strict separation of voices, no impersonation in the dramatic sense. Yet the relation of these responsorial

[15]

chants to the Cornish Ascension drama, for example, is structurally very close indeed.

For the beginnings of true drama, however, we must turn to the Easter Introit trope of the tenth century, known as the *Quem Quaeritis* from its opening line:

> INTERROGATIO: Quem quaeritis in sepulchro,
>   O Christicolae?
>
> RESPONSIO: Jesum Nazarenum crucifixum,
>   O caelicolae.
>
> ANGELI: Non est hic; surrexit, sicut praedixerat.
>   Ite, nuntiate quia surrexit de sepulchro.
>
> QUESTION (*of the angels*): Whom seek ye in the sepulcher,
>   O followers of Christ?
>
> ANSWER (*of the Marys*): Jesus of Nazareth, which was crucified,
>   O celestial ones.
>
> THE ANGELS: He is not here; he is risen, just as he foretold.
>   Go, announce that he is risen from the sepulcher.

From this simple Easter dialogue came more complex dramatic impersonations which emerged finally in the full-blown Latin Resurrection plays of the twelfth century.

Meanwhile there were similar developments from the liturgy marking the other major feasts of the *temporale*, notably the Nativity. The play of the shepherds (*Pastores*) dramatized the biblical account from the Gospels (Luke 2:1–20), beginning with the song of the angels and ending with the visit to the manger. But when the shepherds enter the stable, two midwives question them: "Whom seek ye in the manger, O shepherds? Tell us." To which the shepherds reply: "The Savior, the Christ, the infant Lord," etc. Thus it is not difficult to see the influence of the Easter *Quem Quaeritis* in the shaping of the Christmas play. Other episodes followed, and by the end of the twelfth century vernacular dramas had begun to appear, notably the Anglo-Norman *Mystère d'Adam* and *La Seinte Resureccion* (ca. 1175).

Until recently, histories of the medieval drama have emphasized the evolutionary development of drama, beginning in the liturgy, expanded into Latin dramas, moved outside the church, translated into the vernacular, and taken over by the craft guilds who produced the great mystery cycles of the fourteenth and fifteenth centuries. This notion of evolution applied to the drama is, of course, a figure of speech, as our historians well understood, but on the level of popular exposition it leads easily to oversimplification, and perhaps also has had the effect of obscuring regional differences in the rise of the medieval drama. In any case, there has been a reaction against the use of the Darwinian metaphor, and the emphasis of today's students has been rightly placed on close study of the plays themselves and on methods of production.

But the pendulum should not be allowed to swing too far. There *is* a historical relationship between liturgical drama and the later mystery cycles, and the study of the one can lead to a better understanding of the other. Before turning to the vernacular plays themselves, therefore, we may approach them indirectly by examining a single feature of the Latin liturgical drama for Easter: the characterization of Mary Magdalene in the *Quem Quaeritis* and *Hortulanus* episodes of the Resurrection.

As we have seen, the *Quem Quaeritis* in its simplest form has the three Marys speak in unison and does not attempt to draw together all the texts from the Gospels relating to the Resurrection. But by the twelfth century this small beginning had been greatly expanded. Preceding it there was now the episode of the *Unguentarius*, the merchant who sells his spices and ointments to the three Marys, and who is deduced from Mark 16:1–2 and Luke 23:56, 24:1. Following the *Quem Quaeritis* were added the episodes of the *Hortulanus* (Gardener), which treats the appearance of Christ to Mary Magdalene (John 20:11–17), and the *Peregrinus* (Pilgrim), which presents the appearance of Christ to Cleophas and his companion on the road to Emmaus (Luke 24:13–35).

This conjunction of episodes led to an anomaly in the characterization of Mary Magdalene. The Gospels tell us that she was one of the Marys who visited the tomb, saw the angels, and reported the Resurrection to the disciples (Matt. 28:1–10; Mark 16:1–8; Luke 24:1–10). But other passages go further, specifying that she was the first to see the Lord (Mark 16:9–11 and John 20:1–18). Thus the Magdalene is constrained to rejoice with the other Marys in the *Quem Quaeritis*, only to return to her previous mood of sorrow at the beginning of the *Hortulanus* episode. As long as the liturgical character of these sequences was dominant, this was no problem, but as the dramatic aspect became stronger, the inconsistency in her characterization became more evident.

To illustrate how Mary Magdalene was treated at a particularly

[17]

interesting stage in the development of liturgical drama, I have chosen what Karl Young has called a "crude fragment" of a play from the abbey of Ripoll in Spain in the twelfth century. Although the text is something of a mixture, it has a visible narrative progression: *Unguentarius, Quem Quaeritis, Hortulanus,* and *Peregrinus.* Because of our special interest in Mary Magdalene, I quote only the *Quem Quaeritis* and *Hortulanus* sections, ending with her speech to the disciples.

ANGELUS: Quem queritis in sepulcro, Christicole?
MARIAE: Ihesum Nazarenum crucifixum, O celicole.
ANGELUS: Non est hic, surrexit sicut predixerat; ite, nunciate quia surrexit dicentes,
MARIAE: Alleluia, ad sepulcrum residens angelus nunciat resurrexisse Christum.
    Te Deum laudamus.

. . . .

[MARIA MAGDALENE]: Rex in acubitum iam se contulerat, et mea redolens nardus spirauerat; in hortum veneram in quem descenderat, at ille transiens iam declinauerat. Per noctem igitur hunc querens exeo; huc illuc transiens nusquam reperio.
ANGELI: Mulier, quid ploras? Quem queris?
MARIA: Occurrunt vigilis ardenti studio, Quos cum transierim, sponsum invenio.
ORTOLANUS: Mulier, quid ploras? Quem queris?
MARIA: Tulerunt Dominum meum, et nescio ubi posuerunt eum. Si tu sustulisti eum, dicito michi, et eum tollam.
ORTOLANUS: Maria, Maria, Maria!
MARIA: Raboni, Raboni, Raboni!

. . . .

MARIA REDIENS DICAT: Dic, impie Zabule, quid valet nunc fraus tua?
DISCIPULI: Dic nobis, Maria, quid vidisti in via?
MARIA: Sepulcrum Christi viventis, et gloriam vidi resurgentis: Angelicos testes, sudarium et vestes.

ANGEL: Whom seek ye in the sepulcher, O followers of Christ?
MARYS: Jesus of Nazareth who was crucified, O celestial ones.
ANGEL: He is not here, he is risen as he foretold; go, proclaim that he is risen saying,
MARYS: Alleluia, an angel seated in the sepulcher proclaims that Christ is risen.
    We Praise Thee O God [hymn].

. . . .

[MARY MAGDALENE]: The King had withdrawn himself to his couch and my nard had given forth its fragrance; in the garden I came, where he had gone down, but he had turned aside and gone. Through the night therefore I go seeking for him.
ANGELS: Woman, why weep you? Whom seek you?

[18]

MARY: The watchers run forth with ardent longing. When I have overtaken these, I shall find my bridegroom.
GARDENER: Woman, why weep you? Whom seek you?
MARY: They have taken away my lord, and I know not where they have laid him.
GARDENER: Mary, Mary, Mary!
MARY: Rabboni, Rabboni, Rabboni!
. . . .
MARY RETURNING SAYS [*to the disciples*]: Say, impious Zebulun, what good now is your treachery?
DISCIPLES: Tell us, Mary, what have you seen on the way?
MARY: I saw the sepulcher of the living Christ, and the glory of him risen; angelic witnesses, napkin and garments.

In the passage quoted we see the sudden transition from the *alleluia* of the three Marys to the lament of Mary Magdalene which opens the *Hortulanus* episode. It was this disjunction between the two segments that was to make trouble later on in the cycle plays. But I choose this particular text for purposes of illustration because, despite the difficulty, considerable attention has been given to the scene, and it has been elaborated in a most interesting way. Richard Axton has pointed out that the Magdalene's lyrical lament is adapted from the Song of Solomon. This would seem to reflect a time when dialogue was being expanded, yet only by the importation of appropriate biblical texts. Creation of new dialogue was not yet acceptable, but the use of the Song of Solomon here is quite skillful. Particularly impressive is the exploitation of chapter 5, verse 6: "I opened to my beloved, but my beloved had withdrawn himself, and was gone: my soul failed when he spake: I sought him, but I could not find him: I called him, but he gave me no answer." But when the Gardener speaks, Mary returns to her text (John 20:15), and the dialogue then leads to the recognition. The language of love from the Song of Solomon is usually given to the Virgin in accordance with biblical exegesis, but its use here for Mary Magdalene is very effective indeed.

Another abrupt transition comes when, after the Magdalene has recognized her Lord, she returns immediately to tell the disciples of his Resurrection. Her announcement has what may seem at first glance an unusual form: "Say, impious Zebulun, what good now is your treachery?" The context tells us that this is a joyful announcement of the Resurrection, but why it should take this form is not immediately evident. There is no "Zebulun" present to hear the remark addressed to him, nor does the historical tribe of Zebulun in ancient Israel seem to have been noted for impiety or treachery. In fact, "Zebulun and Naphtali were a people that jeoparded their lives unto the death" at the Battle of Megiddo in the days of the judges (Judg. 5:18). But since the Magdalene's words clearly have to do with the Resurrection, the key to unlocking their meaning should be hidden in one of the messianic prophecies, and indeed we find it when we turn to Isaiah's famous prediction (Isa. 9:2): "The people that walked in darkness, have seen a great light: they that dwell in the land of the shadow of death, upon them hath the light shined."

This is the text that inspired the story of the Harrowing of Hell in the Gospel of Nicodemus, and these are the words spoken by Isaiah himself in the apocryphal narrative when he is freed from limbo. But how should one know that Mary was alluding to this passage? The answer is evident in the verse preceding (Isa. 9:1): "Nevertheless the dimness shall not be such as was in her vexation; when at the first he lightly afflicted the land of Zebulun, and the land of Naphthali, and afterward did more grievously afflict her by the way of the Sea, beyond Jordan in Galilee of the nations."

Yet even here there is no evidence that Zebulun is treacherous in any sense, since the verse simply says that Zebulun and Naphthali were "afflicted" (*aggravata*). But if the Lord afflicts a people, there is usually a reason, and we find one very quickly by looking back a few more verses (Isa. 8:21): "And they shall pass through it, hardly bestead and hungry: and it shall come to pass, that when they shall be hungry, they shall fret themselves, and curse their King, and their God, and look upward."

It is evident that if the last verses of chapter 8 are applied to the first verse of chapter 9, then we are to understand that Zebulun's blasphemy in cursing God in his distress brought on the darkness in which he was forced to walk. But when Christ redeemed man by triumphing over death, even the perverse wickedness of a Zebulun could not hold back the light, or prevent the darkness from being dispelled. Hence the message that Mary Magdalene wished to convey with her enigmatically triumphant question: "Say, impious Zebulun, what good now is your treachery?" This was perhaps too learned a device to make good theater; but it shows us nevertheless that someone with a flair for the dramatic was at work reshaping the previously inflexible dialogue in the liturgical drama of the twelfth century.

[20]

The particular episode that we have been examining in the Latin play from Ripoll appears in all four of the English cycles. The Ludus Coventriae shows perhaps most clearly the surviving influence of the liturgical sequence of *Quem Quaeritis* and *Hortulanus*. In play number 36 the three Marys go to the tomb, discover it empty, and are told by the angel that Christ is risen and that they are to proclaim the resurrection. Each of the Marys in turn expresses her joy at this news, beginning with the Magdalene:

> Ah, mirth and joy in heart we have
> For now is risen out of his grave,
> He liveth now our life to save
> That dead lay in the clay.

They then tell Peter and the apostles the good tidings. This leads to the race between John and Peter to the sepulcher, after which they joyfully return and tell the others. At this point Mary Magdalene goes back to the tomb weeping, and says that her heart is breaking. Then follows the *Hortulanus* episode. There is nó explanation for her sudden change of mood from joy to sorrow.

The Chester play of the Resurrection (no. 18) uses the same materials, but with significant differences in detail. When the Marys hear the good tidings, they are excited, but the Magdalene, at least, still seems skeptical:

> Ah, hie we fast for anything,
> And tell Peter this tiding;
> A blissful word we may him bring,
> Sooth if that it were.

The doubtful sound of the last line provides a transition to positive distress in her report to the disciples:

> Ah, Peter and John, alas, alas!
> There is befallen a wondrous case;
> Some man my Lord stolen has,
> And put him I wot not where.

Peter and John race to the tomb as expected, but soon leave the stage to Mary Magdalene, who is still mourning the loss of her Lord's body. The *Hortulanus* episode then follows naturally and is thus well motivated.

The corresponding episode in the Towneley (Wakefield) cycle occurs in the Resurrection play (no. 26), but events are deployed differently. When the Marys are told the good news by the angels, Mary Magdalene urges her companions to tell the others that Christ is risen, and though it is evident from her words that she understands him to have been resurrected, she remains behind mourning nevertheless. At this point her story is interrupted by an episode showing the consternation of the soldiers and Pilate over the disappearance of the body from the tomb, after which the scene in the garden takes place, turning Mary's sorrow to joy: "I am as light as leaf on tree."

The York and Towneley cycles are closely related, and a general comparison of the two suggests that Towneley (the plays performed in Wakefield) was indebted to York for most of its texts, as might be expected, since drama developed in York much earlier than in Wakefield. But in the particular matter we are pursuing, it is interesting to observe that York shows a better characterization of the Magdalene, while Towneley retains the abrupt transition from joy to sadness. I first quote her speech from the Towneley text:

> My sisters free, since it is so,
> That he is risen the death thus fro [from],
> As said to us these angels two,
>   Our Lord and leech [physician],
> As ye have heard where that ye go
>   Loke that ye preach.

Here is the corresponding stanza from York:

> My sisters dear, since it is so,
> That he is risen death thus fro,
> As the angel told me and you too—
>   Our Lord so free—
> Hence will I never go
>   Ere I him see.

It seems unlikely that the superior York version would have been taken over in the Towneley text and revised backward, so to speak, to resemble the earlier liturgical plays. Perhaps the truth is that the York play originally had what we find in the Towneley stanza, but then later, after the borrowing had occurred, the York reviser made the improvement in the characterization of Mary Magdalene that we see in the surviving York text.

From this single episode we have found unmistakable evidence that the vernacular cycle plays in England were in some sense

[22]

influenced or affected by the Latin liturgical drama of an earlier period. But what was the nature of this relationship? The response to that question, once made confidently in evolutionary terms, is currently being debated by students of the drama, and no clear answer has yet emerged. Hence the following sketch of the emergence of the cycle plays must be regarded as to some extent tentative.

The Rise of Vernacular Drama

We may surmise that the drama could easily have spread from Easter and Christmas to other days and events memorialized in the Church calendar. And to some extent this did occur. Not only do we find a great variety of biblical plays, but there also emerged some based on the lives of saints. Nicholas was very popular, along with Mary Magdalene, whose life story is augmented with additional details from *The Golden Legend*. Probably the lives of many local saints were dramatized, but very few of these escaped the iconoclasm of the Reformation in England. The best surviving example is "The Life of Saint Meriasek" (*Beunans Meriasek*), a Cornish play depicting the life of a patron saint of Camborne. Ironically, this text may have escaped destruction simply because the English censors could not read it. In any case, these saints plays often reflected a local interest and could not command attention on the scale of the biblical drama of the *temporale*, which we are considering here.

What provided the original impulse for the growth of the great cycles, such as those of York and Chester? One theory is that it was the feast of Corpus Christi, which was added to the Church calendar about the end of the thirteenth century. This feast was proclaimed by Pope Urban IV in 1264, but it was not actually instituted until 1311, and became established in the English church about 1318.

The purpose of Corpus Christi was to celebrate the salvation that comes to the Church through the greatest of its sacraments—the bread and wine of the Eucharist. There was, of course, a commemoration of the Last Supper on Maundy Thursday of Holy Week, but the pope felt that a more joyous time for the celebration of God's gift to man of Himself was needed, hence he set aside the Thursday following Trinity Sunday for Corpus Christi, a movable feast that could fall anywhere between May 23 and June 24, depending on the date of Easter.

An important force behind the establishment of this feast was the doctrine of transubstantiation, promulgated in 1215, affirming that Christ was literally present in the bread and wine of Communion when it was blessed by the priest. The popularity of this teaching was immediate and widespread. Its influence in literature was everywhere apparent, to the end of the Middle Ages, explicitly in dramas such as the "Croxton Play of the Sacrament," and implicitly in earlier literature of greater sophistication. Even Arthurian romance, which was mainly secular in its orientation, shows traces of the doctrine. Thus in Malory's version of the grail quest Lancelot is given a glimpse of the grail being used in the service of the Mass:

> Then looked he up into the midst of the chamber and saw a table of silver, and the holy vessel covered with red samite, and many angels about it, whereof one held a candle of wax burning, and the other held a cross and the ornaments of an altar. And before the holy vessel he saw a good man clothed as a priest, and it seemed that he was at the consecration of the mass. And it seemed to Sir Lancelot that above the priest's hands were three men, whereof the two put the youngest by likeness between the priest's hands; and so he lifted him up right high, and it seemed to show so to all the people.

Lancelot's vision of the body of Christ in the hands of the priest illustrates the visionary intensity stimulated by the doctrine. Also it may be recalled that one of the two chapels in Fairford Church is dedicated to Corpus Christi; indeed the central window of that chapel depicts a transfiguration scene somewhat reminiscent of the vision of Lancelot in Malory.

With the added momentum of the doctrine of transubstantiation, the feast of Corpus Christi seems to have been celebrated from the beginning with a good deal of public pageantry, notably a procession in which the Sacrament was carried through the streets of the town or village and thence to the church for services in honor of the occasion. Our particular interest in Corpus Christi stems from the fact that at some point the cycle plays became associated with this feast. Some even argue that the plays were first created to be one feature of the procession. According to this theory the drama soon outgrew the procession of which it was a part, and had to be shifted to another date. The trouble with this is that it is very difficult to learn from civic documents whether the "pageants" referred to are stages on wheels for a processional performance of plays, or merely what we would call a "float" in a Corpus Christi "parade" (*tableau vivant*). One scholar has recently argued that fourteenth-century Corpus Christi processions were almost exclusively nondramatic, and that the plays did not enter into the celebrations until the fifteenth century. Whatever the truth of the matter, it is worth noting that what I have been calling a "cycle play" was known in medieval times as "the play called Corpus Christi," and in a stimulating book by that title, V. A. Kolve argues for the intimate association of these plays with the feast.

An alternative to the theory of Corpus Christi origin is persuasively presented by Rosemary Woolf in her book, *The English Mystery Plays* (1972). She emphasizes the instructional purpose of the plays, and points to the fact that Septuagesima marked the beginning of a traditional Lenten period of instruction of catechumens in the Church which reached its climax at Easter, and that the plays may have originally been used in this period for educational purposes before being transferred to another time. Only after the drama had been regularly performed on Corpus Christi did the name of that feast attach itself to the plays, and (unlike Kolve) Woolf sees no other evidence pointing to the feast as a source of inspiration for the drama.

In view of the conflicting theories of eminent scholars, it is not easy to paint a clear picture of the rise of the cycle plays, but let me try a different tack. When do we know that vernacular plays were first being produced in Britain? A doubtful case can be made for the Anglo-Norman *Adam* (ca. 1160), but this may have been a continental play. Very likely the earliest major productions (to judge from surviving texts) were from the mid-fourteenth century, such as the Cornish *Ordinalia* and a fragmentary English morality play, *The Pride of Life*. Allusions to popular religious plays at York and Beverley begin about 1375, and thereafter the evidence begins to mount. The biblical drama seems to be reflected in *Piers the Plowman* (as we shall see), and Chaucer says that Absolom in "The Miller's Tale" played "Herod on a scaffold high." We may take it as established, therefore, that a variety of plays were being performed in Britain from at least as early as 1350. The Cornish drama was cyclical (though apparently not attached to Corpus Christi and not produced by the guilds), but other early plays may well have been single productions like *The Pride of Life*.

The final question we face is this: what served as the magnet to draw together the scattered biblical episodes of the Church calendar into a cycle of plays designed for performance on a single occasion? While stressing the importance of the Church calendar, we should not overlook the fact that medieval drama was also enormously stimulated by the growing popularity of universal histories, such as were examined in Chapter Six of *The Bible in Early English Literature.* Ranulph Higden was working on the early version of his *Polychronicon* at the very time when the feast of Corpus Christi was establishing itself in England. Indeed, one legend has it that Higden himself composed the Chester cycle in 1328. This attribution is now discredited, but there can be no doubt that the Christian philosophy of history reflected in the *Polychronicon* was a shaping influence in the cycle plays, and perhaps also in the actual selection of particular biblical stories for dramatization. As Kolve points out, the division of world history into seven ages appears to provide one means of selection, particularly in the choice of Old Testament episodes. But this principle should not be carried too far. Biblical exegesis itself was an inevitable influence. It is highly unlikely that the choice of Abraham and Isaac (Gen. 22) was "accidental," as has been suggested; it appears in all the cycles because the story was universally understood to foreshadow the sacrifice of Christ. This is a principle of choice that operates in the biblical drama even when the typological interpretation is not made explicit in the play.

With the example of universal histories could be included biblical compendia such as the *Historia Scholastica, Cursor Mundi,* and various expanded passion narratives in legendary form. To this list scholars now add the great illustrated bibles, such as *The Holkham Bible Picture Book,* to exemplify the fact that a visual equivalent to the cycle plays was being unfolded in the realm of medieval art. With this kind of foundation, it would almost seem strange, given the development of later liturgical drama already discussed, if the vernacular plays had not appeared, with or without their attachment to the feast of Corpus Christi. In the absence of any other established theory, therefore, I am inclined to regard the emergence of the cyclical drama as a phenomenon more or less parallel to the rise of other types of vernacular literature in the later Middle Ages, notably the lyric, which, as we shall see, grew out of a tradition of medieval Latin poetry and had close ties with the liturgy and with drama.

But to think of the cycle plays simply as one more example of the emergence of vernacular literature in the later Middle Ages is to ignore their unique feature—the fact that they were staged. Until recently the characteristic method of their production was thought to be "processional staging." According to this view, every episode in the cycle had its own "pageant" or stage-on-wheels, which was drawn through the streets of the town and stopped at each of several "stations" where the play was performed for the assembled audience. This method was thought to have been devised so that larger numbers of people could see and hear the play, and perhaps also to facilitate a division of labor for such an enormous production: the local guilds could be given civic responsibility for the plays appropriate to their craft; thus the shipwrights would produce Noah and the Flood, the bakers the Last Supper, and the cooks the Harrowing of Hell.

The idea that an entire cycle, from Creation to the Last Judgment, could be performed on a single day with processional staging has been challenged by Alan H. Nelson, and, though the problem is still unresolved, common sense would seem to be on his side. Such a plan bristles with technical difficulties. Of course there is nothing wrong with the idea that single plays may have been performed in this way. In the city of York the wheeled pageant has been revived for street productions of "Abraham and Isaac" and other such episodes on a single one-level stage. In a production I witnessed there some years ago the audience stood at a designated station in the center of town, having been informed of the time by posted public notices and the cry of a herald who preceded the pageant through the streets. The stage was in effect a horse-drawn wagon carrying the actors and a few modest props: in the case of "Abraham and Issac," an altar and a lamb.

There is evidence of this kind of staging in the medieval Coventry play of the Slaughter of the Innocents (Matt. 2 : 1–18), in which Herod takes on the ranting character alluded to by Hamlet when he cautioned his players against trying to "out-Herod Herod." In this play the three kings who visit the Christ child are warned by an angel not to tell Herod where he may be found, and so the kings depart in secret. At this point a messenger comes running to Herod, telling him that the three kings have left by another way. Herod speaks:

[27]

Another way? Out! out! out!
Hath those false traitors done me this deed?
I stamp! I stare! I look all about!
Might I them take, I should burn them at a gleed!
I rant! I rave! and now run I wood [mad]!
Ah, that these villain traitors hath marred thus my mood!
They shall be hanged if I may come them to!

This speech is followed by a curious stage direction: *Here Herod rages in the pageant and in the street also.* We get from this a vivid picture of Herod, and it is not difficult to see how he became one of the most popular of all the characters in the biblical plays. It may well be that he made a deep impression on young William Shakespeare, whose home in Stratford was not far from Coventry, and who could have witnessed the cycle plays there.

But in the final analysis it seems that the case for full processional staging of the cycle plays is in doubt, and that we should look elsewhere for indications of how the plays were performed. Where the evidence shows that pageants were used, as in Chester and York, we have at least two other alternatives: the pageants may have been employed for nondramatic *tableaux vivants* in a religious procession (Corpus Christi), or they may have served as mobile scaffolds, rolled into position around a central playing place (*platea*) for fixed stage performance.

What seems most likely is that the commonest form of production was what we have seen to be the case with the Cornish *Ordinalia*: a theater in the round, with scaffolds arranged about the circumference of the *platea*. The particular form of this may have varied from region to region, because the notion of a "playing place" was a flexible concept and not a rigidly prescribed tradition. In one town the "place" may have been the interior of a church or cathedral, in another a public square or green, in more rural areas (like Cornwall) a round in an open field constructed or adapted for the occasion. In reading the plays, therefore, one must be prepared to imagine different kinds of theatrical settings, depending on internal evidence of the text and the few stage directions that may have been provided.

The English Cycle Plays

Four complete cycles of biblical drama survive in English, and one, as we have seen, in Cornish. The four English texts with which we are concerned here are customarily called the Chester,

York, Towneley, and Ludus Coventriae cycles. This terminology is a little confusing, since in the first two cases the place of performance is referred to, but "Towneley" names the family that once owned the surviving manuscript, and "Ludus Coventriae" is a phrase from the manuscript designating the type of play—meaning a play like that of the famous (lost) Coventry cycle. Modern scholarship has established that the Towneley plays were performed at Wakefield (not far from York). The Ludus Coventriae (now often called "N-town") had no connection with Coventry, but may have been intended for a traveling company, or the text itself may have traveled. Its origins were in East Anglia, possibly in Norfolk or Bury Saint Edmunds. The proclamation which introduces this cycle specified that

> A sunday next yf þat we may
> At vj of þe belle we gynne oure play
> In N. town. . . .

The "N" probably stands for *nomen*, and the speaker at that point would be expected to insert the name of the town appropriate to the occasion. Thus we have three cycles associated with places (Chester, York, Wakefield) and one "floating" cycle of no fixed abode (N-town).

The survival of manuscript copies of the medieval drama was to some extent a matter of chance. As we have seen, Coventry undoubtedly had a full cycle, with perhaps as many as seventeen pageants, and yet only two of them remain. Other single plays survive, suggesting the existence of complete cycles at other towns such as Newcastle-upon-Tyne. A play of "Abraham and Isaac" turned up in a Dublin manuscript, which according to Hardin Craig may have been performed originally in Northampton; and another on the same subject was found in the Brome manuscript, a curious fifteenth-century commonplace book now in the Yale University library. The major cycles are preserved in late copies, and Chester, which may have been the first English-speaking community to produce a cycle, has the latest copies of all.

For the reasons just mentioned, it is very difficult to date these plays or to know how often they were revised before achieving the form we see in the surviving manuscripts. The Chester cycle was traditionally said to have been composed by Higden in 1328. Salter may be right in suggesting perhaps 1375, while Clopper argues for 1422 as the earliest verifiable date. Yet the earliest complete copy of this cycle (a manuscript in the Huntington Library) is dated 1591, over two centuries after the origin of the plays. The gap is smaller in the other cycles, which are preserved in manuscripts of the fifteenth century.

There is a wealth of biblical materials in these cycles, but there is room here for only a brief sampling of what lies in store for anyone who will take the time to study them. To a considerable extent the shape of biblical tradition that we have seen developing in the early literature and in the universal histories reappears in the drama. But there is a difference. The medieval playwright was able, by virtue of his medium, to add a human dimension to the dynamics of salvation history. Typology still seeks to control the significance of these plays, but somehow on stage, men acquire a freedom to act that makes them appear as spiritual adventurers rather than blind instruments in the hand of God. Patriarchs and prophets, apostles and saints are seen with all their doubts and fears, as well as their triumphs.

The Chester Cycle

An interesting device for establishing a unified theological perspective appears in the second play of the Chester cycle, produced by the drapers, dealing with Adam and Eve and Cain and Abel (Gen. 2–4). There is a legendary addition to this otherwise conventional treatment of the biblical narrative that suggests a useful comparison with the Cornish drama. The Cornish *Origo Mundi*, as we saw, makes extensive use of the legend of Seth to show the relevance of the story of the Fall to the coming Redemption. The Chester dramatist for the same basic purpose uses another legend we have encountered: the dream of Adam. When he awakens from his deep sleep (Gen. 2:21), Adam says to God:

> Ah, Lord, where have I long been?
> For since I slept, much have I seen—
> Wonder that without ween [doubt]
> Hereafter shall be wist [known].

It is curious that Adam should have this dream soon after his creation, because in it the Fall is anticipated and remedied before it occurs. He does not disclose its contents to the audience, however, until after he and Eve have been expelled from Paradise. While he slept, Adam says, he was ravished to heaven, where he was given grace to foresee future events:

[30]

> I wot by things that I there see
> That God will come from heaven on high,
> to overcome the devil so sly
> and light into my kind;
> and my blood that he will win
> that I so lost for my sin;
> a new law there shall begin
> and so men shall them [in]sure.

He goes on to predict destruction of the earth by water and fire, and the Last Judgment. But the purpose of this legendary insertion seems to be the same as that of Seth's journey to Paradise in the Cornish drama: a reminder, at the time of the Fall, of the oil of mercy promised to mankind through the Redemption. As a footnote to this, it is perhaps worth pointing out that Adam's vision may have been suggested originally by the visionary sleep of Abraham, which also contained a revelation of future events (Gen. 15:12–16).

The inner struggle of the Patriarch Abraham to obey God and sacrifice his beloved son Isaac is movingly portrayed in the barbers' play of the Chester cycle (no. IV). Indeed the inner conflict looms so large that an expositor is needed at the end of the play to remind us of the higher meaning:

> By Abraham I may understand
> the Father of heaven that can fond [did seek]
> with his Son's blood to break that bond
> that the devil had brought us to.
> By Isaac understand I may
> Jesus that was obedient aye,
> his Father's will to work alway
> and death for to confound.

But a look at the play will show that this theme is not forgotten, even in passages seemingly devoted entirely to the pathos of Abraham's dilemma. We may also consider the relationship of this play to the Brome "Abraham," preserved as a separate drama in a commonplace book of the late fifteenth century. Is the Brome text derived from the Chester play, or is it the other way around? Both views have been argued, but neither has been decisively established.

The Chester play as it stands has obviously been designed to fit the cycle in which it appears. Its first 144 lines dramatize and interpret the story of Abraham and Melchizedek (Gen. 14), while the next 64 lines depict the covenant between God and Abraham and the promise of a son (Gen. 15:1–6). Then begins the story proper of Genesis 22 with God's command for the offering of Isaac (lines 209–28). The heart of the story that follows (lines 229–429) is closely paralleled in the Brome Abraham (lines 105–315). The Chester play then ends with the intervention of the angel, the offering of a lamb (despite the ram mentioned in Genesis 22:13), closing remarks by the expositor, and the announcement by a messenger of the play of Balaam to follow.

The Brome play of Abraham is clearly noncyclical in that it is entirely devoted to the story in Genesis 22. The opening thirty-two lines depict the love of Abraham for Isaac with little attention to the surrounding narrative of Genesis (except for a brief reference to Adam and Eve) and no allusion to the Covenant. What is stressed throughout is the love of a human father for his child. Then in rapid succession we are shown God in heaven directing an angel to relay his command to Abraham, and Abraham on earth in prayer asking God what kind of offering he would like to receive (lines 33–58). The angel presents the command and Abraham accepts it, but unlike the Chester patriarch he protests his love for Isaac to such a degree that the angel is constrained to urge him not to be dismayed, whereupon Abraham summons Isaac from his prayers (59–104). The heart of the play then follows (105–315) corresponding closely with Chester (229–420). The ending of the Brome, however, is quite different. Over a hundred lines (316–434) are devoted to the substitute sacrifice (a ram this time, as indicated in Genesis 22:13) and the relief of Isaac at his escape from death (358–66):

> Ah, sheep, sheep! blessed mot thou be
>   That ever thou wert sent down hither!
> Thou shalt this day die for me,
> In the worship of the Holy Trinity.
>   Now come fast and go we together
>   To my father on high;
>   Though thou be never so gentle and good,
>   Yet had I liefer thou sheddest thy blood
>   Iwis, sheep, than I.

There is much more in this vein, and at the end of the play a Doctor points the moral of uncomplaining obedience to God's commandments. There is no mention in the Brome play of the typological interpretation offered by the Chester expositor, although this higher meaning can be inferred from certain passages in Brome that are parallel to the Chester play.

This brief comparison reveals some important differences. The Brome play seems to explore more fully the emotional resistance of Abraham to God's command, and the childlike and joyful relief of Isaac when he becomes convinced that he is not to be sacrificed. Both belong to the human dimension of the story. The Chester play, while it has this dimension also, does not lose sight of typology, even to the point of using a lamb (signifying Christ) for the sacrifice instead of the ram called for by the story. Yet these differences are such that it is difficult to deduce from them which play is the earlier.

A closer view of the relation between the two plays is provided by looking at certain passages in the middle where the texts are very similar. Thus at the start of the journey the Chester Abraham speaks to his son (249–50):

> Now Isaac, son, go we our way
> To yonder mount, if that we may.

To which the boy replies (251–52):

> My dear father, I will assay
> To follow you full fain.

Compare this with the Brome treatment of the same moment in the story (120–26):

> ABRAHAM: Ah, Lord of heaven, my hands I wring,
> This child's words all to-wound my heart.
> Now Isaac, son, go we our way
> Unto yon mount, with all our main.

> ISAAC: Go, my dear father, as fast as I may,
> To follow you I am full fain,
> Although I be slender.

The Chester text is austere in comparison with the Brome play's exploration of the boyish innocence of Isaac.

Both plays present Isaac as selflessly encouraging Abraham to do his duty while at the same time pathetically urging his father not to tell Sarah what he has done.

> Chester (317–22):

> Father, at home your sons you shall find
> that you must love by course of kind.

[33]

Be I once out of your mind,
Your sorrow may soon cease.
But yet you must do God's bidding.
Father, tell my mother for nothing.

Brome (198–206):

Ye have other children, one or two,
   The which ye should love well by kind;
I pray you, father, make ye no woe,
For be I once dead and from you go,
   I shall be soon out of your mind.
Therefore do our Lord's bidding,
   And when I am dead, then pray for me;
But, good father, tell ye my mother nothing,
Say that I am in another country dwelling.

One wonders whether the calculated and effective pathos of the Brome text would ever have been cut out in revision merely to achieve the different stanza form we see in Chester. Similarly, there seems to be a marked difference of purpose in the handling of Isaac's request for his father's forgiveness before he dies: the Chester Abraham says "I forgive thee here" (380), while in Brome he says, "In all thy life thou grieved me never once" (270). In other words, there is nothing to forgive.

There can be little doubt that the Brome play, with its meticulous attention to pathetic effects, would be regarded as superior to Chester by a modern audience. And in an artistic sense it is indeed the better constructed of the two. This suggests that the Chester play, despite the modern appearance of its language (owing to lateness of the manuscripts), represents a form of the play earlier than that of the fifteenth-century Brome manuscript. And this is supported, I think, by the tendency of the Chester play to retain the typological emphasis which Brome has discarded in the interest of pathos and psychological realism.

The cappers' play (V), which immediately follows the Abraham and Isaac play in the Chester cycle, is devoted mainly to the amusing story of Balak and Balaam (Num. 22–24). The comedy is dramatically effective, but the story was doubtless included because of Balaam's prophecy that "there shall come a Star out of Jacob" (Num. 24:17), a messianic prophecy that provides a convenient transition to the following Nativity play (VI). Yet the manuscripts are curiously divided here, all but one of them giving the messianic theme only perfunctory attention, and ending with an account of the corrupting influence of the Moabite women (Num. 25). Furthermore, this story is not even dramatized, but is given in summary by the Doctor, so that the ending of the play in these manuscripts has only the lamest of connections with the Nativity which follows.

As it happens, the very latest of all the Chester manuscripts (Harley 2124) has what seems to me the earlier form of the cappers' play. Like the other version, it has a brief opening section on Moses and the Ten Commandments followed by the main action, the effort of Balak, king of Moab, to induce Balaam to curse Israel. The real difference may be seen in the ending, where, after Balaam delivers the Star out of Jacob prophecy, the Harley manuscript presents a series of Old Testament messianic prophecies by Isaiah, Ezekiel, Jeremiah, Jonah, David, Joel, and Micah. This use at the end of the Balaam narrative of the *processus prophetarum* to round off the Old Testament plays has been criticized, but it strikes me as an effective way to make the transition to the New Testament sequence. Limitations of space prevent our looking at examples from this play, but assuredly it is rewarding and entertaining drama. The introduction of the prophets has the effect of freezing the action, yet when the expositor has completed his interpretation, the frustrated king of Moab is given one final stanza to express his exasperation (433–40), after which he presumably stalks off stage to the great amusement of the audience.

The one New Testament play from Chester that we may consider briefly is "The Last Judgment" (XXIV), staged by the websters, which brings this great cycle to a close. Despite all that is said about a last judgment in the Bible, there is actually not much to provide a basis for dramatic action, and most judgment plays therefore simply present a trial scene in which Christ separates the sheep from the goats (based on Matt. 25:31–46), followed in some cases (as we know from surviving property lists) by a spectacular blaze representing the destruction of the world. The basic patterning of events is thus similar to what is depicted in the west window of Fairford Church: Christ on the throne of judgment, Saint Michael weighing the souls, Saint Peter welcoming the saved to Paradise, and Satan welcoming the damned to Hell.

The Chester "Last Judgment," however, is especially interesting because it has one feature the other plays lack: a series of speeches by representative ranks of society occupying nearly half of the entire drama. The spokesmen are arranged in two groups, the Saved and the Damned. Thus we have the speeches of a pope, emperor, king, and queen, all saved; and these are followed by speeches of a pope, emperor, king, queen, justice, and merchant, all damned. The Saved pray for mercy, and the Damned bewail the certainty that they are lost.

The balancing of these social ranks is not commonly found in medieval representations of the Last Judgment so far as I know. They do appear, however, in a wall painting of the Doom over the chancel arch in the parish church of South Leigh, just west of Oxford. Whether the drama has influenced the artist in this instance or vice versa is difficult to say, though I tend to believe, with M. D. Anderson, that in doubtful cases it is usually the drama that comes first. A clearer instance of influence, involving drama and poetry, will be found in the last chapter, when we reach an important passage near the end of *Piers the Plowman* which seems to have been inspired by a satire on social ranks like that in the Chester "Last Judgment."

The Wakefield Master

Among the thirty-two plays that form the Wakefield cycle are six that appear to have come from the pen of a single anonymous dramatist known as the Wakefield Master. The six are (1) "The Killing of Abel," (2) "Noah and His Sons," (3) "First Shepherds' Play," (4) "Second Shepherds' Play," (5) "Herod the Great," and (6) "The Buffeting." These plays have been edited as a group by A. C. Cawley, and they are among the liveliest in the entire corpus of medieval drama. The author's skilled sense of stagecraft shows up particularly well, I think, in the Noah play, and, as everyone agrees, in the "Second Shepherds' Play," which has been revived frequently in modern times and has become a popular favorite in the Christmas season.

Noah begins his play with a prayer to God recapitulating the history of the world and expressing his concern that God will take vengeance because of the sins of mankind. In response, God announces the flood, but stipulates that Noah and his family will be saved from the general destruction. He then instructs Noah on building the ark and housing his family and the animals. Noah expresses his thanks, whereupon the Lord blesses him and departs.

This opening follows the text of Genesis closely, but after God's exit (line 18) the mood changes when Noah expresses concern about how his wife will take the news of the impending flood:

> Lord, homeward will I haste as fast as that I may;
> My wife will I frast [ask] what she will say,
> And I am agast that we get some fray
> Betwixt us both,
> For she is full tethee [peevish],
> For little oft angry;
> If any thing wrong be,
> Soon is she wroth.

His fears are fully justified, for before he can tell his wife what God has said, she greets him with a series of accusations: he leaves her alone to do all the work, fails to provide food for their table, constantly fears the worst, and she adds wickedly, "God send thee once thy fill!" After more in this vein, Noah loses patience and tells her to hold her tongue, whereupon they exchange blows and curses. Suddenly Noah stops and says that he will "keep charity," for he has things to do. The wife sits down to spin, and Noah goes to build the ark.

When the ark is ready for boarding, we are given the famous scene to which Chaucer's Miller alludes in *The Canterbury Tales* (I, 3539–40):

> The sorwe of Noe with his felaweshipe,
> Er that he myghte gete his wyf to shipe.

In the Wakefield play, Noah's wife is not only reluctant to board the ship, she flatly refuses and sits down on a hill and continues to spin, daring anyone to interrupt her. Noah calls her attention to the threatening weather, his sons' wives plead for her to come in the ship, all to no avail, until finally she notices the water level rising with the remark, "I sit not dry!" and hurries into the ship. Filled with exasperation at her stubbornness, Noah gives her a whipping, in the course of which each delivers an aside to the audience on the woes of marriage. The wife admits she wishes her husband were dead, and Noah admonishes all married men to chastise their wives' tongues while they are young.

There are no stage directions here, but the dialogue suggests that a knockdown, drag-out fight occurs on the ship. The wife loudly complains of mistreatment: "Out, alas, I am gone! Out upon thee, man's wonder!" To which Noah replies: "See how she can groan, and I lie under!" suggesting that the wife at least temporarily has the upper hand, and is perhaps even perched on her helpless husband. But the three sons shame their parents into abandoning the struggle, and the whole family joins in the task of navigating the ark, which is now water-borne. The remainder of the play follows the biblical account, and concludes soberly with the grounding of the ark on the hills of Armenia.

In some other versions of the Noah play a typological meaning can be found, but there is little basis for seeing the Wakefield Noah as a type of Christ or his ark as the Church. The shrewish wife, however, can be understood as "another Eve," an idea from extrabiblical tradition that appears in the Newcastle Shipwrights' play, which represents the Devil as tempting Noah's wife in an obvious echo of the temptation of Eve. In any case the "storm" between Noah and his wife is introduced skillfully by the Wakefield Master in parallel with the storm of the flood, imparting momentum and conflict to a play that might otherwise have tended to be static, since the flood itself could not be effectively represented on stage. And the play ends peacefully, with a hint that God's mercy will be available to mankind in the final judgment.

The Wakefield Master has given us two excellent Nativity plays, a duplication not found in any other cycle. Perhaps, as has been suggested, they were meant to be acted in alternate years. Both include considerable comedy, although the "First Shepherds' Play" is briefer and more traditional in its recitation of the messianic prophecies (332–403). In the present survey, however, our attention is devoted to the "Second Shepherds' Play," by far the more popular of the two, to judge by the frequency of its revival on the modern stage and its inclusion in most English literature anthologies.

The biblical basis of the "Second Shepherds' Play" is the traditional narrative in Luke 2:8–18: angels appear to the shepherds and direct them to the manger in Bethlehem. But only about the last hundred lines of the play present this story. The remainder— well over six hundred lines—is devoted to the encounter of the shepherds with a rascal named Mak, who steals one of their sheep and, by a clever ruse, almost gets away with it. This episode has often been criticized as a digression, while at the same time it has been admired as the excellent comedy it undoubtedly is. But students of the drama are now more inclined, for good reason, to see the comic episode as an important feature of the play as a whole, a preparation for and commentary on the Nativity itself.

The play opens effectively with a speech by each of the three shepherds. These speeches accomplish several things at once. They introduce the shepherds to the audience, gain immediate attention with their pointed social satire, initiate a "game" (as we shall see) between actors and audience, and impart momentum to the story. To appreciate some of these points, it will be necessary to pay close attention to matters of staging, for a careful reading of the "Second Shepherds' Play," even apart from its few stage directions, shows that the Wakefield Master wrote with a skilled sense of how his play should be acted.

The first shepherd comes on stage alone and begins his speech by complaining of the cold weather, poverty, and taxes. He then launches into an extended denunciation of purveyors, those ruthless stewards of the nobility charged with "requisitioning" supplies from the poor on behalf of their lords. There would be many in the audience who had suffered at the hands of the purveyors, and would immediately identify with the shepherd in his complaint against them. But lest he launch into a sermon on the subject, the first shepherd stops short, seeming to recollect himself, and explains the reason for his remarks (46–47):

> It does me good, as I walk thus by mine one [alone],
> Of this world for to talk in manner of moan [complaint].

He then sits down to wait for his companions.

The entrance of the second shepherd is handled in such a way that he does not see the first, who is presumably seated off to one side. Thus we get a second set speech, beginning very much like that of the first shepherd, with a complaint about the weather. But the second shepherd has a different preoccupation: his interest is in warning the young men in the audience against marriage. Wedded men have a hard life, he says, and often wish they could be free of their wives. So beware, and remember before you marry that "had I known" will be of no use to you after the ceremony. This seems to remind him of his own situation, and he launches into a description of his wife (100–108):

> For, as ever read I epistle, I have one to my fere
>   [for my mate]
> As sharp as a thistle, as rough as a briar;
> She is browed like a bristle, with a sour-loten cheer
>   [sour-looking face];
> Had she once wet her whistle, she could sing full clear
> Her Paternoster [Lord's Prayer].

[39]

> She is as great as a whale,
> She has a gallon of gall;
> By him that died for us all,
> I would I had run til I had lost her!

This is obviously spoken with great feeling and seems to hint that the speaker might continue at great length, but at this point he is interrupted by the first shepherd.

The nature of the interruption, however, is very unusual, and offers a good illustration of the "game" that the actors sometimes play with the audience in medieval drama. The first shepherd's interruption consists of a single line (109):

> God look over the row. Full deafly ye stand!

As Cawley suggests in a note to this line, the first statement is probably spoken to the audience, while "Full deafly ye stand" is directed at the second shepherd. But what does the speaker mean by saying to the audience "may God watch over this company"? No doubt it is a blessing, as Cawley points out, but it is by no means a perfunctory one, if we follow carefully what is happening on stage.

When the second shepherd is launched into his set speech, the first shepherd tries to get his attention, but his companion is absorbed in his harangue and fails to notice him. As the monologue of the shepherd threatens to continue endlessly, the first shepherd's dumb-show efforts to get his attention become more frantic, until at last he breaks character and speaks his blessing to the audience. The import of this blessing is: please excuse me, good people, but I will have to step out of my role and shout, or this fellow will go on forever. Then to the second shepherd: "FULL DEAFLY YE STAND!" This sort of device on the medieval stage suggests that the notion of drama as "play" or "game" was then still a fresh idea in the minds of both dramatist and audience.

The third shepherd is much younger than the other two, and comes on stage crossing himself and complaining that there have never been such winds and rains "since Noah's flood." Although he goes on to express fear of the dark, his words perhaps are prophetic of the vision of angelic hosts that the shepherds are to experience later (136–37):

> We that walk in the nights, our cattle to keep,
> We see sudden sights when other men sleep.

[40]

With these words he spies the other two shepherds, and a bantering conversation ensues in which the third shepherd, though a boy, holds his own very well. This opening section of the play concludes with the three shepherds singing a song.

The pace quickens with the entry of Mak, the sheep stealer. He comes in disguised with a cloak over his tunic, pretending to be a yeoman of the king, complete with southern accent. The shepherds quickly penetrate this disguise and are understandably curious why Mak is roaming so late at night. The second shepherd pointedly remarks (222–25):

> Thus late as thou goes,
> What will men suppose?
> And thou has an ill noise [bad reputation]
> Of stealing of sheep.

But Mak protests his innocence and is allowed to stay with the shepherds, although, as a precaution, they place him between them when they go to sleep.

The audience is no doubt eagerly awaiting Mak's next move, and it is not long in coming. He rises up cautiously, casts a spell over the shepherds (which makes them snore all the louder), and triumphantly takes a fat sheep home to his wife, Gill. She pretends to be spinning (late as it is) and is slow to open the door, but when Mak says that he has brought her something, she replies, "Oh, come in, my sweeting!" Despite that homely tone of the dialogue, we sometimes find in it curious biblical echoes. Thus when Gill, alarmed at the sight of the stolen sheep, tells Mak he is likely to hang for theft, he replies (309–14):

> Do way!
> I am worthy my meat,
> For in a strait I can get
> More than they that swink and sweat
> All the long day.
> Thus it fell to my lot, Gill; I had such grace.

Mak's "grace" apparently was to be one of those hired at the eleventh hour by the householder in the parable of the vineyard (Matt. 20:1–16), against whom the other laborers complain, "These last have wrought but one hour, and thou hast made them equall unto us, which have borne the burden, and heat of the day" (Matt. 20:12). With such biblical texts he seeks to prop up his career as a stealer of sheep.

Gill's fear of discovery by the shepherds infects Mak, and, when he seems undecided what to do, she has the inspired idea of concealing the sheep in the cradle, while she lies as if in childbed and groans. Mak enthusiastically approves the plan, and hastens to rejoin the shepherds in the field before they waken. Meanwhile Gill congratulates herself on the brilliance of her suggestion, and points out triumphantly to the audience (341–42):

> This is a good guise and a far cast;
> Yet a woman's advice helps at the last!

Gill is no less ingenious than Mak in her adaptation of biblical references; here she offers her own good advice to replace the bad counsel of Eve.

The plan at first appears to be flawless. Mak resumes his place with the sleeping shepherds and pretends to be so sound asleep himself that they have to lift him up bodily from the ground. After staggering about sleepily, Mak reports a dream: he thought Gill bore another child to add to his already large family. Now he must go home and see whether it is true. Before leaving, he invites the shepherds to look in his sleeves to assure themselves that he has stolen nothing. They of course cannot find anything, but they remain suspicious enough to inspect their flocks to see if any animals are missing.

Meanwhile Mak and Gill put the sheep in the cradle and prepare themselves for the expected search. The shepherds, having ascertained that a sheep is missing, decide forthwith to visit Mak's home, even though they cannot see how he could have been the culprit. As they approach the cottage, they hear Gill groaning and Mak singing a lullaby "out of tune." Mak lets them in, urging them to speak softly, lest they awaken the newborn child. When the shepherds express a suspicion that somehow Mak or his wife has stolen their sheep, the confident thief points to the cradle beside the bed and says (521–22):

> As I am true and leal [loyal], to God here I pray
> That this be the first meal that I shall eat this day.

Mak continues to live dangerously, for when the shepherds curiously approach the cradle, he remarks (531–33):

> Wist ye how she had farne, your hearts would be sore.
> Ye do wrong, I you warn, that thus come before
> To a woman who has farne—but I say no more.

The word "farne," used twice in this passage, can mean simply "fare," but it may also mean "give birth," referring to animals rather than human beings, and survives in modern English "farrow." Thus the shepherds have more than a hint that Gill has given birth to an animal, but of course they are not quick enough to seize the clue offered them.

The byplay continues while the shepherds search the cottage for some sign of the sheep. They ask whether the child is a boy or a girl, and who served as godparents. Mak gives answers with growing uneasiness, wishing in an aside to the audience that they were gone. After they finally do leave the house, the first shepherd suddenly remembers that they did not give the child a present. The third shepherd, who has been suspicious all along, volunteers to return with a gift of sixpence. Despite Mak's protest, he approaches the cradle (584–85):

> Give me leave him to kiss, and lift up the clout.
> What the devil is this? He has a long snout!

The shepherds indulge in an amusing doubletake, and then one by one they express their amazement and their reluctant admiration for this "high fraud." When Mak finally confesses his guilt, they toss him in a blanket as punishment, and the play concludes with the shepherds' presentation of gifts to the Christ child in Bethlehem.

In this brief summary, we can only glimpse the rich comedy of the "Second Shepherds' Play," but perhaps enough detail has been provided to show that the sheep-stealing episode offers numerous parallels to the Nativity, including the "birth," visit by the shepherds, and offering of gifts to the "child." It has even been suggested that the same props (cottage, cradle, etc.) were used for Mak's house and the stable in Bethlehem, thus underlining the parallelism. This might strike a modern audience as parody, but to medieval spectators such a parallel provided a comic commentary on the shortcomings of fallen man, on whose behalf the Savior came into the world. The episode thus functions in a manner analogous to that of Noah's wife in the play previously considered, although the shepherds' play is a finer, more complex achievement, both in its theological conception and as sheer entertainment.

In a sensitive theological reading of this drama, Míceál Vaughan has recently and persuasively pointed to a trinary structure in

"The Second Shepherds' Play," reflecting three comings of Christ traditionally celebrated during Advent. Advent represents the beginning and the end of the Christian calendar, that point in the circle of the year where the serpent bites its tail. But in addition to the commemoration of the two principal "advents," the Nativity and the Last Judgment, a personal coming of Christ to each believing worshiper was also recognized and taught. Thus in the apocalyptic overtones of the sheep-stealing episode, in the manifestation of the spirit of Christ in the shepherds who show generosity and mercy in their treatment of Mak, and in the actual Nativity scene at the end, the three comings of Christ celebrated in the liturgy of Advent are faithfully echoed in the play. Although the fallen world is unflinchingly exposed to our view, the confounding of Mak's deception is brought about by a charitable impulse: even the suspicious third shepherd returns for the purpose of offering the "child" a gift. Thus, as Vaughan remarks, "a gracious act of charity exposes and spans the narrow void between deception and revelation."

The Morality Play

Along with the major cycles based on the Bible, there developed a very different kind of drama usually known as the "morality," in which the leading characters are personified abstractions. The most famous example is *Everyman*, which dramatizes the moment when Death summons an individual to his reckoning before God. The earliest of such plays is a fragment known as *The Pride of Life* (or *The King of Life*) dated on linguistic grounds about 1350, at least as early as any of the surviving cycles. The first major, full-scale morality is *The Castle of Perseverance* (ca. 1400), to which we will return in a moment. Later plays of this type are *Mankind* (ca. 1460), *Wisdom* (ca. 1475), and of course *Everyman*, possibly of Dutch origin, which in its surviving English form dates from about 1490. The form continued through the sixteenth century and had an important influence on the secular drama, but we will limit our concern here to its medieval manifestations.

In one sense the morality may seem remote from the biblical drama we have been considering. The cast of characters in *Everyman*, for example, includes such names as Fellowship, Kindred, and Good Deeds, a company quite different from those we find in the cycle plays. Yet dramatizations of this kind spring ultimately from the tradition of biblical exegesis, largely through the medium of the pulpit. They represent the counterpart on the medieval stage of the tropological level of interpretation, the application of Scripture to the moral life of the individual. Thus *Everyman* itself has been convincingly shown by Kolve to be in part a dramatic adaptation of the parable of the talents (Matt. 25:14–30).

The morality play is a very distinctive dramatic form, yet literary historians offer a surprising variety of views on its origin and development. One early theory, sketched by the famous eighteenth-century ballad editor Thomas Percy, was that the morality grew out of the cycle plays themselves. There is someting to be said for this view, since allegorical figures sometimes do appear in the cycles. In the N-town "Massacre of the Innocents," for example, the soldiers report to Herod that they have killed the children in accordance with his orders, and conclude with the flattering assurance that he is now the greatest lord among all the nations. Herod responds by saying that never before in his life was he as merry as he is now, and he invites his soldiers to join him in feasting at table. At this moment, Death appears dramatically on stage, unseen by the revelers, and announces his intention of slaying Herod. One suspects the influence here of the parable of the rich man (Luke 12:16–21), but Herod is beyond redemption and unable to hear the warning: *Thou fool, this night thy soul shall be required of thee.* The king and his soldiers are struck down by Death in the midst of their feast, and as the play ends they are carried off by the Devil to Hell.

From instances such as this, one might suppose that the idea for a morality play developed from the use of abstractions in the biblical cycles. But there is a chronological difficulty with this, since as we have seen there are moralities (notably *The Pride of Life*) as early as any of the cycle plays, whereas the occurrence of abstractions in the cycles tends to be late. The N-town cycle, for example, is probably the latest of the four, and much more "literary" than the other cycles.

Some of our literary historians seem to feel that the inspiration for the morality play came, as it were, out of the blue. J. M. Manly saw it as the result of a chance combination of allegory with the dramatic method; A. W. Ward, in the *Cambridge History of English Literature* (V, 22), mentions numerous possible influences but sees it arising from a love of allegory; G. R. Owst gives all the credit to medieval preachers; and Hardin Craig, in his *English Religious Drama of the Middle Ages* (p. 345), reaffirms Manly's theory of chance variation. In passing, however, Craig makes some important observations, notably that the English morality play differed from those on the Continent in having a central protagonist, Mankind.

More recent students of the drama have narrowed the quest for the origin of the morality play by calling attention to important models. Edgar T. Schell questions the validity of Creizenach's comparison of the morality with Prudentius's *Psychomachia* (fourth century) and persuasively offers us instead Deguilleville's *Le Pèlerinage de la vie humaine* (ca. 1330), which was Englished by Lydgate as *The Pilgrimage of the Life of Man* in the fifteenth century. David J. Leigh, in a study of the Doomsday mystery play, makes the valuable point that plays of the Last Judgment are unique in being the only cycle drama to depict events outside historical time. For this reason (he says) they tend to engage in nonrepresentative action, using largely nonhistorical characters, and seek audience involvement to an unusual degree. The anonymous "souls" that always appear come very close indeed to the abstractions of the morality play, and Leigh suggests tentatively that the morality began as an offshoot of the Doomsday drama. The suggestion is interesting, but leaves unsolved the problem of the origin of the Mankind figure.

The excellent study by Robert Potter, *The English Morality Play* (1975), begins with a key point: "But it is the figure of mankind who stands at the center of these plays, and the shape of his life which unfolds to determine the pattern of events" (p. 7). He sees the morality as a form of "repentance drama" derived from the penitential tradition of the medieval church, but gaining strength also through utilization of folk ritual which works in harmony with its theological purpose. Indeed Potter sees the origin of the morality play as closely related to ritual and ritual drama (p. 15). The protagonist, however, remains something of a puzzle: "The deadly sins are quite probably the ancestors of the mankind figures, the representative central characters of the moralities" (p. 28), but "in chronological terms . . . this theory is open to question" (p. 42). Actually the fragmentary *Pride of Life* (ca. 1350) offers some support for his theory, but I think there is another possible source of influence in the shaping of the Mankind figure that has not been previously considered.

The possibility of literary influence on the development of the morality play has been neglected, despite the fact that the indebtedness of drama to other forms of literature has not been uncommon in the English stage tradition. At the time of the growth of drama in the fourteenth century, the most important and creative poetic form was the dream vision, which we shall encounter in later chapters devoted to Chaucer, the *Pearl* poet, and *Piers the Plowman*. The distinctive feature of this form was a central figure, the Dreamer, through whose eyes and understanding all the events and ideas of the poem are viewed. In some cases (as in *Piers the Plowman* especially) the Dreamer actually matures and reaches old age in the course of the poem. J. V. Cunningham has shown how this poetic tradition subtly determined the shape of the General Prologue to *The Canterbury Tales*. In a somewhat analogous way, the dream vision may well have been an important shaping influence in the development of Mankind as the central character of the English morality play. This can be most readily perceived, I think, in a comparison of *Piers the Plowman* and *The Castle of Perseverance*. The former will be the subject of our last chapter and need not be discussed here in detail, while the latter is the most imposing of the morality plays we are considering and deserves to be viewed for its own sake. But in the following discussion of *The Castle* it will be well to take occasional note of certain features reminiscent of dream vision poetry in general, and *Piers the Plowman* in particular.

The Castle of Perseverance

In a general sense, *The Castle of Perseverance* could be said to be based on Christ's promise to his followers (Matt. 24:13): "But he that shall endure [*perseveraverit*] unto the end, the same shall be saved." But the play as a whole is determined by the life of Mankind, the central figure, who comes on stage literally at birth: "This night I was of my mother born," he says to the audience, "full faint and feeble I come before you." About the middle of the play we are informed that he is forty years old (line 1578), near the end he dies in a bed located beneath the Castle (line 3008), and, as the stage directions inform us, his Soul (Anima) rises from under the bed—evidently played by a different actor—and takes the place of his body for the remaining 642 lines of the drama.

Like the Cornish cycle discussed earlier, *The Castle of Perseverance* has with its text a diagram showing how it is to be staged. Richard Southern has made a careful study of this, and we do well to follow his suggestions in the interpretation of the plan. The area first was to be enclosed by a circular fence or ditch, designed to exclude those who do not pay for admission. At the center of the circle is the Castle, with Mankind's bed beneath, and around the perimeter, but inside the barrier, are located five "scaffolds," which are platforms occupied by the main characters of the play. At the four points of the compass we find God (east), World (west), Flesh (south), and Belial or the Devil (north). The fifth scaffold is for Covetousness, placed in the northeast, between God and the Devil. Since God speaks only at the end of the play, the forces arrayed against Mankind would appear to be formidable indeed.

The diagram surpasses those of the Cornish drama in the fullness of its instructions. In the circle representing the enclosing ditch, for example, is written: "This is the water about the place, if any ditch may be made where it shall be played, or else that it be strongly barred all about; and let not over-many stytelerys be within the place." The "stytelerys" (sticklers) are presumably the marshals assigned to control the crowds; some would of course be necessary for this purpose, but too many would apparently obstruct the view of the audience ringed around the edges of the circular playing place (*platea*) or green. Richard Southern postulates some fluidity in the audience, allowing them to encroach on the *platea* and perhaps to some extent move with the action from scaffold to scaffold. His theory is supported indirectly by another statement in the diagram: "This is the Castle of Perseverance, that standeth in the midst of the place; but let no man sit there, for letting [hindering] of sight; for there shall be the best of all." Evidently the marshals are being instructed to keep the audience away from the central area of the Castle, where they would obstruct the view.

Other instructions on the diagram relate in interesting ways to details of production. Thus we are told, "he that shall play Belial, look that he have gunpowder burning in pipes in his hands, and in his ears and in his arse, when he goeth to battle." The costuming and choreography of the beautiful conclusion of the play is referred to: "The four daughters [of God] shall be clad in mantles: Mercy in white, Righteousness in red all together, Truth in sad [dark] green, and Peace all in black; and they shall play in the place together till they bring up the Soul." Also, as we have noted, "Mankind's bed shall be under the Castle, and there shall

[48]

the Soul lie under the bed till he shall rise and play." Finally, there is one other instruction which Southern found to be some-what enigmatic: "Covetousness' cupboard, by the bed's feet, shall be at the end of the Castle." This he paraphrased as follows: "Covetyse's cupboard (?), (which is required) at the end of *The Castle* (that is, near the end of the play), shall be by the foot of the bed (under the tower)." But there remains some uncertainty concerning the actual uses of this cupboard in the play. To this problem we shall return when we reach that scene near the end in which I believe the cupboard was meant to be employed in the action.

The cast of characters is large, but organized in such a way as to facilitate our understanding of them. They are deployed in a hierarchical arrangement. Mankind himself is accompanied by a Good Angel and an Evil Angel. His three major antagonists are the World, the Flesh, and the Devil (Belial), each with his own staff of subordinates: the World has Lust-liking, Folly, and Boy; the Flesh has Gluttony, Lechery, and Sloth; and Belial has Pride, Wrath, and Envy. Notice that the Flesh and the Devil have be-tween them six of the traditional seven Deadly Sins, while World has a rather undistinguished trio of assistants who have only a minor part in the action. But this is because World's true agent is Covetousness (*Avaricia*), who has, as we noted, a scaffold of his own, and who plays a crucial role in the temptation of Man-kind. Indeed a particular feature of *The Castle of Perseverance* is its emphasis on Covetousness as the most sinister and dangerous of the sins. In his book *The Seven Deadly Sins* (1952), Morton Bloom-field makes the interesting point that in the early Middle Ages, in a strongly hierarchical society, pride was appropriately singled out as the worst of the sins; but toward the close of the medieval period, with the rising power of the merchant class, the emphasis in the pulpit shifted and covetousness went to the head of the list. This shift is well illustrated in our play.

Other facilitators of the action are Back-biter, who teaches Man-kind the sins, and Shrift and Penance, who help him purge him-self of them. His greatest single group of defenders is the army of virtues: Humility, Patience, Charity, Abstinence, Chastity, In-dustry, and Generosity. As Southern points out, these are not the usual Seven Virtues. Instead they are the traditional "reme-dies," each opposed to one of the seven Deadly Sins. We find them, for example, in the seven sisters who serve Truth in *Piers the Plowman* (B V 627–38). It is these Virtues who defend Mankind in the Castle against the onslaught of the army of sins. Toward the end of the play, seven more characters appear to complete the cast: Death, who strikes the fatal blow; the Soul of Mankind, who rises up when he dies; the four Daughters of God (Mercy, Truth, Righteousness, Peace), who debate whether Mankind should be saved; and finally God Himself, who hands down the decision.

The action of the play, covering the whole life of Mankind, has numerous ups and downs. The barest outline of events will have to suffice. Mankind listens to his two counselors and decides to follow the Evil Angel. He is met by Lust-liking and Folly and escorted to World's scaffold. World shows him every courtesy, and Back-biter teaches him the seven sins. From this gang he is then rescued through the agency of Shrift and Penance and brought into the Castle of Perseverance in the company of the Seven Virtues. Thus the lines are drawn and the battle between the vices and virtues begins: Pride is pitted against Humility, Wrath against Patience, Envy against Charity, and so on. The fiercest battle is between Covetousness and Generosity. The sins are pelted with roses (emblems of Christ's Passion) and are forced to retreat. Mankind remains safe in the Castle, and for a time it appears that Virtue will be triumphant. But finally Covetousness approaches the Castle and entices Mankind to leave the protection of the Virtues. As old age creeps up on him, Mankind asks for more and more wealth, until finally Death strikes the fatal blow, and the World and his forces take back all their wealth, leaving Mankind to die alone and in misery. But the Soul arises and appeals for mercy. The four Daughters of God debate the question and God decides in favor of Mankind, giving him a place of honor at His right hand.

At times the language and action of *The Castle of Perseverance* echo *Piers the Plowman*. World boasts that he is freshly fed "with fair folk in the field" (*CP* 187, *PP* B Prol. 17). Covetousness enfeoffs Mankind with the seven Deadly Sins (888ff.) in a manner reminiscent of the charter proclaimed by Simony and Civil for the marriage of Meed in *Piers the Plowman* (B II 75ff.). Back-biter's box, wherein he bears about man's bane in the form of letters of defamation (*CP* 670–72), is the evil counterpart of the packet of Patience, containing the remedy for all the ills and strife of mankind (*PP* B XIII 151ff.). In *Piers* the debate of the Four Daughters precedes the Resurrection of Christ; in *The Castle* it precedes the salvation of Mankind. Both the poem and the play feature a siege: in one the attack of the army of Antichrist on Piers' Barn of Unity representing Holy Church (B XX), and in the other the assault on the Castle by the Deadly Sins (1878–2531). In *Piers*, Covetousness is so fierce a fighter that Conscience gives a cry of reluctant admiration and says he wishes that Covetousness were on his side (XX 121–42). In *The Castle*, as we have seen, it is Covetousness who turns the tide of battle against the Virtues.

It is interesting to compare the fate of the Dreamer in *Piers the Plowman* with that of his counterpart Mankind in *The Castle of Perseverance*. The Dreamer appeals for help to Kind (Nature), and is directed to the Barn of Unity, where he goes, by means of contrition and confession, and joins the forces of good still holding out against the army of Antichrist. The defenses of Holy Church are crumbling, but the Dreamer at least has taken the fundamental step necessary for his own salvation.

The case is quite otherwise with Mankind, who remains concerned to the very end with the "necessities" of this life, and relies on the World to supply them. At first Covetousness is obliging and gives him a thousand marks (2727), as well as title to "cliff and coast, tower and town" (2756). It is at this point, I take it, that the playwright intended for the cupboard of Covetousness to come into play. We have seen that it was to be placed at the foot of Mankind's bed, but there was some uncertainty as to its use, since no other directions are given, and in the dialogue Mankind speaks of burying his gold "under the ground." But since, as Southern points out, World later sends to retrieve the gold, I think it more likely that Mankind simply stored his money and deeds in the cupboard, from which it is later removed by the Boy appropriately named "I-Know-Not-Who" (2957–58). Thus Mankind dies looking at the empty cabinet at his feet. This vividly dramatizes the case of a man who has virtually become the personification of the sin by which he was overcome. The cabinet is his "chest," that emblem of Covetousness popularized in medieval iconography, and cited in exemplary fashion as a warning by the enigmatic old man in Chaucer's "Pardoner's Tale" (VI 734–36):

> Mooder, with yow wolde I [ex]chaunge my cheste
> That in my chambre longe tyme hath be,
> Ye, for an heyre clowt to wrappe in me!

[51]

Having lost everything, Mankind finally confesses his folly, and struggles feebly to avoid falling into despair: Good men, take example at me; look out for your spiritual welfare while there is time. My face is fading like a flower; I am dying, my heart is breaking, and I can say no more. Then, having successfully resisted the ultimate danger of despair, he adds:

> I put me in God's mercy.

These simple words thus provide the basis for his eventual salvation, when God welcomes him to Paradise:

> My mercy, Mankind, give I thee.
> Come, sit at my right hand!

Thus the Dreamer of fourteenth-century vision poetry is effectively transformed on stage into Mankind, the central protagonist of the English morality. It is perhaps this remarkable literary development that contributed most to the superiority of the morality plays in England to those that emerged on the Continent.

CHAPTER TWO

Medieval Lyrics and the Church Calendar

IN the following discussion, we shall approach Middle English lyrics from the point of view of content and purpose, rather than form. Rarely have these lyrics as a whole been approached in this way, despite the fact that they are what we would call "occasional" poems. Most if not all of these lyrics were composed to celebrate particular days or seasons of the Church calendar, both the *temporale* and the *sanctorale*. Not every lyric can be dated, of course, but in the ensuing remarks I shall try to show how the lyrics as a whole tend to reflect the ecclesiastical calendar of the Middle Ages.

The calendar that we will be following begins with Advent (the four weeks before Christmas), continues through the Christmas season to its climax on Epiphany (January 6), and concludes its first phase with Candlemas (February 2). From Septuagesima through Lent there was a period of religious instruction and fasting (in February and March) which preceded Holy Week and led up to Good Friday and Easter, the high point of the religious year. Then came the celebration of Ascension, Pentecost, Trinity Sunday, and the feast of Corpus Christi in May and June, thus completing the sequence of moveable feasts tied to the date of Easter. Then followed a selection of feast days such as the Nativity of John the Baptist or Midsummer's Day (June 24), Mary

Magdalene (July 22), the Name of Jesus (August 7), the Assumption of the Virgin (August 15), and Holy Cross Day (September 14). Finally, Advent completed the calendar year by stressing not only the Nativity but also the second advent of Christ at the Last Judgment. The modern reader who approaches the Middle English lyrics in this fashion has an excellent opportunity to achieve a sympathetic understanding of the religious life of medieval people. In the ensuing discussion most of the lyrics are taken from the editions of Carleton Brown, but the English is modernized. Roman numerals indicate the century to which the lyric belongs, and the arabic numeral identifies the particular lyric in that volume. For an explanation of the other abbreviations used, see the section in the Bibliographical Essay for this chapter.

One of the most popular themes in lyrics devoted to the Virgin was the celebration of the joys she experienced in being the mother of God. The earliest and most common list of joys is that found in a thirteenth-century English lyric (XIII 41): the Annunciation, Nativity, Resurrection, Ascension, and Assumption. Since the calendar dates represented here range from December to August, it is somewhat arbitrary to place all of these under Advent; yet the importance of the Virgin in the celebration of Advent provides some justification.

As the popularity of this theme increased, a variety of forms developed. Thus a fourteenth-century version of the five joys opens in the manner of a *chanson d'aventure* (XIV 11):

> As I rode out this other day
>   by a green wood in search of pleasure,
> In my heart I thought of a maid,
>   the sweetest of all thing.
> Listen and I will tell you
>   about that sweet one.

Borrowing the language of secular love, the speaker goes on to identify this maid as the Virgin mother and to declare that he has fallen in love with her:

> With all my life I love that maid,
> She is my solace night and day,
> My joy and also my best pleasure
>   And also my love-longing;
> All the better for me is that day
>   When of her I sing.

[54]

He then enumerates the five joys, in this instance the Annunciation, Nativity, Epiphany, Resurrection, and Assumption.

In oral tradition the song of Mary's joys appears in numbers from five to twelve, the latter number perhaps first established by the merging of earthly and heavenly joys, although this distinction was soon forgotten. After the Reformation, the heavenly joys, associated with the Assumption and Coronation of the Virgin, were replaced by earthly joys such as this one (OBC 70):

> The next good joy that Mary had,
> It was the joy of four;
> To see her own son, Jesus Christ,
> To read the Bible o'er.

We have seen how a traditional theme such as the five joys was given a *chanson d'aventure* setting and amorous vocabulary (XIV 11). The subject of the Annunciation provides us with a similar, even more impressive example of romance influence on the Middle English lyric. I refer to the following poem of only six lines preserved in a manuscript of the fourteenth century (XIV 130):

> At a spring-well under a thorn,
> There was remedy for ill, a little before now;
> There beside stands a maid,
> Full of love ybound.
> Whosoever will seek true love,
> In her it shall be found.

At first glance the subject seems to be entirely secular, but such is not the case. A key phrase is "remedy for ill" (bote of bale), which in the language of love can refer to the lady's acceptance of the lover's plea and ultimately of their sexual union. But although this remedy, we are told, has already been provided (a lytel here a-forn), the person standing before us is a "maid" (virgin), a point designed to alert us that the remedy for ill has a religious meaning, namely the redemption of mankind from the sin of Adam. Like some of the very best lyrics, this one presents us with a tableau: a framed portrait of the Virgin standing beside a spring under a thorn tree. Shortly before this picture was made, we are told indirectly, this maid was visited by the Holy Ghost, thus assuring a remedy for the ills of mankind through the Incarnation.

The ambiguity of the landscape in this portrait has a function analogous to that of the phrase "remedy for ill." Our first impression is one of bleakness, suggested by the thorn tree. Despite the presence of the "spring well," the heroine seems a lonely figure against an austere background. But there are latent biblical allusions here that soon overcome our initial impression. The traditional image of the Virgin as a well of mercy (as Chaucer's prioress calls her) is but one indication of the significance of the "spring-well," a symbol of promised redemption. We may recall the water from the rock in Exodus (17:6), and the waters of Shiloah that flow gently (Isa. 8:6), to mention two examples. The tree is the blossoming thorn, symbolic of the Redemption, derived from the thorns that sprang up after Adam's fall (Gen. 3:18), and the blossoming rod of Aaron (Num. 17:8), which together with the rod of Jesse (Isa. 11:1) generated the flowering rod of Joseph in the New Testament Apocrypha. Both the blossoming thorn and the spring-well appear in a fifteenth-century carol preserved in the manuscript of Richard Hill (EEC 123A). I quote the burden and the first two stanzas:

> *Alleluia, alleluia,*
> *Glory be to God the Father.*
> There is a blossom sprung of a thorn
> To save mankind, that was forlorn,
> As the prophets said before;
> *Glory be to God the Father.*
> There sprang a well at Mary's foot
> That turned all this world to good;
> Of her took Jesus flesh and blood;
> *Glory be to God the Father.*

The fact that the fourteenth-century lyric mentions only the thorn, and not its blossoming, helps explain our initial impression of a desert background, against which the maid appears as a beautiful but lonely figure. Then, in a pivotal line, she is described as "full of love ybound." Now the word "ybound" can have very unfavorable connotations, as in the famous Nativity song (XV 83): "Adam lay ybounden." But our initial feeling that the maid is bound, perhaps in chains, like Adam, is contradicted by the statement that she is full of love. The constraints of love are voluntary. Thus it dawns on us that this maid is the one who lovingly responded to the message of Gabriel: "Be it unto me according to thy word" (Luke 1:38). Then, in the final two lines of the lyric, the presence of the observer of this tableau is recognized for the first time:

> Who-so will seek true love,
> In her it shall be found.

We who have tended to view this scene in a worldly way as a lonely and desolate place discover that we were mistaken, and we are now invited to receive the love of this maid, a love that is not weak but strong, available to all, and one which endures forever. This lyric is a remarkable blend of secular and religious ingredients, and an excellent illustration of the difficulty of classifying Middle English lyrics as "secular" or "religious."

Undoubtedly the most famous of all lyrics devoted to the Annunciation is the following (XV 81):

> I sing of a maiden that is matchless,
> King of all kings as her son she chose.
>
> He came as still where his mother was
> As dew in April that falleth on the grass.
>
> He came as still to his mother's bower
> As dew in April that falleth on the flower.
>
> He came as still where his mother lay
> As dew in April that falleth on the spray [branch].
>
> Mother and maiden, was never one but she—
> Well may such a lady God's mother be.

This lyric depicts the moment announced by Gabriel when "the Holy Ghost shall come upon thee, and the power of the Highest shall overshadow thee" (Luke 1:35). It appears to be inspired in part by an earlier Annunciation lyric (XIII 31), but differs from it in important ways. For example, the earlier lyric relates that the king of all kings chose the Virgin as his mother, whereas this song represents Mary as choosing him to be her son, thus emphasizing the Virgin's voluntary acceptance of her role as mother of the Redeemer.

The three central stanzas, by a remarkable employment of incremental repetition, delicately depict the solemn moment of union between the divine and the human. The child-to-be first approaches the place "where his mother was," then comes to the "bower" (bedroom), and finally to "where his mother lay." The dew similarly approaches—falling on the grass, the flower, and the spray. We are told that He who approaches is her Son, and yet his approach is also that of a lover, as is delicately suggested by the dew imagery, which has amorous meaning in secular song, as well as redemptive significance in biblical texts such as Isaiah 45:8. The word "still" effectively and repeatedly expresses the courtesy of the divine lover, and his unfailing deference to the will of the virgin mother. The last stanza affirms the uniqueness of this moment and the fitness and nobility of Mary as the mother of God. She who was called "maiden" is now referred to as "such a lady," a word which hints at her eventual assumption and coronation as Queen of Heaven.

The complete harmony of sacred and sexual significance in this lyric is a remarkable achievement, reminiscent of the Song of Solomon as traditionally interpreted. In part this may be explained by a freedom in the treatment of sexual themes available to poets before the Reformation (which we no longer have, despite our "free speech"). It is interesting to compare "I Sing of a Maiden" with another lyric in the same manuscript (Sloane 2593) entitled "I Have a Gentle Cock" (N 77), which has a structure very similar to "I Sing of a Maiden," but has a purely amorous significance.

Our review of the Advent season would not be complete without an acknowledgment of the importance of the feast of Saint Nicholas (December 6). The origin of this saint is obscure. He appears to have been a fourth-century bishop of Myra in Lycia, which was in Asia Minor, but the stories about him seem to be no earlier than the ninth century and are largely fictional. Some of the best-known episodes are preserved in *The Golden Legend*. When his parents died, Nicholas inherited great riches, and he determined to distribute his wealth to the honor and glory of God. It was then that he heard of a poor neighbor whose three virgin daughters were on the point of giving themselves up to prostitution to keep the family from starvation. Horrified at this, Nicholas came secretly at night and threw a bag of gold into his neighbor's house. When the man awoke in the morning he found the gold, gave thanks to God, and used it as a dowry to arrange the marriage of his eldest daughter. Nicholas repeated this a second and a third time, thus providing enough gold for the marriage of all three daughters. The three bags of gold are remembered in this saint's emblem (three balls), which in turn eventually become the sign of the moneylender.

The same fifteenth-century songbook that has the unique text of "I Sing of a Maiden" also has a carol devoted to Saint Nicholas, which begins as follows (EEC 316):

> In Patros, there born he was,
> The holy bishop Saint Nicholas,
> He wist mickle [knew much] of God's grace
> Through virtue of the Trinity.

Among the various episodes of the Saint's life alluded to in the carol is the one about the three daughters:

> He married three maidens of mild mood;
> He gave them gold for their food;
> He turned them from ill to good
> Through virtue of the Trinity.

The song ends with a simple prayer to God for salvation. The significance of this carol in its relation to the Church calendar, however, is best seen in its burden, presumably repeated after each stanza:

> *Make ye merry as ye may,*
> *And sing with me, I you pray.*

Already here we can see signs that Saint Nicholas is being taken over by the spirit of the Advent season, and has thus begun the process that will transform him into Saint Nick, Sinte Klaas, or Santa Claus, the jolly old elf who brings gifts to children and embodies the spirit of Christmas.

The earliest Christmas song is a carol of about 1350. The carol is a composition having a "burden" to be sung after each stanza, and it seems to have originated as a song designed for use in a ring dance. The participants join hands and move in circular fashion around something or someone in the manner of "Here we go 'round the mulberry bush." The history of this form has been carefully researched by Richard L. Greene, editor of the early English carols. Greene cites as the earliest known Christmas carol a text found in a manuscript of the mid-fourteenth century (MS Bodley 26), which has the following burden (EEC 12):

> *Hand by hand we shall us take,*
> *And joy and bliss shall we make,*
> *For the devil of hell man hath forsaken,*
> *And God's Son is made our mate.*

[59]

This burden contains some interesting clues. From it we learn that the song was intended to accompany a dance in celebration of the Nativity, which is here viewed in the light of its theological implications (the salvation of man). The fourth line may seem strange in its insistence that God's Son is made our "mate," but the meaning of this is clarified when we take note of the context for the song in the manuscript. The notes immediately preceding the Christmas carol are as follows (folio 201b): "This is that meal spoken of in Apocalypse 19:9 of the blessed who are invited to the feast of the Lamb." The biblical passage referred to contains a proclamation of the marriage of Christ and the Church (the Saints), ending with this exclamation: "Blessed are they which are called unto the marriage supper of the Lamb" (Rev. 19:9). This messianic feast in heaven is of course far removed in time from the Nativity, but if we remember the dual emphasis of the liturgy of Advent on the first *and* second comings of Christ, an allusion to his return at the end of the world in a Nativity song should not be surprising. When the Child is born, can the marriage supper of the Lamb be far behind? The second stanza of this carol recapitulates the entire history of the Redemption:

> Sinful man, be blithe and glad,
> For thy marriage thy peace is proclaimed
>   When Christ was born!
> Come to Christ—thy peace is proclaimed;
> For thee was his blood shed,
>   That were forlorn.

Thus the festive banquet associated with Christmas was not designed for self-indulgence, but was meant to be a foretaste of the marriage supper of the Lamb at the world's end. It is perhaps significant that the earliest Christmas carol could as easily be classified as a Doomsday song.

Another lyric presents a dialogue between the Virgin and Christ child, a format which was to become especially popular in the fifteenth century. The opening reminds us of the *chanson d'aventure* (XIV 56):

> As I lay upon a night
> Alone in my longing,
> Methought I saw a wonder sight,
> A maid a child rocking.

[60]

The child speaks first, asking his mother to sing him a song:

> "Sing now, mother," said that child,
> "What me shall befall
> Hereafter when I come of age,
> As do these mothers all.
>
> "Every mother truly
> That can her cradle keep
> Is wont to lullen lovely
> And sing her child asleep."

Thus the child invokes the custom of lullaby singing, and in the first stanza calls upon Mary to predict his future. The gift of prophecy has been attributed to parents from the earliest times. Lamech, father of Noah, predicted that his son would bring from the ground a means of comfort after toil and labor (Gen. 5:20), apparently alluding to Noah's later invention of wine (Gen. 9:30–31). In the lyric, however, Mary does not prophesy, but merely recapitulates for the child the story of Gabriel's visitation and the appearance of the angels to the shepherds. So Jesus himself prophesies, relating the Circumcision, Epiphany, Purification, his visit to the Temple at the age of twelve, and finally the major events of his adult life including the baptism, temptation, the sending out of disciples, and the people's desire to make him king. Mary expresses delight at this last, but Jesus goes on to warn her of his death on the cross, reminding her of what Simeon had said, namely that "a sword shall pierce through thy own soul" (Luke 2:35). When Mary responds to this with an outburst of grief, Jesus comforts her with references to his Resurrection and Ascension, the Assumption of the Virgin herself, and his return to judge the world at Doomsday. The first person narrator then concludes this lyric as it began:

> Certainly this sight I saw,
> This song I heard to sing,
> As I lay this Yule's day
> Alone in my longing.

Few Nativity songs have as full a narrative as this (thirty-seven stanzas), but the notion of the Christ child as prophet of his own future shows up frequently in later carols, lyrics, and ballads, as for example in "The Cherry Tree Carol" (Child 54A10):

[61]

> Then Mary took her babe
> And set him on her knee,
> Saying, my dear son, tell me
> What this world will be.

From sacred song the idea of infant prophecy passes into secular tradition, and finds its way into the American ballad about that steel-driving man "John Henry," who, as a child sitting on his mama's knee, prophesies that "steel is gonna be the death of me."

The later Nativity carols almost without exception show the growing importance of Christmas festivities in the fifteenth century. Here is the opening of a carol in the collection made by James Ryman, a Franciscan, in 1492 (EEC 3):

> *Farewell Advent, Christmas is come;*
> *Farewell from us both all and some.*
> With patience thou hast us fed
> And made us go hungry to bed;
> For lack of meat we were nigh dead;
> Fare-well from us both all and some.

The singer complains that Advent (personified) had fed all those in his house with nothing but "stinking fish not worth a louse," since salt fish and salmon were "too dear," with thin plaice that was nothing but skin and bones, and with mussels "gaping after the moon." He goes on to call Advent ungrateful and rude, and orders him to leave town: "Go hence, or we will break thy pate!" At the end, all are exhorted to be merry in this time of Christ's natal feast.

Of course no discussion of the Christmas season would be complete without reference to that perennial favorite "The Twelve Days of Christmas." Everyone knows this song, which is built on an enumeration of the gifts the lover provides on each of the twelve days, and unwinds like "The House that Jack Built." The "twelve days" of course refer to the sequence of holy days in the calendar from the Nativity to Epiphany, which were in medieval times the subject of carols such as the following from a fifteenth-century manuscript (EEC 8):

> *Make we mirth*
> *For Christes birth,*
> *And sing we yule til Candlemas.*
> The first day of yule have we in mind,
> How God was man born of our kind,

> For he the bonds would unbind,
>   Of all our sins and wickedness.
> The second day we sing of Stephen,
>   That stoned was and steyed [ascended] up even
> To God, that he saw standing in heaven,
>   And crowned was for his prowess.

It goes on to devote stanzas to Saint John (December 27), the slaughter of the Innocents (December 28), Saint Thomas of Canterbury (December 29), Circumcision (January 1), Epiphany (January 6), and adds a final stanza on the Purification of the Virgin— that is, Candlemas (February 2). No doubt this kind of numerical recitation of the days of Christmas provided the frame for the modern secular adaptation familiar to us today. But there is another lyric that may also have played a part in the creation of this song. "I Have a New Garden" is an attractive love lyric preserved in the fifteenth-century Sloane manuscript, a collection noted for having a number of songs that survive in oral tradition. The pear tree in this lyric has an unmistakable amorous significance (N 78):

> In the midst of my garden
>   Is a pear tree set,
> And it will grow no pear
>   But a pear Janet.
>
> The fairest maid of this town
>   Prayed me
> To graft her a shoot
>   Of my pear tree.
>
> When I had grafted them
>   All at her will,
> The wine and the ale
>   She did in fill.
>
> And I grafted her
>   Right up in her home;
> And by that day twenty weeks
>   It was quick in her womb.
>
> That day twelve-month
>   That maid I met:
> She said it was a pear Robert,
>   But not a pear Janet.

In "The Twelve Days of Christmas" the pear tree loses its sexual significance and simply takes its place in the sequence of odd but harmless gifts that "my true love gave to me." It is unfortunate

[63]

that no intermediate texts survive to reveal to us the evolution of this fascinating Christmas song.

To round out the Christmas season according to its fullest definition, we have still to consider Plow Monday (the first Monday after Epiphany), the Conversion of Saint Paul (January 25), and Candlemas (February 2). Although two of these have a clearly religious origin, all three feasts have a secular significance extending back perhaps to pre-Christian times.

Plow Monday marks the beginning of winter planting season. It is a time for invoking God's blessing on the harvest to come, as expressed in this popular couplet (MS Trinity Cambridge R 3.14, flyleaf):

> God speed the plow
> And send us corn enow [enough]

A similar sentiment is expressed in a fifteenth-century carol intended for singing on Plow Monday (EEC 418.2 st 8):

> However January blow
> Whether high or low
> God speed the plow alway!

Planting time was also a time of concern about the weather and any other factors that might be a threat to the success of the agricultural season. In our day of supermarkets and frozen foods it is difficult to imagine how important it was to understand and perhaps predict the conditions that assured a good harvest. Also, for Englishmen, the factors favoring a safe journey overseas were constantly scrutinized. The author of the alliterative poem *Piers the Plowman* spoke gloomily in the late fourteenth century of the failure of the art of prediction among his contemporaries, in particular singling out shipmen and shepherds for their inability to read the signs in the heavens (B-text XV 353-64).

Under such conditions, a society dependent on the success of agriculture must live in a constant state of anxiety. But through the centuries a system of prediction had established itself in association with the Church calendar. One of the most crucial times in winter, when the hardships of cold weather loomed uncertainly ahead, was Saint Paul's Day (January 25), which from time immemorial was an occasion for prophesying the year ahead (N 110):

> If St. Paul's day be fair and clear,
> Then shall betide a happy year.
> If it chances to snow or rain,
> Then shall be dear all kind of grain.
> And if the wind be high aloft,
> Then war shall vex the kingdom oft.
> And if the clouds make dark the sky,
> Both neat [cattle] and fowl that year shall die.

The feast of the Purification of the Virgin (February 2) is called Candlemas because of the tradition in the Church of the blessing and distribution of candles, which were carried in a procession memorializing the purification of Mary after the birth of Jesus (Luke 2:22–39). The lighted candles were no doubt intended as a reminder of the words of Simeon concerning the Messiah: "a light to lighten the Gentiles" (Luke 2:32), echoing Isaiah's prophecy (49:6): "I will also give thee for a light to the Gentiles, that thou mayest be my salvation unto the end of the earth." Following the example, as it seemed, of the Virgin, women who had given birth adopted the custom of carrying candles to church when they returned for their purification or "churching" as they called it. Robert Chambers, in his *Book of Days*, tells a story showing how this practice, so familiar in medieval times, was used as a grim figure of speech by one of the greatest of English kings:

William the Conqueror, become, in his elder days, fat and unwieldy, was confined a considerable time by sickness. "Methinks," said his enemy the king of France, "the king of England lies long in childbed." This being reported to William, he said, "When I am churched, there shall be a thousand lights in France!" And he was as good as his word; for, as soon as he recovered, he made an inroad into the French territory, which he wasted wherever he went with fire and sword.

Perhaps even more than Saint Paul's Day, Candlemas was a time for predicting the year's weather, specifically the duration of winter:

> If Candlemas day be dry and fair,
> The half o' winter's to come and mair;
> If Candlemas day be wet and foul,
> The half of winter's gone at yule.

The Reformation, of course, severely undermined observance of the feast days of the calendar, which was regarded as a popish invention. Even Christmas itself came under attack. But old traditions die hard. America's civil religion does not recognize Candlemas, but we still have a special affection for February 2, and call it ground-hog day.

The importance of Candlemas as a time for sowing and planting tempts me into a digression on the longevity of traditional songs associated with agriculture. A case in point is the planting and raising of barley, a popular crop in England from the early Middle Ages used for brewing. A reference to the barley harvest forms the basis of riddle number 28 in the Exeter book (A.D. 1000):

> Part of the earth   is fairly enriched
> With the hardest   and with the keenest
> And most terrible   of treasures of men.
> Carved and scoured,   dried and turned,
> Bound and wound,   bleached and softened,
> Decked and prepared,   it is drawn from afar
> To the doors of men.   Mirth of mortals
> Is in it then,   and remains and endures
> To all those   who erstwhile live long,
> Enjoy their desires,   and do not abuse it.
> Then after its death   begin they to deem
> And mouth many things.   Much it is to think on
> For learned men   who this one may be.

The brewing process is here cryptically described, and the "death" of the grain is followed by its "resurrection" in the bodies of inebriated men, an idea derived from Saint Paul's comparison of the body to a grain of wheat (1 Cor. 15:37).

Songs that play on the effects of drink in the manner of the Exeter riddle appear as early as "Allan-a-Maut," which is recorded in the Bannatyne manuscript of the mid-sixteenth century. A hundred years later a broadside was published with the title "A Pleasant new Ballad to sing both even and morne, of the bloody murther of sir *John Barley-corne*" (Evans IV 34). This amusing song depicts a conflict between Sir John of the title and three antagonists named Thomas Goodale, Richard Beer, and Sir William White-wine. Because of the popularity of Sir John, all the others gang together and swear that he shall die. The slaying is accomplished in a manner reminiscent of the Exeter riddle:

> Then with a plow they plowed him up,
>   And thus they did devise
> To bury him quick within the earth

And swore he should not rise.
With harrows strong they combed him,
And burst clods on his head,
A joyful banquet then was made
When Barleycorn was dead.

The process of growing and harvesting of the barley follows the calendar:

He rested still within the earth,
    Till rain from skies did fall,
Then he grew up in branches green,
    Which sore amaz'd them all.

And so grew up till midsummer [June 24],
    He made them all afraid,
For he was sprouted up on high,
    And got a jolly beard.

Then he grew till St. James tide [July 25]
    His countenance was wan,
For he was grown unto his strength,
    And thus became a man.

The song goes on to describe how Sir John was cut down, stacked, carted, beaten, sifted, sacked, steeped, rubbed, dried, and then taken to the mill. The song here very much resembles a similar passage in the Old English riddle:

Corfen, sworfen,   cyrred, þyrred,
bunden, wunden,   blæced, wæced,
frætwed, geatwed,   feorren læded. . . .

From the mill Barleycorn is taken to be washed in a vat, "beaten into barm," and finally put into a barrel:

And then they set a tap to him,
    Even thus his death begun,
They drew out every drop of blood,
    Whilst any drop would run.

But at last, Sir John has his revenge: when his enemies have drunk his blood, he deprives them first of their tongues, then their legs, and finally their sight:

Some lay groaning by the walls,
    Some fell in the street down right,

[67]

> The best of them did scarcely know
> What he had done o'er night.

This song has remained popular to the present day in some dozen different versions, from the broadside of 1645 to a modern song in an album by Traffic entitled "John Barleycorn Must Die."

Having considered so many secular traditions associated with Candlemas, we should not lose sight of the fact that the religious meaning of the feast, at least in the Middle Ages, was not forgotten. A standard carol for Candlemas survives from the fifteenth century (EEC 140 st 4):

> This holy day of Purification
> To the temple thou bare our salvation,
> Jesu Christ, thine own sweet son,
>   To whom therefore now sing we:
> (burden): Revertere, revertere,
> The queen of bliss and of beauty.

The burden just quoted derives from the Song of Solomon 6:13, "Return, return, O Shulamite; return, return, that we may look upon thee," where, as we have seen, the interpretation of the bride as the Virgin Mary is frequently found in medieval commentaries and sermons. In another carol, in the early sixteenth-century manuscript of Richard Hill, the spirit of Christmas speaks and bids farewell to one and all (EEC 14):

> Now have good day, now have good day!
> I am Christmas, and now I go my way.
> Here have I dwelled with more and less
> From Hallowtide till Candlemas,
> And now must I from you hence pass;
>   Now have good day!

With this delightful carol, which gives us the fullest possible definition of the holidays extending from Hallowtide (November 1) to Candlemas (February 2), we take leave of the joyous season of Christmas and turn our attention to the more somber period of Lent leading up to the observances of Holy Week and Easter. Yet even here, as we shall see, secular themes blend easily with sacred ones in the celebration of this holy time.

Septuagesima to Holy Week

The time of year that begins with Septuagesima and extends through Lent was traditionally a period of religious instruction for acolytes and spiritual preparation of the whole congregation for Easter. The annual schedule of Bible readings began on Septuagesima with Genesis, and the entirety of biblical history was taught as an allegorical account of man's spiritual quest, both individually and collectively, as is recapitulated in *The Golden Legend*:

> At Septuagesima beginneth the time of deviation or going out of the way, of the whole world, which began at Adam and dured unto Moses. And in this time is read the Book of Genesis. The time of Septuagesima representeth the time of deviation, that is of transgression. The Sexagesima signifieth the time of revocation. The Quinquagesima signifieth the time of remission. The Quadragesima [first Sunday of Lent] signifieth of penance and satisfaction.

Thus in this time the individual penitent lives through the stages of the collective history of mankind in preparation for the coming of the Redeemer. Of course, the process of spiritual renewal should be continuous, but the logistics of pastoral care in the Middle Ages often made it impossible for the parish priest to examine his charges more frequently than once a year during Lent. For this reason I include here a variety of lyrics concerned with spiritual instruction, even though many of them are in fact appropriate for any time of year.

Lyrics of simple religious teaching are commonplace, but by their very nature are less interesting or creative. There are lyrics devoted to the Ten Commandments (XII 23, 70; XIV 102), the Lord's Prayer (XII 59, 67; XV 53), and various mysteries of the faith (XV 117–21). Only occasionally do these rise above their didactic purpose, as in this epigram (XV 119):

> Wit hath wonder that no reason tell can,
> How maiden is mother, and God is man.
> Leave thy reason and believe in the wonder,
> For faith is above, and reason is under.

Along with the didactic pieces we might expect to find songs arising specifically from the Mardi gras season, but there is nothing here to equal the richness of the Christmas repertoire discussed earlier. There is, however, an interesting composition by the Scottish poet William Dunbar (ca. 1460–ca. 1520), "The Dance of the Seven Deadly Sins" (N 165), the action of which takes place on Shrove Tuesday or, as the Scots call it, "Fasterns Even."

Says Dunbar's poem: On the night of February 15 I lay in a

trance and saw a vision of heaven and hell. In the latter regions
the devil was organizing a dance, composed of wretches who had
not been to confession, in observance of the feast of Fasterns Even.
To take part in this dance there came forth, one by one, the seven
deadly sins. Pride came first, accompanied by a group of impos-
ters, wading through scalding fire. Wrath had with him an army
of boasters, braggers, and wranglers, all dressed in armor and
carrying various weapons. Envy was followed by flatterers, back-
biters, and whisperers of lies, and Covetousness by userers, mi-
sers, and hoarders. Sloth and his sleepy gang were so slow in
the dance that the devil had to lash them and spur them on with
fire. The last dancer was Gluttony, who came in followed by many
a fat drunkard with wagging belly, crying aloud for something to
drink. In response the devil "gave them hot lead to lap."

The poem concludes with an amusing condemnation of Scottish highland culture, including the Gaelic language (Erse):

> Then cried Mahoun [devil] for a highland pageant;
> Syne ran a fiend to fetch MacFadden
>   Far northward in a nook:
> When he the correnoch [outcry] had shouted out,
> Ersemen so gathered him about,
>   In hell great room they took.
> Those termagants, with tag and tatter
> Full loud in Erse began to clatter
>   And croaked like raven and rook.
> The devil so deafened was with their yell,
> That in the deepest pit of hell
>   He smothered them with smoke.

Here the general condemnation of human weaknesses in the dance
of the sins is given a specific local application that undoubtedly
elicited a partisan response. Dunbar's poem is fittingly representative of Shrove Tuesday, both in its festive style and its
confessional theme (the sins).

Ash Wednesday marks the beginning of Lent, a period of fasting for forty days preceding Easter. The word "lent" is a pre-
Christian, Anglo-Saxon word derived from the verb "lengthen,"
in reference to the lengthening of the days during this season.
Thus Lent also means spring, a time when our thoughts turn to
love (XIII 81):

> Lent is come with love to town,
> With blossoms and with birds' song,

That all this bliss bringeth;
Daisies in the dales,
Sweet notes of nightingales,
Each fowl a song singeth.
The thrustle-cock him chideth aye;
Away is their winter woe,
When woodruff springeth.
These fowls sing, wondrous many,
And warble in their winter joy,
So that all the wood ringeth.

This thirteenth-century lyric at first glance seems merely to celebrate the coming of spring. But in the second stanza, amid further description of nature's bounty, we learn that the speaker himself does not join in the spirit of spring, because love has not favored him. The sun and moon give their light, birds sing, the various members of the animal kingdom live in harmony, and even worms "woo under the clods." But then:

Women wax wonder proud,
As well it befits them.
If I shall want [lack] the will of one
This winsome weal I will forgo
And quickly to wood be gone.

What begins as a celebration, affirming the harmonies of nature, ends on a note of love-longing.

Although we mainly think of Lent as a penitential season, it is well to take note of the love songs associated with this time of year. Perhaps the most significant single collection of love songs is the so-called Harley lyrics (ca. 1300), in the British Library manuscript Harley 2253, which contains "Lenten Is Come with Love to Town" quoted above. There are wooing songs, such as "Alysoun" (XIII 77) and "Lady, Have Ruth on Me" (XIII 78); songs in defense of women (XIII 82); dialogues such as "De Clerico et Puella" (XIII 85); and songs of praise such as "The Loveliest Lady in Land" (XIII 83), with its memorable refrain:

Blow, northern wind,
Send thou me my sweeting!
Blow, northern wind,
Blow! blow! blow!

Mingled with these secular love lyrics, however, are songs that speak of the love of God in very much the same idiom. The latter are usually regarded as adaptations of secular love songs for religious purposes. No doubt this is true in some cases, but I think it would be safer to allow the possibility that adaptation of this sort was a two-way street, and that there may be some cases of a religious song providing the inspiration of a secular one.

A good illustration of the problem of distinguishing original from imitation occurs in a comparison of two lyrics found side by side in the Harley manuscript. The first of these begins as follows (XIII 90):

> Little wot it any man
>   How love him hath bound
> Who for us on the cross [with blood] ran,
>   And bought us with his wound.
>   The love of him hath made us sound
>   And cast the grimly ghost [Satan] to ground.
> Ever and aye, night and day, he hath us in his thought,
> He will not lose what he so dearly bought.

Compare this with the opening of the second lyric (XIII 91):

> Little wot it any man
>   How derne [secret] love may stand
> Unless it were a free [noble] woman
>   That much of love had known.
>   The love of her lasts not ever long;
>   She is pledged to me, but puts me in the wrong.
> Ever and aye for my dear I am in great thought [distress];
> I think on her that I see not oft.

Which is the original, and which is the copy? Carleton Brown, in his notes to these lyrics, points out that portions of the religious version appear in manuscripts of the thirteenth century, but concludes that the secular song must be the original, citing "the telltale phrase 'derne love,' which is a clear indication that this religious poem was an adaptation of a secular lyric" (p. 236). The opening of the Caius College manuscript text reads:

> Little wot it any man
> How derne love was founde
> But he that was on cross done
> And bought us with his wound.

It is true that "derne love" is a phrase used to refer to physical love, but there is nothing to prevent a poet from using this phrase figuratively, and there is ample precedent for the idea in medieval commentaries on the Song of Solomon. We need not pursue this case further; I offer it simply as an example of the difficulty of deciding the question of secular or religious priority.

A most interesting case, where secular and religious love are blended in a single lyric, is the "Love Rune" of Friar Thomas de Hales (XIII 43), which begins as follows:

> A maid of Christ asked me eagerly
>   That I make her a love rune,
> Whereby she might best learn
>   How to take another true love,
> One who would be truest of all men
>   And best could keep a free woman.
> I wish not at all to refuse her,
>   I will teach her as I can.

"Rune" can mean "composition" or "song," but also has connotations of magic and the supernatural. As used here, I suspect it is meant to suggest a spell or charm by which a girl hopes to win herself a lover, an ancient practice surviving vestigially in such refrains as "parsley, sage, rosemary, and thyme," and such practices as pulling the petals from daisies to determine if "he loves me" or "he loves me not."

Thomas's "Love Rune" is in twenty-six eight-line stanzas rhyming abababab, and teaches the girl to whom it is addressed to turn from the vanities of this world to the love of Christ. This world's love, says Thomas, is but a frenzy, fickle and frail. Mighty warriors, bold in battle, are gone like a puff of wind, lie cold in the earth, and fade like the meadow grass. All men are mortal: none is so rich or noble that he is not soon snatched away, nor may he buy his life with gold or silver, ermine or fur. And so this world, as thou mayest see, is like a shadow that glides away. Blind is the man who places his love in this world. No matter how extensive his possessions, he shall wither like a leaf on the bough. Man's love is but for an hour; he loves now here, now there. No faithful man is to be found. If you trust him, you are mad. Where are the great lovers of yesteryear—Paris and Helen, Tristan and Iseult? They are as if they had never been.

Ah sweet maid, exclaims Friar Thomas, let me tell thee of a real lover, a true king. He is free of heart, unrestrained in wisdom, and thou needest never fear to put thyself in his protection. He asks no dowry; on the contrary, if thou wouldst offer him thy love, he would bring thee such a garment as neither king nor

[73]

kaiser possesses, and a mansion surpassing all the palaces that Solomon ever built. Thou shalt be in heaven, where no friend turns against another, and there is neither hate nor wrath, pride nor envy, and all shall rejoice with angels in heaven's light, when they see our Lord in his power. Would he not be blessed indeed, maid, who might dwell with such a knight?

Meanwhile, says Thomas, he hath committed to thee a treasure that is better than gold, and biddeth thee lock thy bower and guard it well (Song of Sol. 4:12). This treasure is a gem brought from far away, and there is none better under heaven. It is chosen before all others, it healeth all love wounds. Well were anyone alive who might remain in this state, for if thou hast once lost it, it shall never again be found:

> This same stone that I tell thee of
>   Is called Maidenhood;
> It is a precious gem,
>   That is excellent above all others,
> And bringeth thee without blemish
>   Into the bliss of Paradise.
> While thou guardest it under thy hem
>   Thou art sweeter than any spice.

This gem of virginity is set in heavenly gold and is filled with pure love. All that can should guard it, it shines so bright in heaven's bower. I send thee this rhyme, maid, open and without seal (in contrast to the secrecy of earthly love letters); I pray that thou unroll it and learn it all by heart, and that thou be kind enough to teach it well to other maidens. When thou sittest in longing, draw forth this writ; with sweet voice sing it, and do as it biddeth thee. May God be with thee and bring thee to his bridal feast in heaven.

This "Love Rune" is a very appropriate prelude to the penitential lyrics of the Lenten season, for it reminds us that the often severe sentiment of these lyrics is directed toward a positive end: reconciliation with God and acceptance of his love. So many and varied are these Lenten songs that I have divided them, somewhat arbitrarily, into five categories: *contemptus mundi*, satire, wisdom, death, and penance. Yet nearly all of these categories offer themes that are treated, if only briefly, in Thomas's "Love Rune."

Contempt for worldly values is perhaps best epitomized in this mid-thirteenth-century lyric (XIII 38):

Now thou wretched body that on bier liest,
Where be thy robes of fur and ermine?
There was a day when thou didst change them thrice,
And try to make a heaven of the earth whereon thou liest,
Thou that shall rot as doth the leaf that hangeth on the branch.
Thou didst eat thy food prepared in cauldrons,
While thou lettest the poor stand outside in frost and ice,
Thou wouldst not bethink thee to be wise,
Therefore hast thou lost the joy of paradise.

Carleton Brown entitles this "Over the Bier of the Worldling," which well expresses the implied position of the speaker of the poem. But the theme of this meditation is clearly aimed at the living, who are to avoid the folly of the worldling, and share what they have with the poor, as the Lord commanded (Matt. 25:31–46). The severity of the poem, therefore, is really no greater than that of the gospel: "Depart from me, ye cursed, into everlasting fire, prepared for the devil and his angels" (Matt. 25:41).

Lyrics of the satirical group likewise attack the worldly point of view, but with an ingredient of comedy lacking in "Over the Bier of the Worldling." A good example is the piece entitled "On the Follies of Fashion" (XIII 74), in which common women are attacked for seeking to imitate the fashions of ladies. Items mentioned are the pleating of linen "bosses" (ruffles?) and elaborate headdress. In particular, women who wear the "bosses" are assured that they shall go to hell, where they are pictured in a way that ridicules the fashion they are so proud of:

Now they lack no linen to make into bosses;
They sit like a hunted swine that hangeth his ears.
Such a jousting device each wretch shall wear,
Even though it go out of fashion, this harlots' gear.
　Up aloft
　The devil may sit soft
　And hold court very oft.

We tend to think of carols as exclusively serious and lyrical, but in fact satirical carols are not uncommon. The fifteenth-century manuscript Sloane 2593 contains a goodly number of these, commenting sardonically on various human failings. One offers ironic thanks to the power of the purse (EEC 390):

Sing we all and say we thus:
Thank you, my own dear purse.
When I have in my purse enough,

I may have both horse and plow,
And also friends enough—
    Through the power of my purse.

When my purse beginneth to slack,
And there is nought in my pack,
They will say, "Go! farewell, Jack,
    Thou shalt no more drink with us."

Thus are all my goods forlorn,
And my purse tattered and torn;
I may play me with a horn
    Instead of my purse.

Farewell, horse, farewell, cow,
Farewell, cart, and farewell, plow;
As I played me with a bow
    I said, "God, what is all this?"

Driven by an empty purse to the risky business of poaching in the king's forests, the speaker finally asks that question about the rat race which we find implicit in all medieval satire: What is this world? What is it all about?

In another carol from the same manuscript the speaker is in search of Truth (EEC 385). He searches unsuccessfully among great lords, in the chambers of ladies, among lawyers, and even in Holy Church. In a last despairing effort he turns to the religious orders:

Religious, who should be good,
If Truth come there, I hold him mad;
They would rend him coat and hood
    And make him flee all bare.

Suddenly the carol ends with a discovery:

A man who would of Truth espy
He may find him easily
In the bosom of Mary,
    For there he is, forsooth.

Thus all satire is forgotten, and the tone of the ending reminds us of Friar Thomas's "Love Rune." When an attitude of contempt of the world is strong, as in this carol, satirical indignation must eventually give way to an expression of faith in divine protection.

Under the heading of "Wisdom" I include those lyrics that seek to impart directly those teachings that are merely implicit in satirical pieces. The Boethian nature of this wisdom is evident in a fourteenth-century quatrain (XIV 42):

> The lady Fortune is both friend and foe:
> The poor she maketh rich, the rich poor also;
> She turneth wo into weal, and weal all into wo.
> No man should trust this weal, the wheel it turneth so.

The speaker takes the famous wheel of fortune from Boethius's *Consolation of Philosophy* as a device for teaching us to scorn the gifts of the world, and catches our attention with his pun (weal, wheel). A more detailed statement of Boethian philosophy is contained in this twelve-line poem from a manuscript of the fifteenth century (XV 192):

> The law of God be to thee thy rest,
> The flesh thy sacrifice, the world exile,
> God thy love and thy treasure best,
> Heaven thy country through all the while.
> Repentance take thou into thy breast
> For thine unkindness and wickedness vile,
> And abide at home within thy nest
> Lest showing pity thou be trapped with guile,
> Except that sometimes like a hasty guest
> Thou arise to do good, but for no long while.
> Have done, glutton, flee to this (celestial) feast!
> For herein of all winning lieth cross and pile.

Despite the essential seriousness of this prescriptive lyric, it ends with an unexpected flash of humor. In the last two lines the speaker gives us a glimpse of the worldly object of the poem's wisdom: he is a glutton and a gambler, a devotee of fortune's wheel. A freer translation of the final couplet makes this point clear:

> Begone, glutton, to the Feast that never fails!
> There all are winners, both heads and tails.

The ultimate inducement to the worldling to give up his mad pursuits, of course, is the contemplation of death. Poems on this subject exist in profusion, and we may here notice only a few representative examples. Despite the variety, however, most death lyrics are in a sense commentaries on a single parable of Jesus (Luke 12:16–20).

> And he spake a parable unto them, saying, The ground of a certain rich man brought forth plentifully: And he thought within himself, saying, What shall I do, because I have no room where to be-

stow my fruits? And he said, This will I do: I will pull down my barns, and build greater; and there will I bestow all my fruits and my goods. And I will say to my soul, Soul, thou hast much goods laid up for many years; take thine ease, eat, drink, and be merry. But God said unto him, Thou fool, this night thy soul shall be required of thee: then whose shall these things be, which thou hast provided?

This text was taken seriously as a measure of the value to be placed on worldly possessions. The poet's contribution is often simply a blunt and sardonic reminder of the finality of death (XIII 30):

> When the turf is thy tower
> And the pit is thy bower,
> Thy flesh and thy white throat
> Worms shall consume.
> What helpeth thee then
> All the world to win?

Some of these lyrics were of course much more philosophical and explicitly didactic, as was the song translated from French by the Franciscan friar William Herebert (ca. 1333), which Brown has entitled "Make Ready for the Long Journey" (XIV 23). It is in seven stanzas, with refrain, containing instructions in preparation for death. Man must keep his bags packed, for he knows not when he must leave on his journey. This world is filled with sorrows, and wealth and power are no use, for when the spirit departs, the body is wound "in grit or hair" (earth or, at best, a shroud). Think, man, consider carefully what you should trust in before you come to court (judgment). If you have done good here, then you will be well received; otherwise, beware! Whether you are young or old, strong or famous, you shall not escape: "Death is hid, man, in thy glove." One good deed before death is better than ten afterward. When the ghost is taken from the body, "the barns shall soon be emptied" (Luke 12:18); when the body is in the ground, the soul shall be left bare of friends.

The emphasis on good works in the death lyrics is of course derived from Jesus' teaching concerning the corporal works of mercy (Matt. 25:31–46), but its use in these lyrics seems to have made a deep impression on the minds of people down through the centuries. In this connection it is interesting to recall "The Lyke-wake Dirge," recovered from oral tradition by John Aubrey in the seventeenth century. This was a song sung at funeral wakes, and it describes the journey of the soul of the departed across the

"whinny-moor" (field covered with briars) and the "bridge o
dread" (Aubrey, pp. 177–78):

> When thou from hence away dost pass
> *Every night and all*
> To whinny-moor thou comest at last
> *And Christ receive thy soul.*
>
> If ever thou gave either hosen or shoon
> *Every night and all*
> Sit thee down and put them on
> *And Christ receive thy soul.*
>
> But if hosen nor shoon thou never gave none
> *Every night and all*
> The whinnies shall prick thee to the bare bone
> *And Christ receive thy soul.*

A similar test awaits the departing soul at the "bridge o dread":

> If ever thou gave either milk or drink
> *Every night and all*
> The fire shall never make thee shrink
> *And Christ receive thy soul.*
>
> But if milk nor drink thou never gave none
> *Every night and all*
> The fire shall burn thee to the bare bone
> *And Christ receive thy soul.*

This is impressive evidence of the impact of medieval death lyrics
on the folk imagination.

The few examples cited above are (except for the dirge) from
the thirteenth and fourteenth centuries. But by far the largest
number of death lyrics were composed in the fifteenth century,
a time when death became a major preoccupation. Carleton Brown
includes a series of sixteen examples from this period in his edition (XV 149–64). The opening line of some of these will perhaps
indicate the variety of lyrics represented there: "Farewell, this
world! I take my leave forever" (149); "O vanity of vanities, and
all is vanity" (151); "O Death, how bitter is the thought of thee"
(154); "Wake, man, sleep not, rise up and think that earth thou
art" (155); and "World's bliss, have good day!" (160). Laments,
exhortations, apostrophes, and meditations are among the forms
included here. There is even one in which Death menaces maidens engaged in dressing themselves, which the editor entitles, "A
Mirror for Young Ladies at Their Toilet" (XV 152):

[79]

Mayest thou now be glad, with all thy fresh array,
To look on me, who soon will stain thy face?
Pity thyself, and all thy sin erase!
Soon shalt thou flit and seek another place;
Short is thy season here, though thou go gay.

One is reminded of that gothic emblem, picturing a beautiful young woman looking in a mirror, which when viewed at a distance has the appearance of a death's head.

It is interesting to observe that as we come closer to the Renaissance, there is an occasional example of the lyric on death that might better be called an elegy. By this I mean a poem or song in which the didactic purpose is largely suppressed and a feeling of melancholy prevails. Such is the case with "Lament for the Makaris" (makers = poets), a poem of twenty-five stanzas by Dunbar, said to have been composed "when he was sick." Contributing significantly to this mood of melancholy is the Latin refrain line, taken from the seventh lesson in the third nocturn of the Office of the Dead, and repeated at the end of each stanza: *"Timor mortis conturbat me"* (Fear of death disturbs me). The first half of the poem is a roll call of all ranks of society, none of whom can escape death (Kinsley, no. 62):

He takes the champion in the stour [battle],
The captain, closed in the tower,
The lady in bower, full of beauty;
Timor mortis conturbat me.

He spares no lord for his puissance,
No clerk for his intelligence;
His awful stroke may no man flee;
Timor mortis conturbat me.

Art-magicians and astrologers,
Rhetoricians, logicians, and theologians,
Have no help from their conclusions sly;
Timor mortis conturbat me.

In medicine the great practitioners,
Leeches, surgeons, and physicians,
Themselves from death they may not flee;
Timor mortis conturbat me.

In the second half of the poem Dunbar reels off the names of the great writers of the past, beginning with the most famous:

He did most piteously devour
The noble Chaucer, of makers flower,
The monk of Bury [Lydgate], and Gower, all three;
    Timor mortis conturbat me.

As he goes on to list the other "Makaris," Dunbar provides effective variations in his description of how death goes about his work. "That fell scorpion has infected/Master John Clerk and James Afflek"; Blind Harry and Sandy Traill death has "slain with his shower of mortal hail"; and in Dunfermline, death "has whispered [roune] to Master Robert Henryson." And when the list is completed Dunbar concludes:

Since he has all my brothers tane [taken],
He will not let my life alane,
Perchance I may his next prey be;
    Timor mortis conturbat me.

Since for death remedy is none,
Best is that we for death dispone [prepare],
After our death that live may we;
    Timor mortis conturbat me.

Thus the didactic note appears at the end, but it is not strong enough to counterbalance the grim recitation that precedes it, and we are left with a distinct and lingering mood of lamentation.

Before leaving the subject of death, let me call attention to a poem which is one of my favorites, and yet one which is rarely anthologized. For this reason I quote it in full (Padelford 17):

THE EPITAPH OF LOBE, THE KING'S FOOL

O Lobe, Lobe, on thy soul God have mercy!
For as Peter is *princeps apostolorum* [prince of apostles],
So to thee may be said clearly,
Of all fools that ever was, thou art *stultus stultorum* [fool of fools].
Sure thy soul is *in regna polorum* [in the heavens]
By reason of reason thou haddest none.
Yet all fools be not dead, Lobe, though thou be gone.

The loss of thee, Lobe, maketh many sorry,
Though it be not all for thine own sake;
But the King and the Queen thou madest so merry
With the many good pastimes that thou didst make.
Could thy life be bought, I dare undertake,
Gold nor silver there should lack none.
Yet fools there be enough, though thou be gone.

Thou wast a fool without fraud,
Shaped and born of very nature.
Of all good fools to thee may be laud [praise],
For every man in thee had great pleasure;
For our King and Queen thou wast a treasure.
Alas! for them where could we get such a one?
Yet all fools be not dead, though thou be gone.

Thou wast neither Erasmus nor Luther:
Thou didst meddle no further than thy pot;
Against high matters thou wast no disputer;
Among the innocents elect was thy lot.
Glad mayest thou be thou haddest that knot [hump],
For many fools, seeing thee, think themselves none.
Yet all be not dead, Lobe, though thou be gone.

Duke apWilliams, prepare his obsequies,
Nature constraineth you to do him good;
The mad lady Appleton offer the mass-penny,
And ye as chief mourner in your own fool's hood!
Your wits were much alike, though nothing of blood,
Save in him was much goodness and in you is none.
Yet ye be a fool, and Lobe is gone.

Now Lobe, Lobe, God have mercy on thy merry noll [head],
And Lobe, God have mercy on thy foolish face,
And Lobe, God have mercy on thy innocent soul,
Which among innocents I am sure hath a place,
Or else my soul is in a heavy case [bad way].
Yea! Yea! and more fools many a one,
For folly be alive, Lobe, though thou be gone.

Now God have mercy on all,
For wise and foolish all dieth;
Let us truly to our minds recall
That to say we be wise our deeds denieth.
Wherefore the end my reason thus applieth:
God amend all fools that think themselves none,
For many be alive, though Lobe be gone.

The mention of Erasmus and Luther suggests that this poem probably dates from the reign of Henry VIII, near the time of the Reformation. The author is unknown, but one feels that he must have been a high-ranking member of the court. Certainly his wit and his emotions are both strongly present in this epitaph. To say that the death of Lobe is used as the occasion for satire would be to overstate the case, for the poem seems to me to radiate a genuine grief, out of which the satire spontaneously emerges. "Duke apWilliams" and "lady Appleton" of the fifth stanza appear to be general pseudonyms for all of the (Welsh?) courtiers who show themselves to be fools. But the anonymous "chief mourner" addressed in the last four lines seems to be a particular person, the main object of the poet's wrath. You and Lobe were alike in intelligence, says the poet, though you were not alike in blood, because you are of the nobility and Lobe was not; but the real difference between you is that in Lobe was much goodness, and in you is none. Throughout this searing stanza the poet addresses the nameless nobleman with mock politeness (ye, your, you) in contrast to his familiar, affectionate manner in speaking to Lobe (thou, thy, thine). But in the final two stanzas, his outward hostility vanishes, and the poet gazes inward to examine the state of his own soul, in a return to the didactic purpose we have found to be characteristic of the medieval lyrics in this group.

Such meditations on man's mortality were designed to lead to repentance, and there are numerous penitential lyrics that in various ways express the speaker's contrition, the confession of his sins, and his resolve, with the help of Christ, to sin no more. But these ingredients are not always fully present. One of the earliest such lyrics is highly ambiguous (XIII 8):

> Fowls in the frith [wood],
> The fishes in the flood,
> And I must wax wood [mad].
> Much sorrow I walk with
> For the best of bone and blood.

The meaning of the last line is uncertain ("For beste of bon and blod"), and yet this line is obviously crucial to the meaning of the whole. "For *beast* of bone and blood" has been suggested, but in the above modernization I have made explicit what I take to be the meaning of "beste": the *best*. Nevertheless one might still ask, who is "the best of bone and blood"? If we read the poem as a lover's complaint, "the best" would be his beloved. Yet I am inclined to think (with Edmund Reiss) that this is a religious lyric, and "the best of bone and blood" means Christ. The speaker sees the animal kingdom living in harmony, each member knowing his place, while only man resists the harmony of God's creation. In the words of Isaiah (1:3): "The ox knoweth his owner, and the ass his master's crib: but Israel doth not know, my people doth not consider." Yet through Christ, God has shown man the way, and when the speaker thinks of Christ's sacrifice on the cross, he is sorry for his sins. This interpretation is perhaps too exact, because it ignores interesting ambiguities in the poem. The speaker's mood is such that he is unwilling to be as explicit as we have made him. It is impossible to tell whether he is experiencing contrition, which will lead to repentance, or merely attrition, a state of mind that recognizes sin but is unable to do anything about it. This uncertainty adds to the lyric's force, for it creates the impression that we are being allowed to experience, with the poet, a genuine spiritual crisis.

Quite otherwise is a poem of the later thirteenth century that begins as follows (XIII 66):

> No more will I wicked be,
> Forsake I will this world's fee,
> This wild clothing, this fool's glee;
> I will be mild of cheer,
> Of knots shall my girdle be,
> I will become a friar.

Other lyrics in this group take the form of appeal and exhortation, as in this brief poem from the middle of the fourteenth century (XIV 50):

> Heaven, it is a rich tower,
> Well be him that it may win,
> Of mirth more than heart may think,
> And the joys shall never end.
> Sinful man, unless thou amend
> And forsake thy wicked sin,
> Thou must sing aye "wellaway"!
> For cometh thou never more therein.

Often Jesus himself delivers the appeal, as in this piece from John Grimestone's Commonplace Book of 1372 (XIV 63):

> I am Jesus, that came to fight
> Without shield and spear,
> Else were thy death dight [certain]
> Were it not for my fighting here.
> Since I am come, and have thee brought
> A blisful boot of bale [remedy for ill],
> Undo thy heart, tell me thy thought,
> Thy sins great and small.

Another lyric from the same source beautifully dramatizes Jesus' appeal to the sinner, together with the sinner's response and his resolution to repent (XIV 68):

> "Undo thy door, my spouse dear,
> Alas! why stand I locked out here?
>   For I am thy mate.
> Look, my locks and also my head
> And all my body with blood bedewed,
>   For thy sake."
>
> "Alas! alas! evil have I sped,
> For sin Jesus is from me fled,
>   My true companion.
> Without my gate he standeth alone,
> Sorrowfully he maketh his moan
>   In his manner."

This first half of the poem takes the form of a dialogue in which Jesus stands at the door and knocks, asking to be admitted. One thinks immediately of "Behold, I stand at the door and knock" (Rev. 3:20), which Brown chooses for his (Latin) title. But Jesus' use of the word "spouse" should alert us that here is another of those remarkable adaptations of the Song of Solomon, so popular in medieval lyrics and the drama (5:2): "I sleep, but my heart waketh: it is the voice of my beloved that knocketh, saying, Open to me, my sister, my love, my dove, my undefiled: for my head is filled with dew, and my locks with the drops of the night." With a single, startling change, when the dew on the beloved's head becomes drops of blood, we are made to realize that the bridegroom of Solomon's Song has become the crucified Christ. But the sinner's response is one of disappointment; because of sin, "Jesus is from me fled." Again we find that the form of the dialogue reflects the biblical text (Song of Sol. 5:6): "I opened to my beloved; but my beloved had withdrawn himself and was gone." But the Lord is not really gone, for in the latter part of the poem the speaker addresses him in passionate language:

> Lord, for sin I sigh sore,
> Forgive, and I'll do so no more,
> With all my might I forsake my sin,
> And open my heart to take thee in.
> For thy heart is cleft our love to catch,
> Thy love has chosen us all to fetch;
> My heart it pierced if I were kind,
> Thy sweet love to have in mind.

[85]

> Pierce my heart with thy loving,
> That in thee I may have my dwelling.
> Amen.

Although the Song of Solomon provides the main biblical source for this lyric, an image of the crucified Christ is also central, and indeed provides the impetus for the speaker's repentance. This may serve as a reminder that the biblical account of the Crucifixion inspired by far the greatest number of lyrics, and it is to these that we now turn.

The Passion

On the day before his Passion (Maundy Thursday) Jesus shared a Passover meal with his disciples, during which he let it be known that one of them would betray him. Readers of the Bible have always been fascinated by the question of the motivation of the traitor Judas, and in a remarkable thirteenth-century lyric (sometimes called the first popular ballad) a unique account of the betrayal is set forth (XIII 25):

> It was on a Holy Thursday that our Lord arose,
> Full mild were the words he spoke to Judas:
> "Judas, thou must [go] to Jerusalem our food to buy;
> Thirty pieces of silver thou bearest upon thy back;
> Thou comest far in the broad street, far in the broad street,
> One of thy kinsmen there thou mayest meet."

The notion that Jesus sent Judas to buy food perhaps originated in John's report of speculation among the disciples, when Jesus dismissed Judas, namely that the latter was told to "buy those things that we have need of against the feast" (John 13:29). *Not* mentioned here in the Bible are the thirty pieces of silver, and Jesus' reference to the "broad street," perhaps an allusion to the wide gate and broad way of the Sermon on the Mount (Matt. 7:13). That Jesus tells Judas that he may meet a kinsman on his way perhaps echoes other precise predictions made to the disciples (e.g., Mark 13:13–16), but the significance of the remark becomes clear in the next episode:

> He met with his sister, the deceitful woman:
> "Judas, thou wert worthy that men stoned thee with stone,
> Because of the false prophet that thou believest upon."
> "Be still, dear sister, thine heart it may break!
> If my Lord Christ knew this, revenge he would take."

> "Judas, go thou on the rock, high upon the stone,
> Lay thy head in my bosom, and sleep thou anon."
> As soon as Judas of sleep was awoken,
> Thirty pieces of silver from him were taken.

As Peter Dronke has suggested, the word "sister" is here used sardonically as a reference to Judas's mistress. This lends additional significance to Jesus' description of her as "one of thy kinsmen." That Judas himself should be betrayed by a woman finds ample precedent in the story of Adam and Eve (Gen. 3:1–19), but the device of putting him to sleep in her lap so as to betray him is reminiscent of Delilah's treachery when she caused Samson to "sleep upon her knees" (Judg. 16:19). Without pressing the comparison too far, we might even say that when Judas, in distress over the loss of the money, madly pulls out his hair ("He drew himself by the top, so that it ran with blood") this is reminiscent of what was done to Samson to deprive him of his strength: a man was ordered "to shave off the seven locks of his head."

Next Pilate comes forth and asks Judas if he is willing to sell his Lord. The conversation between them is in the popular style, and illustrates well why Professor Child regarded this piece as a forerunner of the ballad tradition:

> "Wilt thou sell thy Lord that is called Jesus?"
> "I will not sell my Lord for any kind of trade,
> Unless it be for the thirty pieces, that he to me paid."
> "Wilt thou sell thy Lord Christ for any kind of gold?"
> "Nay, unless it be for the pieces that he will recall."

We thus discover that the reason for Judas's betrayal is not to be found in some uncommon flaw, but in a simple, even ridiculous human weakness. His mistress has stolen his silver, and he dreads that Jesus will discover the loss, since he would be forced to return without the food he was told to buy. Paradoxically, he is willing to betray his Lord in order to avoid being found out by his Lord, so he takes the thirty pieces of silver from Pilate and buys the food. Now the scene shifts back to the Last Supper for the end of the story:

> In came our Lord as his apostles sat at meat:
> "Why sit ye, apostles, and why will ye not eat?
> I am bought and sold today for our meat."
> Up stood him Judas, "Lord, am I the one you seek?
> I was never in the place where men evil of thee speak."

[87]

> Up stood him Peter, and spoke with all his might:
> "Though Pilate come with ten hundred knights,
> Yet I would, Lord, for thy love fight."
> "Still be thou, Peter, well I thee know;
> Thou wilt forsake me thrice ere the cock him crow."

In his very denial, Judas clumsily reveals his guilt. But then, lest we tend to think of him as a uniquely evil sinner, the poet concludes with a reference to the weakness of Peter, prince of the apostles. Judas is not allowed to become a scapegoat, and we are indirectly reminded through Peter that Christ "was wounded for our transgressions" (Isa. 53:5).

The largest single category of lyrics consists of those devoted to Good Friday. And aside from the occasional piece devoted to other incidents of that day—such as Christ's prayer in Gethsemane (XIV 62)—most of these are concerned with the Crucifixion, which is viewed from every conceivable vantage point. From this abundance we may only look at a few representative examples.

One of the finest lyrics of the cross is a quatrain appearing in a treatise composed by Saint Edmund Rich at the monastery in Pontigny, France, where he died in 1240. The treatise is entitled *Le Merure de Seinte Eglise* (The Mirror of Holy Church), and in chapter XXIV is related the commitment of the Virgin to Saint John (John 19:25–27). Mary's sorrow is first compared to that of Naomi (Ruth 1:20); then she is quoted as saying (from Song of Sol. 1:6), "Look not upon me, because I am black, because the sun hath looked upon me" ("car le solail me ad descolurée"). Immediately following this we are told that "un Engleis" (Saint Edmund?) composed the following quatrain in the form of a pietà ("en teu manere de pite") (XIII 1):

> Now goeth sun under wood;
> Me rueth, Mary, thy fair rode [face],
> Now goeth sun under tree;
> Me rueth, Mary, thy son and thee.

The speaker reveals the Crucifixion indirectly by concentrating on the Virgin's face, metaphorically darkened by the sun, in reality shadowed by grief. Indeed there is no direct reference to the cross, although the first three rhyme words suggest it (wood, rood, tree). But in the final line the speaker expresses pity for "thy son and thee," thus making it clear that we are witnessing sunset on Calvary. The play on words and compression of language makes this a most remarkable Passion lyric.

At the other end of the spectrum is the kind of Crucifixion poem that is strongly narrative and detailed in its treatment of the story. A favorite of mine is the one which Carleton Brown entitles "A Springtide Song of the Redemption" (XIII 54). Summer is come and winter gone, says the poet. The day lengthens and the birds sing. But despite the joy all around me, a sorrow fiercely binds me for a young man who is gentle. Through bush and bank he sought me, and he found me bound because of an apple from a tree. Then he broke the bond that was so strong through his wounds. He was sold to Jews: they did not know who he was. "Let us nail him on a tree upon a hill," they said, "but first we must shame him a while." They made sport of this king, struck him, wounded him on a cross, and gave him a bitter drink. He took death on the cross, he who was life for us all, and saved us from the pains of hell. The sixth stanza describes the Crucifixion scene:

> Maiden and mother there stood
> Mary full of grace,
> She let her tears, all of blood,
> Fall in that place.
> The trace
> ran of her blood,
> changed her flesh and blood
> and face.
> He was drawn [torn]
> Like a deer slain
> in the chase!

Mary's tears of blood are traditional, but the marring of her face seems a more explicit way of evoking pity than the delicate in-direction of "Now goeth sun under wood." By far the most strik-ing effect of this stanza, however, is the hunting image of the last three lines applied to the crucified Christ. Peter Dronke rightly calls attention to the forcefulness of this image, and points out that there is no counterpart for it in the Passion narrative. But the close association of the Twenty-second Psalm with the Cru-cifixion leads me to think that this hunting image was suggested by references to the "dogs" surrounding the speaker (Ps. 22:16, 20), who was traditionally identified as the crucified Christ.

In certain other lyrics the speaker addresses the crucified Christ, expressing his love for him or asking the Lord to help him. Here is one which Brown entitles "A Prayer of the Five Wounds" (XIV 52):

> Jesus Christ, my lover sweet,
> That for me died on the tree,
> With all my heart I thee beseech
> For thy wounds two and three,
> That as firmly in my heart
> Thy love rooted might be,
> As was the spear in thy side,
> When thou suffered death for me.

Then there is this impassioned prayer in the Ellesmere manuscript (XV 98):

> O Jesus, let me never forget thy bitter passion,
> That thou suffered for my transgression,
> For in thy blessed wounds is the very school
> That must teach me by the world to be called a fool.
> O Jesus, Jesus, grant that I may so love thee,
> That the wisdom of the world be clean gone from me,
> And burningly desire to come see thy face,
> In whom is all my comfort, my joy and my solace.

And here is one (adapted from Augustine's *Confessions,* VIII, 5) that belongs in this category, I think, though it does not mention the cross (XIV 5):

> Lord, thou didst call me
> And I naught did answer thee
> But in words slow and sleepy:
> "Stay yet! stay a little!"
> But "yet" and "yet" was endless,
> And "stay a little" a long way is.

More rarely the speaker will address the cross itself (XIV 40):

> Steadfast cross, among all others
> Thou art a tree of great price,
> In branch and flower such another
> I know of none in wood nor grove.
> Sweet be the nails,
> And sweet be the tree,
> And sweeter be the burden that hangeth upon thee!

This particular lyric is from the fourteenth century, but it is the kind of meditation on the cross destined to become much more popular in the fifteenth century, when crucifixes began to multiply in chruchyards and by roadsides. Examples also of popular piety are lyrics devoted to the Hours of the Cross (XIV 34, 55; XV 93, 94) and to the seven words (XV 96).

We have already noted the importance of the Virgin as a witness to the Crucifixion (based on John 19:25), but there are numerous lyrics in which we actually see events through the eyes of the Virgin. Often we feel the poet is trying to communicate to us what Mary experienced when (in the words of Simeon) "a sword will pierce through your own soul also" (Luke 2:35). Medieval artists were able to depict this figurative sword literally piercing the Virgin's breast as she stands beneath the cross, but poets accomplished this by presenting a sharp grief that borders perilously on despair (XIV 64):

> Sweet son, have pity on me, and burst out of thy bonds;
> For now me thinketh that I see, through both thy hands,
> Nails driven into the tree, so ruefully thou hangest.
> Now it is better that I flee, and leave all these lands.

After describing in piteous terms his cruel suffering on the cross, Mary concludes:

> Sweet son, pity me and bring me out of this life,
> For me thinketh that I see thy death, it nigheth swiftly;
> Thy feet be nailed to the tree—may I no more thrive,
> For all this world without thee shall not make me blithe.

An even more explicit death wish is expressed dramatically in a lyric in which the Virgin addresses the executioners (XIV 60):

> Why have ye no pity on my child?
> Have pity on me, full of mourning,
> Take down from the cross my dear child,
> Or pierce me on the cross with my darling.
>
> More pain to me may not be done
> Than let me live in sorrow and shame;
> As love bindeth me to my son,
> So let us die, both the same.

Perhaps the most striking representation of the Virgin's grief was the pietà, which depicts that moment after the deposition from the cross (not recorded in the Bible) when the Virgin cradled

[91]

the body of her son in her arms before it was taken to be buried in the tomb by Joseph and Nocodemus (John 19:38–42). The pietà was an outgrowth of the devotional tradition of the later Middle Ages, hence is most popular in the fifteenth century. An excellent illustration is a carol of the fifteenth century (EEC 161), of which I give the refrain and first stanza:

> *Suddenly afraid, half waking, half sleeping,*
> *And greatly dismayed, a woman sat weeping.*
>
> With favor in her face far passing my reason,
> And of her sore weeping this was the occasion:
> Her son in her lap lay, she said, slain by treason.
> If weeping might ripe be, it seemed then in season.
>   "Jesus!" so she sobbed
>   How her son was mocked
>   And of his life robbed;
> Saying these words, as I tell thee:
> "He who cannot weep, come learn from me."

The refrain provides a dream-vision framework, and the carol sets forth the process whereby the dreamer is taught to weep from the example set by the Virgin.

The "cradling" of Christ's body by the Virgin in the typical pietà often suggests that in her grief she sees her son once again as a child. Some depictions even show the slain body in her arms as unnaturally small, no doubt to suggest this to the viewer. This feature of the pietà, if kept in mind when reading (or hearing) certain medieval lyrics, can be very helpful. Indeed I believe it holds the key to an understanding of one of the most famous and mystifying of all, the "Corpus Christi" carol (EEC 322A):

> *Lully, lullay, lully, lullay,*
> *The falcon hath borne my mate away.*
>
> He bare him up, he bare him down,
> He bare him into an orchard brown.
>
> In that orchard there was an hall
> That was hangèd with purple and pall.
>
> And in that hall there was a bed,
> It was hangèd with gold so red.
>
> And in that bed there lieth a knight,
> His wounds bleeding day and night.

> By that bed's side there kneeleth a may,
> And she weepeth both night and day.
>
> And by that bed's side there standeth a stone,
> *Corpus Christi* written there-on.

This carol presents us with a tableau of the Passion, much in the manner of an Annunciation lyric considered earlier in this chapter, "At a Spring-well under a Thorn" (XIV 130). The unusual feature is the refrain, which in the first line suggests a lullaby, and in the second line a lament (death has taken away my beloved). The frame of the carol thus seems to alternate between Christmas (lullaby) and Good Friday (lament). But if we recall the diminutive Christ figure of the pietà, we have a possible explanation for this ambiguity. The first line of the refrain may simply reflect the Virgin's sorrowing recollection of her son's birth at the moment of his death. Alternatively, of course, it is possible to see this as a Nativity carol incorporating a prophetic account of the Christ child's eventual death. The refrain holds these alternatives in delicate balance.

Unlike most medieval lyrics, the "Corpus Christi" carol has had a continuous life in oral tradition down to the twentieth century. After the Reformation, of course, the culture in which this song was preserved lost its sense of a Church calendar, except for Christmas and Easter. But it is interesting to note that the modern versions of the carol (of which there are four) tend to tie it more explicitly to Christmas. Thus a traditional version from Derbyshire ends (EEC 322C6):

> Over that bed the moon shines bright
> Denoting our Saviour was born this night.

Most interesting is an American version, recovered in North Carolina in 1936, which has an interlaced refrain clearly showing that this song was used for the Christmas season (EEC 322E):

> Down in yon forest be a hall,
> *Sing May, Queen May, sing Mary,*
> It's coverlidded over with purple and pall,
> *Sing all good men for the new-born baby.*

In this same version there is also a stanza strikingly reminiscent of the diminutive Christ figure of the medieval pietà:

[93]

On that bed a young Lord sleeps,
His wounds are sick and see he weeps.

Here is indeed a remarkable survival of medieval tradition in the Appalachians. The evidence of oral versions thus shows us that the "Corpus Christi" carol was in the long run associated with Christmas rather than Easter, whatever may have been the intended occasion of the original version.

Another popular form of Crucifixion lyric was the dialogue between Jesus and the Virgin. The earliest of these begins thus (XIII 49):

> "Stand well, Mother, under rood [cross],
> Behold thy child with glad mood;
> Blithe, Mother, mayest thou be."
> "Son, how may I blithe stand?
> I see thy feet, I see thy hands
> Nailed to the hard tree."

In the dialogue that follows, Jesus seeks in vain to comfort his mother by explaining why his death is necessary. Toward the end he makes a traditional point about the significance of the Virgin's grief:

> "Mother, have pity on mothers' care
> Now thou knowest the pain they endure,
> Though thou be a pure maiden."

The implication is that although Mary experienced no pain at the birth of Jesus, she more than made up for that in witnessing his death, and therefore readily qualifies as one able to understand the pain that mothers must endure. Other dialogues of this sort are briefer, and focus on Jesus' commitment of the Virgin to the care of Saint John (John 19:26–27) (XIV 67, 128). There are, in addition, dialogues between abstractions such as Natura Hominis and Bonitas Dei (Nature of Man and Goodness of God) (XV 107), and narrations of this kind too numerous to mention.

A final and very popular category of Crucifixion lyric is the one in which Christ speaks to man from the cross. In its simplest form, Christ appeals to man to be moved to repentance by his suffering (XIV 4):

> Man and woman, look at me,
> How much pain I suffered for thee;

[94]

Look upon my back how sorely I was beaten;
Look to my side, what blood I have let.
My feet and my hands be nailed to the rood;
From the thorns pricking my head runneth my blood.
From side to side, from head to foot,
All over my body thou findest blood.
Man, thine heart, thine heart, turn thou to me,
For the five wounds that I suffered for thee.

This penitential theme is of course quite traditional, and implicitly in harmony with the dialogues we have already noted, in which Christ explains to the Virgin that his death is necessary for the salvation of man.

A striking change occurs in the tone of Jesus'. remarks, however, in lyrics such as the one that Brown entitles *"Popule meus quid feci tibi"* (XIV 15). This remarkable song is constructed to resemble what modern biblical scholars call the "covenant lawsuit" in the Old Testament prophets. The Latin title comes from such a passage in the prophet Micah (6:3–4):

> O my people, what have I done unto thee? And wherein have I wearied thee? Testify against me. For I brought thee up out of the land of Egypt, and redeemed thee out of the house of servants; and I sent before thee Moses, Aaron, and Miriam.

Besides listing what he has done for Israel, God sometimes matches this with an account of Israel's ungrateful reaction, as in these verses from Amos (2:10–12):

> Also I brought you up from the land of Egypt, and led you forty years through the wilderness, to possess the land of the Amorite. And I raised up of your sons for prophets, and of your young men for Nazarites. Is it not even thus, O ye children of Israel? saith the Lord. But ye gave the Nazarites wine to drink; and commanded the prophets, saying, Prophesy not.

The medieval lyric opens in the typical form of the "covenant lawsuit," but the speaker of course is Jesus on the cross (XIV 15):

My folk, what have I done to thee,
Or in what thing have I vexed thee?
Come now and answer me:

Forth from Egypt I led thee,
And thou ledest me to the rood tree.
My folk, what have I done to thee? etc.

[95]

> Through wilderness I led thee,
> And forty years protected thee,
> And angels bread I gave to thee,
> And into rest I brought thee.
> My folk, what have I done to thee? etc.
>
> What more should I have done
> That thou hast not already won?
> My folk, what have I done to thee?

The remainder of the song consists of comparisons between God's aid to Israel and Israel's ungrateful response. I fed and clothed thee, says Jesus, and thou didst give me vinegar to drink, and stung me with a spear. I divided the sea, and drowned the pharaoh for thee, and thou didst sell me to princes. I led thee in a pillar of cloud, and thou didst lead me to Pilate. With each accusation the refrain line from Micah 6:3 is repeated: "O my people, what have I done to thee?" and the song ends with this final accusation:

> Much honor I bestowed on thee;
> And thou dist hang me on the rood tree.
> My folk, what have I done to thee?

At first glance it would seem that this view of the Crucifixion contradicts the usual emphasis on its necessity. But in many another Passion lyric the same accusing tone is directed at mankind as a whole, coupled with an exhortation for man to put away his sins. In one lyric, the cross is put forward as a specific remedy for each of the sins in turn (XIV 127).

Another Old Testament verse used to provide words for Christ on the cross is from Lamentations (1:12): "Is it nothing to you, all ye that pass by? behold and see if there be any sorrow like unto my sorrow. . . ." Such is the inspiration for a short lyric in John Grimestone's Commonplace Book (XIV 74):

> Ye that pass by the way,
> Abide a little while!
> Behold and see, my brothers,
> If any like me may be found.
> To the tree with three nails
> I hang firmly bound,
> With a spear all through my side
> That in my heart has made a wound.

This is perhaps the most characteristic, though not the best, of the Passion lyrics we have considered, in its simple appeal to the onlooker.

By way of concluding our review of the Passion lyrics, I call attention to one that has been highly praised by Rosemary Woolf, and is indeed a worthy example of the genre. Carleton Brown calls it "A Song of Sorrow for the Passion" (XIII 64):

> I sigh when I sing
> For sorrow that I see,
> When I with weeping
> Behold upon the tree
> And see Jesus the sweet
> Lose the blood of his heart
> For the love of me;
> His wounds they wax wet—
> Mary, mild and sweet,
> Have mercy on me!

This is the characteristic ten-line stanza, and four of the six end, like this one, with a reference to the Virgin. The second stanza is almost photographic in its highlighting of detail:

> High upon a down
> Where all folk see it may,
> A mile without the town
> About the mid-day,
> The rood was up-reared.
> His friends were all afraid:
> They clung as the clay.
> The rood standeth in stone.
> Mary herself alone,
> Her song was welaway.

The narrator goes on to describe the Crucifixion and his reaction to it, in a manner that is highly emotional. Jesus he calls "my lover," and he is barely able to endure the sight of his suffering:

> The nails be all too long,
> The smith is all too sly,
> Thou bleedest all too long,
> The tree is all too high.

The ability of the speaker to think of such details as the "sly" smith who made the nails lends an authenticity to this meditation

[97]

not often found. And these details build up to a conclusion which is traditional and yet vividly expressed.

> Well often when I sleep
> With sorrow I am sought;
> When I wake and turn,
> I think in my thought:
> Alas! how men be mad—
> While beholding the cross
> (I lie not) they do sell
> Their souls into sin
> For the joy of this world,
> Despite such a dear redemption.

The Passion lyric is often filled with commonplaces, but this example shows us that it could become the vehicle for considerable freshness in both thought and emotion.

Easter to the Feast of Mary Magdalene

The two great feasts of the Church calendar that survive in modern times, at least in the English-speaking world, are of course Christmas and Easter. Indeed, Easter clearly overshadows Good Friday for all except the devout few who still attend Friday services tied to the Hours of the Cross. It is therefore no small surprise to discover that in comparison with the vast array of Passion poems, English lyrics devoted to the Resurrection are very few indeed. There are Friar William Herebert's translation of the Easter hymn *Iesu Nostra Redemptio* (XIV 24) and an anonymous translation of two stanzas of another hymn, *Aurora lucis rutilat* (XIV 37), both of the fourteenth century; two fifteenth-century Resurrection lyrics (XV 112, 113); and a five-stanza poem by William Dunbar, "On the Resurrection of Christ," which is perhaps the best example in this group. But one is left with the feeling that the canon of medieval English lyrics is curiously deficient in songs celebrating Christ's victory over death.

The period from Easter to Trinity Sunday in general exhibits a decline in the production of occasional poetry, at least in comparison with what we have seen to be the case in Holy Week. Saint George (April 23) was of course popular in England, yet we have but a single carol devoted to him (EEC 311.1), although he is referred to in other carols (EEC 308, 309a, 323, 431.1, 433.1). Ascension is an important feast, but I found only two lyrics in Carleton Brown that could be associated with that occasion (XIV 25, 119).

For Pentecost (Whitsun) we have merely two translations of the famous hymn *Veni Creator Spiritus* (XIV 18, 44). Lyrics and carols on the Trinity are more numerous, but not very inspiring (XV 49–52, 55; EEC 279.1–305).

Of all the pieces mentioned above, the best in my opinion is a ten-stanza lyric composed for the Sunday before Ascension, which begins as follows (XIV 119):

> In summer before the Ascension,
>   At Evensong on a Sunday,
> Dwelling in my devotion,
>   For the peace fast did I pray;
>   I heard a verse that pleasèd me,
>   That was written with words three,
>   And thus it is, shortly to say:
>   *Mane nobiscum, domine!*

The Latin line ("Abide with us, Lord") is adapted from the gospel account of the appearance of Jesus to certain disciples on the road to Emmaus. They had not recognized him, but were strangely drawn to him, and when he made as if to leave them, they persuaded him to stay (Luke 24:29): "But they constrained him, saying, Abide with us: for it is toward evening, and the day is far spent." The addition of the word *domine* in the refrain line of course reveals the identity of the stranger that the disciples have not yet recognized (stanza 3):

> When thou from death was risen and gone,
>   Then as a palmer forth thou didst pass;
> Then met thou pilgrims making moan,
>   But yet they wist not who thou was.
>   Thus then saith Cleopas:
>   "The night is nigh, as we may see,
>   The light of day is waxen less,
>   *Mane nobiscum, domine.*

The allusion here to Christ as pilgrim (palmer) is traditional, and we shall have occasion to notice it again later in this chapter. The remainder of the lyric is devoted to a series of appeals to the Lord to abide with us throughout this life and in the life to come—appeals which are enhanced by repetition of the haunting refrain line: *Mane nobiscum, domine!*

The feast of Corpus Christi was not established in England until about 1318, hence it is to be expected that lyrics on this subject (the Eucharist) will be late in appearing. Indeed, there is only one fifteenth-century prayer (XV 115) and a cluster of carols of the same date (EEC 317–21). Typical of the carols is this one from Richard Hill's Commonplace Book of about 1500 (EEC 319):

> *Mirabile misterium:*
>   In form of bread is God's Son.
>
> Man, that in earth abideth here,
> Thou must believe without fear
> In the sacrament of the altar
>   That God himself decreed at his supper.
>
> Though it seem white, it is red;
> It is flesh, though it seemeth bread;
> It is God in his manhood,
>   As he hung upon a tree.
>
> This bread is broken for you and me
> Which priests consecrate, as you may see,
> Which fleshly man in Deity
>   Died for us upon a tree.

The emphasis on transubstantiation in the second stanza is typical of the "Corpus Christi" lyric, which is otherwise unremarkable.

One carol that perhaps belongs with this group, however, is worthy of special notice for its representation of a remarkable religious service (EEC 323):

> Merry it is in May morning,
> Merry ways for to go.
>
> And by a chapel as I came,
> Met I with Jesus to churchward going,
> Peter and Paul, Thomas and John,
>   And his disciples everyone.
>
> St. Thomas the bells did ring,
> And St. Nicholas the Mass did sing;
> St. John took that sweet offering,
>   And by a chapel as I came.
>
> Our Lord offered what he would,
> A chalice all of rich red gold,
> Our Lady the crown of her head;
>   The son out of her bosom shone.
>
> St. George, that is our Lady's knight,
> He tended the tapers fair and bright,

> To mine eyes a seemly sight,
> And by a chapel as I came.

The simplicity of this song is striking, and it may be, as Greene and others have suggested, that it belongs to the folksong tradition, although oral versions seem not to have survived. Certainly the picture of Jesus as a priest officiating at Mass is not the sort of thing one would expect from the learned composers of the medieval lyrics considered in this chapter.

The Nativity of Saint John the Baptist, or Midsummer Day (June 24), is likewise something of a disappointment. For Saint John himself we find a single brief prayer (XV 122). The fact that his day is also the observance of midsummer might lead us to expect a cluster of popular songs, but such is not the case. All we have are two carols of holiday seduction (EEC 452–53). I quote the burden and first stanza of EEC 453:

> Alas, alas the while!
> Thought I on no guile
>   So have I good chance.
> Alas, alas the while
>   That ever I could dance!
>
> Led I the dance on Midsummer Day;
> I made small trips, sooth for to say.
> Jack, our holy water clerk, came by the way,
> And he looked upon me; he thought he was gay.
>   Thought I on no guile.

The speaker continues to protest her innocence in the refrain line while Jack in turn dances with her, kisses her, promises her a pair of gloves, invites her to his room, and gets her with child. The song ends with a proverb: "Ill-spun yarn ever it will out," followed by the now rueful refrain line: "Thought I on no guile."

Although the calendar following Holy Week has thus far been somewhat disappointing, one day that we have now reached is particularly rich in literary associations, and that is the feast of Mary Magdalene (July 22). The particular lyric that belongs to her is "Maiden in the Moor Lay" (N 138), a beautiful song which editors have until recently categorized as a secular composition. That it is in fact a religious lyric devoted to the Magdalene is I think beyond dispute, but to see why this is so we need to examine the wider tradition that her remarkable popularity produced in the later Middle Ages.

Mary Magdalene in Popular Tradition (July 22)

1. Bible

Considering the attention that Mary Magdalene has received through the centuries, from the earliest biblical commentaries to the latest rock opera, there is actually very little space devoted to her in the four Gospels. She is one of a number of women from Galilee, accompanying Jesus and his disciples, who had been healed of evil spirits and infirmities: "Mary called Magdalene, out of whom went seven devils" (Luke 8:2). Along with other women, variously identified, she is a witness to the Crucifixion (Matt. 27:56, Mark 15:40, Luke 23:49 and 24:10, John 19:25). With some of these same women she observes the burial of Jesus' body by Joseph of Arimathea (Matt. 27:61, Mark 15:47, Luke 23:55), and on Easter morning, bringing spices and ointments (Mark 16:1, Luke 23:56 and 24:1), she and the other women discover the empty tomb and are instructed by the angel(s) to tell the disciples that Jesus is risen (Matt. 28:1–8, Mark 16:1–8, Luke 24:1–10). According to Matthew, the risen Lord himself appears to the women as they are departing from the sepulcher (Matt. 28:9–10), but the most important of all accounts of the Resurrection depicts an encounter between Christ and Mary Magdalene alone, in which she mistakes him for the gardener (John 20:1–18). This last passage in the Gospel of John contains the seed of important developments to come, as we shall see, in the legendary life of Mary Magdalene.

But preachers and commentators have never been satisfied with the scanty information on the Magdalene provided by the Bible, and during the Middle Ages there was a quest for additional facts. What about the other women named Mary in the New Testament: could any of them be our heroine? An affirmative answer was provided as early as the sixth century by Gregory the Great in his sermons on the Gospels. Gregory unhesitatingly identified as Mary Magdalene the woman who anointed Jesus and bathed his feet with her tears (Matt. 26:6–13, Mark 14:3–9, Luke 7:36–50, John 12:1–8), and in this he was followed by most Western interpreters. Because of the clear identification of this woman in John 11:2 and 12:1–8, it follows that the Mary who is the sister of Martha and Lazarus is also understood to be the Magdalene, and it is she who is said to have chosen the better part (Luke 10:38–42). On the basis of this passage in Luke, therefore, Martha and Mary (Magdalene) are often referred to as typical representatives of the active and contemplative lives. And because of the importance of spices and ointment in Mary Magdalene's life (anointing Jesus and later bringing spices to the tomb with the intention of anointing his body), she is often depicted in medieval illustrations carrying a jar of ointment. All these details merge to form a distinctive portrait of our heroine.

But could there not also be some references to the Magdalene that are simply anonymous? Since she was at one time a sinner (Luke 7:37), and had seven devils (Luke 8:2), commentators searched the scriptures for likely candidates. By the close of the Middle Ages, Mary Magdalene had been identified with the woman taken in adultery (John 8:1–11) and, most important for popular tradition, with the woman of Samaria (John 4:1–42). For the sake of completeness, we may add one other identification, based on the account of the marriage feast in Cana (John 2:1–10), and provided in *The Golden Legend*:

> Some say that St. Mary Magdalene was wedded to St. John the Evangelist when Christ called him from the wedding, and when he was called from her, she had thereof indignation that her husband was taken from her and went and gave herself to all delight, but because it was not covenable that the calling of St. John should be the occasion of her damnation, therefore our Lord converted her mercifully to penance, and because he had taken from her sovereign delight of the flesh, he replenished her with sovereign delight spiritual tofore all other, that is the love of God.

In the biblical passage, of course, the bridegroom is not identified and the bride not even mentioned. We have now reached the point where scriptural evidence comes to an end, and legend begins.

2. Legend

The Golden Legend is a late medieval collection of the lives of saints honored in the Church calendar. The feast day of Mary Magdalene is July 22, and the story of her life is a combination of biblical and legendary materials which may be summarized as follows.

Mary Magdalene was born of noble parents: her father was Cyrus and her mother Eucharia. From them Mary inherited the castle Magdalo, her sister Martha had Bethany, and her brother Lazarus inherited property in Jerusalem. But Mary, a very beautiful woman, squandered her inheritance and indulged in bodily delight to such an extent that she became known as a sinner. While in this sinful condition she first heard the preaching of Jesus, and, overwhelmed by repentance, she came to him in the house of Simon, washed his feet with her tears, dried them with her hair, and anointed them with precious ointments. Reproving Simon for his unspoken objection, Jesus forgave Mary her sins and took from her the seven devils. Hereafter she became his hostess, in charge of procuring supplies for his journeys, and he often spoke up for her: to the Pharisee who said she was not clean (Luke 7:39), to Martha who said that she was idle (Luke 10:40), and to Judas who said that she was a waster of goods (John 12:4–6). In addition to all the favors she received during his lifetime, Mary Magdalene was the first to whom Christ appeared after his resurrection, and she was made "apostolesse of the apostles," in that like them she was sent out, after the ascension of the Lord, to preach the word of God.

During the persecution that accompanied the preaching of the gospel, Mary Magdalene and her companions were seized by the infidels and placed in a rudderless ship, with the intention that they should be drowned at sea. Included in the group were Saint Maximin (in whose care Mary had been entrusted by Saint Peter), Lazarus, Martha, Martha's maid servant Marcella (the "certain woman" of Luke 11:27), and Sidonius (the man blind from birth of John 9:1), together with many other believers. But with the aid of divine providence, the ship sailed into Marseilles, where the preaching of Mary Magdalene converted the pagan inhabitants to Christianity. The king and queen of the province agreed to adopt the new religion on condition that Mary intercede with God on their behalf, praying that they might have a child. When Mary's prayers were answered and the lady conceived, the king vowed to go on pilgrimage to the holy land, to hear the gospel from the lips of Saint Peter himself. Despite his protests, the queen, great with child, insisted on accompanying him on the ship, and during a storm at sea, she died in childbirth. The sailors were about to throw mother and child overboard in order to calm the seas, when the distraught pilgrim persuaded them to leave the dead mother and her babe on a nearby island. The ship then continued on to Palestine, where the king met Saint Peter, who informed him of the faith and showed him all the holy places where Jesus Christ lived and died. After two years, when returning home, the king persuaded the shipman to stop by the island where his wife and child had been left. There he found both of them, miraculously alive. The queen joyously reported that during his pilgrimage Mary Magdalene had visited her and brought her in spirit to Jerusalem, where she too saw all the holy places that Saint Peter had shown her husband. The reunited couple then sailed rejoicing to Marseilles, where they kneeled before Mary Magdalene and recounted all that had happened. When they were baptized by Saint Maximin, they ordered all the idols of the city destroyed and installed Lazarus as bishop of Marseilles and Maximin as bishop of Aix.

Meanwhile Mary Magdalene, "desirous of sovereign contemplation," retreated to a place in the desert where she lived alone for thirty years without the comfort of running water, trees, or herbs. Yet without food she was miraculously sustained each day by "celestial refection." At each of the seven canonical hours (Ps. 119:164), she was lifted up in the air by angels, "and heard the glorious song of the heavenly companies with her bodily ears." By this means "she was fed and filled with right sweet meats, and then was brought again by the angels unto her proper place, in such wise as she had no need of corporal nourishing." Toward the end of this thirty-year period of Mary's miraculously sustained life of contemplation, a solitary priest in the vicinity was privileged to witness one of her exaltations. Approaching her cave, he called out to her, asking who she was, and she informed him that she was Mary Magdalene, who had washed the feet of the Savior with her tears and dried them with her hair. She then directed him to Saint Maximin, who met Mary in his oratory on the day after Easter, and there, after receiving communion, she died and ascended to heaven. A heavenly odor surrounded her body for seven days, after which it was buried by the blessed Maximin with instructions that he should be buried with her after his death.

According to medieval tradition, Mary Magdalene's tomb was in the church of Saint Maximin, about thirty miles from Marseilles, in the archbishopric of Aix, where she had lived as a contemplative. With her were buried Maximin, Marcella, and Sidonius. Nearby is the place of La Baume, a cave in a rock where the Magdalene lived for thirty years without earthly food or drink.

The legendary life of Mary Magdalene seems to have been quite popular between the twelfth and sixteenth centuries. In praise of her, Latin hymns were composed, as well as lyrics in all the major European languages. Her popularity on the medieval stage came early, in the *Hortulanus* episode of the Resurrection (based on John 20:1–18), and continued in the vernacular drama, as we shall see, which included not only the cycle plays but also an entire saint's play devoted to the life of Mary Magdalene based on *The Golden Legend*.

3. Drama

The Digby play of *Mary Magdalene* (late fifteenth century) provides the most memorable dramatic form of our heroine's life. It is epic in scope, and offers us a panorama of events against a landscape extending from Jerusalem to Marseilles. The staging of this play was no doubt accomplished by the use of a medieval theater in the round, consisting of a central playing place, ringed by a series of platforms representing the residences of the main characters. This arrangement allowed the audience surrounding the place to follow the action easily, when a messenger, for example, is sent by the Emperor in Rome (on one stage) through the "place" to Jerusalem, where he delivers his message to Herod (on another stage). The "castle" of Magdalen may have been one of these stages, or, as has been suggested, its importance may have dictated its placement in the center of the circle. To complicate matters, not all of the stages represented "real" (earthly) places. There were separate platforms for Heaven, Hell, and also for that evil trinity, the World, the Flesh, and the Devil, who provide the psychological warfare that results in the possession of Mary Magdalene by seven devils (the seven deadly sins). There were likewise special effects that would surely challenge the ingenuity of a modern director. The personified sins carry out an assault on Castle Magdalen; after the devils are driven out of Mary, Satan has them whipped for their failure and orders their "house" (the scaffold of Hell?) set on fire; another conflagration is indicated when Mary prays to God to destroy the idols of Marseilles, for the stage directions tell us that "here shall come a cloud from heaven and set the temple on fire."

Despite the rapid shifting of locales, the first half of the play focuses steadily on the biblical period of Mary Magdalene's life. After her father's death, she squanders her wealth in riotous living, and is enticed by Pride, in the form of a gallant named Curiosity, to live a life of voluptuousness. The temptation takes place in a tavern, and serves as a prelude to Mary's conversion in Simon's house. The staging of the conversion, while not as spectacular as the fire scenes already mentioned, is an intriguing example of medieval stagecraft at its best. Mary enters the "place" alone as if waiting to meet some of her lovers:

> Ah, God be with my valentines,
> My sweet birds, my loves so dear!

Failing to see any of them, she decides to rest a while:

> Me marveleth sore they be not here.
> But I will rest in this arbor
> Among these balms precious of price,
> Till some lover will appear
> That me is wont to hold and kiss.

Since the time of Gregory the Great (sixth century), the Old Testament Song of Solomon has had important associations with the life of Mary Magdalene. Indeed, it provides the lesson for the Mass on Saint Mary Magdalene's Day (Song of Sol. 3:1–4). Here we need only notice that the sinful Mary is presented to us in an earthly bower which is the counterpart of the spiritual garden of the Song of Solomon (e.g., 5:1). Meanwhile, on the stage representing Simon's house a banquet is being prepared, and while this is going on, the Good Angel enters and wakens Mary:

> Woman, woman, why art thou so unstable?
> Full bitterly this bliss it will be bought,
> Why art thou against God so variable?
> Why thinkest thou not God made thee of nought?

In response to the Angel's exhortation Mary vows to give up her sinful life and follow Jesus:

> I shall pursue the prophet, whereso he be,
> For he is the well of perfect charity;
> By the oil of mercy he shall me relieve.
> With sweet balms I will seek him this time,
> And surely follow his lordship in each degree.

She then enters Simon's house to anoint Jesus' feet, and the subsequent events follow the gospel account (Luke 7:36–50), with one notable exception. When Jesus says to Mary, "go in peace," seven devils suddenly emerge from a place of concealment (perhaps under the banquet table?), rush out of the house along with the Bad Angel, and "enter into Hell with thunder."

The Passion narrative that follows this dramatic exorcism is compressed so as to include little more than those events involving Mary Magdalene. She returns to the castle, joyously informing Martha and Lazarus of her deliverance by the "prophet" (John 4:19) whom she had called "the well of perfect charity" (John 4:6–15). Indeed the Magdalene's lines are often chosen freely from the Scriptures, as when she says to Lazarus: "Though I were never so sinful he said 'Return!' " a line that nicely combines Song of Solomon 6:13, "Return, return, O Shulamite," with Ezekiel 33:11, "I have no pleasure in the death of the wicked but that the wicked turn from his way and live." But her joy is soon overshadowed by her brother's sickness and death. There follows the episode of the raising of Lazarus as reported in John 11:1–45, which ends on a note of triumph and harmony. Mary, Martha, and all of the Jews present who have witnessed the miracle say with one voice, "We believe in you, Savior, Jesus, Jesus, Jesus!"

Abruptly the King and Queen of Marseilles appear on their platform, speak boastfully, and order spices and wine for their refreshment. This brief episode serves two purposes: first, to introduce us to the main setting for the second half of the play; second, to represent the passage of time between the raising of Lazarus and the resurrection of Christ which now follows. A devil "in horrible array" comes on stage to describe the Harrowing of Hell in the words of Psalm 24:7–10, after which the three Marys—Mary Magdalene, Mary Jacobi, and Mary Solome (Mark 15:40, etc.)—appear with spices and ointments on their way to the tomb. As they pass the stations of the cross, each Mary in turn delivers an appropriate lament, till they come to the sepulcher, where an angel tells them that Jesus is risen, and instructs them to report to the disciples. After Peter and John have visited the empty tomb, Mary returns alone, and there follows that luminous scene from the Gospel of John (20:1–18) in which she encounters the risen Lord and mistakes him for the gardener. When Jesus speaks her name, Mary recognizes him:

> Ah, gracious Master and Lord, you it is that I seek!
> Let me anoint you with this sweet balm:
> Lord, long has thou hid thee from my spice.
> But now I will kiss thee, for my heart's ease.

Jesus of course forbids her to touch him, and tells her to announce his resurrection to the disciples. Thus far the dramatist is following the gospel very closely, but then comes an interesting addition to the scriptural account, drawn ultimately from a sermon of Gregory the Great. Mary says:

> When I saw you first, Lord, verily,
> I thought ye had been Simon the gardener.

Jesus answers:

> So I am, forsooth, Mary;
> Man's heart is my garden here.
> Therein I sow seeds of virtue all the year;
> The foul weeds and vices, I rend up by the root.
> When that garden is watered with pure tears,
> Then spring virtues, and smell full sweet.

The garden imagery of the Song of Solomon thus receives an allegorical elaboration which, as we shall see, is destined to reappear in popular tradition. When Jesus vanishes, Mary rejoins her companions, and the three Marys together encounter the risen Lord (Matt. 28:9–10), thus completing the story of the Resurrection.

A rapid-fire shifting of scenes, from Marseilles to Jerusalem to Rome and back to Jerusalem, launches the second half of the play, based on the legendary life of Mary Magdalene after the Lord's ascension. Jesus sends the angel Raphael to Mary, appointing her "as an holy apostylesse" to go and convert the King and Queen of Marseilles. From this point the drama follows *The Golden Legend* rather closely, except that no companions accompany Mary on the journey, a change that serves to keep the spotlight almost exclusively on our heroine. There is also a spectacular bit of stage business which no doubt enhanced the popularity of this play. When Mary goes down to the sea in quest of transportation to Marseilles, the stage directions specify that "here shall enter a ship with a merry song." How this was to be done is not specified, but it has been plausibly suggested that the ship was a pageant-wagon of the type used in the cycle plays, with the addition of sails and oars. The entrance of this vessel into the circular playing place, with the sailors singing a sea chantey, must have been a memorable experience for the medieval audience. Later the ship does an encore, taking the King of Marseilles to Palestine and returning with him to Marseilles.

Another popular feature of the play is its association of the role of Mary Magdalene with that of the Virgin Mary, the mother of Jesus. As a prelude to his appointment of his "apostolesse," Jesus sings the praises of his mother, and then sends the angel Raphael with his message to the Magdalene in a scene reminiscent of Gabriel's appearance to the Virgin (Luke 1:26–38). Later, when the King of Marseilles returns home with his queen and child miraculously alive, he kneels before Mary Magdalene and greets her with "Hail be thou Mary! The Lord is with thee," words very near to those used by Gabriel in greeting the Virgin (Luke 1:38), and he adds, "Hail, tabernacle of the blessed Trinity," a characterization one would think ought to be limited to the Virgin mother. The queen echoes her husband in unmistakable terms:

> Hail, thou chosen and chaste of women alone!
> It passeth my wit to tell thy nobleness!
> Thou relievedst me and my child on the rock of stone,
> And also saved us by thy high holiness.

Of course, it might be argued that the King and Queen, now Christian believers, are attributing their deliverance to the Virgin mother, and rendering thanks to her. But no such alternative is possible later on in the play, when the priest addresses Mary Magdalene in the desert:

> Hail, creature, Christ's delectation!
> Hail, sweeter than sugar or cypress!
> Mary is thy name, by angel's relation.
> Great art thou with God for thy perfectness.

The scriptural bases for addressing the Magdalene in terms usually limited to the mother of Christ may be found in the link we have already noted between Mary Magdalene and the Song of Solomon, because the Song of Solomon is even more commonly associated with the Virgin Mary in medieval hymns, lyrics, and carols. In any case, the merging of the two Marys, as we shall see, becomes an important feature in the popular tradition of Mary Magdalene.

The Digby play has a rapid pace and spectacular effects, but it is also held together by skillful thematic development of Mary's character. Not only does she turn from sin to repentance, she also moves from an active to a contemplative life and from physical to spiritual sustenance. The biblical source for this motif is, as we have already noted, the Mary/Martha episode of the Gospel of

Luke (10:38–42), where Mary is said to have chosen the better part. But she is not a contemplative from the beginning. Most of the second half of the play, covering her life as an apostoless, shows her as leading a very active life indeed. Only when the King and Queen have returned alive with their child does Mary announce her intention to retire to the desert:

> Now will I labor forth God to please,
> More ghostly strength me to procure.

Along with this movement toward contemplation, the play frequently makes a contrast between physical and spiritual food, stressing the importance of the latter in religious experience. As early as the moment of her conversion in Simon's house, Mary addresses Jesus as her "contemplative repast." When she first arrives in Marseilles, however, Mary is rebuffed by the King. Forced to lodge outside the gate of the city, she weeps for hunger and thirst and prays to Christ for relief. In heaven Jesus speaks to his angels:

> My grace shall grow and down descend
> To Mary, my lover, that to me doth call,
> Her condition for to amend.
> She shall be relieved with sustenance corporal.

But when she later abandons the active life and begins her life of contemplation in the desert, Mary vows to give up corporal sustenance:

> Of worldly foods I will leave all refection;
> By the food that cometh from heaven on high,
> That God will send me, by contemplative.

To which Jesus replies:

> With ghostly food relievèd she shall be.
> Angels! Into the clouds do ye enhance her;
> There feed her with manna for her sustenance.

Four angels obediently descend to the desert where Mary is kneeling, and the stage directions tell us what happens next: "Here shall two angels descend into wilderness; another two shall bring an oblé [Mass wafer], openly appearing aloft in the clouds. The two beneath shall bring Mary and she shall receive the bread, and then go again into the wilderness." In such a manner is the Magdalene kept alive for thirty years in the desert, a miracle of contemplative fasting that was widely admired in the Middle Ages and a motif very popular in the lives of the saints. The mysterious Grail King of Chrétien's *Perceval* was kept alive for fifteen years in this manner, and actual cases of miraculous fasting were reported in medieval chronicles. Francis Petrarch, the Italian poet laureate and author of a treatise on the contemplative life, reported that he once made a pilgrimage to the cave where Mary Magdalene's thirty-year fast took place. Little wonder that this story attracted attention from high and low, for in it is embodied an important part of Christ's teaching which in the Middle Ages was incorporated in the doctrine of the Eucharist (John 6:58): "This is that bread which came down from heaven: not as your fathers did eat manna, and are dead: he that eateth of this bread shall live forever." Thus Mary Magdalene's miraculously sustained life in the desert was a foretaste of the eternal life to come promised by her Lord.

4. Lyric

Songs of Mary Magdalene were numerous in the Middle Ages, but our concern in the space remaining will be with the few that are important for popular tradition. A case in point is the familiar carol:

> I saw three ships come sailing in
>   On Christmas day, on Christmas day;
> I saw three ships come sailing in
>   On Christmas day in the morning.

An early version of this was printed in 1666 under the title "Sunny Bank," after the opening line "As I sat on a sunny bank." It is not clear at first glance why the Virgin Mary and Christ should be sailing by ship into (landlocked) Bethlehem on Christmas day, as the carol affirms. But the suggestion that the song originally celebrated Mary Magdalene's sea journey to Marseilles seems to me quite likely. When the influence of the Church calendar declined after the Reformation, the song detached itself from July 22 (Magdalene's day), and was drawn into the still-powerful orbit of Christmas, with predictable results. The affinity of the two Marys that we have already noted simply made it all the easier for the Virgin Mary and Christ to replace Mary Magdalene and her companions in the ship(s).

[112]

But by far the most important and interesting example, for our purposes, is "Maiden in the Moor Lay," a beautiful lyric preserved in a manuscript of the fourteenth century (N 138):

>Maiden in the moor lay,
>   In the moor lay,
>Seven-night full,
>   Seven-night full—
>Maiden in the moor lay,
>   In the moor lay,
>Seven-night full and a day.
>
>Well was her meat.
>   What was her meat?
>The primerole and the—
>   The primerole and the—
>Well was her meat.
>   What was her meat?
>The primerole and the violet.
>
>Well was her drink.
>   What was her drink?
>The chill water of the—
>   The chill water of the—
>Well was her drink.
>   What was her drink?
>The chill water of the well-spring.
>
>Well was her bower.
>   What was her bower?
>The red rose and the—
>   The red rose and the—
>Well was her bower.
>   What was her bower?
>The red rose and the lily flower.

All students of lyric poetry have been deeply impressed by this enigmatic lyric, but have been just as deeply divided over how to interpret it. It appears among the "secular lyrics" edited by R. H. Robbins, but, as Joseph Harris has recently and impressively demonstrated, it is undoubtedly based on the legendary life of Mary Magdalene, and celebrates her victorious ascetic life in the desert. Coming to this text from our study of the Magdalene tradition in legend and drama, it should be possible to see not only that the maid is Mary but also that in the poem her desert has blossomed as the rose (Isa. 35:1) and has become a place of beauty resembling the garden of the Song of Solomon. We are reminded of Jesus' words to Mary at the moment of his resurrection:

> When that garden is watered with pure tears,
> Then spring virtues, and smell full sweet.

To this idea of the garden of penitence the poet adds the flower symbolism so popular in medieval tradition: the primrose for her zeal as an apostoless, the violet for her humility as a confessor, the rose for her constancy as a martyr, and the lily for her purity as a virgin. These are all flowers that are equally suited to the Virgin Mary, of course, denoting a conjunction of the two Marys which we have already encountered. But the flowers are not merely decorative. They are said to have been eaten by the Maid, thus incorporating another feature of the life of Mary Magdalene that we noted in the Digby play: her subsistence in the desert on nothing but spiritual food. Perhaps the most significant feature of all in this lyric is the climactic position of the lily flower with which the poem concludes. Can a former prostitute ever again be said to be a virgin? The poet's answer is affirmative. The final miracle, attributable to the Magdalene's heroic asceticism, is that she is refined and made pure in the sight of God.

It is important to remember that "Maiden in the Moor Lay" is the product of a period when the contemplative life was highly esteemed. And even though this lyric, in one form or another, seems to have remained popular both in England and on the Continent down to the Reformation, changing attitudes toward the efficacy of a life of contemplation necessarily affected the form and tone of the Magdalene ballads that were later composed under its influence.

5. Ballad

Two hundred years after "Maiden in the Moor Lay" was first written down, a ballad of Mary Magdalene was recorded in western Europe, originating in Catalonia and spreading through the Romance area. Whereas the lyric presented a highly symbolic tableau, the ballad relies heavily on a narrative derived from biblical and legendary materials. In one version from Catalonia, for example, the Magdalene's conversion takes place when she hears Jesus preach. After the service she follows him to Simon's house, where she is given her penance: she is to live seven years in the wood of La Baume, eating only roots, drinking only dew, and making her bed on the ground. At the end of seven years she returns to Jesus, who asks her how she fared, and she replies,

[114]

"I fared very well." Her response satisfies Jesus, who sends her to heaven.

This simple narrative undergoes a small but significant elaboration in another version from Catalonia. After seven years, on her way home from the desert, the Magdalene pauses to wash her hands and face in a well. Looking down at her reflection in the water, she notes regretfully how "black and hardened" she has become as a result of her austerities—she who used to wear the red gold. Perceiving that she has not yet completely overcome her worldliness, Jesus sends her back to the desert for seven more years, after which she dies and goes to heaven, where she receives the crown of salvation from the Virgin Mary herself. Although there is no specific identification of the well in the Romance ballad, I suspect that the "fount of stone" where Mary washed her face and hands is none other than Jacob's well, where Jesus met the Samaritan woman (John 4:6). Hence it seems likely that this particular variant generated the later ballad of the Samaritan woman which appears in the seventeenth century in England and Scandinavia. Indeed the English ballad "The Maid and the Palmer" begins with the maid washing at a well (Child 21A):

> The maid she went to the well to wash,
> Dew fell of her lily white flesh.

But here the original purpose of this episode, which was to reveal that the maid's penance is not yet complete, has been lost, and she turns out merely to be doing the laundry:

> While she washed and while she wrang,
> While she hanged on the hazel wand.

On the other hand, the function of this episode is clearly preserved in the Finnish ballad of Mataleena, who goes to the well, sees the reflection of her face, and bewails her lost charms.

In the English ballad, "an old palmer" (Jesus) comes to the well, greets the maid, and asks her for a drink. She excuses herself by saying that she has "neither cup nor can," but Jesus says that if her lover were there, "cups and cans thou would find soon." The maid swears by God and by Saint John that she has no lover, to which Jesus replies:

> Peace, fair maid, you are forsworn!
> Nine children you have borne.

[115]

> Three were buried under thy bed's head,
> Other three under thy brewing lead.
>
> Other three on yon play green;
> Count, maid, and there be nine.

This is a remarkable departure from the biblical text, in which Jesus speaks only of the Samaritan woman's five "husbands" (John 4:16–18), but it is a feature common to both the English and Scandinavian forms of the ballad. That it could be somehow secondary or derivitive I find difficult to believe, for it appears regularly in all versions, providing the motive for the woman's recognition of Jesus as a prophet (John 4:19):

> But I hope you are the good old man
> That all the world believes upon.

She says this in acknowledgment that he has told her the truth about her dead children, and repenting her sins, she now asks the "old palmer" to assign her penance. Here the English ballad gives us another surprise:

> Penance I can give thee none,
> But seven year to be a stepping stone.
>
> Other seven a clapper in a bell,
> Other seven to lead an ape in hell.

These remarkable penitential transformations perhaps derive ultimately from the example of Nebuchadnezzar, whose dream is thus interpreted by Daniel (Dan. 4:25):

> That they shall drive thee from men, and thy dwelling shall be with the beasts of the fields, and they shall make thee to eat grass as oxen, and they shall wet thee with the dew of heaven, and seven times shall pass over thee, till thou know that the most High ruleth in the kingdom of men, and giveth it to whomsoever he will.

The transformation of the Babylonian king into a beast with hairs "grown like eagles' feathers" and "nails like birds' claws" (Dan. 4:33) is perhaps not far removed from the bizarre metamorphoses of the English ballad.

By contrast, the Scandinavian ballads retain a penance closely resembling that of the Romance *Mary Magdalene*. In a Swedish text, for example, Mary confesses to having killed her children, and Jesus assigns her the usual austerities found in the original ballad. Then after eight years, Jesus questions Mary:

> Hear thou, Magdalene, dear daughter mine,
> How does thy meat seem to thee?
>
> Well it seems to me my meat,
> As if I had dined at the king's board.
>
> Hear thou, Magdalene, dear daughter mine,
> How does thy drink seem to thee?
>
> Well it seems to me my drink,
> As if I had drunk the clear wine.
>
> Hear thou, Magdalene, [dear daughter mine],
> How dost thy bed seem to thee?
>
> Well it seems to me my bed,
> As if I had lain in a flower bed.

As Joseph Harris has pointed out, this form of questioning is quite reminiscent of "Maiden in the Moor Lay":

> Well was her meat.
> What was her meat?

In any case, the bed of flowers seems reminiscent of the flowery garden of virtues that Jesus plants in the heart of man. Only the eating of the flowers, unique to the lyric, is missing here. Still, such exotic symbolism is not likely to survive long in popular tradition.

But we have left for last the most interesting question: do we find in the ballad any trace of the lyric's dramatic revelation— that Mary's heroic asceticism has refined and purified her, restored her virginity? The answer is to be found in the final stanza of the English ballad, where Jesus says to the maid:

> When thou hast thy penance done,
> Then thou'st come a maiden home.

And yet this statement, in its context, seems to fall far short of an affirmation. Rather it has the sound of those paraphrases for "never" which are characteristic of balladry: "when the blackbird turns to white," "when the sun sets on yonder hill," and so forth. In short, Jesus seems to be telling the maid that she will come home a virgin when hell freezes over.

The negative tone of the ending of "The Maid and the Palmer" should come as no surprise when we notice the evolution that the ballad has undergone during its transmission in popular tradition. What begins as a lyrical celebration of the miraculous transforming power of the contemplative life in the fourteenth century becomes, after the Reformation (in England at least), a reappraisal of Mary Magdalene based on her identification with the woman of Samaria. However ancient the roots of "The Maid and the Palmer" in its present form, it radiates a Protestant skepticism toward the idea that a prostitute, through the exercise of penance, can ever "come a maiden home."

This interpretation of the Magdalen ballad tradition would not be complete without mention of the fact that ballad scholars customarily have regarded the murdered children of "The Maid and the Palmer" as an intrusion from another ballad entitled "The Cruel Mother." My fundamental reasons for rejecting this kind of theory are stated elsewhere, in a book on the literary history of the popular ballad, but I would like to append here the basis for rejecting this view of the relationship of these two particular ballads. For one thing, chronology is often ignored by these critics; yet it is very important, for it is often the only factual evidence we have. In this case, the earliest text of "The Maid and the Palmer" is 1650, while the first broadside edition of "The Cruel Mother" appeared thirty-six years later in 1686.

Moreover, the internal evidence of antiquity of "The Maid and the Palmer" is very strong, which is not the case with "The Cruel Mother." Why is Jesus called a "palmer"? The word "palmer" meant pilgrim, from the custom that travelers had, particularly those who had been to the holy land, of carrying with them as an emblem or souvenir a palm leaf, which attracted attention because it was exotic, at least to northern eyes. The identification of Jesus as *peregrinus* (pilgrim) comes from the passage in Luke relating his appearance to two of his disciples on the road to Emmaus (Luke 24:18, A.V. stranger). In the early Latin liturgical drama this episode was acted out in church at an appropriate time in connection with the Easter services. A cleric was dressed to play the part of the risen Lord "carrying a walet with a long palm, prepared well in the manner of a pilgrim, having a cap on his head, dressed like the disciples in a tunic, and barefoot." By the time "The Maid and the Palmer" was copied in the Percy Folio Manuscript, such liturgical practices had long been discontinued, hence it seems likely that the ballad's use of the word "palmer" for Christ is evidence of considerable antiquity.

A final point of some interest is the refrain associated with "The Maid and the Palmer." The Percy Folio version has an interlaced nonsense refrain, printed in full only with the first stanza:

> The maid she went to the well to wash,
> *Lillumwham, lillumwham!*
> The maid she went to the well to wash,
> *What then? what then?*
> The maid she went to the well to wash,
> Dew fell of her lily white flesh.
> *Grandam boy, grandam boy, heye!*
> *Leg a derry, leg a merry, mett, mer, whoop whir!*
> *Driuance, larumben, grandam boy, heye!*

This is a pattern of refrain found commonly in traditional folk-song, as early as "The Three Ravens" (1611) and as recent as the American doughboy song of the First World War, "Mademoiselle from Armentières." Whatever may have been the original refrain for our ballad, I am convinced this was not it.

Fortunately there is a Scottish version of "The Maid," to which our attention has been called recently by David Buchan:

> The may's to the well to wash and wring,
> *The primrose of the wood wants a name*
> An' ay so sweetly did she sing.
> *I am the fair maid of Coldingham.*

The first refrain line is repeated identically throughout, while the second varies slightly depending on the speaker.

> O fair may bethink ye again,
> *The primrose etc.*
> Gie a drink o' cauld water to an auld man.
> *If ye be etc.*

Starting with the sixth stanza, in fact, as Jesus begins his recitation of the maid's dead children, the final refrain line becomes a relentlessly repeated denial:

> O seven bairns hae ye born,
> *The primrose o the wood wants a name*
> An' as many lives hae ye forlorn.
> *An' ye're nae the fair maid of Coldingham.*

and there is no indication, even ironic, that she will "come a maiden home." Particularly interesting is the mention of the primrose in the first refrain line. Could this be the "primerole" of "Maiden in the Moor Lay"? I am inclined to think so, in which case the flower refrain is one more indication of the antiquity of this ballad.

An objection to my use of the Scottish version in the argument might be that it is a much later text (early nineteenth century), and that what we really see here is the continuing influence of "The Cruel Mother," which has a flower refrain:

> She sat down below a thorn,
> *Fine flowers in the valley*
> And there she has her sweet babe born.
> *And the green leaves they grow rarely.*

This ballad goes on to tell the tragic story of a girl who gives birth alone in the forest, stabs the babe with her penknife, and buries it by the light of the moon:

> As she was going to the church,
> She saw a sweet babe in the porch.
>
> "O sweet babe, and thou were mine,
> I would clad thee in silk so fine."
>
> "O mother dear, when I was thine,
> You did not prove to me so kind."

Critics have in particular been impressed by the haunting effect of this ballad, when sung, arising from the contrast between the somber story and the beautiful interlaced flower refrain. A version collected by Greig even included this as one of the refrain lines:

> *Hey the rose an' the linsie, O*

which comes very close to the rose and lily flower of "Maiden in the Moor Lay."

All of this evidence suggests to me that "The Cruel Mother" owes its origin to an actual case of child murder in the latter half of the seventeenth century in York (as the original broadside specifies), and that the author modeled his ballad on a form of "The Maid and the Palmer" having a flower refrain like that of the Scottish version of "The Maid." If so, this development represents the final rejection of that religious optimism so characteristic of the life of Mary Magdalene in popular tradition. In its

place we find, despite the hint of divine grace in the flower refrain, an attitude of awesome severity:

> Oh little children can you tell,
> *High alow and alonely*
> Where I shall go, to heaven or hell?
> *Down by the greenwood sidie O.*

> Oh yes, dear mother, we can tell,
> *High alow and alonely*
> It's us to heaven, and you to hell.
> *Down by the greenwood sidie O.*

The medieval religion of love, which envisioned the salvation of
Mary Magdalene, has here given way to a cult of righteousness,
which, in the seventeenth century, was the wave of the future.

The Feast of the Name of Jesus to Advent

The feast of the Sweet Name of Jesus (August 7) was established even later than Corpus Christi, and is not found listed in
English calendars until the end of the fourteenth century. During
the fourteenth century mystics such as Richard Rolle composed
moving meditations on Jesus' name, and some lyrics of the period are in this vein (e.g., XIV 48, 89). But it is not until the fifteenth
century that we find a lyric specifically associated with this day
of the calendar. Carleton Brown entitles it "A Prayer of the Holy
Name" (XV 125), and it is curiously lacking in the mystic fervor
one associates with this tradition:

> O Christ Jesus, meekly I pray to thee,
> To let thy name, whether I ride or go,
> In every peril and in every adversity,
> Be my defense against my mortal foes,
> To make them stand still as any stone;
> And that seek falsely to war against me
> Make thou their malice fully to obey.

The speaker goes on to ask for protection against "wicked spirits
horrible and black" that busily lie in wait for him day and night,
and he vows to impress the name of Jesus in his forehead so that
it will "drive them out of sight." It is almost as if the name is
being used here as a talisman against evil, a function which once
more suggests a popular origin, or at least a popular function, for
this curious prayer.

If we consider lyrics of the Assumption of the Virgin (August

15) to be only those based on the liturgy for that feast, then we
have only three fifteenth-century lyrics to represent this popular
holiday (XV 37–39). But if we widen our net to include pieces in
which the Virgin is addressed specifically as Queen, we then have
a much larger group to choose from (e.g., XV 21). But the one I
find most appealing is a *chanson d'aventure* of the fourteenth century which Brown entitles (after the refrain), *Quia Amore Langueo*
(XIV 132):

> In a tabernacle of a tower
> As I stood musing on the moon
> A crowned queen, most of honor,
> Appeared in ghostly sight full soon.
> She made complaint thus on her own
> That man's soul was wrapped in woe:
> "I may not leave mankind alone
>   *Quia amore langueo.*

The refrain means "because I languish [am sick] with love," and
is taken from the Song of Solomon (5:8): "I charge you, O daughters of Jerusalem, if ye find my beloved, that ye tell him, that I
am sick of love." The speaker is the Virgin Mary, now in heaven,
and in a dozen such stanzas she invites sinful man to come to
her and ask forgiveness. I long for the love of man, my brother,
she says. I am his advocate—why should I despise my own dear
child? If he fall into sin, yet we must pity him till he rise.

Toward the end, the Virgin explains why she was placed in so
privileged a position in heaven:

> Why was I crowned and made a queen?
> Why was I called of mercy the well?
> Why should an earthly woman be
> So high in heaven above the angels?
> For thee, mankind, the truth I tell!
> If thou ask my help, then I shall do
> That for which I was ordained—keep thee from hell,
>   *Quia amore langueo.*

After this explanation of the Virgin's role as intercessor, the poem
ends with an appeal to man to "creep under my wing." Then in
a return to the love motif of the Song of Solomon, she concludes,
"Take me for thy wife and learn to sing, *Quia amore langueo*."

Holy Cross day was September 14, but it is difficult to say which
if any of the songs involving the cross were composed for that
occasion. But there is one strangely haunting quatrain of the late

thirteenth century that unmistakably belongs here (Stevick 23):

> Well, who shall these horns blow
> Holy Rood thy day?
> Now he is dead and lieth low
> Was wont to blow them aye.

It is rare that a few words from someone long gone can communicate such vivid emotion. In this respect the lyric seems to me very like the anonymous epitaph on Lobe, the king's fool, which we considered earlier.

Having spent so much time on the summer feasts, we must now skip past those of the fall season and return to Advent, the season with which we began this circuit of the calendar year. In the beginning we noted the importance of Advent for celebrating the coming of the Savior, the birth of Christ. But Advent is also important for remembering the *second* coming of Christ at the Last Judgment, and this latter function of the season is well represented in lyrics devoted to meditations on Doomsday.

One of the earliest such lyrics appears in the Trinity Cambridge manuscript 323 (mid-thirteenth century), which Carleton Brown prints as two poems entitled respectively "Doomsday" (XIII 28a) and "The Latemest Day" (XVI 29A). In this manuscript, however, the text appears as a single poem in quatrains, hence I treat it here as such. It begins as follows:

> When I think on doomsday full sorely I dread
> How each man, after his works, shall have his meed.
> I have sinned against Christ in thought and in deed:
> Lord Savior, God's son, what shall be my reed [advice]?

The poet goes on to provide a traditional description of the coming of the end of the world. The end shall come with fire on a Saturday night, the time specified not only in early commentaries but also in songs that have survived to modern times, like the following stanza I remember from childhood:

> Saturday night about twelve o'clock
> This old world's gonna reel and rock,
> Pharaoh's army got drownded,
> O Mary don't you weep.

Four angels shall blow their trumpets, the poet continues, and then Christ shall come to give his judgment. Rich men shall sing "alas," and no one will be saved by force of arms or wise words. The righteous shall be welcomed, and the wicked shall be condemned to eternal fire (Matt. 25:31–46). Each man will have to answer for his own sins. The soul may well complain because of his sins committed by the body, and she does so by pointing out the terrible fate that awaits it after death:

> Now shall thine "hell" be fashioned with a spade,
> And thou, wretch, shall be brought therein;
> They will sweep out thy house and burn thy belongings,
> All thy chests shall be ransacked.
>
> The house where thou shalt dwell is quickly built,
> Both the beams and the roof shall lie on thy chin;
> Then worms shall dwell inside thee,
> Nor shalt thou ward them off with button or with pin.

The soul goes on to point out vindictively the many disadvantages of dwelling in the grave—the rotting of the body, the loss of friends and wealth, and the fading of the very memory of the person. A long *ubi sunt* passage (stanzas beginning "Where are . . .") is climaxed by the soul asking the body these questions:

> Where are thy dishes with their sweet servings?
> Where is thy bread and ale, thy casks and camels?
> Now thou shalt dwell in the pit with fiends;
> Alas! why did thou not understand this before now?

Having denounced the body at length, the soul now realizes that for her the worst is yet to come:

> While thou haddest the power to do at thy will,
> Thou wert always busy to ruin us both;
> And now thou, wretch, shalt lie very still,
> But I must pay very dearly for thy sins.

This leads to a final outcry against the injustice of it all:

> Lie, accursed body, may thou never arise!
> Whenever I think on thee, I tremble;
> I shall shudder in fire, and shiver in ice,
> And be tortured because of thee in a terrible way.
>
> On doomsday we shall be naked in a bitter bath,
> Made of brimstone and boiling pitch,
> Wherein Satan the fiend tears us with his rake,
> And then the fiery dragon will swallow us.

[124]

Three more stanzas describe the frightening features of the Devil, with horns on both his head and his knee, a terrible countenance, eye sockets like a brewing cauldron with fire springing from them. One look at him and anyone would die of fright. To avoid such an encounter the author urges that we keep ourselves from the seven sins, and make our peace with holy Church. In contrast to the fire and brimstone passage, the poem closes with a prayer for forgiveness and divine guidance:

> Let us pray our Lord for his sweet might
> That he ever be our shield from the foul wight [Devil],
> And let us hate the evil and love the right,
> And bring us at our ending into heaven's light.

We turn now, in conclusion, from this lengthy, serious Doomsday poem to a series of shorter pieces which will conclude our survey of the medieval English lyric. One of these is a doomsday prayer, rescued from obscurity by Robert D. Stevick, and included in his edition of *One Hundred Middle English Lyrics* (no. 20):

> Nought hath my soul but fire and ice
> And the body earth and tree [wood]:
> Bid we all the high King
> That shall wield the last doom
> That he let us that same thing,
> That we may do his will;
> May he excuse us from the tithing
> That the sinful shall undertake
> When death leadeth them to the mirth
> That never shall be undone. Amen.

I have as usual modernized the language, but some problems of interpretation still remain. Here, in paraphrase, is my understanding of this remarkable prayer: As a sinner, I can expect nothing at the Last Judgment except earth and wood (a coffin) for my body, and fire and ice for my soul (compare the description of hell's pains in the preceding poem). Since like me all have sinned, we all should pray the high king that shall reign at the final doom that he withhold for us that judgment until we do his will; and may he excuse us from the tithing that the sinful must undertake when Death leads them in the dance that shall never cease. A paraphrase cannot convey the wit and intensity of this lyric. Key words are "tithing" and "mirth"—words not usually associated with death and Doomsday. In the first instance one is reminded of Saint Ambrose's use of the word "tithe" to refer to the slaughter of Saint Maurice and his companions, reported in *The Golden Legend*. A more recent parallel appears in the ballad "Tam Lin" (Child 39A24):

> And pleasant is the fairy land,
> But an eerie tale to tell,
> Ay at the end of seven years
> We pay a tiend [tribute, tithe] to hell . . .

In God's system of justice even the devil, it seems, is allowed to collect his tithe. Most startling, at the end of our poem, is the use of the word "mirth" to describe the tortures of the damned. Despite the early date of this poem (1275), Edmund Reiss may be right in suggesting a hint here of the Dance of Death. In any case, this is a poem of unusual compactness and originality.

Another remarkable lyric devoted to the Last Judgment appears in a collection made by Bishop Sheppey while he was at Oxford before the middle of the fourteenth century. Carleton Brown entitles it "How Christ Shall Come" (XIV 36):

> I saw him with flesh all bespread—
> He came from the east;
> I saw him with blood all beshed—
> He came from the west;
> I saw that many with him he brought—
> He came from the south;
> I saw that the world of him ne rought [did not care]—
> He came from the north.
>
> I come from the wedlock as a sweet spouse,
> that have my wife with me in-nome [taken in].
> I come from fight a stalwart knight,
> that my foe have overcome.
> I come from the cheaping as a rich chapman,
> that mankind have bought.
> I come from an uncouth [unknown] land as a poor pilgrim,
> that far have sought.

This poem is a striking collage of biblical passages forming a description of the Last Judgment. In the first stanza, the poet speaks as an observer who sees simultaneously the Crucifixion and the Second Coming. We see Christ stretched on the cross and yet at the same time we see him coming from "the four corners of the land" (Ezek. 7:2), bringing many with him (Matt. 25:31), while "the world knew him not" (John 1:10). Then Christ himself describes his own coming, first as the bridegroom with his bride the church (based on the Song of Solomon and Revelation), second as a knight who has overcome his foe in battle (Ps. 24:7–10), third as a merchant who has redeemed mankind (using the parable of the pearl of great price, Matt. 13:45), and finally as a poor pilgrim, an image we have seen earlier to be derived from the Emmaus episode (Luke 24:18). Traditional as are these figures, their use here to describe the second coming of Christ is highly original and effective. The themes of love and war, wealth and poverty somehow blend to form a single, luminous figure of the Messiah. Placing the poor pilgrim in climactic position is especially effective, suggesting as it does the gentle, continuing quest of the Savior for the redemption of all mankind.

The fifteenth century offers us a final example of the doomsday lyric, and perhaps the passage of time is responsible for a new note of urgency and subtle warning of the judgment to come. The speaker is Christ and the time is somewhere between Easter and Doomsday (XV 111):

> I have labored sore and suffered death,
> And now I rest and draw my breath;
> But I shall come and call right soon
> Heaven and earth and hell to doom:
> And then shall know, both devil and man,
> What I was and what I am.

CHAPTER THREE

Chaucer's Parliament of Fowls and the Hexameral Tradition

THAT Geoffrey Chaucer was familiar with the Bible is generally taken for granted. Its influence on his poetry can be seen
both in the grand design of major works like *Troilus and Criseyde* or *The Canterbury Tales* and in detailed passages such as may
be found in "The Man of Law's Tale" or "The Merchant's Tale."
Thus the fall of Troilus is an echo of the fall of Adam, and in the
pilgrimage to Canterbury is prefigured that perfect glorious pilgrimage to what the Parson calls "Jerusalem celestial."

When we examine the artistry of individual tales, the influence
of the Scriptures is likewise evident. Thus when Constance, in
"The Man of Law's Tale," is set adrift by the Syrians in a rudderless boat, Chaucer inserts a highly rhetorical passage—not in
his source—which begins as follows (*CT* II 470–76):

> Men myghten asken why she was nat slayn
> Eek at the feeste? who myghte hir body save?
> And I answere to that demande agayn,
> Who saved Danyel in the horrible cave
> Ther every wight save he, maister and knave,
> Was with the leon frete er he asterte?
> No wight but God, that he bar in his herte.

This addition continues for four more stanzas, in which the narrator repeats this pattern of rhetorical questions. Who kept her
from drowning in the sea? Answer: Who kept Jonah in the fish's
maw, until he was "spouted up" at Nineveh? Where might this

woman have meat and drink three years and more? Answer: Who fed the Egyptian Mary in the cave, or in the desert? In a similar passage later in the tale the victories of David over Goliath and Judith over Holofernes are invoked to explain Constance's overthrow of the evil steward who assaulted her on the ship.

A very different use of the Bible can be found in "The Merchant's Tale," where the lecherous old January addresses his young bride in the language of the Song of Solomon (*CT* IV 2137–48):

> . . . in a morwe unto his May seigh he:
> "Rys up, my wyf, my love, my lady free!
> The turtles voys is herd, my dowve sweete;
> The wynter is goon with alle his reynes weete.
> Com forth now, with thyne eyen columbyn!
> How fairer been thy brestes than is wyn!
> The gardyn is enclosed al aboute;
> Com forth, my white spouse! out of doute
> Thou hast me wounded in myn herte, O wyf!
> No spot to thee ne knew I al my lyf.
> Com forth, and lat us taken oure disport;
> I chees thee for my wyf and my comfort."

The contrast between the purity of the biblical verses and the impurity of the elderly husband is compounded by the obtuseness of the narrator (the merchant), who seems not to recognize the scriptural source in his comment on January's song: "Swiche olde lewed wordes used he."

These are but a few examples of the complex and fascinating ways that Chaucer makes use of the Bible in his poetry. But my present purpose is to call attention to scriptural influence of a different and less obvious kind: a poem written directly under the influence of the Bible, with a structure and theme in accord with this influence. We have such a work, I believe, in Chaucer's best dream vision poem, the *Parliament of Fowls*. But the *Parliament* is such a complex work that before considering its indebtedness to the Bible, we need to take note of its principles of order and its use of multiple literary sources.

The *Parliament of Fowls* is first of all a dream vision, modeled on the great French poem of Guillaume de Lorris and Jean de Meun, the *Roman de la Rose* (ca. 1237–77). Chaucer's *Book of the Duchess, House of Fame,* and Prologue to the *Legend of Good Women* were all written in this form, and some of the best poetry by Chaucer's contemporaries, notably the *Pearl* and *Piers the Plow-*

man, were likewise cast in the form of visions. One of the advantages of this was the central figure of the dreamer, through whose eyes the entire vision is perceived. The dreamer's reactions to events in the poem often provide a cue for the reader, but equally important is the poet's tendency to depict the dreamer as slow to comprehend, a trait that gives the reader a sense of discovery, a feeling that he is perceiving the truth of things ahead of his guide. This device is notably present in the *Book of the Duchess*, and, I believe also, in the *Parliament of Fowls*.

The *Parliament* also reveals traces of another literary form, known as the *demande d'amour*. In this type of poem a question is posed in regard to love which is designed to lead to a discussion by the assembled company. The evidence of Chaucer's works suggests that he often read his poems before a courtly audience, and indeed examples of the *demande d'amour* are not lacking in his tales. In "The Knight's Tale," for instance, the two rivals for the hand of Emelye—Palamon and Arcite—are imprisoned by Duke Theseus where they can see the beautiful Emelye taking her daily stroll in the garden, but they are unable to speak to her. Soon Arcite is released from prison by the intercession of a friend, but on condition that he leave the country. Thus Palamon could see Emelye, but remained in prison, while Arcite was free, but could no longer set eyes on the lady. At this point in the tale the Knight addresses the pilgrims (CT I 1347–48):

> Yow lovers axe I now this questioun:
> Who hath the worse, Arcite or Palamoun?

This marks the end of part one of the tale, and possibly an interval during which the listeners could discuss the dilemma of the lovers among themselves. A similar use of the *demande d'amour* occurs in "The Franklin's Tale," where the question is which of three persons in the narrative shows the greatest generosity.

Fused with the *demande d'amour* in the *Parliament of Fowls* is the "bird debate," a form perhaps best known in the early English poem *The Owl and the Nightingale*. The latter is of course limited to a dispute between the two birds of the title, whereas Chaucer's *Parliament* allows for a wide-open debate among representatives of all classes of fowls. Before the argument gets out of hand, however, we see traces of the *demande d'amour* in the claims of the three tercel eagles for the right to marry the formel. Which of the three eagles has the greatest claim on her? But in this case we are left with no answer when the formel chooses not to marry "as yet."

One may conclude that a dream vision, employing the *demande d'amour* in a bird debate, would suffice for any poet, but Chaucer goes one step further: the *Parliament* is also a Valentine poem. Indeed, the connection of the poem with February 14 is a most important feature and may have led to the idea of a bird parliament as its main ingredient (*PF* 309–10):

> For this was on seynt Valentynes day,
> Whan every foul cometh there to chese his make. . . .

Where did Chaucer get the idea that birds marry on Saint Valentine's Day? Some think he originated the concept. It is true that we have no allusion to the belief prior to this date (ca. 1380), but independent references in the centuries following suggest that it may have been a feature of traditional folk belief even before Chaucer's time. "And, cousin, upon Friday is St. Valentine's Day, and every bird chooseth him a mate" (Paston letters, 1477); "Saint Valentine is past: Begin these woodbirds but to couple now?" (Shakespeare, *MND* 4.1.145). Even in modern times the belief survives in America. Among the childhood memories of my wife is the vivid recollection of being told by her parents that the birds marry on Valentine's Day. She and her sister would spend much of the day looking out the window and occasionally seeing processions of birds (including the famous Kentucky Cardinal, vivid red against the late winter snow) that they truly believed to be acting out their own form of marriage service.

Thus we have a Valentine poem in which a dreamer sees a vision of a parliament of birds, convened by the goddess Nature so that the fowls may choose their mates for the coming year. This seems straightforward enough: but there is more. The parliament scene does not begin until we are nearly halfway through the poem. Students of Chaucer have been puzzled by a long introduction that seems to have little to do with the main episode. There is first a waking interval in which the dreamer announces his theme (love) and tells of reading an old book by Cicero, the *Dream of Scipio*, which he proceeds to summarize. He tells how the elder Africanus appeared to Scipio the younger in a dream, took him up into the heavens, and showed him the stars, the planets, and the little spot of earth where he lived. Africanus urged

Scipio always to seek the welfare of all people (the common "profit") and promised him if he did so an eternal reward in heaven.

The evening comes, depriving the dreamer of light to read by, and, feeling restless, he finally goes to sleep and dreams that Africanus is standing at his bedside. After an appeal for inspiration to Cytherea (Venus), the poet begins a description of the vision itself. He dreams that Africanus leads him to a gate, over which is written in letters of gold and black some verses that are alternately enticing and threatening. The first message directs the dreamer to a "blissful place," where all hearts will be healed; the second message warns of the mortal strokes of "Disdain and Danger." When the dreamer hesitates, Africanus shoves him through the gates and leaves him to make his way through the garden alone.

Inside, the dreamer finds himself in beautiful surroundings, reminiscent of medieval descriptions of Paradise: beautiful streams, trees, birds singing, a land of temperate climate and soft breezes. Suddenly, in this beautiful setting, the dreamer sees a tableau: Cupid, with his bow and arrows under a tree, along with various courtly and allegorical figures. Nearby is the Temple of Venus, in which we are shown Priapus and his worshipers and finally Venus herself inside, seductively described. Two young people kneel before her, asking her blessing. Broken bows hang on the wall, left by former devotees of "Diana the chaste" who are now among those converts to Venus's religion, whose hot sighs fill her temple. And Chaucer ends this episode with a list of unfortunate lovers, whose stories and whose deaths, he says, were painted on the walls of the sanctuary. The atmosphere of this episode is oppressive, and it is with some sense of relief that we follow the dreamer back outdoors to the beautiful garden, where we now find Nature, "vicar of the almighty Lord," presiding over the congregation of birds.

From this brief résumé we can see that Chaucer's *Parliament* divides readily into three parts: the first is the waking prologue, devoted primarily to a recitation of the contents of Scipio's dream; the second is the tableau in and around the Temple of Venus which is drawn primarily from Boccaccio's *Teseide*, the same source used by Chaucer for the Knight's tale of Palemon and Arcite; and the third, of course, is the parliament itself, the most original part of the poem, although Chaucer tells us that his idea for using

Nature as the presiding goddess comes from a Latin poem by Alanus de Insulis entitled *The Complaint of Nature* (*PF* 316–18):

> And right as Aleyn, in the Pleynt of Kynde,
> Devyseth Nature of aray and face,
> In swich aray men myghte hire there fynde.

Thus we see, as readers of Chaucer have long been aware, that the three distinct parts of the poem seem to be rendered even more distinct by the fact that they are derived, at least in part, from three quite different authors: Cicero, Boccaccio, and Alanus. The poem is almost invariably praised as one of Chaucer's best, but his "juxtaposition" of these three episodes is often seen as puzzling or mystifying. What does Africanus have to do with Venus? And where do they both stand in relation to Nature? In recent decades, much attention has been devoted to these problems.

But many of these questions can be set aside, I believe, if not entirely dissipated, when the three parts of the *Parliament* are seen as aspects of a single structure governing the poem as a whole. It is my contention that this structure is biblical, and that Chaucer's *Parliament of Fowls* is a "Creation" poem, with its organizing principles derived from commentaries on the first chapter of Genesis, a body of medieval exegesis generally known as the hexameral tradition. When this structure is perceived, the poem holds together very well. It remains a Valentine poem, light and yet serious, on the subject of love, both human and divine, an appropriate subject for Saint Valentine's Day. It is not a sermon, but it has a text: *Crescite et multiplicamini, et replete terram* ("Increase and multiply, and replenish the earth").

A favorite subject of early Christian exegesis was the first chapter of Genesis, containing an account of the first six days (*hexaemera*) of creation. One of the first and most important of these was the Greek *Hexameron* of Saint Basil the Great, Bishop of Caesarea, 370–79. The model provided by Basil was followed closely by Saint Ambrose in his Latin *Hexameron*, delivered as a series of nine sermons on the Six Days of Creation, probably in Holy Week of 387, the very time of his baptism of Saint Augustine. The great Augustine provides a *Hexameron* of his own in his *Confessions* (XI–XIII), and in his commentary on Genesis (*De Genesi ad Litteram*), but this is quite different from the approach of Basil and Ambrose in its emphasis on the metaphysical and theistic aspects of cre-

[133]

ation. Augustine pays little attention to the physical side of God's creation; hence very little in the life of birds and beasts can be found in his commentary or in those *hexamera* written under his influence.

In the twelfth century, there were some new developments in the hexameral tradition, particularly in the direction of viewing creation as a continuous development involving the working out of natural causes. The new school of thought is perhaps best illustrated in a cosmological work by Bernardus Silvestris, *De Universitate Mundi.* This treatment of the Creation is highly philosophical, strongly indebted to Plato's *Timaeus,* and abandons the six-day structure of Genesis. It was Bernardus's student, Alanus de Insulis, to whom Chaucer refers (as we have seen) as author of the Latin poem *De Planctu Naturae* ("the Pleynt of Kynde"), which contains such an elaborate portrait of the goddess Nature. Thus it was to the twelfth-century Platonists that Chaucer owes his conception of the goddess who presides in the *Parliament of Fowls,* the "vicar" or executive officer under God in the establishment of creation.

But the Platonists have no really large role, philosophically, to play in the poem; the major authorities for Chaucer were, and continued to be, the philosophers and theologians of the early Middle Ages. Boethius remained a central influence throughout Chaucer's life. Augustine, too, was important, but in considering the *Parliament* we must be prepared to replace him with Ambrose, whose account of the creation was more central to the hexameral tradition, and, in short, more biblical. In saying this, I do not wish to lose sight of the fact that Chaucer knew Cicero, Macrobius, Boccaccio, and all the other writers customarily cited in any discussion of the sources of the *Parliament of Fowls.* There is no doubt that these writers provided the passages attributed to them. What I wish to emphasize is that the influence of the hexameral tradition on the poem is present, but at a deep level: so deep that it governs its structure while scarcely ever showing itself on the "surface" of the text.

Before testing our theory of the structure of the *Parliament,* we must become acquainted with the pattern of exegesis represented by the hexameral tradition, and for this we may take Ambrose's *Hexameron* as a model. The work is divided into six books, representing the six days of creation, although two sermons are devoted to the first, third, and fifth days, making a total of nine sermons. The organization follows Basil very closely, but there is much originality in Ambrose's work, which is well worth considering in its own right. In the following summary I can only hint at the riches that await the student who wishes to read Ambrose for himself.

The First Day (Gen. 1:1–5)

In the beginning God created the heaven and the earth. How can we find the truth about creation among the warring opinions of the ancients? The danger in these is that they tend to confer divine honors on the sky, the earth, and the sea, which is idolatry. But Moses, inspired by the Holy Spirit, clearly shows us in his opening words that God gave all created things their beginnings, and was not one who imitates matter under the guidance of some "Idea." Thus he who seeks to comprehend God through science is a fool. Scripture tells us that the Pasch (Passover) shall be the beginning of months (Exod. 12:2), and the pattern of the seasons also suggests that Easter was the time when the world was created. Therefore, for those of you listening to me who are acolytes, it is also a time of passing over from vices to virtues, when you renounce the devil and cross the Red Sea into the new life of the Church. Thus there is more to creation than what can be seen. The Angels, Dominations, and Powers came into being at some time before the heavens and the earth, and the latter themselves show forth the attributes of the Creator, as the prophet declares (Ps. 18:1). Moreover, with heaven and earth were created those four elements from which came everything in the world: earth, air, fire, and water. But most important is that the earth is dependent on the power of God: "The Lord established it by the support of his will" (Ps. 94:4). The simplicity of this faith is worth all the proofs of science.

And the earth was without form and void; and darkness was upon the face of the deep. Some might argue that this means matter existed from the beginning, but they would be wrong. For if it did exist, where was it? in what place? The earth may be thought of as invisible only in the sense that at this point it had not yet been given its appropriate form and beauty. By "darkness" we should not understand the powers of evil, lest we seem to say that their wickedness was brought about by God; for evil is not a substance, but an accident, a deviation from good. But it is clear that evil is not meant when we go on to read: *And the spirit of God moved upon the face of the waters.* Then whence came evil? Our adversary is within us. Look closely on your intentions: you yourself are the cause of your wickedness. Why do you summon an alien nature to furnish an excuse for your sins? We ourselves give in to sin instead of doing deeds of charity. Why then do you accuse Nature? We should guard against the sins of youth and irrational passions of the body through our wills, and not ascribe the fault to others.

The Second Day (Gen. 1:6–8)

And God said, Let there be a firmament. . . . How marvelous it is that a world of dissimilar elements is united by laws of concord and love! Do not, therefore, estimate with your eyes nor weigh with your mind the problem of creation. Some say, for example, that God created only one heaven. But the Apostle shows us that there were at least three (2 Cor. 12:2), and David introduced the "heavens of heavens" into the chorus of those who give praise to God (Ps. 148:4). In imitation of him philosophers speak of the harmonious movement of five planets, which, along with the sun and moon, form the seven spheres whose contrary motion produces a heavenly melody. Yet when asked for proof of these things, they have little to offer. So let us leave them to their theories, and adhere closely to the doctrine laid down by the celestial scriptures.

Marvel not that the firmament should *divide the waters from the waters,* a fact that is confirmed in Psalm 148:4 ("Praise him . . . ye waters that be above the heavens"). God controls the waters, as he proved by dividing the Red Sea and rolling back the Jordan. Moreover, the waters remain suspended in the heavens because God has balanced the universe with weights and measures: thus water and fire prevent each other from raging out of control. But it is God who controls the heavens, as when he allowed no rain because of sin in the time of Elijah. Some speak of the waters as "purificatory powers," and I can accept that, while still maintaining that the waters we have been discussing are real. Moreover, we do not believe the stars to be unseen powers of nature, but to have real existence. Even dragons praise the Lord (Ps. 148:7), because their nature and aspect, if examined closely, are not without a certain modicum of beauty. Indeed, the Father and the Son together artfully made the world, and saw that it was good. But let us bring an end to the second day, lest darkness overtake us, and so that you may refresh yourselves with food and drink.

The Third Day (Gen. 1:9–13)

And God said, Let the waters under the heaven be gathered together. . . . Even as the waters obeyed God, I see that you, my listeners, are gathered together in the Church of the Lord. Indeed the gathering of the waters very well expresses the formation of the Church. From every valley and marsh, the people of the Gentiles came together on dry land to become the congregation of the faithful. The valley is a theater, a circus, wherein are found the vanity and strife of the world; and the marsh is self-indulgence, intemperance, and incontinence, the home of the passions. But the people of God love each other, and rejoice in the protection of this holy temple.

The dry land now showed itself when the covering of water was removed. To those who object that this is not possible, I reply in their own terms: the voice of God is the efficient cause of Nature. But let them also answer me: have they not seen springs shoot up from below or water rise out of the ground? Behold a still greater marvel: the waters flow, but do not overflow (Eccles. 1:7). As God says to Job: Hitherto shalt thou come, but no further, and here shall thy proud waves be stayed (Job 38:11). What prevents the Red Sea from inundating Egypt? (the threat of which perhaps led to cancellation of plans for a canal). There are many seas, and yet one sea. But what is meant by the phrase "dry land?" Each of the four elements has its own peculiar property: the earth is dry and cold; air, warm and humid; fire, warm and dry; water, cold and humid. Thus each is joined to one other element by qualities shared in common. In this manner, these elements, by a circuitous process, meet together in a dance measure of concord and association. Hence the Latin *elementa* is found in Greek as *stoicheia*, denoting agreement and harmony. But God also saw that the sea was good, for in it is found much that is both useful to man and beautiful in itself.

And God said, Let the earth bring forth grass. . . . Thus God shows that germination, a law of nature, can operate without the sun, which is not the cause and therefore should not be worshiped.

[137]

He also provides food for animals, before providing for man. What is man? The prophet says that "all flesh is grass" (Isa. 40:6). Today he is a youth, tomorrow the ills of this world take their toll. When he suffers a change of fortune, he is deserted by everyone. Rather let us sow the seed of the spirit! What a miraculous thing it is when the plant springs from the death of the grain! (John 12:24). How great is God's kindness in providing us the fruits of the earth! How wonderful the beauty of the flowers, and how beneficent the health-giving juices of the herbs! And nothing is created without a purpose. Even poisonous plants turn out to have medicinal uses. Do seeds degenerate? No, they invariably pass on the integrity of their stock, and often provide an abundance, even while we are asleep (Mark 4:26–9).

And the earth brought forth the fruit tree yielding fruit after his kind. . . . Immediately the trees were assembled, the forests arose, and the peaks of the hills were clothed with leaves. There were the pine, cypress, cedar, pitchpine, fir, laurel, and oak, each with its characteristics; for Nature maintained in every case, through future ages, the prerogatives that had been impressed on it at the moment of creation. We see a lesson in the flourishing of the vine, but in fact all of the trees have a certain utility for man, and their fruit is useful for medicine as well as for sustenance of the body.

Let the earth bring forth, said God, and immediately the whole earth was filled with growing vegetation. And to man it has been said, *Love the Lord thy God,* yet the love of God is not instilled in the hearts of all. Deafer are the hearts of men than the hardest rock. We deny our debt for the earth's plenitude when we do not give homage to its author.

The Fourth Day (Gen. 1:14–19)

And God said, Let there be lights in the firmament of the heaven. . . . Cleanse your eyes in order to behold the sun on the fourth day, delayed in creation so that no one should believe that it was a god. When you admire the sun, give praise to its Creator! With the voice of her gifts does Nature cry out: "Good indeed is the sun, but good only in service, not in command; good as one who assists at my fecundity, not as one who creates. With me he groans, with me he is in travail, in order that there may come the adoption of sons and the redemption of the human race by which we, too, may be freed from servitude (Rom. 8:21–22). By my side he praises the Author; along with me he says a hymn to the Lord God." Mystically the sun is interpreted as Christ, and the moon as the Church. For the Church, like the moon, may grow dim (in time of persecution), but it never undergoes a loss of substance, just as the orb of the moon is often seen to be intact, even when only the horns are shining. The fire of the sun both illuminates and burns. Thus it illuminated Moses when God appeared to him in the burning bush (Exod. 3:2), but it destroys the wicked, to whom the Lord says, "I am a consuming fire" (Deut. 4:24).

And let them be for signs, and for seasons, and for days and years. The sun, moon, and stars divide time in various ways, and will some day provide signs of the coming of the end of the world. But some men vainly seek to read the signs of the heavens in order to determine the future of each newborn child. Of what use are the commandments of the Lord if all our actions are determined by some natal star? How do we determine the precise date of a child's birth? Suppose that there is an astrologer near at hand. (Can a man be present at a child's birth?) While the astrologer is setting up his horoscope, the precise moment of birth escapes him. And is it not ridiculous to derive a standard for conduct from the beasts of the Zodiac? How can they say that the "planets" determine the destiny of our lives? A man was in no way guilty, it is said, but an unfavorable sign looked upon him! How like a spider's web is the wisdom of the astrologers. The very laws and statutes of the world reveal that men themselves are held responsible.

The seasons, days, and years, with which we are all familiar, are fixed by the sun and moon, the Romans by solar and the Hebrews by lunar calculation. These two great heavenly bodies appear impartially to all peoples, and never vary in size. Despite the power of the sun, the Creator arranges that it warms but never burns. The moon disperses dew, and waxes and wanes according to plan; while it does not directly affect the weather, it does affect the tides. Morally we should learn from the moon that nothing lasts in this world; mystically the moon makes known the mysteries of Christ and the Church. And from the important service assigned to the moon by God we know that no charms produced by the superstitions of the astrologers can move or bring harm to the Church itself. No more should we pay attention to the belief that the fourth day is unlucky for the start of a journey or enterprise, especially when it is the day on which we celebrate our Redemption.

The Fifth Day (Gen. 1:20–23)

And God said, Let the waters bring forth abundantly the moving crea- ture that hath life, and fowl that may fly above the earth in the open firmament of heaven. At this command the waters immediately poured forth their offspring. The rivers were in labor. Fish leapt, dolphins frolicked, and there were shellfish, oysters, and sea ur- chins. Alas, that such became an enticement for the appetite of man! The earth was replete with plants, the sea with living things. There are serpents, fish that swim, seals, crocodiles, and water horses (hippopotamuses), using their feet as oars. God made the largest and the smallest: the whale and the snail. It is impossible to enumerate all the species of sea life, but in passing let us take note of the fact that things that are an object of fear on land be- come harmless in the sea: even water snakes are bereft of poison. The same may be said of ravens and wolves; and the sea lions flee from the calves. But this is not to be wondered at, since even in the Church the effect of water (in baptism) is such that the guilt of the wicked, when washed away, is assimilated to inno- cence.

We would do well to learn from the habits of the fish, both in what to imitate and what to avoid. Fish are always diligent in the protection of their young, a quality that men have lost. There are no unnatural betrothals, such as the union of donkey and mare abetted by man, all in the name of efficiency. It is true that fish prey on each other—the larger on the smaller—but this violent way of living comes from inner compulsion, whereas with us it springs from avarice and not from nature. Beware, you rich man, of imitating the habits of predatory fish! Beware the hook and the net! But the faithful need not fear the hook of Peter, for it does not kill, it consecrates. Only let not the storms of this world over- whelm you, but hide yourselves in the depths. "Be therefore wise as serpents" (Matt. 10:16). Speaking of serpents, let us be wise in this matter of marriage. Observe the mating of the sea viper. Wives, embrace your husband with affection; husbands, lay aside your rudeness and be a guide, not a dictator. All of us can learn from the deceitful character of the polypus, that conceals itself by turn- ing the color of the rock on which it awaits its unwary victim.

[140]

How cleverly the crab hunts the oyster! But who can match the ability of the sea urchin to forecast a change in weather? Can an astrologer do so much? What teacher has instructed it? It is God who created all these. He has made all things in wisdom, and if he has not neglected the lowly sea urchin, how much more will he bestow on mankind, O ye of little faith?

By force of habit each species of fish keeps itself within the bounds of its prescribed habitat, while man seeks constantly to alter his environment. Men use and abuse the sea, dredging and building, making oyster beds and fish ponds. Each wants what is his neighbor's. The Lord will punish them! How alien to the fish is this monstrous greed. Consider the whale, who lives far from the haunts of men, delights in his own habitat, and prefers to live out his life in solitary fashion. Some fish do migrate, but out of necessity for spawning. Who arranges their itinerary? Can men move together with such precision? Fishes follow the law of their Commander, while men do not. They know "the time to be born" (Eccles. 3:2), while man alone ignores such times. Thus it falls to women to give birth in seasons of inclemency. An unsettled and arbitrary desire to produce offspring leads to an uncertain time for childbirth. Both man and fish migrate, but for different reasons: man for greed, fish for love of offspring. The sea is full of wealth for our use, and beauty for our delight. How much more pleasant is travel on water than on land! Water was a means to salvation for Jonah, and be assured that water has been given to us, more than to the Ninevites, as a source for the remission of sins.

And God created . . . every winged fowl after his kind. . . . Peering into the depths of the sea, I nearly forgot the race of winged creatures. It is customary for the birds at nesting time to charm the sky with song, in that their allotted task is done, and to sing the praises of their Creator, even as we sing his praises in the Psalms of our divine service. There are three classes of these creatures: those of the earth, the air, and the water. Turning first to the birds of the air, what shall I say of the parrot, the blackbird, nightingale, turtledove, pigeon, and crow? Among the waterfowl are the halcyon, gull, heron, and goose, reminding us that the birds came originally from the water, and that swimming, after all, is not so very different from flying. Some birds live by plunder, like the hawk and the eagle; some are stationary, while others migrate, like the thrush, stork, and crane. Some are wild, and some are tame. Some are imitative, like the blackbird and the parrot. Some are guileless like the dove, or artful like the partridge. The cock is inclined to be boastful, the peacock to be vain. Some love to consult together in groups, thus helping to form by this combined strength a state of their own under a king. Other birds love to look out, each one for his own interest, avoiding a systematic rule, and, when captured, long to quit a slavery that is disdainful to them. Birds that have become examples for our own way of life are the crane, the stork, and the swallow. Hawks appear harsh toward their offspring, but in fact are training them for a life of plunder. A similar point can be made about the eagle. Yet the waterfowl, who often adopts the rejected nestling of the eagle, gives us an example of charity. The turtledove, faithful beyond death, illustrates the joys of widowhood. The vulture is said to conceive without the union of the sexes, and thus rebukes those who question the truth of the Virgin birth. The bees live under the control of laws in a sort of commonwealth. Who taught them their organization and the construction of their cells? But while we are occupied with such diversity, behold how the birds of night flit around us! Let us now sing the mysteries of the Lord and await the morning, which shall be the sixth day.

The Sixth Day (Gen. 1:24–31)

Enter with me into this mighty and wonderful theater of the whole visible creation. Let me show you from all these examples how the Creator of the universe has conferred more abundant benefits on you than on all the rest of his creatures. It is for you, therefore, that the wreath of victory is designed. While you share with the rest of creatures your corporal weakness, you possess above and beyond all other creatures a faculty of the soul which in itself has nothing in common with the rest of created things. You may ask, "How long are we to learn of other living creatures while we do not know ourselves? Tell us what is to be for our benefit that we may know ourselves." That is a just complaint. But we must follow the order of Scripture and first review the creation of the animal kingdom, for through the study of other creatures we shall be better able to understand ourselves. Consider the habits of these animals: the horse, donkey, fox, lion, leopard, the lowly ant, the dog, the bear, the serpent, tortoise, sheep, and hedgehog. Among all these beasts the mightiest is the elephant. But there is a balance in the animal kingdom, and God has included some as scourges for our correction, as a good teacher disciplines his students.

Your soul is made in the image of God, whereas your body is related to the beasts. In one there is the holy seal of imitation of the divine. In the other there is found base association with beasts and wild animals. Before he sinned Adam conformed to the image of God; but after his fall he lost that celestial image and took on one that is terrestrial. Because your soul is a priceless thing, be on your guard and shun the temptations of the world. The human body excells all things in grace and beauty, and is constructed like the world itself. This is revealed in a careful study of it, extending from head to toe. But this brings us to the end of our discourse, the completion of the sixth day, after which our Creator rested, to whom be the glory forever. Amen.

With this overview of Ambrose's *Hexameron* in mind, we may now trace its influence in Chaucer's design for his Valentine poem. In brief, the three main sections of the *Parliament* seem to correspond generally to features of the second, third, and fifth days of creation. Thus the dream of Scipio belongs with speculations on the nature of the firmament created on the second day (Gen. 1:6), the Temple of Venus with its tableau of intemperate love corresponds to the marsh of self-indulgence in Ambrose's allegorical treatment of the gathering of the waters on the third day (Gen. 1:9), and the description of the garden, together with the entire parliament of birds, is derived from the scriptural account of the creation of vegetation on the third day (Gen. 1:11–12) and of fishes and birds on the fifth day (Gen. 1:20–23). Such modifications of this general comparison as may be necessary can be dealt with as we now examine each segment of the poem separately and in detail.

To begin with, let us examine the two introductory stanzas announcing that the theme of the poem is love. In doing so, let us assume that Chaucer has been asked (or has decided) to write a poem for Valentine's Day. He must now decide what kind of poem it shall be. It is not enough to say that the subject will be "love." What kind of love? The poem as a whole tells me that he chose as his underlying theme the love of God that holds the universe together, that is, "the laws of concord and love" which, according to Ambrose, "form a union of . . . discordant elements" (II.1.1). The idea is perhaps best expressed by Boethius in his *Consolation of Philosophy*, which I quote (with modernized spelling) from Chaucer's own translation (II, m.8):

> . . . all this accordance of things is bound with love, that governeth earth and sea, and hath also commandment to the heaven. And if this love slacked the bridles, all things that now love them together would make battle continually, and strive to fordo [destroy] the fashion [form] of this world, the which they now lead in accordable faith by fair movements. This love holds together people joined with an holy bond, and knitteth sacrament of marriages of chaste loves; and love enditeth laws to true fellowship. How well were mankind, if that love that governeth heaven governed your spirits!

This famous passage from Boethius well expresses the implicit theme of the *Parliament of Fowls*. Chaucer's task, however, is to communicate this theme without preaching, and without disturbing the delicate balance between whimsy and seriousness in a Valentine poem. The opening stanzas, therefore, are not philosophical: instead they speak of the human love we normally associate with Saint Valentine's Day (1–14):

> The lyf so short, the craft so long to lerne,
> Th'assay so hard, so sharp the conquerynge,
> The dredful joye, alwey that slit so yerne:
> Al this mene I by Love, that my felynge
> Astonyeth with his wonderful werkynge
> So sore, iwis, that whan I on hym thynke,
> Nat wot I wel wher that I flete or synke.
>
> For al be that I knowe nat Love in dede,
> Ne wot how that he quiteth folk here hyre,
> Yit happeth me ful ofte in bokes reede
> Of his myrakles and his crewel yre.
> There rede I wel he wol be lord and syre;
> I dar nat seyn, his strokes been so sore,
> But "God save swich a lord!"—I can na moore.

Thus does Chaucer announce his theme, while at the same time dissociating himself from those who serve a tyrannical Cupid, whose "miracles" and "cruel wrath" are strongly reminiscent of the vengeful God of the Old Testament. Having mentioned that he read about love in books, Chaucer has prepared us for the bookish summary of Cicero's *Dream of Scipio* that follows.

Books play an important part in Chaucer's dream vision poems. In the *Book of the Duchess* and the Prologue to the *Legend of Good Women* the dreamer reads a book before falling asleep, and while this does not happen in the *House of Fame*, the first section of that poem is given over to a summary of Virgil's *Aeneid*. It almost seems as if Chaucer needs the support of one of his beloved authors to ignite his own creativity. In the *Parliament* he tells us that not long ago he was reading a book "written with letters old" for the purpose of learning "a certain thing" not specified (22–25):

> For out of old feldes, as men seyth,
> Cometh al this newe corn from yer to yere,
> And out of olde bokes, in good feyth,
> Cometh al this newe science that men lere.

Chaucer does not specify the object of the dreamer's search, but the effect of his words is to put us in a searching mood, so that we may, with the dreamer, read what is to come in the hope of finding a certain thing: the meaning of the poem.

The book that the dreamer is reading is the *Dream of Scipio*, which originally appeared as a part of Cicero's *Republic*, but circulated independently in the Middle Ages with a popular commentary by Macrobius (ca. 400). Cicero no doubt owed his inspiration for the *Dream* to the tale of Er in Plato's *Republic*, and in his commentary Macrobius makes the following observation about the two works:

> In our reading of Plato's *Republic* and Cicero's *Republic*, my son Eustachus, my joy and boast in life, we noted this difference at a glance: the former drafted plans for the organization of a state, the latter described one already in existence; the one discussed an ideal state, the other the government established by his forefathers. In one respect, however, imitation has produced a striking similarity, namely, that whereas Plato, at the conclusion of his work, has a man who apparently had died and was restored to life to reveal the conditions of souls liberated from their bodies, introducing as well an interesting description of the spheres and constellations, the Scipio of Cicero's work treats of the same subjects, but as revelations which came to him in a dream.

Chaucer summarizes this dream as follows:

> When the younger Scipio arrived in Africa, he visited King Massinissa, an old friend of the family, who told him much of his ancestor, the elder Africanus. In his sleep that night Scipio dreamed that Af-

ricanus took him up to the heavens where from a starry place, he showed him Carthage, and prophesied a great deal about his future career as a leader of Rome. When Scipio asked him if there was a life after death, Africanus told him yes, saying that our life in this world is but a kind of death, and that rightful folk, after they die, shall go to heaven, and pointed out to him the universe [57–63]:

> Thanne shewede he hym the lytel erthe that here is,
> At regard of the hevenes quantite;
> And after shewede he hym the nyne speres,
> And after that the melodye herde he
> That cometh of thilke speres thryes thre,
> That welle is of musik and melodye
> In this world here, and cause of armonye.

Then Africanus urged him to take no delight in this world, and showed how brief is our span of life here compared to the length of the Mundane Year, when all the stars will return to their original positions at the beginning of time. When Scipio asked how he might come to the bliss of heaven, Africanus replied: First know thyself to be immortal, look that you seek always the "common profit," and then you shall not fail to come to that blissful place. To this he added a warning [78–84]:

> "But brekers of the lawe, soth to seyne
> And likerous folk, after that they ben dede,
> Shul whirle about th'erthe alwey in peyne,
> Tyl many a world be passed, out of drede,
> And than, foryeven al hir wikked dede,
> Than shul they come into this blysful place,
> To which to comen God the sende his grace."

This somber warning of Africanus comes to us at one remove from the dreamer's book (like a play within a play), yet it is in harmony with the poem's theme, directing our search away from the tyrannical love of the senses toward the love that governs heaven. The magnificent representation here of the Ptolemaic universe, with the music of the spheres expressing the harmony of God's creation, was the generally accepted world view throughout the Middle Ages from the time of Macrobius until the rediscovery of Aristotle in the twelfth century. And for most, including Chaucer, it remained valid perhaps down to Shakespeare and beyond. But it is interesting that the early Church Fathers, including Basil and Ambrose, appeared skeptical of this tradition, or at least felt it important to declare that in any conflict of opinion Moses (the author of Genesis) should take precedence over

Creation

Pietà

Harrowing of Hell

Ij illoteme. Duo ex discipu
lis ihu ibant ipa die i cas
tellum q̄ erat i spacio sta
dioru sexaginta ab uehi
noie emaus. Et ipi loq̄

(Top) *Road to Emmaus;* (bottom) *Ascension*

Plato and his successors. Thus Basil, in his *Hexameron* (III.3), after describing the spheres and their melody, offers a skeptical comment: "Then, when those who say these things are asked for a sensible proof, what do they say? That, having become accustomed to this sound from our birth, we fail to notice the sound through our early familiarity with it and because of habitually hearing it, like men in smithies who have their ears incessantly dinned." The explanation alluded to by Basil comes from Plato (*Republic*, X.14.615), whereas Cicero, in his *Dream of Scipio*, meets the same objection by citing the example of the people living near the great falls of the Nile River at Catadupa, who are said to have become deaf from the great sound of the waters. It is interesting that Ambrose, in his commentary on the music of the spheres, chooses the example of the Nile used by Cicero to illustrate his own skepticism. But this Christian resistance to pagan science soon gives way in the later commentaries in the hexameral tradition.

Darkness descends on the dreamer, forcing him to give up his book (88–91):

> And to my bed I gan me for to dresse,
> Fulfyld of thought and busy hevynesse;
> For bothe I hadde thyng which that I nolde,
> And ek I nadde that thyng that I wolde.

Like the dreamer, we too are restless, because despite the opening announcement of the theme of love, the old dream of Scipio has not really satisfied us. In an earlier poem Chaucer sent his dreamer to bed in a restless and dissatisfied frame of mind (*Book of the Duchess*, 1–43), and the suggestion there, as in the *Parliament*, I think, is that the dream must be expected to provide a resolution to the unstated problem. And sure enough, when our dreamer goes to sleep, he dreams that Africanus appears at his bedside. Out of appreciation for the reading of his "olde bok totorn," Africanus promises to reward the dreamer for his labor.

What form this reward is to take we do not know, but suddenly Chaucer inserts an invocation to Cytherea (Venus), that seems to suggest that the reward will have something to do with love. Despite the strong suggestion that the dream was caused by reading Cicero, the dreamer now acknowledges to Cytherea that *she* caused him to have the dream, and asks her aid in writing the poem. Yet his attitude toward her is reminiscent of that expressed in the opening stanzas toward the god of love. Cytherea frightens whomever she pleases with her firebrand (114), and his appeal to her is made "as surely as I saw thee north-north-west," a strange expression in the context, unless, as has been suggested, Chaucer wished here to date his poem by astronomical reference. But in fact the planet Venus could never be literally seen in England that far north, and I am inclined to group this line with the other disclaimers in the poem of any direct knowledge of the love that Venus represents. The purpose of this stanza, nevertheless, is to provide another assurance to the reader that despite the long philosophical prologue, love is indeed the poet's theme.

Africanus brings the dreamer to a gate forming the entrance to a walled park, over which were written two very different inscriptions (127–40):

> "Thorgh me men gon into that blysful place
> Of hertes hele and dedly woundes cure;
> Thorgh me men gon unto the welle of grace,
> There grene and lusty May shal evere endure.
> This is the wey to al good adventure.
> Be glad, thow redere, and thy sorwe of-caste;
> Al open am I—passe in, and sped thee faste!"

> "Thorgh me men gon," than spak that other side,
> "Unto the mortal strokes of the spere
> Of which Disdayn and Daunger is the gyde,
> Ther nevere tre shal fruyt ne leves bere.
> This strem yow ledeth to the sorweful were
> There as the fish in prysoun is al drye;
> Th'eschewing is only the remedye!"

These two stanzas vividly present the paradoxical nature of human love, at once attractive and threatening. The dreamer hesitates, he says, as if caught between two magnets of even strength, until Africanus scornfully declares that the inscriptions have nothing to do with him; they concern only one who is "Loves servaunt" (160–61):

> For thow of love has lost thy tast, I gesse,
> As sek man hath of swete and bytternesse.

With a few more words in this same comic vein, Africanus promises to show him something to write about, and leads him into the park, after which his guide silently disappears from the dream (171–75):

> But, Lord, so I was glad and wel begoon!
> For overal where that I myne eyen caste
> Were trees clad with leves that ay shal laste,
> Ech in his kynde, of colour fresh and greene
> As emeraude, that joye was to seene.

Here the pace of the poem quickens; the dreamer's restlessness is gone, replaced by a fresh and eager scrutiny of all the delights of the garden.

Students of Chaucer's *Parliament* have sometimes been undecided about the identity of this garden: does it represent the original, unfallen state of nature in Eden? the earthly home of fallen man? or the heavenly home of the redeemed after death? But the hexameral tradition shows us that it is wrong to seek a single identity for the garden. It is at one time Eden, where the trees are clad with leaves that "ay shal laste" (173), as in the passage quoted above, with all the freshness that Ambrose sees in the vegetation at the moment of creation, when God said, *Let the earth bring forth grass. . . .* In another passage, Ambrose shifts to the moral level and deplores the inadequacy of mankind in relation to the perfection of God's Creation. In still another passage, Ambrose looks ahead to the time of judgment, which shall come in the twinkling of an eye. In short, the levels of meaning employed by the preacher provide the pattern for Chaucer's shifting depiction of his garden as Eden, the world, and the heaven of the redeemed. Yet the poet never loses sight of the creation setting, and occasionally gives us an echo of the scriptural text, such as "each in his kind" (174), reminiscent of the refrainlike repetition of *after his kind* in the first chapter of Genesis (1:11, 12, 21, 24, 25).

The subtle shift from Eden to the world is well illustrated as we move from the ideal description of the eternal foliage already quoted above to the famous catalogue of trees in the following stanza (176–82):

> The byldere ok, and ek the hardy asshe;
> The piler elm, the cofre unto carayne;
> The boxtre pipere, holm to whippes lashe;
> The saylynge fyr; the cipresse, deth to playne;
> The shetere ew; the asp for shaftes pleyne;
> The olyve of pes, and eke the dronke vyne,
> The victor palm, the laurer to devyne.

It is clear that the purposes enumerated for the trees relate to a fallen world, as we see in the use of the elm in making coffins, holm oak for whips, cypress for mourning death, yew for making bows, and aspen for arrows. In fact, so far as we know, connecting these particular trees with the ominous uses attributed to them was original with Chaucer, and that suggests that the fallen state of man they imply is an important part of his intention here. The other trees in this list are quite traditional, and can be found in similar lists in classical and vernacular poetry, often with the same characteristics or functions attributed to them.

By Chaucer's time, elaborate reference works were available for the expansion of such lists, and it is interesting to note that the great encyclopedia of Bartholomew the Englishman, *On the Properties of Things* (*De Proprietatibus Rerum*), was translated in Chaucer's lifetime by his countryman John Trevisa. This work was organized, very handily for the student of God's creation, according to the Great Chain of Being: book I treats God, book II the orders of angels, book III the soul, book IV the body, and so on through the heavens, times and seasons, and the elements; book XII presents birds; then come water, lands, countries, followed by stones and metals; book XVII covers plants and trees; book XVIII is concerned with the animal kingdom; and, last of all, book XIX deals with "accidents"—that is, colors, liquids, and odors. The work indeed is something of a compromise between the order of the Chain of Being and the order of creation in Genesis.

Corresponding to Chaucer's "saylynge fyr," Bartholomew says that "of this tree is good ship timber." Bartholomew also speaks of the olive of peace and the palm of victory. Ambrose, too, in his commentary on the third day of creation, mentions these and other trees—many more than we find in Chaucer—together with their characteristics. For example, he says of the fir (III.ii.47): "The fir tree also advanced in procession, a tree which was not satisfied to have its roots in the earth and its head on high, but was destined, while mariners are safe, to undergo perils from wind and wave on the sea." And he goes on to emphasize that the function of each tree, impressed on it at the moment of creation, was maintained by Nature thereafter in future ages.

But after presenting his inventory of trees, with its hint of violence and death, Chaucer resumes once more his description of the garden in its ideal state. The next two stanzas, in fact, correspond closely to the creation scene depicted in *The Holkham Bible Picture Book* (2ᵛ), to which Dr. Hassall has given the title "The

Creator and His Creatures" (p. 59). Here is Chaucer's description (183–96):

> A gardyn saw I ful of blosmy bowes
> Upon a ryver, in a grene mede,
> There as swetnesse everemore inow is,
> With floures white, blewe, yelwe, and rede,
> And colde welle-stremes, nothyng dede,
> That swymmen ful of smale fishes lighte,
> With fynnes rede and skales sylver bryghte.
>
> On every bow the bryddes herde I synge,
> With voys of aungel in here armonye;
> Some besyede hem here bryddes forth to brynge;
> The litel conyes to here pley gonne hye;
> And ferthere al aboute I gan aspye
> The dredful ro, the buk, the hert and hynde,
> Squyrels, and bestes smale of gentil kynde.

This is the peaceable kingdom as it existed before the Fall, a tableau designed to display the magnificent variety of God's creatures. From this Genesis tapestry Chaucer will select the birds as the centerpiece of his valentine. At the moment, however, they are on their good behavior, singing with angel voices, and bringing forth their young in obedience to Nature's commands.

The description of the beauties of the garden continues, even intensifies, as the dreamer hears music of such a ravishing sweetness that he thinks even God the Creator had never heard anything better. And in the leaves the breeze makes a soft sound that blends with the birds' song. The weather is neither hot nor cold; wholesome spices abound, and no man is afflicted with illness or old age; and there are a thousandfold more joys than a man could tell (209–10):

> . . . ne nevere wolde it nyghte,
> But ay cler day to any manes syghte.

There is an ambiguity in this description which I think is intentional. The ravishing sound suggests the music of the spheres; the soft wind perhaps reminds us of the Spirit (wind) of God that *moved upon the face of the waters* on the first day (Gen. 1:2). The wholesome spices parallel the health-giving plants enumerated by Ambrose in his description of the vegetation on the third day of creation (III.8.37). On the other hand, many of these same features are found in the traditional Earthly Paradise, and one is left in doubt about the precise nature of this garden—a doubt that is not dispelled by the curious statement at the end regarding eternal day. For although in the process of creation there is evening and morning, Ambrose is careful to point out (I.10.37): "Scripture teaches us that the everlasting day of eternal reward is to be one in which there is no interchange or intermission of day and night." Thus in two stanzas of description are blended features of Eden, the Earthly Paradise of lovers, and Heaven of the redeemed. As I have suggested, the ambiguity is deliberate: Chaucer is now leading us gently into the precincts of the Temple of Venus.

Students of the *Parliament* have seen many and various meanings in the temple scene, but there can surely be no doubt that here we are being shown the worship of human love. This is a point not always obvious to the modern reader, especially if he is aware that he is reading a valentine, since modern literature has very little to say about the limits of human devotion to sexual love, and modern valentines in particular recognize no such limits at all. But medieval man, and this includes Chaucer, saw things differently, and we are destined to learn in the parliament scene that Nature favors no union of the sexes that does not have reproduction as its object. In this she is in harmony with the grand design of Creation itself. Chaucer does not turn philosophical on this subject in his *Parliament*, but the teaching that is implicit here we find stated explicitly by Theseus in "The Knight's Tale."

After the funeral of Arcite, there is an extended period of mourning during which the sorrow of his friend Palamon and his intended bride Emily continues unabated. Finally, Theseus decides that it is up to him to see that life goes on, and to make Palamon and Emily realize that they are in love with one another and should be married. The argument of Theseus comes largely from Boethius, but clearly sets forth for the lovers their place in God's creation, and the reason it is God's will that they be joined together (CT I 2987–98):

> "The Firste Moevere of the cause above,
> Whan he first made the faire cheyne of love,
> Greet was th'effect, and heigh was his entente.
> Wel wiste he why, and what thereof he mente;
> For with that faire cheyne of love he bond
> The fyr, the eyr, the water, and the lond
> In certeyn boundes, that they may nat flee.
> That same Prince and that Moevere," quod he,

> "Hath stablissed in this wrecched world adoun
> Certeyne dayes and duracioun
> To al that is engendred in this place
> Over the whiche day they may nat pace, . . ."

He then goes on to present the familiar explanation of God's creation as stable in its foundation (God), but descending through the spheres until, below the circle of the moon, it is susceptible to corruption. For this condition, God has established a system of generation (3011–15):

> "And therfore, of his wise purveiaunce,
> He hath so wel biset his ordinaunce,
> That speces of thynges and progressiouns
> Shullen enduren by successiouns,
> And nat eterne, withouten any lye. . . ."

In short, for society to continue, people must reproduce. Of course Theseus is too good a diplomat to put the case quite so bluntly, and it is only after many more lines of consolation that he finally comes to his point and proposes that Palamon and Emily should be married, with which happy event the Knight's story comes to an end.

But of course Chaucer knew very well that love is an awesome power, and cannot always be made to conform to the doctrines delivered to mankind. In this second section of his poem, therefore, he provides a tableau of the follies of human love, drawing, as we have noted, on Boccaccio's *Teseide*, the very same Italian poem that was his source for "The Knight's Tale."

Critics have not been slow to point out the significant fact that Chaucer, in the process of translation, has turned Boccaccio's garden of love into a description that conveys more strongly the author's disapproval. Both poets have the figure of Cupid "our lord," under a tree beside a well, where his daughter is engaged in tempering the heads of his arrows. But among various other personifications that both poets include—such as Plesaunce, Aray, Lust (delight), Courtesy, Beauty, Youth, and so forth—Chaucer alone specifies (220–21):

> . . . the Craft that can and hath the myght
> To don by force a wyght to don folye. . . .

And it is Chaucer who adds the personifications Messagerye and Meede, representing the activities of go-betweens and even bribery in the furthering of a love affair. The scene has a glittering surface, but it does not satisfy. And when we reach the temple, the women dancing around it seem engaged in a ceremony that has lost its meaning (232–38):

> Aboute that temple daunseden alwey
> Women inowe, of whiche some ther weere
> Fayre of hemself, and some of hem were gay;
> In kertels, al dishevele, wente they there:
> That was here offyce alwey, yer by yeere.
> And on the temple, of dowves white and fayre
> Saw I syttynge many an hundred peyre.

But if Chaucer is writing a hexameral poem, as I have contended, what possible justification does he have for inflicting on the landscape of creation this Temple of Venus with its swarm of white doves? But the answer to this question is obvious when we remember how the pendulum of Ambrose's rhetoric swings back and forth between the beauties of creation and the desecrations of mankind. A case in point is his allegorical treatment of the marsh in connection with the gathering together of the waters on the third day (III.1.4–5):

> The marsh is self-indulgence, the marsh is intemperance, the marsh is incontinence, where are found wallowing places for lusts, the grunts of beasts, and the lairs of passions. Whoever falls therein is dragged down and does not emerge. Here men's feet find no foothold, but waver uncertainly. Here waterfowls are begrimed when they bathe, and above us are heard the mournful cries of doves.

Of course Ambrose's method allows him immediately to swing back to a positive theme, a strategy that Chaucer here denies himself. Ambrose continues by contrasting the true kind of love practiced by the faithful:

> Rather, all love each other in mutual love, all cherish one the other, and support themselves as one body, although of diverse members. They find delight not in the baleful songs sung by theatrical performers, songs which lead to sensual love, but in the chants of the church. Here we hear the voice of the people singing in harmony the praises of God. The sight of their piety gives us pleasure. Here are people who find no delight in tapestries of purple or costly stage curtains. Their pleasure lies rather in their admiration of this most beautiful fabric of the world, this accord of unlike elements, this heaven that is "spread out like a tent to dwell in" (Isa. 40:22) to protect those who inhabit this world.

[154]

This positive idea is of course implicit in Chaucer's view of creation, but he is not a preacher, and the emergence of a positive theme in the *Parliament* comes only gradually.

Meanwhile the dreamer continues his tour of Venus's garden, and enters her temple, which echoes with hot sighs, engendered by desire and stimulated by jealousy. The oppressive atmosphere is temporarily relieved by the sight of Priapus, god of gardens, whose frustration when he attempted to assault the nymph Lotis is amusingly described by Ovid (*Fasti*, i, 415ff). When all the company was asleep, Priapus slipped to her side, drew back the coverlet, and was about to begin the attack, his phallic "scepter" at the ready, when a nearby saddle ass suddenly brayed, waking the sleepers, who laughed aloud to see the pose of the startled would-be lover. That Chaucer does not see Priapus here merely as the god of gardens is evident in his allusion to Ovid's story (253–59):

> The god Priapus say I, as I wente,
> Withinne the temple in sovereyn place stonde,
> In swich aray as whan the asse hym shente
> With cri by nighte, and with hys sceptre in honde.
> Ful besyly men gonne assaye and fonde
> Upon his hed to sette, of sondry hewe,
> Garlondes ful of freshe floures newe.

It is quite evident that the men who are *trying* (as Emerson Brown has taught us to say) to set flowers on the head of this god are engaged in an act of devotion to his powers, and see nothing comical in his slavery to passion, or their efforts to crown him.

Meanwhile the dreamer moves past this tableau and comes at last to Venus (260–73):

> And in a prive corner in disport
> Found I Venus and hire porter Richesse,
> That was ful noble and hautayn of hyre port.
> Derk was that place, but afterward lightnesse
> I saw a lyte, unnethe it myghte be lesse,
> And on a bed of gold she lay to reste,
> Til that the hote sonne gan to weste.
>
> Hyre gilte heres with a golden thred
> Ibounden were, untressed as she lay,
> And naked from the brest unto the hed
> Men myghte hire sen; and, sothly for to say,

> The remenaunt was wel kevered to my pay,
> Ryght with a subtyl coverchef of Valence—
> Ther was no thikkere cloth of no defense.

There is an attempt here at richness of description, but it is clear that Venus, secluded in a dark corner of the temple, is the pejorative embodiment of seductiveness. And in addition to Riches (her favors require wealth), she is attended by Bacchus and Ceres, representing wine and food, traditional inciters of passion. Forgotten is the garden where night never comes (209–10), for we are told that Venus rested until the hot sun began to sink in the west. Before her, two young folk on their knees were crying for her help. "But thus I let hire lye," says the dreamer rather unceremoniously and goes on to describe the interior walls of the temple, covered with the broken bows of maidens who have renounced their allegiance to Diana, chaste goddess of the hunt, and with wall paintings depicting the life and sad death of famous unfortunate lovers, most of whom had found a place in Dante's Hell of the Lustful.

With no further ado, the dreamer leaves the Temple of Venus and emerges once more in the place "That I of spake, that was so sweet and green," where for the first time he sees Nature, whose beauty surpasses that of every other creature, just as the light of the sun is greater than the stars. In contrast to the interior setting of the Temple of Venus, Nature's halls and bowers are made of branches, according to her design and measure. Before her are assembled every kind of bird capable of reproducing itself, ready to receive her judgment. Chaucer chooses this moment to announce the subject of his poem, and the birds of his Genesis tapestry suddenly come alive (309–15):

> For this was on seynt Valentynes day,
> Whan every foul cometh there to chese his make,
> Of every kynde that men thynke may,
> And that so huge a noyse gan they make
> That erthe, and eyr, and tre, and every lake
> So ful was, that unethe was there space
> For me to stonde, so ful was al the place.

There is no formal description of Nature herself; instead Chaucer invites us to read *The Complaint of Nature* by Alanus de Insulis (316–18):

> And right as Aleyn, in the Pleynt of Kynde,
> Devyseth Nature of aray and face,
> In swich aray men myghte hire there fynde.

In his Latin poem, Alanus describes Nature as beautifully adorned, with a diadem made of the seven planets and a robe on which are depicted her creatures, including the birds. But Alanus also depicts Nature weeping for the sins of men (the subject of the poem is in fact her complaint), and her garment is torn, indicating man's fall from grace. Chaucer, significantly, makes no use of this part of his source. In fact, he takes little more than the figure of Nature herself. Yet this feature is extremely important, for it enabled Chaucer to remove from his creation scene the traditional figure of God the Creator, and present instead "the vicar of the almighty Lord," who can more appropriately function as the sometimes schoolmarmish presiding officer of a parliament of birds that occasionally, as we shall see, gets out of hand.

First we should look carefully at Chaucer's classification of the birds in Nature's garden (323–29):

> That is to seyn, the foules of ravyne
> Weere hyest set, and thanne the foules smale
> That eten, as hem Nature wolde enclyne,
> As worm or thyng of which I telle no tale;
> And water-foul sat lowest in the dale;
> But foul that lyveth by sed sat on the grene,
> And that so fele that wonder was to sene.

The "foules of ravyne" correspond to those birds that Ambrose says (V.14) "live by plunder" like the hawk and the eagle. The "foules smale" that eat worms are simply classified in the *Hexameron* as birds that "search for different kinds of food as they come upon them," and are distinguished, as in the *Parliament*, from birds that "find their food in seeds." The fourth and final category is "water-foul," such as the swan, crane, and heron. The classification Chaucer employs is thus precisely that of Ambrose.

The inventory of birds reminds us of Chaucer's earlier catalogue of trees. Just as each tree was identified with some function or purpose, so nearly all the birds we will be noting have some phrase or clause of identification. Moreover, as we shall see, the birds are not all models of good behavior, and this is important: Chaucer thus announces early on that the world of the parliament is the world of fallen man. To some extent this fits the pattern of the hexameral tradition, for although Ambrose often uses the benign features of his birds to put man to shame, he also freely acknowledges that some birds are passable imitations of their fallible human counterparts (V.14): "There are also other birds: some guileless like the dove (*columba*), or artful like the partridge. The cock is inclined to be boastful; the peacock, to be vain." But we should also note that while Chaucer's poem follows the pattern of God's creation very closely, there is no sixth day, no creation of man: such inferences as we may wish to make about the poet's attitude toward fallen humanity will have to come from the behavior of the very human birds in his parliament. In this Chaucer diverges sharply from the hexameral model, and thus avoids any overt appearance of passing judgment on mankind.

Now let us examine Chaucer's gallery of birds, as he intended we should, and carefully note the characteristics of each. In so doing we shall find echoes of the hexameral tradition as well as details from the medieval encyclopedias. Perhaps surprisingly, we may also notice features attributable to Chaucer's own observation of birds, first called to our attention some years ago by Beryl Rowland. We shall follow the order of the catalogue in the *Parliament*, lines 330–64.

First come the fowls that live by plunder (330–40):

> There myghte men the royal egle fynde,
> That with his sharpe lok perseth the sonne,
> And othere egles of a lowere kynde,
> Of whiche that clerkes wel devyse conne.
> Ther was the tiraunt with his fetheres donne
> And grey, I mene the goshauk, that doth pyne
> To bryddes for his outrageous ravyne.
>
> The gentyl faucoun, that with his feet distrayneth
> The kynges hand; the hardy sperhauk eke,
> The quayles foo; the merlioun, that payneth
> Hymself ful ofte the larke for to seke; . . .

Chaucer here mentions five varieties of eagle, and implies there are many more that clerks can devise in the encyclopedias. Bartholomew, who limits himself to "birds and fowls of which special mention is made in the text of the Bible or in the gloss" (XII, 1), lists only four: *aquila* (the eagle), "queen of fowls"; *aucipiter* (the goshawk), "a royal fowl"; *alietus* (the falcon), a "bold and hardy" bird, sometimes confused with the smaller sparrowhawk; and *herodius* (the royal falcon). Concerning the eagle, he says that

[158]

its power of sight is strong, for it can look directly at the sun without blinking an eye; and he cites Ambrose's statement in the *Hexameron* that the eagle tests the sight of its young by holding them facing the sun. If their eyes water, they are driven out of the nest.

Exactly what Chaucer means by calling the goshawk a "tyrant" is not clear. He may refer to its harshness toward its offspring, described by Ambrose and included in Batholomew, but it is also possible that he refers to the fact, reported by Bartholomew, that the goshawk, because he takes other fowls for his prey, is called *aucipiter*, "a raptor and ravisher."

From the hierarchy of fowls of ravine, we now turn to a more varied list, beginning with examples of the seed fowl, waterfowl, and scavenger. The "dove with hire yën meke" is the *columba* (not to be confused with the turtledove), that Ambrose calls "guile-less" (*simplices*), and Bartholomew "mild and meek," much given to lechery. We met a flock of these birds earlier, hovering over the marsh of self-indulgence in the *Hexameron* (III.1.4) and perched on Chaucer's Temple of Venus in *Parliament* (237–38).

The swan, of course, is well known for its inclination to sing at the moment of death, duly reported by Ambrose and Bartho-lomew, but the notion of its "jealousy" may well be one of those features that Chaucer observed with his own eyes. Robert Burton, in his *Anatomy of Melancholy* (3.3.1), affirms the "jealousy" of the swan, and refers his readers to Chaucer's *Parliament*; and D. A. Bannerman, a modern ornithologist, declares from observation that nesting pairs of swans will quickly drive off an intruder, and at times may even fight to the death. Though I am not an expert, I was once charged by a swan on the Isis in Oxford, and was sufficiently impressed by that experience to believe them capable of anything.

Chaucer says the owl is the harbinger of death, or, more precisely, "crying of the owl by night bodeth death," as we find in Bartholomew. The owl is at the low end of the scale of plunderers, and in daylight is a weak-eyed victim of harassment by other birds. Ambrose, however, restricts his comments to the owl's poor vision in daylight, comparing it to the wise of this world, who have eyes and see not.

In the following stanza, we meet a dazzling variety of birds: the crane, a giant bird with a voice like the sound of a trumpet; the thieving chough and the jangling magpie; the scornful jay, and the enemy of eels, the heron; the false lapwing, full of treachery; the starling, which can betray secrets; the tame robin and the coward kite; the rooster that serves as a clock in small villages. Most of these descriptions are self-explanatory. The lapwing will drag its wing to distract intruders from its nest, but this seems a defensible maneuver, one that can scarcely account for the harsh words in Chaucer's description. Bartholomew calls the lapwing (*upupa*) "ungentle and unkind," dwelling always in graves or in dirt, and adds this obscure but ominous observation: "and its heart is good to evil-doers, for in their evil-doing they use its heart." Also suggestive of treachery is Lucio's admission in Shakespeare's *Measure for Measure* that "'tis my familiar sin / With maids to seem the lapwing and to jest,/Tongue far from heart" (1.4.32–33). Starlings could be taught to speak, hence Chaucer's reference to their betrayal of counsel may be to a story of the type he later used as the Manciple's tale, in which a crow witnesses the adultery of his master's wife and later reports it to the master on his return home. "The tame ruddok, and the coward kyte" appear together nowhere in our sources, but one wonders whether Chaucer might have chosen them as his own representatives of one of Ambrose's categories (V.14.49): "Some birds submit themselves to be handled. They are accustomed to the table, and are delighted to be fondled. Other birds shrink from this through fear." The tameness of the English robin is something I have witnessed myself in the garden of a friend, who demonstrated the fact to me by enticing a particular robin that lived there to come to her and eat from her hand. Chaucer may well have observed this kind of behavior. The fearfulness of the kite (*milvus*) is well expressed by Bartholomew: "he is a ravishing fowl and hardy among small birds, and coward and fearful among great birds." What a menagerie of birds this is. In this one stanza only two of the ten birds listed could be classified as friendly: the tame ruddock and the cock who tells time for villagers. It is a curious fact that our final impression of the parliament will be a positive, harmonious one; yet the catalogue of birds in its details quite clearly shows us not only nature red in tooth and claw but feathered symbols of many of humanity's darkest traits.

And there is more (351–57):

> The sparwe, Venus sone; the nyghtyngale,
> That clepeth forth the grene leves newe;

> The swalwe, mortherere of the foules smale
> That maken hony of floures freshe of hewe;
> The wedded turtil, with hire herte trewe;
> The pekok, with his aungels fetheres bryghte;
> The fesaunt, skornere of the cok by nyghte.

For those readers with an eye on the development of Chaucer's art, it is fascinating to read the *Parliament,* with its bird portraits and (as we shall see) its all too human squabbles in the parliamentary debate, and at the same time to look ahead to the portraits of the pilgrims in *The Canterbury Tales* and the clashes of opinion that Chaucer dramatizes in the intervals between the telling of the stories. I mention this only in passing, being prompted to it by Chaucer's listing of "the sparwe, Venus sone," a bird put to use in the prologue to the *Tales* for the portrait of the Somonour (*CT* I 626):

> As hoot he was and lecherous as a sparwe.

The importance of Chaucer's dream visions in paving the way for the General Prologue to *The Canterbury Tales* is a subject all its own, and has been well explored by J. V. Cunningham, a poet as well as a scholar.

The nightingale is commonly known as a harbinger of spring, but it is curious that Chaucer would single out the swallow's eating of bees among the many features of that bird that he might have chosen. Ambrose makes much of the swallow's solicitude for her children (*Hexameron* V.17) and her industry in building the nest, a feature echoed by Bartholomew. The turtledove is, of course, widely known as a model of fidelity in marriage, and Ambrose credits it with faithfulness beyond the grave (V.19):

It is related that the turtle dove (*turtur*), when widowed by the loss of her consort, was utterly weary of the bridal bed, and even of the world itself, for the reason that her first love, turning traitor, cheated her by death. . . . Therefore she renounces any other marriage alliance and does not break the laws of chastity or her pledges to her beloved, reserving for him alone her love, for him alone cherishing the name of wife. Learn, women, how great are the joys of that widowhood which even the birds are said to observe.

Chaucer ignores the pride of the peacock, mentioned by Ambrose and elaborated in Bartholomew's encyclopedia, citing only its bright feathers, suitable for angels. But the last line is something of a puzzle (357):

The fesaunt, skornere of the cok by nyghte.

It has been suggested that the pheasant sometimes breeds with the common hen, which could be interpreted as scorning the cock; or Alanus, in his *Complaint of Nature,* speaks of the wild cock as scorning the sluggishness of the domestic cock, another kind of scorning. But what is the significance of the phrase "by nyghte"? It is this detail that inclines me toward the explanation of Beryl Rowland, who points out that although the wild pheasant some-times feeds with domestic chickens during the day, when night comes and the cock tries to herd it in to roost with the others, it will refuse to obey. This, too, is something that Chaucer may have seen for himself. Although we know he loved old books, there is ample evidence that he also was very observant.

The roll call of birds is completed in a final stanza (358–64):

> The waker goos; the cukkow ever unkynde;
> The popynjay, ful of delicasye;
> The drake, stroyere of his owene kynde;
> The stork, the wrekere of avouterye;
> The hote cormeraunt of glotenye;
> The raven wys; the crowe with vois of care;
> The throstil old; the frosty feldefare.

The goose is called a "watcher" (sentinel) in reference to the story of geese alerting the Roman citizenry and thus saving the capitol from surprise attack in 389 B.C. Ambrose makes the same allusion, and in the process is unable to resist a belittling comment on pa-gan religion (*Hexameron*, V.13.44): "Who does not marvel at the night sentry watches of the geese, who give evidence of their vigilance by their constant cackling? That was the way in which they defended even the Roman Capitol from the Gauls. You, Rome, rightfully owe to them the preservation of your empire. Your gods were sleeping, but the geese were awake."

The cuckoo is "unkind" (unnatural) because it lays its eggs in the nests of other birds; and the young cuckoo, crowding out the original nestlings, sometimes even kills its foster parent, as is cruelly recited by the Fool in *King Lear* (1.4.235–36): "The hedge-sparrow fed the cuckoo so long / That it had it head bit off by it young." The popinjay, a bird frequently seen perching in trees of the Earthly Paradise, is notorious for its self-indulgence. The drake, according to Vincent of Beauvais, has been known to kill his mate in the fury of his wantonness; on the other hand, some birds (like the peacock in Bartholomew) are said to seek out the eggs of the female and break them, "that he may so occupy him the more in his lechery," and Chaucer may have seen this trait somewhere attributed to the drake, "destroyer of his own kind."

Ambrose devotes a chapter to the stork (V.16), praising the orderliness of its ranks, its attitude of hospitality to crows (who serve as escorts), and the piety of the young in caring for their parents; and he uses these virtues to show, by comparison, the shortcomings of mankind. It is in Bartholomew's description of the stork that we find the explanation for Chaucer's epithet, "the avenger of adultery": "And if the male aspieth in any wise that the female hath broken spousehood, she shall no more dwell with him, but he beateth her and sticketh her with his bill and slayeth her if he may, as Aristotle saith." The cormorant has been identified with the *onacrocalus*, which is called the "mirdrommel" by Bartholomew (Oxford English Dictionary: mire-drum, or bittern), and is called "a bird of great gluttony," having a long bill and a place to store food in his jaws.

It is interesting that Chaucer distinguishes between raven and crow, birds that were easily confused, with the result that their descriptions in the encyclopedias are often very similar. Thus both the crow and the raven in Bartholomew are said to have powers of divination. This may explain why Chaucer calls the raven "wise." But the raven is also identified as the clergy in biblical exegesis, as in Gregory's commentary on Job 38:41, "Who prepareth for the raven his food, when his young ones cry to God, wandering because they have not meat?" and in commentaries on Psalm 147:9, "He giveth to the beast his food, and to the young ravens which cry." No doubt this same tradition led Anthony Trollope, in *Barchester Towers* (chap. 43), to have Mr. Harding reflect thus on the large and destitute family of the vicar of Puddingdale: "What wants had he to set in opposition to those of such a regiment of young ravens?"

But perhaps the most fascinating portrait in this stanza is "the crowe with vois of care." Some such description of the crow's voice is common to practically all accounts of this bird, probably because the description came originally from a famous line in Virgil's *Georgics* (1.388): *Tum cornix plena pluviam vocat improba voce.* Ambrose quotes this line, omitting one word (*improba*), and his version is thus translated by Savage (V.12.39): "the raven who with deep tones (*plena voce*) calls down the rain." Savage used "raven" no doubt because *cornix* in Virgil (as well as Cicero and Lucretius) was understood to designate that species. Bartholomew, however, also quotes Virgil, but includes the critical adjective *improba* (omitting *plena*), while his translator calls the bird a crow: "Nunc cornix pluviam vocat improba voce, that is to say, "now the crow calleth rain with (unweary) voice." In search of a better translation of the Latin word *improba*, the editors of Trevisa's translation of Bartholomew decided to emend the word I have put in parentheses. The English manuscripts read "unweary" (which I have used above), "dying," and even "ailing" (in the revised edition of this translation by Stephen Batman in 1582)—all, I think, efforts to translate this peculiar word *improba* describing the voice of the crow. The editors of Trevisa emend to read "unworthy," which is a possible meaning of the Latin, but not really appropriate to the context. The word *improba* was a favorite of Virgil's, as we are informed by his editors, but it is very difficult to translate. It expresses generally an absence of all moderation, of all regard for consequences or the right of others. In a brief summing up of translations, I have found it rendered "unwearied," "insistent," and even "merciless." My search was motivated by a desire to understand what lay behind Chaucer's phrase, "the crowe with vois of care," but the evidence appears far from conclusive. It hardly seems suitable as Chaucer's rendering of *improba*. In the absence of other evidence, I am inclined to suggest that his attribution of a sorrowful voice to the crow may be the result of his own experience with birds. We should recall especially that this particular bird (according to Virgil) is noted for his ability to prophesy rain. My own recollection of the cry of a bird I knew only as the "rain crow," coming from a hillside near my home in Kentucky, was as mournful a sound as I have ever heard. Whether the call of such a bird ever reached Chaucer's ear I do not know.

The possibility of direct observation by Chaucer is supported by his reference to the "throstil old" (thrush) and the "frosty feldefare," which conclude his catalogue. In fact the coloring of the thrush, with its light chest below a brown face, suggesting the beard of an elderly creature, perhaps lies behind Thomas Hardy's description in his poem, "The Darkling Thrush": "An aged thrush, frail, gaunt and small, / In blast-beruffled plume. . . ." And in calling the fieldfare "frosty," Chaucer may either be alluding to its appearance (especially in flight) or to the fact that in England the fieldfare is a winter visitor.

Thus concludes our parade of birds. The picture we have is a mixture of sunlight and shadow, of malice and benevolence—in short a feathered version of fallen man, an impression that is confirmed in the parliament itself, in which all the clamor of a human assembly is presented in microcosm.

Nature, the vicar of the almighty Lord, announces to the assembled fowls that the first to choose their mates on this Valentine's Day shall be the birds of highest rank, beginning with the eagles. (The first of the Canterbury pilgrims to tell a tale was the Knight, highest ranking member of that company.) She calls upon the highest ranking eagle, the royal tercel, to speak first and make known his choice. But before the tercel begins, Nature lays down an important condition, and since there has been some disagreement among readers of Chaucer as to its meaning, we should consider her words carefully (407–10):

> "But natheles, in this condicioun
> Mot be the choys of everich that is heere,
> That she agre to his eleccioun,
> Whoso he be that shulde be hire feere.

I take the meaning of these lines to be as follows: But nevertheless the choice of everyone that is here must be subject to this condition: that whoever he may be that wishes to be her mate, (the marriage can take place only if) she agrees with his choice. The crux, of course, is whether the mate is being forewarned that she *must* accept when chosen or whether she is being given the freedom to accept or decline. I think the latter meaning is the one intended, because Nature goes on to say that whoever at this time may "have his grace" shall be happy, where the phrase "have his grace" surely means "meet with acceptance." As we shall see, the gentle formel perched on Nature's hand, who is the prize sought by the three eagles, eventually exercises her rights and decides, for the time being, not to marry.

The three eagles, beginning with the royal tercel, speak in turn, stating their respective reasons for wanting to marry the formel. In brief, the first says that he loves her the most, the second that he has loved her the longest, and the third that he most desires her. The speeches are very courtly and apparently very long, for the dreamer says that they lasted until the sun began to go down. At this point, the decorum of the parliament is shattered by the impatience of the other birds, who cannot choose their own mates until the eagles finish (491–97):

> The noyes of foules for to ben delyvered
> So loude rong, "Have don, and lat us wende!"
> That wel wende I the wode hadde al to-shyvered.
> "Com of!" they criede, "allas, ye wol us shende!
> Whan shal youre cursede pletynge have an ende?
> How sholde a juge eyther parti leve
> For ye or nay, withouten any preve?"

The birds have a point: it is difficult to see how any one of the eagles could establish his case objectively. The *demande d'amour* motif has ended in a stalemate, and the natives are getting restless (498–500):

> The goos, the cokkow, and the doke also
> So cryede, "Kek kek! kokkow! quek quek!" hye,
> That thourgh myne eres the noyse wente tho.

Without recognition from the chair, three birds volunteer as spokesmen for their kind: the goose for waterfowl, the turtledove for seed fowl, and the cuckoo for worm fowl. The parliament is close to being out of order when Nature intervenes with "Hold youre tonges there!" and directs each group to choose a spokesman, beginning with the "foules of ravyne," who choose the tercelet of the falcon (male hawk). As far as the arguments go, says the tercelet, they are all equally persuasive and could only be decided by combat: "al redy!" the three eagles instantly reply. But the tercelet dismisses this solution and proposes that the formel be given to the eagle who is worthiest of knighthood, highest ranking and noblest of blood, and strongly hints that this would be the royal tercel (552–53):

> "And of these thre she wot hirself, I trowe,
> Which that he be, for it is light to knowe."

After a brief caucus, the waterfowl put forward the goose as their spokesman (561–67):

> And for these water-foules tho began
> The goos to speke, and in hire kakelynge
> She seyde, "Pes! now tak kep every man,

> And herkeneth which a resoun I shal forth brynge!
> My wit is sharp, I love no taryinge;
> I seye I rede hym, though he were my brother,
> But she wol love hym, lat hym love another!"

This goosish reasoning cannot be allowed to stand, and is soundly rebuked by the sparrowhawk, with approving laughter from all of the "gentil foules." It is interesting that in each case where a rebuke is called for, it is delivered by one of the noble class—the fowls of ravine.

The turtledove, elected by the seed fowl, responds in the way we have been taught to expect (582–88):

> "Nay, God forbede a lovere shulde chaunge!"
> The turtle seyde, and wex for shame al red,
> "Though that his lady evermore be straunge,
> Yit lat hym serve hire ever, till he be ded.
> Forsothe, I preyse nat the goses red,
> For, though she deyede, I wolde non other make;
> I wol ben hires, til that the deth me take."

There is, of course, nothing at all wrong with this sentiment as far as the courtly birds are concerned, but the obstreperous duck is unable to keep silent in the face of such idealism, and speaks its mind without the formality of being elected or recognized by the chair (589–95):

> "Wel bourded," quod the doke, "by myn hat!
> That men shulde loven alwey causeles,
> Who can a resoun fynde or wit in that?
> Daunseth he murye that is myrtheles?
> Who shulde recche of that is recheles?
> Ye quek!" yit seyde the doke, ful wel and fayre,
> "There been mo sterres, God wot, than a payre!"

This crude response to the idealism of the turtledove calls forth a sharp rebuke from the high-ranking spokesman of the noble birds (596–602):

> "Now fy, cherl!" quod the gentil tercelet,
> "Out of the donghil cam that word ful right!
> Thow canst nat seen which thyng is wel beset!
> Thow farst by love as oules don by lyght:
> The day hem blent, ful wel they se by nyght.
> Thy kynde is of so low a wrecchednesse
> That what love is, thow canst nat seen ne gesse."

[167]

With the cuckoo, self-appointed spokesman for the worm fowl, we reach perhaps the lower end of the Chain of Being as it applies to birds that, as Ambrose remarks, "love to look out, each one for his own interest" (V.14.49). Because the cuckoo is beneath the contempt of the high-ranking birds, the rebuke to his selfish attitude is delivered by the merlin, one of the more humble birds of ravine (603–16):

> Tho gan the kokkow putte hym forth in pres
> For foul that eteth worm, and seyde blyve:—
> "So I," quod he, "may have my make in pes,
> I reche nat how longe that ye stryve.
> Lat ech of hem be soleyn al here lyve!
> This is my red, syn they may nat acorde;
> This shorte lessoun nedeth nat recorde."

> "Ye, have the glotoun fild inow his paunche,
> Thanne are we wel!" seyde the merlioun;
> "Thow mortherere of the heysoge on the braunche
> That broughte the forth, thow rewthelees glotoun!
> Lyve thow soleyn, wormes corupcioun!
> For no fors is of lak of thy nature—
> Go, lewed be thow whil the world may dure!"

It is significant that the severest denunciation in the entire parliament is directed against an unmistakably antisocial bird. The goose and the duck perhaps give the wrong advice, but they *do* advise; it is only the cuckoo who expresses a completely uncaring attitude, and for this he is angrily denounced by the merlin, and reminded of his own unnatural behavior.

After this bitter exchange, Nature calls a halt to the argument and announces her decision: the formel eagle herself shall decide which suitor to accept. Yet even Nature cannot resist offering the formel some advice (631–37):

> "But as for conseyl for to chese a make,
> If I were Resoun, certes, thanne wolde I
> Conseyle yow the royal tercel take,
> As seyde the tercelet ful skylfully,
> As for the gentilleste and most worthi,
> Which I have wrought so wel to my plesaunce,
> That to yow hit oughte to be a suffisaunce."

This is really the third time we have been prompted to note the qualifications of the royal tercel. First the goddess praised him highly in her opening speech before the parliament (393–99); then the tercelet unmistakably hints at his qualifications in giving his opinion (552–53); and finally Nature explicitly commends the royal tercel to the formel in the stanza just quoted but qualifies her statement importantly by prefacing it with "if I were Resoun." The point is, of course, that the "wonderful werkynge" of love cannot be made to conform to reason's dictates, as is immediately evident in the formel's decision (647–53):

> "Almyghty queen! unto this yer be gon,
> I axe respit for to advise me,
> And after that to have my choys al fre:
> This al and som that I wol speke and seye.
> Ye gete no more, although ye do me deye!
>
> "I wol nat serve Venus ne Cupide,
> Forsothe as yit, by no manere weye."

The goddess graciously accepts this decision and encourages the three suitors to be of good heart and "do wel" until it is time for the formel's decision. She then turns her attention at last to the other birds (666–72):

> And whan this werk al brought was to an ende,
> To every foul Nature yaf his make
> By evene acord, and on here way they wende.
> And, Lord, the blisse and joye that they make!
> For ech of hem gan other in wynges take,
> And with here nekkes ech gan other wynde,
> Thankynge alwey the noble goddesse of kynde.

As we approach the conclusion of this "fifth day" of Chaucer's creation poem, let us turn once more to Ambrose for a final word on our theme (*Hexameron*, V.12.36):

When I arrived at the point where I believed that I had exhausted my subject, and when I felt that I had completed the fifth day, this reflection came into my mind: It is customary for the birds at nesting time to charm the sky with song, in joy that their allotted task is done. This usually happens, following, as it were, a ritual pattern, at dawn and sunset, when the birds sing the praises of their Creator, at the moment of transition from day to night or from night to day. By such an omission I would have lost a mighty incentive for arousing our religious devotion. For what person of natural human sensibility would not blush to terminate the day without a ritual singing of the psalms, since even the tiniest bird ushers in the approach of day and night with customary devotion of sweet song?

And in this same spirit, Chaucer forms a choir of birds to sing a roundel in honor of Nature and for the sake of Saint Valentine. The tune, he tells us, was composed in France, and the thrice repeated refrain bids farewell to winter (680–82):

> "Now welcome, somer, with thy sonne softe,
> That hast this wintres wedres overshake,
> And driven away the longe nyghtes blake!

Today, six hundred years after Chaucer composed his *Parliament of Fowls*, psalms are not so frequently or fervently sung, and when our poets listen to the singing of birds it has seemed to them that

> So little cause for carollings
> Of such ecstatic sound
> Was written on terrestrial things . . .

But Chaucer offers us even today a permanent reminder that human sensibilities can be attuned to the grandeur of nature and that our eyes and ears can register afresh the sights and sounds of God's creation almost as it was in the beginning. His vision was of a harmony that transcends the discord of human conflict embodied in the parliament of birds, a concord that is the same throughout the universe whether in the music of the spheres or in the sublunar song of the birds. "How well were mankind," exclaimed Lady Philosophy, "if that love that governeth heaven governed your spirits!"

CHAPTER FOUR

The Pearl Poet

D ESPITE speculation about the "lost literature of medieval England," we tend to assume that all our great works have
come down to us intact, an assumption seemingly supported by the numerous extant manuscripts, for instance, of the
poetry of Chaucer. But the unique, late fourteenth-century copy
of the works of the *Pearl* poet, subject of the present chapter, is
a reminder of how precarious has been the survival of even the
best early English literature. The first reference to this precious
volume appears in a catalogue of the book collector Henry Savile
(1568–1617), from whom it was acquired by Sir Robert Cotton, in
whose private library it was shelved under a bust of the emperor
Nero. In the mid-eighteenth century, after narrowly escaping destruction by fire in Ashburnham House (the same fire that scorched
the Beowulf manuscript), our manuscript was acquired by the
British Museum (now the British Library), where it was given the
designation Cotton Nero A.x, after its former position in Sir Robert's library. In this modest volume (quarto size) are to be found
the only known copies of four major poems: *Pearl*, *Cleanness* (or
Purity), *Patience*, and *Sir Gawain and the Green Knight*. The last named
was edited by Sir Frederic Madden in 1839 as the first volume of
the Early English Text Society series. If fire had consumed this
manuscript in 1753, we would have had no idea that we were
missing some of the finest poems in Middle English.

Who was the craftsman who produced these remarkable texts?

Without any sure proof, it has generally been assumed (as I do here) that one man was responsible for all four, and possibly one more poem, *Saint Erkenwald*, preserved in a fifteenth-century manuscript in the British Library (Harley 2250). But the identity of the author of these five poems remains a mystery. Years ago a northern candidate was proposed, Huchown of the Awle Ryale (Royal Hall), who was said in Andrew Wyntoun's *Chronicle* (ca. 1420) to have written, among other things, the *Adventure of Gawain*, and who was thought to be the same man referred to by the Scottish poet Dunbar as Sir Hugh of Eglintoun in his "Lament for the Makaris." Another candidate is Ralph Strode, whom Chaucer addresses as "philosophical Strode" near the end of his *Troilus and Criseyde*. Most recently the name of John Massey of Cotton (in Cheshire) has been proposed, perhaps the most promising possibility yet considered; but discussion of this issue continues, and the verdict has not yet been pronounced. In the absence of a name, we can nevertheless be grateful that the work of this poet has been preserved for us. Apart from *Sir Gawain and the Green Knight*, which belongs to the corpus of Arthurian romance, the work of the *Pearl* poet is remarkable in its indebtedness to the Bible, and it is with this aspect of these poems that we shall be mainly concerned.

Cleanness

If any generalization can be made about the *Pearl* poet, it is that his style, though employed invariably for a serious purpose, is uncommonly distinguished by benevolence and humor. Yet we begin our consideration of his work with the one poem in the group that would appear to be an exception to this rule. *Cleanness* is a homily on purity that is dominated by negative examples from the Old Testament, dwelling on the spectacular punishment inflicted on sinners by God in the cases of the Flood, the destruction of Sodom and Gomorrah, and the fall of Babylon. One has a first impression, at least, that the poet who wrote *Cleanness* was an angry man, writing almost out of control. But there are mitigating features that point in another direction, not least his use of the Beatitudes from Christ's Sermon on the Mount. The Old Testament curses are there, and are to be taken seriously, but they are placed in a frame of potential blessings from the New Testament.

The poem employs the alliterative long line similar to that found in Old English poetry, and modern editors further divide the text into four-line stanzas, for which there is some justification in the manuscript (1–4):

> Clannesse who-so kyndly cowthe comende,
> And rekken up alle the resouns that ho by right askes,
> Fayre formes myght he fynde in forthering his speche,
> And in the contrare kark and combraunce huge.

> He who could rightly commend Cleanness
> And recount all the arguments in her support
> Might find fair forms in furthering his speech,
> As well as woe and sorrow that comes from the contrary.

Priests especially, who read and sing in church and handle the elements of Communion at the altar, should be pure, and if they fail in this, they incur God's anger. When Christ enumerated the Beatitudes, he gave this promise to those who maintained purity: *Blessed are the pure in heart, for they shall see God* (Matt. 5:8). So do not think to go to heaven in torn clothes or beggar's apparel with hands unwashed. For what earthly man of high rank would like it if a lad came poorly dressed to his banquet table? Surely such a person would be thrown out of the hall and never allowed to return. And if he were unwelcome to a worldly prince, think how much stricter the high King of Heaven would be in such a matter. Matthew tells of a certain rich man who made a great feast and invited many to come (Matt. 22:1–14). When those first invited made excuses, the lord rounded up folk from near and far to take their places at his table. It is clear that this banquet, made "to marry his heir dear" (52), is envisioned by the poet as the marriage supper of the lamb (Rev. 19:9), which the redeemed shall enjoy in the presence of God. Not everyone in the hereafter has a place of equal honor, but each person's satisfaction is complete (113–20). But as he moved through the hall, the lord noticed one guest in working clothes and asked him why he was not wearing a festive garment. When the guest for shame failed to respond, the lord ordered him thrown out. This episode, so briefly told in the gospel (Matt. 22:11–13), is presented much more emphatically in *Cleanness* (139–60):

> "Tell me, friend," quoth the lord, with a grim face,
> How came you into this house in garments so foul?

> "The habit that you have, no holy day it honors:
> What you wear is not fit for a wedding feast.

How did you dare, undaunted, draw near this house
In so ragged a robe, all rent at the sides?

"Thou art a fellow defiled in that feeble gown,
Thou hast appraised me and my place very poorly indeed,
So presumptuously to approach my presence herein:
Dost thou suppose I be a pauper, that will praise thy dress?"

The beggar was abashed at his bitter words,
And hung down his head, beholding the earth;
He was scared out of his wits, so fearful of harm
That he knew not one word to say in reply.

Then the lord wondrous loud delivered a cry,
And called to his torturers, "Take him," he said,
"Bind both hands behind his back,
And fasten the fetters firmly to his feet;

"Put him stiffly in stocks, and stick him thereafter
Deep in my dungeon where dole lasts forever,
Weeping and wailing and woeful gnashing
Of teeth angrily together, to teach him to dress."

Lest we miss the point, the poet explains that Christ is here comparing this feast to the Kingdom of Heaven, and warns us not to approach that Prince unless our clothes are clean, for "He hates hell no more than them that are soiled" (168). And what does he mean by these clothes? They are the works that we have wrought here on earth. There are many faults, any one of which may cost us eternal life: but of all the sins of mankind, none is more offensive to God than filth of the flesh (203–4):

> For then, as I find, he forgot his gracious ways,
> And grew fierce for revenge, with wrath at his heart.

To distinguish this kind of vengeance from ordinary punishment for sin, the poet cites three notable examples: the fall of Lucifer, the fall of Adam and Eve, and the destruction of the sinfull race of men by the Flood. The first two are cases of what might be called deliberate punishment. Thus the poet describes Lucifer's presumption in saying that he will establish his throne in the north and be like the Most High (Isa. 14:12–14), and then relates his abrupt fall, along with his fellow conspirators, into the pit of Hell (Isa. 14:15). As they fell, they turned into black fiends, falling thick as snow, and hurled into Hell-hole, like a swarming hive. The fall took forty days, and looked like smoke of fine meal under the sieve. And yet all of this was done without anger (229–32):

[174]

This was a cruel calamity and a great vengeance,
And yet God was not angry, nor did the wretch repent,
Nor ever acknowledge, for wilfulness, his sovereyn God,
Nor pray him for pity, so proud was his will.

Similarly in the case of Adam and Eve, although the sentence of death was severe, "the vengeance was made in measure and moderation / And later amended by a maiden" (247–48). But the third case involved "merciless malice and much hostility" (250), because of the "filth" of the folk in the time of Noah:

And then found they filth in fleshy deeds,
And contrived against kind contrary works,
And used them unthriftily, each one on other,
And also with others, willfully, in a wrong wise.

So fiercely was their flesh defouled that the Fiend looked
How the daughters of the people were dearly fair,
And fell in fellowship with them in fleshly wise,
And engendered on them giants with their vile tricks.

Augustine, in his *City of God* (XV, 23), mentions the possibility that the sons of God in Genesis 6:2, 4 may be understood as fiends (cf. Job 1:6, 2:1), but the additional specification by our poet of sins against nature seems designed to emphasize uncleanness as the occasion for God's anger, and the cause of his resorting to the violence of the Flood as a form of punishment. The phrasing of the first stanza quoted above may owe something to Saint Paul (Rom. 1:24ff.); it clearly goes beyond what we are told in Genesis 6. The story of the Flood itself and the survival of Noah and his family in the ark loaded with animals follows the biblical narrative closely, but adds details such as the vain efforts of the population to escape the mounting waters and a vivid description of the storm that drove the ark over the troubled waters. The story closes with the landing of the ark, Noah's sacrifice to the Lord, and the return of the surviving animals to their favorite haunts. Then comes the moral (545–56):

So beware now anyone who wishes to have honor
In the comely court of the King of bliss,
That in the filth of the flesh you never be found
As long as water in this world to wash you is not lacking.

For there is no one under the sun so seemly in his deeds,
But that if he be tainted with sin that remains uncleansed

One speck of a spot may suffice to forfeit
The sight of the Sovereign that sits on high.

For he that would be brought to those bright mansions
Must be clean as the beryl, burnished bright,
That is perfect on every side and has no seam,
Without spot or blemish, like the margery-pearl.

The concluding reference to the pearl of great price (Matt. 13:46) becomes a positive symbol of the cleanness that is the theme of the poem, and at the same time points ahead to the *Pearl*, a poem which, as we shall see, is undoubtedly the poet's greatest achievement.

Part II of *Cleanness* (557–1156) presents the account of the destruction of Sodom and Gomorrah (Gen. 18–19). Although God promised Noah that he would never again send such destruction on the whole earth, this did not mean that he would no longer punish sin severely. Indeed he continues to hate all sins, and especially those of the flesh. He honors the man who is pure in heart, but spurns the sinner and drives him away, or quickly kills him. His sudden anger is well illustrated in a disaster that occurred in the time of Abraham, with whom our story begins.

There follows the famous encounter of the patriarch with three men who come to his tent and are hospitably received. The main purpose of the scriptural account is to present yet another version of God's promise to Abraham, while at the same time showing the latter's hospitality as contrasted with the inhospitable behavior of the people of Sodom in the next chapter. In medieval commentaries, however, Abraham's encounter is seen as an important revelation of the Trinity—God manifesting himself to the patriarch as three men. Hence in addition to wondering whether Abraham will recognize that his visitors are divine, the reader has an additional ingredient of suspense: will Abraham recognize that the three men are One? Our poet does not overlook these dramatic possibilities.

Seated before his door in the heat of the day, under a green oak tree, Abraham sees three lordly men coming down the road. The poet plays with our expectations about these men in a teasing aside to the listener: "Whether they were indeed handsome, noble, and fair to behold will be clear enough before we reach the end of our story!" (607–8). Abraham quickly rises to go meet them "as if to God" and "hails them in unity, and says 'Dear Lord'"

(611–12). Thus we are to understand that the patriarch instinctively recognized their Unity in addressing them in the singular as "Lord" (as in Gen. 18:3). They accept his invitation to dinner, and Abraham serves them himself, with head uncovered and arms uplifted (643). In details such as these last, the poet seems to blend literal and figurative meanings, showing Abraham in an attitude of worship even before the Lord has revealed Himself to him, and perhaps suggesting that we are being shown an early form of biblical Mass.

After promising the patriarch and his wife Sarah that they shall have a son, the Lord sets out on the road to Sodom, accompanied by Abraham. Here the poet follows his original (Gen. 18:16–23) very closely, with one exception. The Lord decides to make Abraham aware of his plans against Sodom and Gomorrah, and spells out, beyond anything in the biblical text, the nature of their sin and why he particularly detests it (693–712):

> "They have learned a lesson that is loathsome to me,
> They have devised the worst of fleshly faults:
> Each male has for mate a man like himself,
> And in effeminate fashion they foolishly mingle.
>
> I designed them a natural skill and secretly taught them,
> And valued it uniquely in the order of things,
> Set druerie [love] therein, the sweetest of gifts,
> And I myself planned the play of paramours,
>
> And devised their dalliance, most delightful of all,
> That when two true lovers have tied them together
> Such mirth should mount between the male and his mate
> Scarcely Paradise itself could prove any better.
>
> As long as each honorably used the other
> At a still stolen hour when none can see,
> The love-flame between them would flare so hot
> That all the woes of the world could not put it out.
>
> Now they have altered my purpose and scorned nature,
> And contemptuously crave a custom unclean;
> I shall smite them smartly for that smut, I think,
> That men shall learn by their example, world without end."

In the bargaining between Abraham and God, the Genesis account leaves it for us to infer, if we wish, that Abraham is concerned about the fate of Sodom because it is the home of his nephew Lot. Our poet makes this explicit by having Abraham appeal directly to the Lord that "Lot lives among yon people, who is my dear kinsman" (772), and adds, "if thou destroyest that town, temper thine ire, if thy mercy may moderate it, to spare the meek man" (775–76).

Lot's hospitable treatment of the two angels, the assault of the townsmen on his house, the destruction of the cities, and the escape of Lot and his family— all follow the Genesis account very closely, with the addition of some judicious details that enhance the vividness of this already vivid story. Like Abraham, Lot is courteous to strangers, but although we may infer that he recognized the divinity of his visitors in serving them unleavened bread (Gen. 19:3), it is only in the poem that we are told the "alert man" recognized them as such when they first approached the city. Lot's wife, when she learns that the strangers are to be served without salt, is indignant (822–28):

And said softly to herself: "These unseasoned fellows
Like no salt in their sauce, yet this is no reason
For others to do without, just because they are so nice [fastidious]."
Then she seasons with salt her sauces each one,
Against the word of the man who had forbidden it,
And held them in scorn who knew well her purpose.
Why was the wretch so mad? She angered our Lord.

This anticipatory example of the disobedience of Lot's wife prepares us for the moment when, fleeing with the rest to escape destruction, she looks back (against the command of the angels) and is turned into a pillar of salt (Gen. 19:26). Hearing the outcry of the doomed people of Sodom, "the wretched woman, who never was obedient, / Looked behind her back as she heard that sound of misery" (979–80). As soon as she had once looked over her left shoulder, she turned to solid stone, salty as any sea. This happened to her for two reasons (997–1000):

First, she served salt at supper before the Lord,
And second, she looked behind though it was forbidden:
For the latter she became stone, for the former turned to salt,
That the beasts of that land ever loved to lick.

The episode concludes with a conventional description of the Dead Sea like that found in *Cursor Mundi*. It is broad and bottomless, bitter as gall, and violates all the laws of nature: heavy objects float in it, and light objects sink. If a man be plunged beneath its surface, he may sink to the bottom, but will live on in that lake until Doomsday. Beside the corrosive waters grow lush trees filled with oranges and pomegranates, red and ripe looking; but when the fruit is opened, there is nothing inside but swirling ashes (1013–48).

With the lurid destruction of the five cities of the plain, we reach the middle, and the turning point, of the poem. In view of the strong negative impact of the preceding biblical examples, the poet wishes, before taking up the sinister case of Belshazzar, to present an interlude (1048–1156) in which a more positive argument for cleanness can be made. The terrible vengeance that we have just witnessed, he says, should lead each person to understand that our Father loves clean conduct. So if you desire to be acknowledged in his court and to see his sweet face, I council you to be pure. Remember Friend's advice to the Lover in Jean de Meun's *Roman de la Rose* (7719ff.): "Pay attention to the way that Fair Welcoming looks at you; . . . adapt yourself to his manner. . . . If he is happy, put on a happy face; if he is angry, an angry one. If he laughs, you laugh, and weep if he does. Maintain your conduct in this way at every hour. . . ." Similarly, says the poet, you should conform to the manners of God. This literary allusion comes as something of a surprise, since in the context of the *Roman de la Rose*, Friend speaks with the voice of worldly wisdom. But it is soon made clear that this is advice of a very different kind, in that the poet goes on to urge us to imitate Christ and to become as clean as a polished pearl.

This is followed by a beautiful lyric passage emphasizing the cleanness of Christ's nativity and his life on earth (1069–80):

> For lo, when first he alighted in the loyal maiden,
> By what a marvelous means he made his entry:
> No virginity was vanquished, nor violence done,
> But much cleaner was her corse when God was conceived;
>
> And when he was born in splendid Bethlehem,
> How pure was their parting, though they were poor!
> No mansion was ever so merry as a manger then,
> Nor any studio as bright as a stable there,
>
> Nor none so glad before God as she that should groan,
> For instead of sore sickness, there was soundness and health,
> There was the scent of roses instead of rottenness,
> And solace and song instead of sorrowful cries.

As we have seen (in the chapter on lyrics), the painlessness of the birth of the Christ child is traditional, and more than compensated for in the pain of the Virgin at the Crucifixion, when the sword predicted by Simeon pierced through her soul (Luke 2:35). The solace and song referred to are provided by the angel musicians (often depicted in medieval art). As soon as the child is born the ox and ass worship him (Isa. 1:3), recognizing him by his cleanness, "for never before had one so clean come from such an enclosure" (1088). And so it is not surprising that one so clean cannot endure anything vile. Yet he did not refuse to touch loathsome lepers, the lame, the sick, and the blind, and when he did so, they immediately became clean. So pure and so good was the skill of his fingers that he never had occasion to employ knife or blade, for when he broke bread by hand it fell apart more cleanly than if it had been cut with a knife (Luke 24:35). How can we sinners come to the kingdom of such a one? But the Master is merciful, for he will be ready to receive you if you cleanse yourself through confession, become pure through penance, a pearl of great price.

The pearl is not the most expensive of ornaments, observes the poet, yet it is highly valued in any display of jewelry. Surely this is because of its pure whiteness, which it never loses unless it is neglected. Even then, its luster can be restored if you simply wash it in wine. In like manner, if any man be corrupted in soul, let him go to confession, where the priest will assign him penance whereby he may be polished brighter than the finest pearl. But once you have been washed and polished, be careful that you do not slip again into sin, for then you incite the Lord to punish you more severely than if you had not washed yourself. For when a soul is consecrated to the Lord, he counts it wholly his own, and takes its loss badly, as if it were plundered by thieves. The Lord strictly forbids that we ever defile any vessel used in his service (2 Tim. 2:20–22), as is well illustrated by something that happened in Babylon, in the time of Belshazzar, who defiled the vessels taken from the temple of the Lord at the fall of Jerusalem. Indeed Belshazzar was treated more severely than his father Nebuchadnezzar, who had taken the precious vessels from the temple by force.

The subtle shift from pearl to vessel as the image of purity occurs, we notice, at a critical point in the poem. It prepares us for the story of Belshazzar, but it also takes us a step beyond the fleshly sins already considered. The Babylonian king is guilty of a more sophisticated violation, the blasphemous use of the utensils taken from Israel's temple at a great feast, where he and his princes, his wives, and concubines drink from the sacred vessels (Dan. 5:1–4). The poet clearly views this as a calculated insult to God, a kind of Old Testament sin against the Holy Ghost. As such it is his ultimate example of the violation of cleanness; and his account of God's angry response to this—the destruction of Babylon—greatly expands the biblical narrative, and, as we shall see, enhances the significance of the story by enclosing it in an atmosphere suggestive of Doomsday.

When the Jews turned to other gods in violation of the covenant, the Lord sent Nebuchadnezzar against Jerusalem. After a lengthy siege, Zedekiah sought to break out of the city but was captured by the Babylonians, who killed his sons, put out his eyes, bound and led him to Babylon (2 Kings 25:1–7). Why did the Lord permit this to happen? The poet wants us to understand that it had nothing to do with the power of Nebuchadnezzar or his army (1225–27):

> Now see how the Sovereign asserted his vengeance!
> It was not because of Nebuchadnezzar, or his nobles either,
> That Zedekiah's pride was so painfully punished,
> But rather his bad behavior, against his blithe Lord.

This is followed by a stanza that has been the despair of editors (1229–32):

> For hade the Fader ben his frende that hym bifore keped,
> Ne never trespast to him in teche of mysseleve,
> To colde wer alle Caldé and kythes of Ynde,
> Yet take Torkye hem wyth, her tene hade ben little.

The problem, I believe, arises from the tendency of editors to read the first two words of line 1231 as "too cold," whereas I think is more likely a misspelling of "to-called" (past participle), with inverse word order to express the conditional: "though all Chaldea and peoples of India were called together." The stanza could then be understood as follows:

> For had the Father remained his friend, who protected him before,
> And had he [Zedekiah] not trespassed against him in the sin of
>   apostacy,
> Though all Chaldea and peoples of India were assembled,
> With Turkey thrown in for good measure, their wrath would
>   have been of little avail [against Jerusalem].

This fits nicely with the preceding stanza, and expresses more forcefully God's guardianship of Israel, very much in the spirit of Psalm 2: *Why do the heathen rage . . . ?*

There follows a vivid description of the capture of Jerusalem, slaughter of its inhabitants, the taking of prisoners, seizure of the temple vessels, and the burning of the city (1233–1308). When the sacred vessels were presented to Nebuchadnezzar, the king was greatly impressed by their beauty (1313–20):

> He accepted them with solemnity, the Sovereign he praised
> Who was noblest of all, the Lord of Israel;
> Such goods, such gowns, such gay vessels
> Had never been brought to Chaldean realms.
>
> He packed them in his treasury in a trusty place,
> Reverently received them, as he rightly should;
> And in this he was wise, as you will learn hereafter,
> For had he regarded them lightly, he might have fared the worse.

This reverence for Israel's sacred vessels is not specified in the Bible, but our poet no doubt inferred it from the openness of Nebuchadnezzar to the teaching of Daniel (especially Dan. 4), to which he refers in this stanza (1325–28):

> And all [was] through the advice of Daniel, when he explained
> That all goods come from God, and gave him examples,
> Til the king fully acknowledged the truth of his words,
> And humbled himself, and moderated his deeds.

When Nebuchadnezzar dies, Belshazzar is installed in his stead, but it is soon evident that he lacks the potential for repentance that his father had. The two kings are deliberately contrasted in the poem, and the idolatry of Belshazzar is emphasized (1337–56). The motivation for his great feast, unspecified in the Bible (Dan. 5:1), is here attributed to a desire to publicize his own wickedness. It may be that the poet wishes us to compare this "mangerie" (1365) with the great feast ("mukel mangerie") given by the rich man (51ff.) near the beginning of the poem. The first is a banquet of the chosen, marred only by the presence of a single guest in working clothes; the second is a banquet of the damned, save for the presence of a single clean man, the holy prophet Daniel, called in to interpret the mysterious handwriting on the wall. The severity of the poem's conclusion is thus mitigated, I believe, when we understand the lurid feast of Belshazzar to be countervailed by the banquet of the redeemed, while at the same time that very feature contributes to our feeling that the fall of Babylon provides a foretaste of the Day of Judgment.

Now follows a magnificent description of Babylon with its palaces and gardens, the coming of the guests, and the banquet itself (1373–1528). The traditional contrast between Jerusalem, the city of God, and Babylon, the city of man, together with the identification of the king of Babylon as a type of Satan (Isa. 14:4ff.), might lead us to expect the poet to paint a diabolic picture, to portray Babylon by means of the iconography of Hell. But this we do not find: rather we are given an impressive sketch of the *golden city* (Isa. 14:4), thereby enhancing the greatness of its fall. In this passage, at least, our poet seems to shun the indirection of allegory in order to emphasize the reality of the events described. We discover the corruption of Babylon not from a description of it, but from the excesses and the idolatrous deeds of Belshazzar and his guests.

The broad city is set in the fairest place under the stars, surrounded by seven rivers on every side. It has a wondrous wall, ornamented and high, with battlements connecting pinnacled towers, all protected by horizontal palings. The enclosed area is very large, each side measuring seven miles along the ground. The palace, surpassing all others, has high buildings, and the hall is large enough that horses can race inside it. When the time appointed for the feast arrives, noblemen meet before the dais, and the great throne, bright with precious gems, is prepared for Belshazzar. The king takes his place, accompanied by his concubines. When everyone is seated, the service begins with a blast of trumpets, gleaming with gold banners, the sound of which echoes along the walls of the palace. Men carry in roast meats on silver platters, decorated on top with ornamental houses pared out of paper and painted over with gold; above are depicted fierce baboons, below other beasts, with birds in the foliage flickering back and forth, and everything enameled in azure and rich indigo; and all this is carried in by hand on the backs of horses to the accompaniment of pipe and drum, cymbals and bells.

When the wine has gone to his brain, the king orders servants to fetch forth the sacred vessels that Nebuchadnezzar brought from Jerusalem, fill them with wine, and let his ladies drink from them, so that they shall see that "there is no bounty among men like that of Belshazzar" (1436). Even the brass altar is brought and set up in the hall. In order to emphasize the seriousness of the violation of the sacred objects, the poet now draws on the diabolic significance of the king of Babylon in biblical tradition (1445–50):

> That which had been blessed before by bishops' hands
> And with the blood of beasts zealously anointed
> In the solemn sacrifice that had a good savor
> Before the Lord of the heavens, lifted in praise,
> Now is set to serve Satan the black,
> Before the bold Belshazzar, with boast and with pride.

Solomon spent seven years and more in the design and creation of these sacred vessels: basins of pure gold, with pitchers to match; cups shaped like castles, with ornamental lids, and carvings of birds and fruit trees all set with precious stones; engraved goblets of gold, and incense bowls fretted with flowers and golden butterflies; and, last but not least, there was the magnificent candlestick (Exod. 25:31–40) with its bases of brass and ornamental branches, which had customarily stood in the Holy of Holies, where the true God "expounded his speech spiritually to special prophets" (1492). What does the Lord think now of this use of his precious vessels? (1493–1500):

> You may well believe that the Lord who rules the heavens
> Was much displeased at that play in this strange place,
> That his gentle jewels were defiled by wretches,
> Which had proved to be precious in his presence before.

> Some in sacrifice had been solemnly anointed,
> Through the summons of Himself that sits on high;
> Now a boaster on a bench imbibes therefrom
> Til he be drunken as the devil, and dotes where he sits.

Belshazzar calls for more wine, and toasts the assembled company with "Wassail!" There is a ringing of metal as the cups are filled: the dotard on the dais drinks what he can, followed by dukes and princes, concubines and knights in order of seniority. They linger over these liquors and glory in their false gods made of sticks and stones. They call on Baal-peor, Belial, and Beelzebub, but forget the giver of all good.

When the mysterious hand writes its "runic" words on the wall, the king's confidence is completely shattered (1537–45):

When bold Belshazzar looked at that fist,
Such a daunting dread rushed to his heart,
That his face became fallow, and his countenance fell;
The strong stroke of astonishment strained his joints.

His knees knock together and his legs grow weak,
With restless hands he scratches his cheeks,
And bellows like a mad bull that roars for dread,
Ever beholding the hand until all was engraved
And the runic words were written on the wall.

Next we find the summoning of the soothsayers, who are unable
to read the writing, and then, at the suggestion of the queen,
Daniel is called. Here the text follows the biblical account very
closely, except that Daniel's recapitulation of the reign of Nebuchadnezzar is expanded by recourse to the earlier passage in which
it is first recorded (Dan. 4). Then follows the interpretation of the
words "Mane, Techal, Phares" (Dan. 4:25–28), and the public recognition of Daniel by the king. At last the banquet is ended (1759–
66):

Then paled the color of the bright skies,
The merry weather grows murky, and the mist drives

Along the horizon by the low meadows;
Each man to his home hurries along,
They sat at their supper, and sang thereafter,
Then each seeks a companion for the rest of the night.

Belshazzar was borne with bliss to his bed:
Let him rest as he pleases—he rose never again.

We see, against the background of gathering darkness, a people enjoying customary conviviality, totally unaware of the coming vengeance; Belshazzar himself is treated to a ceremonial re-
tirement in sharp contrast to the fact that this is his last night on
earth. The poet's technique here reminds us of the prophet Amos,
who thus likens the coming of the day of the Lord (Amos 5:19–20):
"As if a man did flee from a lion, and a bear met him; or went
into the house, and leaned his hand on the wall, and a serpent
bit him. Shall not the day of the Lord be darkness, and not light?
even very dark, and no brightness in it?" The capture of Babylon
in the Bible requires but a single verse: *In that night was the king
of the Chaldeans slain* (Dan. 5:30). Our poet describes the assembling
of the troops (Medes, Persians, and Indian allies), the sudden-

ness of the attack at night, accompanied by an alarming blast of trumpets, and the slaying of men in their sleep. To some extent, as we have noted, the details here suggest biblical descriptions of the great day of the Lord (e.g., Joel 2:1–11), but I think also the poet has in mind Isaiah's prophecy of the overthrow of the king of Babylon (Isa. 13–14). Belshazzar's death serves as a grim example of what happens to those who defile and blaspheme (1787–92):

> Belshazzar in his bed was beaten to death,
> Til his blood and his brain blended on his clothes.
>
> The king in his bed-curtain was caught by the heels,
> Fetched out by the feet and foully despised;
> He who was so doughty that day and drank of the vessel
> Now is no dearer than a dog that lies in the ditch.

While the details here stress the maltreatment of the king's body (the defiler defiled), the general idea for the manner of his death may have come from Isaiah 14:19–20. The poem ends with a prayer that we may have the grace to "serve in his sight" in the hereafter, thus returning to the opening reference to the beatitude that promises the pure in heart that they shall see God. And while it is true, as we have seen, that the poet includes positive arguments in support of cleanness, the final impression we have is a sense of awe at the majestic anger of the Lord in the presence of his opposite. And we can only say, with the prophet: *Woe is me, for I am undone; because I am a man of unclean lips, and I dwell in the midst of a people of unclean lips: for mine eyes have seen the King, the Lord of hosts* (Isa. 6:5).

Patience

Patience resembles *Cleanness* in several ways: both poems are in praise of a particular virtue derived from the Beatitudes; both take their illustrations from the Old Testament; and both are written in the alliterative long line, possibly arranged in quatrains. Moreover, in both, the Beatitudes are used in a similar way as a framing device. Why is it then that the two works convey such different impressions? Surely it is in the choice of biblical exempla that the two differ most significantly: the selection of Jonah as the protagonist in *Patience* is an important key to its success. And yet the reader coming to the poem for the first time may be surprised at the choice of Jonah for this purpose. What has Jonah to do with patience? If anything, he illustrates the contrary, and so we appear to have another similarity to *Cleanness*: a virtue is defined by its opposite. But what a difference there is in the nature of the opposition. The defiling of the human body and of the sacred vessels in *Cleanness* is carried out singlemindedly by defiant and unredeemed men; the impatience of Jonah is a redeemable human failing, and the positive example of patience is provided by God himself in his handling of the prophet. The result is a much more humanly attractive poem, which follows the biblical narrative closely but expands the story in very imaginative ways, particularly in depicting Jonah's three-day voyage inside the whale. In sharp contract to *Cleanness*, in *Patience* the poet gives free rein to his inimitable sense of humor.

To begin with, patience is defined (1–8):

> Patience is a virtue, though it is oft displeasing:
> When hearts are heavy, and hurt by scorners,
> Sufferance may assuage them and lessen the pain,
> For it quells every quarrel and quenches malice.
>
> For he who can suffer sorrow shall find joy after,
> And he who cannot endure woe, the worse he suffers.
> So it is better to abide the blow betimes
> Than ever harp on my hurt, however evil it seems.

This definition is followed by a list of Beatitudes from Matthew 5:3–10. The translation tends to be very close, but in certain instances we can detect the influence of exegetical tradition on how these virtues are interpreted. Thus *pauperes spiritu* (the poor in spirit) is expressed as "poverty in heart," perhaps reflecting the medieval ideal of voluntary poverty as contrasted with the physical condition of poverty; *qui lugent* (they that mourn) appears in the poem as "they . . . that for their harm weep," which means those who are penitent, who weep for their sins; the *pacifici* (peacemakers) are those who "hold their peace," which suggest for them a less active, perhaps quietistic role; but most interesting of all is the final Beatitude (Matt. 5:10): *Beati qui persecutionem patiuntur propter iustitiam* (Blessed are they which are persecuted for righteousness' sake), which the poet translates, "They are happy also that can their heart steer." Immediately following these definitions the poet characterizes each of these virtues as a personified courtly lady, such as Dame Poverty (the poor in spirit), Dame Penance (they that mourn), Dame Pity (they which do hunger and thirst after righteousness), "merry Cleanness" (the pure in heart), Dame Peace (the peacemakers), and Dame Patience (they which are persecuted for righteousness' sake). Thus Dame Patience is in climactic position and has been identified specifically with those who can steer (govern) their hearts, that Boethian ideal that we have seen to be central to medieval thought.

Before leaving the Beatitudes, the poet calls attention to the fact that the first (poor in spirit) and the last (the patient) are promised identical rewards: *for theirs is the kingdom of heaven.* He then rather curiously explains this as follows (41–48):

> For where Poverty proffers herself, she will not be put out,
> But lingers where she wishes, like it or not;
> And where poverty oppresses, painful as it seems,
> No matter how he moans, he must suffer much.
>
> Thus Poverty and Patience must needs be playfellows;
> Since I am beset with them both, it behoves me to suffer.
> So it is better to make the best of it, and praise their ways
> Than to resist and be wroth and fare the worse.

Since the story of Jonah does not involve poverty as an issue, we may wonder why the poet makes such a point of it unless, as some have speculated, he himself suffered from poverty and here refers to that fact. But nothing more comes of this, and I am more inclined to think that he is speaking in very general terms of a poverty of circumstances, a situation that "oppresses," and calls for patience. This broader view is supported by the stanzas immediately following, which constitute a transition from the Beatitudes to the story of Jonah (49–60):

> If a destiny is designed and ordained for me,
> What good is it to show disdain or defiance?
> Or if my liege lord were inclined to bid me
> To ride or to run to Rome on an errand,
>
> What good would grumbling do but get me more trouble?
> For he would make me go, in spite of my objections,
> And then must I endure danger and displeasure for a reward,
> When I should have bowed to his bidding as befits my hire.

The poet then goes on to point out that Jonah was guilty of grumbling against the Lord's commands, and launches into his exemplum, which is designed to show that Jonah's disobedience is attributable to a fundamental defect: a lack of patience.

Long ago in Judea, Jonah was appointed a prophet to the Gentiles, and God whispered in his ear "with a rough voice," telling him to go denounce the sins of Nineveh. The Bible tells us that Jonah's reaction to this command was to flee to Tarshish, but no explicit reason is given. The poet leaves us in no doubt: Jonah fears that he will be arrested in Nineveh, put in prison, and tortured (73–88). On his way to the port of Jaffa, the prophet explains further the basis of his fear (93–96):

> "Our Sire sits," he says, "on his seat so high,
> In his glowing glory, and gives little thought
> If I be seized in Nineveh and stripped naked,
> Pitifully torn on a cross by many a traitor."

In supposing that he might be the victim of a crucifixion, Jonah reminds us of the Christological interpretation of his life, based largely on Jesus' words in Matthew 12:40: *For as Jonas was three days and three nights in the whale's belly, so shall the Son of Man be three days and three nights in the heart of the earth.* To some degree this allegorical reading shows up in the poet's description of Jonah's experience in the whale's belly, but in general the prophet is treated realistically as a fallible spokesman of God. The tendency of exegetes in the allegorical tradition was to be much less critical of Jonah and to explain his flight in other more innocent ways. Again we see our poet avoiding an opportunity to employ allegory in the development of his theme.

In vigorous and salty language, the poet describes the beginning of the sea voyage, the weighing of anchors and hoisting of sails (101–8), and the prophet's relief in escaping the hostility of the Lord. The witless wretch thought that God could see no farther than Samaria. King David knew better than this when he sang (Ps. 94:9): *He that planted the ear, shall he not hear? he that formed the eye, shall he not see?* Then follows a magnificent description of the storm at sea called forth by the Lord (129–52). The desperate mariners slash the lines and begin bailing out the rising water. They jettison their bags, featherbeds, bright garments, chest, coffers, and casks, and end by crying on their gods for help. At length they cast lots to determine which man may have grieved his god and caused such a terrible storm. Here the biblical account is followed very closely. When the lot points to Jonah he admits his guilt and explains the circumstances, but the mariners first make one more effort to save the ship before acquiesing in Jonah's suggestion that they throw him overboard. As soon as this is done, the storm begins to recede, and the ship is saved. After they reach land, praise is lifted aloft to the merciful God in the manner of Moses (Exod. 15:1–18), and they offer sacrifice and make vows (Jonah 1:16). Meanwhile Jonah faces an adventure that would be hard to believe were it not recorded in holy writ.

Part II of *Patience* (245–304) is essentially an expansion of Jonah 1:17, which simply reports: *Jonah was in the belly of the fish three days and three nights.* A wild wallowing whale, driven up from the depths, floats by the ship just as the prophet is being thrown overboard and opens its mouth. While the folk still hold Jonah's feet, the fish seizes him; "without touch of any tooth he tilted [tumbled] into his throat" (252). Then it dives to the sea bottom, past many rough rocks and stormy strands, while the man in its maw is "malskred in dread"—that is, in a state of shock. And little wonder, for if the high King of Heaven had not guarded this wretched man in the warlock's guts, who would believe that any life could be preserved for so long therein? "Lord, cold was his comfort, and his care huge!" (264). For he was aware of every misfortune that had befallen him, how he was snatched into the boiling sea from the boat by a beast, and thrown in at its throat without more ado, "like a mote in at minster door, so mickle [great] were his jowls" (268). Next we have the adventures of Jonah inside the whale (269–80):

He glides in by the gills through slimy filth,
Reeling in through a gut that seemed like a road,
Head over heels hurling along
Til he came to a cavern as wide as a hall.

And there he fastens his feet and feels his way
And stood up in that stomach that stank as the devil.
There in fat and filth that savored as hell
Was built the man's bower who is to suffer no bale.

Then he lurks and looks for a sheltered place
In each nook of his navel, but nowhere can find
Either rest or recovery—nothing but muck and mire,
Whichever gut he explores; but God is ever sweet.

The reference to the whale as a warlock (a term frequently used for the Devil) and the emphasis on the horror of the beast's interior in contrast to the sweetness of God does remind us of the descent into hell comparison called for by Matthew 12:40; but rather

than foreshadowing the Harrowing of Hell, the passage quoted
serves mainly to motivate Jonah's repentance, which immediately
follows (281–88). As soon as he has called upon the Lord, he comes
upon a corner where he is protected from the filth around him,
and he remains there, troubled only by darkness, as safe and sound
as he had been before when he was asleep in the boat (293–
300):

> So in a bowel of that beast he abides alive
> Three days and three nights, ever thinking on the Lord,
> His might and his mercy, his moderation therein;
> Now he knows him in woe, who could not in joy.
>
> And ever wallows this whale through the wild deep,
> In many a rough region, in the pride of his will;
> For that mote in his maw made him, I think,
> (Though small in comparison) feel sick in his heart.

This concludes the highly original passage on Jonah's survival
in the bowels of the fish, and it is interesting that by contrast the
prayer that follows (305–36) is very close to the corresponding biblical text (Jonah 2:2–9): . . . *out of the belly of hell cried I, and thou
heardest my voice* becomes ". . . out of the hole . . . of hell's womb
I called, and thou knew mine unclear steven [voice]." The poet's
addition of the word "unclear" accentuates the wonder of the
Lord's hearing Jonah's faint cry from inside the whale. *For thou
hadst cast me into the deep, in the midst of the seas* becomes "Thou
diptest me of the deep sea into the dim heart [Vulgate *corde*]."
where "dim" adds to the sense of terror of the sea. *Yet I will look
again toward thy holy temple* becomes more hopeful or explicit: "Yet
surely I hope again to tread in thy temple and belong to thyself."
A very unusual departure occurs in verse six, where *yet hast thou
brought up my life from corruption, O Lord my God* is replaced by
the following (323–24):

> Thou must relieve me, Man, while thy justice sleeps,
> Through the might of thy mercy that great is to trust.

Thus God's mercy in relation to his justice is given a position of
central importance in the prayer, and the usual honorific phrase
used in addressing God (*Domine Deus meus*) is replaced by the
simple word "Man" (renk), the same word used elsewhere by
God in speaking to Jonah. Some editors gloss "renk" here as "Sir,"
but I think this tends to obscure a deliberate effect: in his des-

peration Jonah addresses God with the unassuming familiarity of an Abraham.

At the command of the Lord, the whale coughs up Jonah on the shore. I leave it to you, says the poet, to decide whether his mantle was in need of a washing. To make it clear that Jonah has learned his lesson, the poet prefaces God's second command (Jon. 3:1–2) with this little exchange (345–48):

> Then a wind of God's word ruffles the man:
> "Wilt thou never go to Nineveh, no way at all?"
> "Yes, Lord," quoth the lad, "lend me thy grace
> To proceed at thy pleasure, or it profits me not."

Again the word for man (lede) is used suggestively: Jonah has now been restored to his proper role as a "servant" of the Lord. In this capacity he goes obediently to Nineveh and announces its destruction in forty days (Jon. 3:4). To this simple biblical prophecy the poet adds a stanza that seems to have Jonah envisioning the destruction of Nineveh in terms reminiscent of his own recent and disastrous experience in the whale (361–64):

> Truly this town shall tilt to the ground;
> Upside down ye shall dive, deep into the abyss,
> To be swallowed swiftly by the swart earth,
> And all that lives herein shall lose its life-blood.

In proclaiming a fast to the people of Nineveh, the king alludes briefly to the possibility that God may change his mind (Jon. 3:9): *Who can tell if God will turn and repent, and turn away from his fierce anger, that we perish not?* The poet's expansion of this verse shows once more his concern to emphasize God's mercy (396–404):

> Our voices shall rise to him that may well have pity;
>
> Who can know for certain that the Lord will not be pleased,
> He that is courteous in the height of his gentility?
> I am sure his power is so great, though he be displeased,
> That in his mild moderation he may find mercy.
>
> And if we give up these games, our loathsome sins,
> And softly walk in the way he himself ordains,
> He will turn from his fury, and leave his wrath,
> And forgive us this guilt, if we believe him to be God.

It is difficult to modernize lines like these without losing something, particularly the first two lines of the second stanza quoted:

> And if we leven the layk of our layth synnes,
> And stylle steppen in the styye He styghtles Hymselven. . . .

The word *layk* (play, game) usually has light and favorable connotations, but linking it by alliteration and assonance to *layth*
(loathly) ironically undercuts the normal meaning. Yet I think the
idea of play continues in the next line, particularly in the word
styghtles (ordains, makes rules) which survives in the modern word
stickler (umpire). Thus while we should cease playing sinful games,
we are at the same time encouraged to enjoy the quiet game
"stickled" by God, to walk in the way that he has ordained. The
grace of the poet's paraphrase calls to mind two other passages
of Scripture: *For my yoke is easy, and my burden is light* (Matt. 11:30);
*and what doth the Lord require of thee, but to do justly, and to love
mercy, and to walk humbly with thy God?* (Mic. 6:8).

In the face of such an appeal, and the theological soundness of
the king's proclamation, the people repent, and God withholds
his vengeance. This angers Jonah, and in the poem his explanation is more explicit than that of the Scriptures. I knew, he
says, that when I had threatened the Ninevites they would make
their peace with you by prayer and penance; that is why I fled
into Tarshish. Take my life, Lord, for it would be sweeter to die
swiftly "than to preach thy love any longer when you make me
a liar!" (428). Not only does Jonah resent God's granting mercy to
these pagans, he also seems to be suffering from embarrassment
that his prophecy turned out to be wrong.

There remains the final episode in which Jonah retreats to a
booth outside the city where the Lord gives him his final lesson
in patience. The poet lingers over his description of the booth and
its protective vine (453–56):

> The man glanced at the green and gracious leaves
> That ever waved in a wind so soft and cool:
> The bright sun shone around it, but no shaft of light
> Could shine on that man, as much as a mote.

One remembers by contrast Jonah's incarceration in the terrifying
whale. Once again he is to learn something, but this time in much
gentler confinement, as if the grace of God had become a local
habitation for him. The mere symbolic withdrawal of this divine
protection, in the withering of the vine, will be enough to teach
Jonah his final lesson. In God's final words the poet spells out
what is only implicit in the biblical narrative (520–23):

> Were I as hasty as thou, sir, harm would result;
> Could I suffer no more than thou, few would survive.
> I may not be so malicious and still be thought mild,
> For malice must be matched by mercy within.

In this balancing of justice and mercy God himself provides once more a model for the patience that the poem teaches.

Saint Erkenwald

Saint Erkenwald was bishop of London in the last quarter of the seventh century (ca. 675–93), but his association with the rebuilding and rededication of St. Paul's cathedral is found only in this poem, preserved, as we have seen, in a manuscript in the British Library (Harley 2250). While it is by no means certainly the work of the *Pearl* poet, it seems to me to share some of the characteristics of the four other poems, enough so to lead me to include it in this chapter. As a saint's life *Saint Erkenwald* is less directly biblical than *Cleanness* or *Patience,* but its theme is one that reflects a major concern of theologians in the fourteenth century: the salvation of the righteous heathen.

According to legend, Gregory the Great passed by the tomb of the Roman Emperor Trajan and was reminded how this man, though a heathen, was famous for his just life. Could such a man be damned simply because he lived in ignorance of the law of Christ? When he prays to God, Gregory is informed in a dream that his prayer has been answered, that Trajan is saved and is now in heaven. The problem in such cases is the explicitness of verses like Mark 16:16, *He that believeth and is baptized shall be saved; but he that believeth not shall be damned,* balanced against assurances such as those contained in Psalm 24:3–4:

> Who shall ascend into the hill of the Lord?
> Or who shall stand in his holy place?
> He that hath clean hands, and a pure heart;
> Who hath not lifted up his soul unto vanity,
> nor sworn deceitfully.

The medieval solution to this problem seems to have been found in allowing the baptismal requirement to be fulfilled in some way after the fact, as the result of specific petition in individual cases. The importance of the sacraments as a means of salvation was an issue here, and on this there developed some disagreement, as is evident in the treatment of the Trajan legend in *Piers the Plow-*

man, where the righteousness of the emperor overshadows the potency of Gregory's prayer on his behalf. Not so in *Saint Erkenwald*. Here the bishop's role is of central importance, as we shall see, and the salvation of the pagan judge is attributed to his intercession. The present poem, therefore, offers us the more customary and orthodox treatment of the righteous heathen.

When Gregory the Great sent missionaries to Britain, they removed the idols from the pagan temples, cleansed them, and installed saints in their place. A mighty devil once possessed the great minster of New Troy (London), and his sacrifices were the most solemn in Saxon lands. But this devil was removed, and Saint Paul set in his place, and it was in a new Saint Paul's minster that the Bishop Erkenwald had his seat, and taught the law of Christ in London town. But while the workmen were laying foundations for the new work, they found in their digging a marvelous tomb, a sarcophagus of solid stone, "garnished with gargoyles all of grey marble" (48). The borders were embellished with bright gold letters, but none of the clergy that crowded around the tomb could read that writing. Word of the discovery spread rapidly, and people of all ranks hurried to the minster to see this wonder. The mayor ordered the sanctuary closed off, and then bade the workmen to open the coffin. When the lid was laid by, a strange sight greeted the onlookers. The interior was brightly colored, and in it lay a body dressed in royal garments: the gown hemmed with gold, ornamented with many a pearl, a great mantle trimmed with fur, on his cap a rich crown, and in his hand a seemly scepter. But the most remarkable thing was the body's state of preservation (85–92):

> His clothes were as clean, without spot or blemish,
> Either of mould or mote, nor was it moth-eaten,
> And as bright of their color, in brilliant hues
> As if only yesterday in that yard they were newly made.
> And his face was as fresh, and the bare flesh
> That was openly exposed on his ears and hands
> As ruddy as the rose, and two red lips,
> As if in health suddenly he had slipped into sleep.

The evidence of the sarcophagus seemed contradictory: it was buried so deep that it must be the tomb from the dim past; but the state of the body and its clothing suggested someone recently dead. A search of the cathedral records turned up nothing to identify any such royal personage, so it was decided that the bishop should be informed of the mystery.

As it happened, Erkenwald was in Essex visiting an abbey when word of the discovery was brought to him. Immediately he hurried to London and came to Saint Paul's, but instead of listening to accounts of the affair or viewing the corpse, the bishop went straight to his palace and closed the door. For most of the night he knelt in prayer, asking God for a revelation concerning this wonder (122–27):

> "Though I be unworthy," all weeping he said
> In his great humility, "grant it my Lord
> In confirmation of thy Christian faith, cause me to know
> The mystery of this marvel that men wonder upon."
> And so long he cried for grace till there was granted him
> An answer from the Holy Ghost, and afterward it dawned.

It has been suggested (by Clifford Peterson) that the bishop's prayer and subsequent visit to the tomb are envisioned by the poet as taking place on the feast of Pentecost, thus making it especially appropriate for him to seek the aid of the Holy Ghost, who had descended on the apostles at that time (Acts 2:1–4). Indeed the miraculous speaking of the body in the tomb, as we shall see, may be intended to remind us of the speaking in tongues of the apostles. It is also worth noting that a principal service for Pentecost is the mass beginning *Spiritus Domini*, and it is this service that the bishop sings before going to visit the tomb (129–33):

> The bishop solemnly prepared to sing the high mass;
> The prelate in pontificals was priestly attired.
> Mannerly with his ministers the mass he begins
> Of *Spiritus Domini* for God-speed in subtle wise
> With soft quests of the choir in quavering notes.

On the completion of the divine service, Erkenwald proceeds straight to the tomb, still clad in his rich vestments, accompanied by many nobles and officials of church and state. The cloister is unlocked, and the bishop comes to the coffin, where the dean of the cathedral recounts its discovery and the futile efforts to identify the body. The bishop declares that there shall be an end to speculation, and that they must rely on God to provide the answer. When man's power is checkmated, he says, and he stands helpless, God can loose with one finger what all the hands under heaven could not hold. So when we lose the way of wisdom, it behooves us to seek the Comfort of the Creator (John 14:26). Erkenwald then addresses the body in the name of Jesus who died on the cross (185–88):

"Since we know not who thou art, inform us thyself
Who thou wert in this world, and why thou thus liest,
How long thou hast lain here, and what law thou usest,
Whether thou art joined to joy or judged to pain."

Then the bright body in the coffin stirs a little, and, "through some ghost lent life, by him that rules all" (192), he forces out words that have a dreary sound (193–96):

"Bishop," quoth this body, "thy bidding is dear to me;
I must bow to thy boon despite both my eyes.
To the name thou hast named and invoked me with
Hold all heaven and hell, and the earth between."

He then goes on to explain that despite his royal appearance, he was not king nor kaiser, but a man of law, who served as a magistrate of this city under the governance of a pagan prince. As for the length of time he has been dead, "that is a lewd date" [that is an unbelievably long time], too much for a man to reduce to mere numbers. Yet despite this, the body gives them a calculation of it (207–13):

After Brutus had built this borough at first,
Nought but five hundred years, lacking eighteen,
Before your Christ was born, by Christian account,
A thousand years and thirty more and yet thrice eight,
I was of Eyre and Oyer in the New Troy
In the reign of the rich king that ruled us then,
The bold Briton Sir Belinus, Sir Brennius was his brother.

Editors have puzzled over this, but I think that the passage makes sense, and can be paraphrased as follows: After Brutus built London (time unspecified), 482 years before the birth of Christ, or, in other words, 1054 years ago, I was commissioned a justice in both the circuit courts and the king's bench during the reign of King Belinus.

Since the difference between 482 and 1053 is 572, the poet appears to assume A.D. 572 as the date of the exhumation, which is about one hundred years too soon, when we remember the dates of Erkenwald's service as bishop (675–93); but the date for Belinus (482 B.C.) is also about a century too early, and we should not expect the poet to have access to all the records we now use to determine ancient chronology. The point that is designed to startle the onlookers (and impress the reader) is that this body has been lying in its grave for over a thousand years.

The silence that follows the body's disclosure of its age is eventually broken by Erkenwald, who asks why, if he were not a king, the judge was buried with scepter and crown. "In honor of my honesty," the body replies, in an important passage which is the nearest thing to social criticism in the entire poem (237–44):

> My conscience was not encumbered by earthly greed
> In any sinful decision to assent to fraud
> (Were a man never so rich) out of respect for rank,
> Nor for the menacing of any man, nor misfortune nor pity.
> None drew me from the highway, to depart from the right,
> As far as my fidelity made my heart conform.
> Though he had been the death of my father, I did him no wrong,
> Or no favor to my father, though it meant he should hang.

It is for these reasons that all of New Troy mourned the death of this judge, and buried him in such splendor. The bishop then asks why he has been so well preserved through the centuries, wondering whether his body was embalmed. The judge hastens to assure him that he was not embalmed; rather it was "the rich king of reason" (267) who has preserved him uncorrupted: "and if mere men for justice have thus arrayed me, He has allowed me to last who loves justice best" (271–72). This is the nearest the pagan judge comes to an awareness of the biblical God, and I take it that the poet has in mind Paul's argument on behalf of righteous Gentiles who are ignorant of the Torah (Rom. 1:14), but who do the works of the Law, thus showing that it is written in their hearts.

We reach the real theological crux when the bishop asks the judge about the state of his soul, and where it is now "stabled" (274). The bishop continues (275–80):

> He that rewards all men as they have deserved
> Could scarcely not give thee a branch of his grace,
> For as he says in his truth, written in the Psalter:
> "The righteous and innocent are welcome to me." [Ps. 24:3–4]

With this inquiry the body loses that accustomed confidence heretofore evident in his answers and begins to sigh and groan. Instead of answering the bishop, he speaks directly to God, in a

prayer that is central to the poem and most important in leading
up to the miracle that is its climax (283–308):

> "Mighty maker of men, thy might is great:
> How might thy mercy to me be a matter of moment?
> Was I not a poor pagan who knew not thy convenant,
> Nor the measure of thy mercy nor thy mighty virtue,
> But ever a faithless fellow that lacked thy laws
> For which thou hast ever been praised? Alas the hard times!
> I was none of that number that thou didst with pain redeem
> With the blood of thy body upon the bare cross;
> When thou didst harrow hell and hale them out,
> Thy loved ones out of limbo, thou didst leave me there.
> And there sits my soul, that may see no further,
> Languishing in the dark death induced by our father,
> Adam our elder who ate of the apple
> That has poisoned many plightless people forever.
> Ye were touched with his teeth and taken in the glut [Jer. 31:29?]
> But mended with a medicine ye are made to live,
> That is, baptized in the font with faithful belief,
> Which we have missed without mercy, myself and my soul.
> What won we with our good deeds, who ever did right,
> When we are damned dolefully into the deep pit
> And exiled from that supper, that solemn feast
> Where richly they are refreshed who hungered for the right?
> My soul may sit there in sorrow, and sigh full cold,
> Dimly in that dark death, where day never dawns,
> Hungry in hell-hole, and hearken after meals
> Long ere she see that supper, or be summoned to it."

All who hear these words weep for woe, and the bishop im-
pulsively expresses a wish that the body might have its life until
he can fetch water to baptize it with the words "I baptize thee in
the name of the Father, Son, and Holy Ghost." But even as he
speaks these words his tears trill down on the tomb, and one
drop falls on the face of the corpse. Immediately the judge sighs,
praises God, and informs Erkenwald that his tears have served
as the baptism that has released his soul from limbo (332–40):

> "Right now to supper my soul is set at table,
> For with the words and the water that washed us from pain
> Lightly flashed there a gleam, low in the abyss [Isa. 9:2]
> So that quick sprang my spirit with unsparing mirth
> Into the solemn assembly where sup all the faithful;
> And there a marshal met her and made her welcome
> And granted her graciously a place there forever.

> For this I praise my high God and also the bishop,
> That has brought us from bale to bliss: blessed may thou be!"

Suddenly in the silence that follows, the onlookers see the judge's pure complexion vanish, and the skin of his body become as black as mold, decaying into dust (345–48):

> For as soon as the soul was safely in bliss
> Corrupt was that casing that covered the bones,
> For the everlasting life that never shall cease
> Reviles all vainglory that avails so little.

Then everyone praises the Lord as they depart from the sanctuary, and all the bells in the borough ring out at once. Although "mourning and mirth are mingled together" (350), the poem ends on a note of triumph and praise for the role of Saint Erkenwald in bringing about the salvation of the just judge. Medieval saint's lives, various as they are, generally lack the sophistication of this one. And I suppose it is this quality that inclines me to view *Saint Erkenwald* as the work of that master who, for lack of a name, we call the *Pearl* poet.

Pearl

We come now to a unique poem, the *Pearl*, differing not only from works of the early English period generally but also from the other poems of the particular group we are considering in the present chapter. *Cleanness* and *Patience* are biblical homilies, and *Saint Erkenwald* a miracle story, but *Pearl* is not easy to categorize. It is also, in my opinion, the finest work of art in this distinguished group, not excluding *Sir Gawain and the Green Knight*. Before looking at *Pearl* in some detail, therefore, it may be well to consider what are the features that set this poem apart from all others.

The first thing the reader will notice is the form of the *Pearl*: it is in twelve-line stanzas, and not only are the lines distinguished by alliteration (which all of these poems have) but each stanza is marked by end rhyme in a very restrictive pattern (ababababbcbc), which allows the use of no more than three different rhyming sounds in twelve lines of verse. Moreover, the stanzas themselves are arranged in groups of five, connected with an echoing word or phrase that is repeated at the beginning and end of each stanza throughout that section of five stanzas. This echo or linking word is carefully chosen to chime in harmony with a particular theme or subject being emphasized in that part of the poem. And yet, considering the complexity of this metrical structure, it does not call attention to itself, and the reader becomes so absorbed in the poem as to cease to be aware of it, while it no doubt continues to have a subliminal effect and contributes to the total significance of the poem. There are twenty sections of five stanzas each. This would amount to a poem of 1,200 lines, except that one section (XV) has an extra stanza, so that the total is 1,212 lines. The reason for the emphasis on twelves in this structure will be evident when we come to consider the biblical sources of the poem.

Besides having this ornate structure, the *Pearl* is a dream vision, a literary form used by Chaucer (as we have seen) in his early poems, and a form that we shall meet again in *Piers the Plowman.* The pattern for the dream vision perhaps has biblical apocalypse as its ultimate model, but dreams are a common human experience, and the dream structure had already been used with great originality as early as the Old English *Dream of the Rood.* For poets of the fourteenth century the supreme model was the *Roman de la Rose,* and we have noticed above that the *Pearl* poet, in *Cleanness,* alludes directly to a passage from the second part of that work. In *Pearl* the opening is set in pleasant surroundings, in an arbor, where, after a meditation which establishes the mood, the speaker falls asleep and experiences a vision which is the substance of the poem. As in other dream visions, the Dreamer has trouble understanding what he sees, and part of the pleasure for the reader is to appreciate what is being taught before the Dreamer himself does.

The question of just what the poem teaches has been much disputed in recent years, and critics tend to belong to one of two schools, believing either that the poet is occupied with some aspect of mystical experience or that the poem is an elegy on the death of a child who was near and dear to him. If the former is correct, we should expect the focus of concern in the poem to be the disposition of our souls before God. How shall I be saved? Or, even more specifically, how shall I be rescued from spiritual dryness? By experiencing the Dreamer's religious struggle, we may then learn how to direct our steps. But if the poem is an elegy, then it seems to me that we have a very different focus: a poem charged with a sense of the loss of another person dearly loved. Both of these experiences—mystical longing and bereavement—

can be deeply felt, but they are also very different emotions. As I shall try to show, the *Pearl* seems to me clearly to have grown out of a sense of bereavement: the loss referred to by the Dreamer was indeed a little girl who "lived not two years in our land" (483) and never knew "Paternoster or Creed" (485). But even though we call this poem an elegy, we must be careful to avoid thinking in terms of Tennyson's *In Memoriam*. For the *Pearl* provides an unmistakably Boethian consolation in the teaching of the maiden: she assures the Dreamer that his beloved is happy in heaven, but treats severely all of his complaints against Providence. One of the great achievements of the poem is the emotional reconciliation of the Dreamer to his loss without the slightest compromise in Christian doctrine. Readers are often surprised to find an "elegy" so full of theological discussion, but it is precisely this discussion that produces the emotional reconciliation just mentioned. All this is apprehended, however, through the eyes and ears of a very human Dreamer, and it is the identification of the reader with the Dreamer that finally gives the poem its effectiveness. At times we may think that he is slow to comprehend, but in the final analysis, if we are honest, we must confess that we cannot run ahead of him in the overpowering of genuine grief.

The focus of biblical influence on the *Pearl* is the Book of Revelation, which, together with legendary descriptions of Paradise, is used by the author to envision the heavenly setting of the pearl maiden. We have already noted the prominence of twelves in the structure of the text, but it is only gradually that we are shown, in the latter part of the poem, the twelve-gated city as described by John. The picture is built up by hints and suggestions. Medieval readers or listeners would perhaps have sensed the importance of twelve as the perfect number, and may have noted by contrast the use of the temporal number seven in the description in *Cleanness* of Babylon, a city surrounded by seven rivers, with each of its four walls seven miles long. Indeed in the Middle Ages, Babylon was the City of Man par excellence, and Jerusalem the City of God, as is evident in the distinction made by Gregory the Great between citizens of Babylon and of Jerusalem. In this context the twelve gates of Jerusalem guarded by twelve angels with the names of the twelve apostles inscribed on the twelve foundations of the walls garnished with precious stones—all bespeak the perfection of the celestial city. The Book of Revelation is not without its sevens, but it is interesting that most of these are associated either with the apocalyptic destruction of the world or with the Church militant on earth, the seven churches of Asia (1:4), represented by the seven candlesticks and their guardian angels represented by the seven stars (1:20). Hence the poet in his vision of Paradise, as we shall see, stresses perfection in the number twelve, along with the lapidary significance of the precious stones in the foundations and the pearly gates. Multiples of twelve likewise represent perfection, as in the number of servants of God sealed by the angels: twelve thousand for each of the twelve tribes of Israel, making a total of 144,000 living forever in the presence of the Lord and wearing the white robes of martyrdom (7:3–17). There is much more, such as the twelve kinds of fruit yielded by the tree of life (22:2), but it is perhaps time now to turn to the *Pearl* itself, a poem that is much indebted to Revelation, but which is written in a very different spirit. Gone is the tense, electric atmosphere of first-century persecution. We now enter a calmer world, one that knows grief and sorrow, but finds release in quiet and solemn meditation:

> Pearl, pleasant to prince's pay [satisfaction],
> To cleanly enclose in gold so clear:
> Out of orient, I hardily say,
> Proved I never her precious peer.
> So round, so radiant in each array,
> So small, so smooth her sides were,
> Where-so-ever I judged gems gay,
> I set her singly in singlere [as unique].
> Alas! I lost her in an arbor;
> Through grass to ground it from me yot [went].
> I dwindle, fordolked [mortally wounded] of love-danger
> Of that privy pearl without spot.

The associations of "pearl" in medieval tradition were very rich, but the principal one is its signification as the human soul in Paradise, based no doubt on Christ's reference to that "one pearl of great price" (Matt. 13:45–46) bought by the merchant. It is this meaning, no doubt, that led Shakespeare to have Ariel sing, "Those are pearls that were his eyes," in the *Tempest* (1.2. 398), in harmony with the notion that in crossing over from this life to the next we "suffer a sea-change" like the grain of sand that becomes a pearl. But while the *Pearl* poet undoubtedly expects us to think of this traditional meaning, he begins the poem as if he is referring to a literal gem of the type prized by earthly princes. In fact the first eight lines could be said to consist entirely of praise of the pearl, except for a few phrases ("so small, so smooth her sides were") that are suggestive of a human being, in fact a girl. Then suddenly the loss is announced: "I lost her in an arbor," after which we momentarily forget the earlier suggestion of humanity and again think of the pearl as an object: "Through grass to ground it from me yot." The last word is usually taken to be the past tense of *yede* (go), and so translated "went." I suspect it may be, as has been suggested, another verb entirely, one that means "pour," "pour out," and in this context hints obscurely at the poet's sense of loss, in saying that the pearl "trickled" out of his hand to the ground, for, as the wise woman of Tekoah remarks to King David (2 Sam. 14:14), *we must needs die, and are as water spilt on the ground, which cannot be gathered up again.* This is the first slight hint of the mood of mourning that is to dominate the Dreamer in the first section of the poem. But something more explicit is given us in the final two lines. The Dreamer tells us that he is withering away as a result of his loss of "that privy pearl without spot." To speak of a pearl of great price is one thing; but to call it a pearl "without spot" seems to hint at sacrifice, or something other than the "sea-change" implicit in the image. Jephthah's daughter was no doubt thought to have been pleasing to God as a sacrifice because she had known no man (Judg. 11:39), just as an animal offered to God should be without spot or blemish (Num. 19:2). Still, it would be possible to take these words as simply an expression of the unique quality of the lost gem, were it not that the Dreamer also says that he has been wounded to the point of death (fordolked) by "love-danger." True, editors tend to explain this compound as referring explicitly to the Dreamer's own emotional state, as when Cawley and Anderson paraphrase "mortally wounded by the power of my love for my own spotless pearl." But I think it more likely that the poet is here adapting a concept from the *Roman de la Rose* (as we have seen him do in *Cleanness* 1057ff.), where the personification "Danger" represents the standoffishness of the lady. We may then paraphrase "mortally wounded by the coldness of that privy pearl without spot." This underscores an earlier hint (line 11) that the pearl is a person, and goes so far as to suggest that she is a lady who has cooled toward her lover. Here is the first hint that the poem is an elegy, though we have yet to learn that the beloved's alienation is no whim, but the natural consequence of death and burial.

The fact that the loss of the pearl represents the death of someone close to the poet is brought out in the next stanza (13–24):

> Since in that spot it from me sprang,
> Oft have I waited, wishing for that weal
> That wont was whilom to void my wrang [sorrow]
> And heave up my happiness and all my heal.
> That does but thrust my heart thrang [grievously].
> My breast in bale but to bolne and bele [swell and burn].
> Yet thought me never so sweet a song
> As the still stounde [hour] let to me steal.
> Forsooth there float to me fele [many (such songs)],
> When I think on her color, so clad in clot [clay].
> O mold [earth], thou marrest a merry jewel,
> My privy pearl without spot.

The poet's hand is quicker than our eye or ear, for we must slow
down our reading in order to perceive that he is accomplishing
several things in a single stanza. The linking word "spot" now
takes on another meaning: it is the spot (grave) where the pearl
fell. Moreover (and this device continues in the following stanza)
the pearl does not simply trickle down; we are told that it "sprang"
from the Dreamer as if it had a will of its own and was determined to get away. Words of this kind are carefully chosen at the
beginning of the poem to shadow forth the Dreamer's deep resentment at his loss which he will express later in conversation
with the Pearl Maiden. But most of this second stanza is taken
up with a gentle alternation between loving recollection and over-
whelming grief: Often have I waited here (says the Dreamer)
longing for that goodly one who used to set aside my sorrow and
fill me with happiness and well-being. But then my heart becomes heavy, my breast swells and burns with grief. And yet
there seemed never so sweet a song as that which came to me
here in the quiet hours. Indeed many such songs have floated to
me when I think of her color, so clad in clay. O earth! thou dost
harm a marvelous jewel, my privy pearl without spot. Thus sorrow mingles with sweet song, and the spotless pearl is spotted
with mold from the grave.

From this alternation between joy and grief, the poet turns to
a more direct description of the grave that he has been visiting
in the arbor (25–36):

> That spot of spices must needs spread,
> Where such richness to rot is run:

> Blooms bleak [yellow] and blue and red
> There shine full sheer against the sun.
> Flower and fruit may not fade
> Where it down drove in mold's dun;
> For each grass must grow of the grain's dead [death]—
> Else were no wheat to wones [barns] won.
> Of good each good is aye begun:
> So seemly a seed might fail not,
> But that springing spices upward spun
> Of that precious pearl without spot.

The technique of indirection prevails, but it is evident that the "spot" growing with spices is the grave of the beloved. The stanza speaks simultaneously of death and resurrection. Richness runs to rot, but in the wisdom of Nature this produces flowers; the pearl perversely (again!) "drove down" into the earth, but from that same earth springing spices "spun upward." The implicit rectitude of nature's way is made doctrinally explicit in the biblical reference to the death of the grain (John 12:24) and gathering into barns (Matt. 13:30). The speaker is thus revealed as a mourner who knows the Church's teaching on death and resurrection.

We follow the Dreamer as he enters that green arbor in August, in a high season (Lammastide was August 1): beautiful flowers cover the mound (huyle) where the pearl had "trundled down," and a fair odor floats from that place where dwells that worthy one, "my precious pearl without spot" (37–48). Standing before that spot where his pearl had fallen, the Dreamer feels a chilling sorrow that makes him clasp his hands; a terrible grief lurks in his heart, even though reason seeks to reconcile him. I complained of my pearl that was imprisoned there, he says, with fierce arguments that fought with each other. Though the example of Christ brought me comfort, my wretched will remained in woe (57–60):

> I fell upon that flowery flaght [turf],
> Such an odor to my hernes [brain] shot;
> I slid upon a sleeping-slaght [blow, onslaught]
> On that precious pearl without spot.

This concludes the first five-stanza section, and here the dream begins. The Dreamer is overcome by the sweet odor of the flowers growing on the grave and falls asleep. The compound "sleeping-slaght" is sometimes glossed as "deep sleep," but I am convinced that it should be understood more literally as a sleeping-blow, from which a freer paraphrase might be derived: "I was slugged into sleep." Our poet is careful always to provide natural settings for our consideration, but he is also very sensitive to the possibility of divine intervention in every situation. Only in modern times has God retreated from view; in medieval times he was constantly involved in guiding, commending, and rebuking his servants. When he sees that our Dreamer is in danger of giving way to excessive grief, he unceremoniously puts him to sleep in order that he may find consolation in his dream (the poem).

From that spot in the arbor, says the Dreamer, my spirit sprang into space, while my body remained on the mound in a swoon. My ghost went in God's grace to a place where marvels may be found. I don't know where it was; I knew only I was cast where cliffs cleave the heavens. I turned toward the forest where rich rocks were to be seen. No one could believe the gleaming light that glinted from them. For there was never a tapestry woven by men of half so precious adornment (adubbement, the link word for this section) (61–72). The beauty of this landscape is breathtaking (73–84):

> Dubbed were all those down sides
> With crystal cliffs so clear of kind.
> Holt-woods bright about them abides
> Of bolles [trunks] as blue as blee [color] of Ind [India].
> As burnished silver the leaf on-slides,
> That thick did trill on each tine [branch],
> When gleam of glades against them glides,
> With shimmering sheen full shrill they shined.
> The gravel that on ground did grind
> Were precious pearls of orient,
> The sunbeams but blo [dark] and blind
> In respect of that adubbement [adornment].

But this beauty has an artificiality, or perhaps better an unearthliness, that is stressed in the description: A silver reflection seems to "slide" on the polished surfaces of the leaves when they move ("trill") on each branch, caused by reflection of light from the glades (open spaces), making them shimmer and shine "shrilly." One notices the transposition of aural and visual perception in words like "trill" and "shrill" for the motion and shining of the leaves, producing an effect that seems to document the dazed wonderment of the Dreamer in his new and strange surroundings, who is scarcely yet aware that the crunching sound under his feet is made by pearls instead of ordinary gravel.

The ornamental surroundings cause the Dreamer to forget all grief, and the fresh odors of fruit refresh him as well as food. Fowls small and great of flaming colors fly together in the woods, whose song surpasses that of musical instruments, and when they beat their wings, they sing in harmony. No one could have such gracious entertainment as to hear the adornment of their song (85–96). What we have been given here is a traditional description of the approaches to Paradise with its characteristic birds and fruit trees. The next feature of the landscape to be presented is the *pure river of the water of life, clear as crystal, proceeding out of the Throne of God and of the Lamb* (Rev. 22:1). I stress this because this river is perhaps the most important and functional feature of the heavenly landscape of the *Pearl*. It is revealed to us only gradually, because the Dreamer himself does not at first perceive it as a river. Yet it is very important because it is used by the poet as the water barrier traditionally found in the otherworld journey of medieval romance, and it is this water across which the entire conversation between the Dreamer and the Pearl Maiden takes place throughout the poem. It is fascinating to observe how the fact of the water barrier is gradually forced on the Dreamer. At first it is simply one more feature of the beautiful landscape. As he moves forward, more wonders greet him: plains, plants, spices, pear trees, hedges, borders, and river banks. Then "I won to a water by a shore that sheers" (107). This "water" will remain the focus of attention through much of the next four stanzas, and some half-dozen different words are used to refer to it, with a variety of meanings that reflect the Dreamer's uncertainty about what kind of water it is (109–20):

> The dubbement of those dear *depe* [depths]
> Were banks bene [pleasant] of beryl bright.
> Swirling sweet the *water* did sweep,
> With a rownande rourde [whispering voice] rushing aright.
> In the founce [bottom] there stood stones steep [bright]
> As glint through glass that glowed and glight [glinted],
> As streaming stars, when strothe-men [earth-men] sleep,
> Stare in the welkin in a winter night.
> For each pebble in the *pool* there pight [set]
> Was emerald, sapphire, or gem gent [noble],
> So that all the *loch* gleamed of light,
> So dear was its adubbement.

At the same time we are being given hints that this is the *water of life*: it rushes with a "whispering voice," and the (precious) stones in the bottom of the stream are "steep" (113). The latter word is usually glossed as "bright," but this overlooks special connotations of this word in Middle English. Chaucer uses it in describing his monk, who had eyes that were "steep, and rolling in his head, that steamed [gleamed] as the furnace of a lead [cauldron]." These stones in the river of life likewise gleam upward through the water like eyes, or like stars that "stare" from the sky in a winter night. When we try to translate these original words of the poet, we lose the animation of the river that he provides. The presence of gems in the riverbed, of course, should tip us off that we are dealing with the rivers of Paradise which, as the author of *Cursor Mundi* reports (1039–40):

> . . . bring stones from paradise
> So precious nowhere founden is.

As we come to the third section of the poem, the Dreamer's happiness continues to grow as he gazes at the precious adornment of hill and dale, wood, water, and splendid plains. Alongside a "stream" that ceaselessly flows he blissfully makes his way, "bredful my brains" (126)—his brain brimful. The farther he follows those "floaty vales" (127), the more joy fills his heart, as when a man is being tested by Fortune, whether she send solace or sorrow, he on whom she bestows her favor ever wants to have more and more (121–32). The accelerating pace of this section of the poem (III) is marked by the linking phrase "more and more," and is climaxed by the Dreamer's first glimpse of the Pearl Maiden toward the end of the section. But he must first discover the nature of the water barrier that stands between them (133–44):

> More of weal was in that wise
> Than I could tell though I time had,
> For earthly heart might not suffice
> To the tenth dole [part] of that gladness glad.
> Wherefore I thought that Paradise
> Was there over against those banks broad.
> I hoped [thought] the water were a device
> Between mirths by *meres* made.
> Beyond the brook, by slant or slade
> I hoped that mote marked wore [city were set].
> But the water was deep, I durst not wade,
> And ever me longed aye more and more.

Cawley and Anderson gloss lines 139–40 as follows: "I thought the stream was a device [i.e., an artificial conduit] joining pleasure gardens made by the side of pools." Perhaps they were influenced by an earlier editor (Gollancz), who thought the description here was adapted from the *Roman de la Rose*, clearly known to the poet, as we have seen. But I believe this reading fails to appreciate the particular use being made of the word "device," which can occasionally be used to mean apparition or illusion. In context it seems far preferable to say: "I thought the water was a mirage, made by separate pools [meres] among the beauties [mirths] of the landscape." This could mean, then, that the meres only *seemed* to be joined in a single, impassable body of water; when the Dreamer came closer, he expected to be able to wade past them or perhaps thread his way through them to the city on the other side. Line 143 confirms this interpretation: "But the water was deep, I durst not wade."

Now the Dreamer knows that he is confronted with a formidable barrier, but he has not given up. The land on the other side is beautiful, and he wants to cross over to it (149–54):

> About me I did stop and stare,
> To find a ford fast did I fond [try];
> But woes more y-wiss there were,
> The farther I stalked by the strand.
> And ever me thought I should not wond [shrink]
> From woe where weals [joys] so winsome were.

It is at this moment, when he is still trying to find a ford, that the Dreamer looks beyond the "merry mere" and sees a crystal cliff with rays of light shining from it (161–68):

> At the foot thereof there sat an infant
> A mannerly maiden, full debonaire
> Glistening white was her bleaunt [mantle].
> I knew her well, I had seen her before.
> As glistening gold that man did shear
> So shone that sheen [fair one] under the shore.
> At great length I looked toward her there:
> The longer, I knew her more and more.

He is seized with a desire to call out to her, but something holds him back because he "saw her in so strange a place" (175). When she lifts up her fair face, his heart is stung with confusion.

Part IV of the poem is taken up with a description of the Pearl

Maiden, in which it is made clear that this little girl is the precious
jewel that the Dreamer had lost (181–92):

> More than me list my dread arose:
> I stood full still and durst not call;
> With eyes open and mouth full close
> I stood as hende [polite, quiet] as hawk in hall.
> I hoped that ghostly [spiritual] was that purpose;
> I dreaded anent what should befall,
> Lest she escape me whom there I chose [saw],
> Ere I at steven [with voice] her might stall [detain].
> That gracious gay one without gall [bitterness],
> So smooth, so small, so seemly slight,
> Rises up in her array royal,
> A precious piece [person] in pearls pight [adorned].

As the Maiden comes down the bank toward the dreamer he can
see that she is dressed in white (Rev. 7:9), her garment pearl-
trimmed, and she is wearing a crown (Rev. 2:10) decorated entirely
with pearls. Her expression is as grave and dignified as that of a
duke or an earl, her countenance white as whale's bone, and her
bright golden hair down to her shoulders. A wondrous pearl
without spot is set amid her breast, and no man could possibly
measure its value (Matt.13:46). When she reaches the water's edge
opposite him, the Dreamer's joy increases (233–40):

> She was nearer to me than aunt or niece:
> My joy therefore was much the more.
> She proffered me speech, that special spice [person],
> Enclining low in womanly lore [fashion],
> Caught off her crown of great treasure,
> And hailed me with a lote light [friendly word].
> Well was me that ever I was bore [born]
> To answer that sweet in pearls pight [adorned]!

With the next section (V) the Dreamer's education begins, and
in his conversation with the Pearl Maiden he refers to himself as
a "jeweler," which becomes the linking word in these five stanzas. But although we have had hints that the Maiden is in Paradise, and that the two speakers are separated by an impassable
body of water, we quickly learn that the Dreamer, in the high
emotion of the moment, is totally unaware of these things. He
begins by asking her if she is indeed the pearl that he lost, and
asks how it is that she lives a life unstrained by strife while he
has to live in grief and "great danger." From the time that we

two have been separated, he says, "I have been a joyless jeweler" (241–52). The Maiden then looks at him with her gray eyes, puts on her crown again, and calmly informs him that he is mistaken to say that his pearl is lost, when in fact she is so beautifully enclosed in this garden, which he should consider a most fitting casket for his pearl, if he were indeed a gentle jeweler (265–76):

> "But, gentle jeweler, if thou shalt lose
> Thy joy for a gem that to thee was lief [dear],
> Me think thee put in a mad purpose,
> And busiest thee about a reason brief [small matter].
> For what thou lost was but a rose
> That flowered and failed as kind [nature] it gave.
> Now through the kind of chest that did it enclose
> To a pearl of price it is put in proof [has proved to be].
> And thou hast called thy weird [fate-God] a thief,
> Who ought of nought [out of nothing] hath made thee clear.
> Thou blamest the boot [remedy] of thy mischief:
> Thou art no kind jeweler."

The Dreamer replies happily to this, but in doing so he shows that his ignorance is greater than we might have expected (277–88):

> A jewel to me then was this guest
> And jewels were her gentle saws [words].
> "I-wiss," quoth I, "My blissful best [dear one].
> My great distress thou all to-drawest [removest].
> To be excused I make request;
> I trowed [thought] my pearl done out of days [dead].
> Now that I have found it, I shall make feast,
> And wone [dwell] with it in sheer wood-shaws,
> And love my Lord and all his laws
> Who has thus brought me this bliss so near.
> Now were I with you beyond these waves,
> I were a joyful jeweler."

Who has not dreamed or imagined against all reason that some dear departed friend or relative is still alive? The Dreamer here reminds us of Mary Magdalene and her initial reaction to the risen Lord (John 20:16–17) as she is depicted in the medieval drama, where she first greets Jesus as if he had not died. But the Pearl Maiden deals severely with this delusion on the part of the "jeweler" (289–300):

> "Jeweler," said that gem clean,
> "Why borde [jest] ye men? How mad ye be!

Three words hast thou spoken at eene [once]:
Unadvised, forsooth, were all three.
Thou wist not in world what one doth mean;
Thy word before thy wit doth flee.
Thou sayest thou trowest [believest] me in this dene [valley]
Because thou mayest with eyes me see;
Another thou sayest, in this country
Thyself shalt wone [dwell] with me right here;
The third, to pass this water free—
That may no joyful jeweler."

This marks the transition to section VI, in which the link word is "deem," reflecting the fact that in these stanzas the Dreamer's mistaken judgment is subjected to severe scrutiny. It has been pointed out that the Pearl Maiden, particularly in this section, speaks more like an adult than a child, and this is used to argue against the interpretation adopted here—that she represents the soul of a child that died in infancy. But the maturity of the Maiden (if not indeed her omniscience) is perfectly in keeping with the common belief that spirits of the departed, whenever they choose to return and speak to men, are possessed of complete knowledge (1 Cor.. 13:12): *then shall I; know even as also I am known.* Indeed they are often asked to prophesy, and do so. In the ensuing conversation, therefore, we should not be surprised to find the child speaking as an adult, and the Dreamer by contrast as a child.

I have little praise, says the Pearl Maiden, for anyone who does not trust the promise of the Lord concerning the resurrection of the dead. It is wrong to believe nothing unless you can see it (Heb. 11:1). Do you think that you can "dally" (313) or bandy words with God (cf. Job 6:26)? You say you shall dwell in this bailiwick, but methinks you should first ask permission, and even then you may not be granted it. You want to cross this water, but there is something else you must do first: your body will have to sink into the cold clay, as a result of the sin of Adam (301–24).

If you doom me, my sweet, replies the Dreamer, to grief again, then I shall dwindle away. Now that I have found what I lost, must I lose it again? If I am to lose you, I care no more about my life nor do I expect anything but everlasting dole. Beware, responds the Maiden, lest in mourning a lesser loss you lose the greater. Rather you should love God in weal and woe, for anger will get you nowhere. Since you must needs suffer, be not so impatient: for though you "dance as any doe," struggle in the net ("brandish") and bray out your fierce frustration, when you can stir no further, you must abide what God shall deem fit for you. And the Maiden goes on in essence to recommend that the Dreamer come to the conclusion of Job (9:15): . . . *I would make supplication to my judge.* To this the Dreamer replies rather impressively in the next section that his words were blurted out spontaneously as an expression of his pain and grief. His defense is in fact gentle and loving, and is underlined by the linking phrase which he uses first to refer to his beloved pearl: "The ground of all my bliss" (372). By comparison, Job's defense to his friends is rather stern (6:26): *Do ye imagine to reprove words, and the speeches of one that is desperate, which are as wind?* Whereas the Dreamer pleads that the Pearl has been both his joy and his sorrow. Since you went away, I never knew where you were gone; now that I see you, my grief is lessened. Moreover, when we parted we were at one: God forbid we now be angry with one another. "We meet so seldom by stock or stone" (380). He then asks her about her life in heaven.

God bless you, then said that lovely one: for now your speech is dear to me. My Lord the Lamb (Rev. 5:6ff.) who is the ground of all my bliss, ever loves meekness. You know well that when your pearl slipped away from you, I was full young and tender of age; but my Lord the Lamb made me his bride, and crowned me a queen to dwell in bliss forever.

Are you then that Queen of Heaven that all the world honors? asks the Dreamer. The Maiden patiently explains that Mary is indeed Queen of Heaven, but "the court of the kingdom of the living God" is so disposed that everyone there is either king or queen, without anyone depriving any other of sovereignty, and the Virgin Mary holds sway over them all without in the slightest displeasing any of our "gang" (455). As Saint Paul says, we are all members of the body of Christ (1 Cor. 12:12–31).

Now we come to a central question raised by the Dreamer: is it fair for one so young to be elevated so quickly in heaven? And he adds, perhaps thinking of himself (475–80):

> What more honor might he achieve
> That had endured in world strong,
> And lived in penance his life long,
> With bodily bale his bliss to buy?
> What more worship might he fong [receive]
> Than be crowned king by courtesy?

Then by comparison he again refers to the fact that the maiden died at a very young age (483–86):

> Thou livedst not two years in our theed [land];
> Thou couldst never God neither please nor pray,
> Nor never know Paternoster nor Creed—
> And yet queen made on the first day!

There is no limit to His goodness, she replies, and then launches into the parable of the vineyard (Matt. 20:1–16), which, properly interpreted, contains the doctrine that establishes the justice of heavenly reward for individuals having different degrees of merit. Thus when the laborers who had worked all day in the vineyard receive a penny, the same amount paid to those who arrived only at the "eleventh hour" (20:6), they complain to the lord of the vineyard for treating the two groups equally. To this the lord replies (558–61):

> Friend, no moaning will I thee yet [allow];
> Take what is thine own, and go.
> An [If] I hired thee for a penny agret [as a group]
> Why beginnest thou now to threat?

The lord's justification of himself follows the biblical account very closely, but the Maiden then expands on it to make the application to her own case. I have more of joy and bliss, rank and perfection, she continues, than any creature in the world would be able to ask for "by way of right" (580). In other words, heaven is attained not by earning it, but by the gift of God. Not so! counters the Dreamer, *for thou renderest to every man according to his work* (Ps. 62:12). This brings us to the midpoint of the poem, where the Maiden gives the fullest and most important theological justification for her place in Paradise.

There is no "more and less" in God's kingdom, she explains (603–4):

> For there is each man payed inlich [inwardly satisfied],
> Whether little or much be his reward.
> For the gentle Chieftain is no chinch,
> Whether-so-ever he deal nesch or hard [kindly or harshly].

When the Lord rescues a sinner and grants him salvation, his generosity is very large indeed: "the grace of God is great enough" (610). This line becomes the link that holds together this section (XI), in which the Maiden reviews the fall of man and redemption

[215]

by the sacrifice of Christ, from whom flowed the blood and water (John 19:34) of redemption and baptism. This doctrine applies, of course, to the sinner. But what of those (like the Pearl Maiden) who do not live long enough to commit sin? In section XII the new echo line triumphantly proclaims the answer: "The innocent is aye safe by right" (672). She then outdoes the Dreamer in citing Scripture that supports her argument: "the righteous man shall see his face" (Ps. 24:5–6, Rev. 22:4); "Lord, who shall climb thy holy hill? . . ." (Ps. 24:3–4); and Solomon tells how Wisdom guided him (Wisdom 10:9–10):

> By ways full strait she did him constrain,
> And showed him the reign of God awhile,
> As who says: "Lo, yon lovely isle!
> Thou may it win if thou be wight [valiant]."
> But hardily [boldly], without peril,
> The innocent is aye safe by right.
> (691–96)

Having equated the destiny of the innocent with that of the righteous, the Maiden then goes on to give the Dreamer both a warning and a blessing. The warning comes in the words of David (Ps. 143:2): . . . *enter not into judgement with thy servant: for in thy sight shall no man living be justified.*

> Forthi [Therefore] to court when thou shalt come,
> Where all our cases shall be tried,
> (If thou) allege the right, thou may be innome [taken]
> By this ilke [very] speech I have espied.
> (701–4)

This is of course theologically correct, but to the Dreamer, by itself, it would sound very harsh. But it does not stand alone, for the Maiden immediately adds (705–8):

> But may he on rood [cross] that bloody died,
> Dolefully through hands was thright [pierced],
> Grant thee to pass, when thou art tried,
> By innocence, and not by right.

Here the echo line is skillfully used to draw the Dreamer, if possible, into the congregation of the innocent, so that he may indeed come at last into fellowship with his pearl. In touches like this the doctrinal rigor of the Maiden is effectively softened and made more acceptable to earthly ears. Then in the final stanza she returns to the main point, the salvation of innocent children, which is effectively reinforced by Jesus' words concerning them (Luke 18:15–17): . . . *for of such is the kingdom of heaven* (709–20).

Having treated the doctrinal questions involved in the salvation of the Maiden, the poet now turns to a somewhat more graphic depiction of the place of the little child in the paradise of the redeemed, and it is here that his indebtedness to Revelation becomes more and more evident. But first he returns to the gospel in order to explain more precisely the meaning of the pearl of great price (Matt. 13:45–46). This pearl is like the kingdom of heaven, for it is spotless, clean and clear. Lo, says the Maiden, my Lord the Lamb placed it here on my breast in token of peace. I advise thee to forsake the mad world and purchase thy spotless pearl. But the Dreamer, his doctrinal doubts overcome, is now completely absorbed in the beauty of the Pearl Maiden and her role in Paradise (745–56):

> "O maskeles [spotless] pearl in pearls pure,
> That bear," quoth I, "the pearl of price,
> Who formed thee thy fair figure?
> He that wrought thy weed [clothing], he was full wise.
> Thy beauty came never of nature;
> Pygmalion painted never thy vys [visage],
> Nor did Aristotle either, by his lettrure [learning]
> Of carped the kind [Speak of the nature] of these properties.
> Thy color surpasses the fleur-de-lis,
> Thine angel-having [angelic manner] so cleanly courteous.
> Brief me [Tell me], bright one, what kind of office
> Bears the pearl so maskeles [spotless]?"

The matchless Lamb, replies the Maiden, chose me as his mate, though such a union might once have seemed unmeet. When I went from your wet world, he called me to his beatitude (Song of Sol. 4:7–8): "Come hither to me, my sweet lover, for mote nor spot is none in thee." He gave me this beauty, washed my clothing in his blood (Rev. 7:14), crowned me in pure virginity, and adorned me with spotless pearls. Hearing this, the Dreamer characteristically jumps to the conclusion that this union is the same as earthly (monogamous) marriages, and that therefore the Lamb has chosen the Pearl Maiden above "so many a comely under comb" (775). Think, argues the Dreamer, how many deserving ladies endured strife-torn lives for Christ's sake, and now you "drive out all those dear ones," "depress" them from the marriage, and take their place all by yourself "so stout and stiff." This sounds disruptive, but it is actually a tempest in a teapot. The serious differences between the Dreamer and his Pearl are now over and gone; moreover, the Maiden has no need to defend her position to this poor earthling. So she patiently explains that all of the 144,000 white-robed servants of God have become brides of the Lamb, as they are described by Saint John, who saw them "all in a knot" (788) on the hill of Sion (Rev. 14:1), "the new city of Jerusalem" (792). "Jerusalem" now becomes the echo word as the Maiden launches into an account of the role of the Lamb in Paradise. If you would know what kind of person he is—my Lamb, my Lord, my dear jewel, my joy, my bliss, my noble lover—the prophet Isaiah spoke of his gentleness, saying that this guiltless one was led *as a lamb to the slaughter* (Isa. 53:7). Isaiah's words are then subtly interwoven with the New Testament description of the Passion of Christ, climaxed by the echo line: "For us he died in Jerusalem" (816). A second time my beloved was called a lamb by John the Baptist, who said (John 1:29), *Behold the Lamb of God, which taketh away the sins of the world!* The third time was in the Apocalypse (5:1ff.), where the apostle John saw the Lamb reading from the book sealed with seven seals, and at that sight all the hosts did bow "in hell, in earth, and Jerusalem" (840).

From the Lamb and his redemptive act our attention is directed in section XV to the company of saints and their worship of him. Each spotless soul, the Maiden explains, is a worthy wife of the Lamb, and although each day he fetches more of them, there is no strife; indeed, we wish there were five times as many as there are, "the more the merrier, so God me bless!" (850). Our love thrives in great numbers, for those who bear the crest of pearls never even think of quarreling (857–64):

> Although our corpses in clods cling,
> And ye remen for rauthe [cry for pity] without rest,
> We thoroughly have knowing [see 1 Cor. 13:12];
> Of one full death our hope is dressed [Rev. 2:11].
> The Lamb us gladdens; our care is cast [discarded];
> He mirths us all at each mass.
> Each one's bliss is breme [intense] and best,
> And yet never is one's honor ever the less.

This stanza draws on various biblical passages (some indicated above), but it also shows us the author reaching beyond what is explicitly available in Scripture to depict the enjoyment of the beatific vision as a celestial mass conducted by the Lamb himself. The basic source in Revelation is 14:1–5, where the 144,000 virgins sing a new song (Ps. 96:1) before the throne of God, and the remainder of section XV consists of a fairly close translation of these verses (865–900).

Deeply impressed by this vision, the Dreamer nevertheless cannot resist asking one more earth-bound question: where is such a large company of people housed? Surely it would not be good for them to lie out in the open! He is worried that he sees no buildings in the vicinity, and questions her referring to their dwelling place as Jerusalem, since that city is not here, but "in Judea." The Maiden explains the difference between the earthly and heavenly Jerusalems (Gal. 4:21–26), and interprets the name as meaning both "City of God" (cf. Rev. 3:12) and "Sight of Peace" (*Visio Pacis*, the standard medieval etymology). It is toward this city that we press (957–60):

> "That is the borough that we to press,
> From when our flesh be laid to rot,
> Where glory and bliss shall ever increase
> To the meyny [company] that is without mote [spot]."

To this the Dreamer responds (as naïve as ever) by asking to go with her (961–64):

> "Moteless maid so meek and mild,"
> Then said I to that lovely flower,
> "Bring me to that bigly bild [pleasant dwelling]
> And let me see thy blissful bower."

The Maiden gently tells him that God will not allow him to enter his tower, but adds that she has obtained permission from the Lamb for him to have a glimpse of "that clean cloister" from the outside (973–76):

> "If I this mote [city] to thee shall unhide [reveal],
> Bow up toward this burn's head,
> And I anent thee on this side
> Shall sue [follow], till thou to a hill be veved [come]."

These are the last words spoken between the two. Following her directions, the Dreamer reaches the hill, and from there sees the holy city "as devises it the apostle John" (984), the linking line for the stanzas of this section (XVII). The poet's description of the city mainly follows John's account of the new heaven and the new earth that replaces the fiery destruction of the world (Rev. 22), with particular emphasis on the precious stones on each of the twelve foundations. As we have already noted, the emphasis on twelve (the perfect number) in Revelation is preserved and even strengthened in the poem.

In section XVIII the brightness of the holy city is emphasized by using for the echo some variation of "sun and moon" from Revelation 21:33: *And the city had no need of the sun, neither of the moon, to shine in it: for the glory of God did lighten it, and the Lamb is the light thereof.* Here is the poet's version of this passge (1045–56):

> Of sun nor moon had they no need;
> The self God was their lamplight,
> The Lamb their lantern, without dread;
> Through him blysned [glistened] the borough all bright.
> Through wall and wone [house] my looking yede [went],
> For the subtle clarity did not let [obstruct] the light.
> The high throne there might ye heed
> With all the apparelment umbepight [set around],
> As John the apostle in terms tight [described];
> The high God's self it sat upon.
> A river from the throne there ran outright
> Was brighter than both the sun and moon.

Although there was no impurity in that city, the river flowed swiftly through the clean streets. There was no kirk, chapel, nor temple there, for the Almighty was their fit minster, and the Lamb their sacrifice to enjoy (Rev. 21:22). The gates were open to every road (21:25), although none but the spotless may take refuge there (21:27). The moon cannot steal any light from there, for it is never night. Indeed, why should the sun, or moon, or the planets vie with the light that shines from the brook's brim? All around the water are trees bearing the twelve kinds of fruit that renew themselves each month. This is indeed almost more than the Dreamer can bear to contemplate (1081–92):

> Under the moon so great a marvel
> No fleshly heart it might endure,
> As when I blushed [gazed] upon that bayle [city],
> So ferly [wondrous] thereof was the fasure [form].
> I stood as still as a dazed quail
> For ferly [wonder] of that frelich figure [noble allegory];

> So that felt I neither rest nor travail,
> So was I ravished with gleaming pure.
> For I dare say with conscience sure,
> Had bodily burne [man] abiden that boon [favor],
> Though all clerks [clergy] had him in cure [care],
> His life were lost under the moon.

We are reminded that when the Dreamer first saw the Pearl Maiden he "stood as hende [polite, quiet] as hawk in hall" (184). The effect is intensified here in the quail image, which is immediately followed by a troublesome line— troublesome because the word I have printed as "frelich" (following the majority of editors) is actually "freuch" in the manuscript. Cawley and Anderson thus print it, and render "freuch figure" as "frail vision," an attractive possibility. But it seems to me that the poet is stressing the *force* of the vision, not its fragility; hence my agreement with the other editors. There remains, however, the word "figure," which these editors gloss as "form" (Moorman) or "apparition" (Gordon). The latter is more to my liking, but "apparition" has modern connotations we can do without. I am inclined to link the use of figure here with the earlier statement of the poet concerning the appearance of the Pearl Maiden: "I hoped that ghostly [spiritual] were that purpose" (185). More specifically, one thinks of Chaucer's *ABC* (a prayer to the Virgin translated from Deguilleville), in which the burning bush witnessed by Moses was said to be a "sign" of the Virgin's unspotted maidenhood (92–94):

> Thou art the bush on which there gan descende
> The Holi Gost, the which that Moyses wende [thought]
> Had ben a-fyr; and this was in *figure*.

The Dreamer has been taught by the Maiden to distinguish the Jerusalem "in Judea" from the new Jerusalem, which is the dwelling place of the redeemed: hence his reference to the latter as a noble "figure" demonstrates his awareness that he has been allowed a glimpse of *the substance of things hoped for, the evidence of things not seen* (Hebrews 11:1). This is a perilous privilege, and the Dreamer is convinced that no "bodily" man could have seen that vision and lived—reminding us that he has been having an out-of-body experience since the beginning of the dream (61–62):

> From the spot my spirit there sprang in space;
> My body on balk [mound] there abode in sweven [swoon].

[221]

In pointing out the Dreamer's awareness of the nature of his experience implied in his use of the word "figure," I do not wish to overstate the case, because in the final two sections of the poem his intellectual awareness is more than counterpoised by a surge of emotion as he witnesses the entry of the 144,000 in the company of the Lamb into the new Jerusalem (1093–1104):

> Right as the mainful [mighty] moon doth rise
> Ere thence the day-gleam drive all down,
> So suddenly in a wondrous wise
> I was aware of a procession.
> This noble city of rich emprise [renown]
> Was suddenly full, without a summons,
> Of such virgins in the same guise
> As was my blissful one under crown;
> And all were crowned in the same fashion,
> Depaint [Adorned] in pearls and weeds [garments] white;
> In each one's breast was bounden boun [firmly fixed]
> The blissful pearl with great delight.

This great company glides rejoicing through golden streets made of glass, led by the Lamb with seven horns (Rev. 5:6), and dressed in pearly garments. They make their way toward the throne in orderly fashion (1114–16):

> Though they were fele [many], no press in plight [ranks],
> But mild as maidens seem at mass,
> So drew they forth with great delight.

When the Lamb draws near, the elders fall at his feet, and legions of angels cast incense abroad and sing a song in praise of the Lamb, the sound of which extends even to the earth and down into hell (Rev. 5:13). The Dreamer takes great delight in singing praise of the Lamb along with his retinue. While admiring the white garments of the Lamb and his gentle appearance, the Dreamer notices a single detail that runs counter to the happiness of that scene (1135–40):

> But a wound full wide and wet con wyse [did show]
> Anent his heart, through hide torente [the torn skin].
> From his white side his blood outsprent.
> Alas, thought I, who did that spite?
> Any breast for bale [sorrow] ought have forbrent [burned]
> Ere he therein had had delight.

This detail comes from John's statement that he beheld a Lamb *as it had been slain* (Rev. 5:6). But the note of sadness soon disappears, for the Dreamer no longer needs an interpreter: no one could doubt the joy of the Lamb, for there was no hint of hurt or wound in his glorious glances. Indeed all of his followers are filled to overflowing with life everlasting. In this moment of fulness and joy the Dreamer suddenly notices that the Pearl Maiden is no longer opposite him on the other shore (1147–52):

> Then saw I there my little queen
> That I wende [thought] had stood by me in slade.
> Lord, much of mirth was that she made
> Among her feres [companions], who was so white!
> That sight me gart [made] to think to wade
> For love-longing in great delight.

From this emotional height we see the Dreamer's sorrow turned to joy, his "love-danger" (11) turned to "love-longing" (1152). What happens at this critical moment, hinted at in the word "wade" (1151), is quite unexpected and yet completely natural (1153–64):

> Delight me drove in eye and ear,
> My man's mind to madding malt [melted].
> When I saw my frely [fair one], I would be there,
> Beyond the water though she were walt [kept].
> I thought that nothing might me deer [harm]
> To fetch me bur [a blow] and make me halt,
> And to start in the stream should none me steer [hinder],
> To swim the remnant, though I there swalt [died].
> But of that munt [intention] I was bitalt [shaken];
> It was not to my Prince's pay [liking].

He had been told that his body must lie in the cold clay before he could pass over this water (315–20), and yet he seeks to take the plunge here, after we have already seen evidence that he has learned much from the Maiden and from the subsequent vision granted him. Yet it may well be this foolish act that so endears the Dreamer to us, and renders believable his final acceptance of the Church's teachings about the destiny of his little queen.

It was not pleasing to my Prince, he says (echoing the first line of the poem), that I so rashly sought to fling myself into the water. For just as I reached the bank, the violence of my efforts suddenly woke me from my dream, and I found myself in that lovely arbor with my head resting on the mound where my Pearl had slipped away from me. It was painful to be taken so suddenly from that fair region, but I cried, "O Pearl, what you have told me in this vision is very precious" (1185–88):

> If it be very and sooth sermon [a true tale]
> That thou so stickest [art set] in garland gay,
> So well is me in this dole-dungeon
> That thou art to that Prince's pay [pleasure].

Indeed, if I had followed the instruction of Pearl, I might have been privileged to see more of God's mysteries. But man always wants more than he can have by right: therefore my joy was torn away from me, and I was cast out of those regions that last forever. Lord, mad are those who strive against thee! Thus we now see that the Dreamer is able to make the selfsame theological points that were earlier made for him by the Pearl Maiden, and his last view of her is beautifully expressed in the image of the new Jerusalem as a gay garland in which his Pearl is set as a precious ornament. The final stanza then sends us back into the world with a benediction (1201–12):

> To pay [please] the Prince or set him saght [be reconciled]
> It is full ethe [easy] to the good Christian;
> For I have found him, both day and naght [night],
> A God, a Lord, a friend full fine.
> Over this hyul [mound] this lote I laght [this lot I had],
> For pity of my pearl enclyin [inclined, bent];
> And then to God I it betaught
> In Christ's dear blessing and mine,
> Who in the form of bread and wine
> The priest us showeth each day.
> May he give [grant] us to be his homely hyne [servants]
> And precious pearls unto his pay [pleasure].

The *Pearl* poet was writing in the late fourteenth century, a time of crisis and uncertainty in England, probably during the reign of Richard II (1377–99). Some critics see in his poetry indications of the tensions of that age, but I must confess that I do not find it so. *Cleanness* perhaps comes closest to explicit dissatisfaction with the callousness of his contemporaries (especially the priesthood?), but through most of the poems shines the light of faith and calm reason, which inevitably prevail over the human weaknesses depicted in the prophet Jonah, in the excited and ignorant throng of *Saint Erkenwald*, and in the misguided but malleable Dreamer of the *Pearl*. If this is a time when the Age of Faith was beginning to crumble, and Church doctrine was being subjected to uneasy scrutiny, it does not manifest itself in these poems. Rather it seems to me that the biblical faith handed down by the saints shines throughout strong and clear. But England in the fourteenth century was made up of individuals, not all the same, and as we turn now to the last chapter of this survey, we come to a great work, one which not only is our finest example of a "biblical poem," but one that above all reflects the agony of its age.

CHAPTER FIVE

Piers the Plowman *as History*

O F all the literary works we have examined, none is more "biblical" than the English alliterative poem *Piers the Plowman*. Indeed, it could almost be said that this text offers itself to us as Scripture, as an extension of the Bible: Morton Bloomfield has even called it "a fourteenth century apocalypse." Certainly it is evident, even to the casual observer, that the text is sprinkled with quotations from the Latin Bible, and a closer inspection reveals passage after passage of biblical paraphrase and imitation. But as our knowledge of the poem has increased in modern times, the exact nature of its indebtedness to the Bible has become a more complex and difficult problem, for a number of reasons that should be mentioned before we turn to the poem itself for some answers.

For one thing, the text of *Piers the Plowman* exists in significantly different forms. For centuries it was known to the reading public only in the edition printed by Robert Crowley in 1550; but in the latter half of the nineteenth century, Walter W. Skeat, whose parallel text edition I will use for purposes of citation, proved that the poem existed in at least three distinct forms: the "A" version, a relatively short poem of some 2,500 lines; the "B" version (Crowley's edition), consisting of a revised and expanded A text plus a continuation of 4,000 lines; and the "C" version, about the same length as B, but substantially revised throughout.

In itself the existence of three versions of the poem need not be an obstacle, but in fact their relationship has been a matter of serious disagreement in this century, involving such important matters as dating and authorship. There is no room in this chapter for discussion of these issues, except to remark that authorship, chronology, and historical background are as important for understanding *Piers the Plowman* as they are for study of the biblical book of Isaiah. So let me simply say that in my opinion the theory of dual authorship provides the best hypothesis: one man wrote the A version and another wrote B and C. The first poem was completed in 1362, and the B revision and continuation, contrary to present scholarly opinion, in 1383; it is harder to date the final version, but the earliest likely date would be 1387, with completion of it perhaps as late as the 1390s. It seems unlikely that the two authors were acquainted, and it is entirely possible that the "collaboration" was posthumous—the A poet having died during the two decades that elapsed before the appearance of the B version. In a homemade conclusion to the A text (preserved in full in only one manuscript) a certain John But says of the author that "Death dealt him a dint," and there is no reason to doubt the truth of this. So the A poet probably did not live to see what drastic changes were made in his text.

In the fourteenth century, a poem became public property as soon as its text was made available to others for recopying. In France in the thirteenth century, Guillaume de Lorris wrote the *Roman de la Rose*, to which Jean de Meun wrote a continuation forty years later. In the case of *Piers the Plowman*, no particular name was decisively attached to the poem in the century of its birth. William (or Robert) Langland (or Langley), Willelmus W., John Malverne, and others are found in various manuscripts. One sixteenth-century writer referred to "that nameless," but modern students of the poem have settled on William Langland, and often speak as though there were evidence outside the manuscripts of his actual existence. I abstain from the use of this name, despite the awkwardness that results from the lack of a "handle," for two reasons: one is that using the name carries with it the implication that one man wrote all three versions, and the other is that I believe real names were deliberately not used at the time because of the explosiveness of the material the poem contains. We may never know for certain who wrote *Piers the Plowman*, any more than we are likely to uncover the names of authors of the numerous commentaries, sermons, and tracts that today are classified as Wycliffite or Lollard literature—and for similar reasons.

Valuable work has been done in recent years on *Piers the Plowman* as a doctrinal poem, but almost invariably at the expense of its historical significance. This chapter attempts, modestly enough, to redress the balance. Just as the Book of Isaiah remains an enigma to the reader with no knowledge of the history of Israel from the eighth to the sixth century B.C., so it is with *Piers the Plowman* without some awareness of the issues and events of English history in the latter half of the fourteenth century. Even as the Babylonian Exile is a watershed in biblical studies, likewise in *Piers the Plowman* a single great historical event looms over all: between the A and B versions of the poem falls the shadow of the Peasants' Revolt of 1381.

Our main concern will be to look at the versions of the poem in sequence, specifically the A and B texts, since space limitations prevent consideration of C. What will emerge from this, I hope, is at least the beginning of a synoptic view, which will allow us to see the complex and differing ways in which both poems (A and BC) draw on the Bible for inspiration. If this effort is successful, we will discover that the author of A, like Amos, calls out in a voice of prophetic anger for the establishment of justice in the gate. Twenty years later a reviser who has lived through the violence of 1381 radically rewrites the poem in order to paint an ominous picture of Armageddon.

England in Midcentury (1346–62)

The notorious reign of Edward II (1307–27) ended dramatically with the king's deposition and subsequent murder in Berkeley Castle in September 1327. Under the circumstances, things did not look promising for his son Edward III (1327–77). But the young king, who was as different from his father as could be imagined, quickly took over leadership of the nation and marshaled his forces for a war with France, which began in 1337 and led to a spectacular victory at Crécy in 1346. Other military triumphs followed, over both Scotland and France, and the successful outcome of the siege of Calais in 1347 enabled the English fleet to dominate the Channel, and from this seaport launch their attacks directly against France. The highlight of Edward's continental campaigns, now increasingly under the leadership of his son Edward (the Black Prince), was undoubtedly the capture of the French King John at Poitiers in 1356. Thereafter the English began to suffer reverses, along with a certain amount of fatigue, climaxed by Black Monday (April 14, 1360), when the king and his forces outside Paris were overawed by a dark cloud, which brought with it a freak hailstorm and bitter weather resulting in numerous deaths by freezing. The following month, Edward III signed a treaty at Brétigny waiving his claim to the French throne. But the English king did not come away entirely empty-handed: in addition to retaining Calais and certain territories, he obtained the promise of 3,000,000 crowns from the dauphin as ransom for the return of his father King John.

Through much of the fourteenth century, the Papacy was established in costly exile in Avignon, far removed from Rome and the customary sources of its income. Moreover, the Avignon popes tended to side with France in the conflict with England, so that their efforts to bring about peace had little effect. Even before the Great Schism (1378–1417), which began with an exchange of anathemas between Urban VI in Rome and Clement VII in Avignon, it was evident that the control of the Papacy over both church and state in western Europe was rapidly slipping away. So much for the great dream of Innocent III.

As papal power declined, ecclesiastical appointments to high position in the English church came increasingly under the control of the English crown. Church historian W. A. Pantin has pointed out a striking feature in the evolution of episcopal appointments in the thirteenth and fourteenth centuries: in the earlier period the reform bishops were distinguished scholars, while in the fourteenth century the bishops tended more and more to be strong administrators and astute politicians rather than learned men. This important change made itself felt throughout the ecclesiastical establishment, all the way down to the parish level, and is even reflected in the satirical portraits of worldly churchmen in the prologue to Chaucer's *Canterbury Tales*. Especially in the latter half of the century, it was evident that the Christian Church in England was rapidly becoming a temple of the kingdom (Amos 7:15).

Despite its growing worldliness, the Church itself nurtured articulate critics of the established order. Some of this criticism appeared in the (largely anonymous) literature of social satire, but much of it was uttered fearlessly from the pulpit by legions of conscientious preachers, as G. R. Owst has shown. An impartial observer in the fourteenth century would have seen in the English church a house divided against itself: on the one hand, there were the "regular" clergy, living on vast and wealthy estates, acquisitive, socially conservative, and bent on preserving the status quo; on the other hand, there were the "secular" clergy, from whose ranks came the priests who served their parishes in the manner of Chaucer's humble parson. Neither of these groups had a monopoly on righteousness, but it was clearly from the secular clergy that a challenge to the social order would have to come. Between these two groups stood the friars, and the stresses that produced the cleavage between seculars and regulars also brought about a division within the fraternal orders, particularly the Franciscans, whose members disagreed on the question of apostolic poverty. The Conventuals took a more conservative line, while the Spiritual Franciscans insisted that Christ and the Apostles had not owned property, and that this was intended as a model for the Christian life. Clearly their position was not designed to make the "possessioners" feel comfortable, and in 1323 a bull issued by Pope John XXII declared this a heretical interpretation.

By midcentury it was clear that the Spiritual Franciscans had lost control of the fraternal movement. The orders retained a kind of fictional poverty, largely by assigning custody of their houses and property to laymen while retaining actual possession. According to the rule, they were not to touch money; they got around this by wearing gloves. Still, this is only one side of the picture. The friars had produced a succession of great scholars during the early days of reform, mainly the thirteenth century; and even in the period we are studying they retain a strong emphasis on education, at least enough to arouse jealousy in the secular clergy, whose ranks were not without their share of ignorant priests. The hostility between these groups was particularly evident in Oxford, and the former chancellor of the University, Richard FitzRalph, delivered sermons critical of the friars in London from the pulpit of Saint Paul's in 1356–57, and these were matched with sermons by fraternal preachers highly critical of the secular clergy. To the pious London worshiper it must have seemed that Manasseh was devouring Ephraim, and Ephraim Manasseh. But behind all these conflicts and passionate arguments lay a genuine concern for the proper role of the Church in dealing with the escalating problems of wealth, poverty, war, and corruption as they affected both church and state.

In the midst of war, schism, oppression, and greed, were there any signs of God's displeasure? Indeed there were. Across the face of Europe and to the shores of England in 1348–49 came the pestilence known as the Black Death. An entire population stood helpless in the path of the King of Terrors. A general power was given to all priests, both secular and regular, to hear confession and grant absolution, while the mortality rate for the clergy itself was awesome. Prices at first slumped, because no one sought to buy anything out of a general fear of death; and the ordinary functions of society broke down, since, according to Knighton, "there was such a great scarcity of servants that no one knew what he ought to do" (Dobson, p. 60). The scholarly Thomas Bradwardine, newly consecrated archbishop of Canterbury, arrived in London in August 1349 and was dead within two days. *Timor mortis conturbat me.* Countless generations had been told repeatedly that the social order to which they belonged had been established by God. Now for the first time it may have become possible for many to question the permanence of that order, and to think that there might be alternatives to it. The plague changed everything; there is scarcely a single development in the remainder of the century that does not owe something to its impact. It is no coincidence that in a few short years there emerged the popular rhyme:

> When Adam delved and Eve span,
> Who was then the gentleman?

Whatever might have been in the hearts and minds of the people, it was the king and council who first responded to the catastrophe, and this response took the form of a statute designed to force laborers to remain on the job and to freeze wages at pre-plague levels. The initial action of 1349 was followed in 1351 by the Statute of Laborers, which spelled out a harsh enforcement designed to hold the workers in check. Needless to say the law was not well received, since in a much reduced population, laborers were very much in demand, and the natural tendency was for wages to rise, as indeed they did, despite repeated legislation by a succession of parliaments.

When ancient Israel suffered a catastrophic earthquake, Isaiah quoted their reaction as, *The bricks have fallen down, but we will build with hewn stones,* a far cry from the response demanded by the prophet: *For the people turneth not unto him that smiteth them, neither do they seek the Lord of hosts* (Isa. 9:10, 13). In like manner, the

English leadership turned to mechanisms for preserving the status quo in the face of disaster rather than seek the Lord. This absence of moral seriousness in fact seems to have characterized English government policy for the remainder of the reign of the aging Edward III. Neither the vicious return of the pestilence in 1361 nor the growing resentment of an oppressed people seems to have affected the policies of either church or state. But at this very moment, a prophet arose whose messsage is preserved for us in the earliest version of the poem known as *Piers the Plowman*. And it was this version—*not* the revisions that appeared later— which was to be embraced and exploited by the leaders of the Peasants' Revolt.

Piers the Plowman: The A Version (*1362*)

A glance at the poem as a whole shows us that it is in reality two poems; the first, called the *Visio* (Vision), contains an introductory section (a prologue and passus I or book I); an allegorical action set in London at Westminster (passus II–IV); a pivotal confession of the cardinal sins (passus V); a second allegorical action in a rural setting introducing Piers, the good plowman (passus VI–VII); and finally a dramatic conclusion in which Piers is given a pardon by St. Truth, and the Dreamer awakens (passus VIII). This *Visio* is followed immediately by a second and related poem entitled "The Life of Dowel Dobetter and Dobest," consisting of a prologue, passus I, and passus II (Skeat A passus IX– XI), usually referred to as the *Vita* (Life), after the first word of its Latin title. Although the *Vita* is also in the form of a dream, there is no real allegorical action. Instead, various allegorical spokesmen seek to answer the Dreamer's questions concerning what constitutes a truly upright life and where in the various ranks of society it may be found.

In the opening of the *Visio*, the poet tells us that on a May morning in Malvern hills he paused beside a stream, weary with wandering, and soon went to sleep to the sound of its waters (A Prol. 11–19):

> Then 'gan I mete a marvelous sweven [dream]
> That I was in a wilderness, wist I never where;
> But as I beheld into the east, on high to the sun,
> I saw a Tower on a toft [hill] truly made;
> A deep dale beneath, a dungeon therein,
> With deep ditches and dark, and dreadful of sight.

A fair field full of folk found I there between,
Of all manner of men, the mean and the rich,
Working and wandering, as the world asketh.

In this prologue the poet shows us the everyday world of four-teenth-century England against a backdrop of eternity: Heaven and Hell, as represented by the tower and the dungeon. Thus the standard Christian values are to be used to judge the behavior of the folk in the field. It is quickly apparent that some are good and others bad. Some plow the land and work hard, while "was-ters" greedily consume what the workers produce. Worthy an-chorites stay in their cells, unlike those who wander about the countryside living a life of self-indulgence. There are good min-strels, a legitimate profession, but there are also "japers and jan-glers, Judas' children," who play the fool even though they have the intelligence to work for a living if they would. There are beg-gars who feign handicaps for food, fight in the alehouse, and lead lives of ribaldry and sloth.

In his roll call of the professions, the Dreamer presents a series of vignettes reminiscent of Chaucer's portraits in the General Pro-logue of *The Canterbury Tales*. Indeed a storytelling pilgrimage like that of Chaucer is briefly described (A Prol. 46–49):

Pilgrims and palmers plight them together
For to seek St. James and saints at Rome;
Went forth on their way with many wise tales
And had leave to lie all their life after.

At the end of their journey, instead of the customary indulgence, these pilgrims are granted permission to tell lies for the rest of their lives: the poet's contempt for such pilgrimages is quite ev-ident, both here and later on in the poem.

In the field we see friars preaching to the people for personal profit, glossing the gospel to make it conform to their greed. These friars, unlike their predecessors, are well dressed, and make it their business to hear the confessions of great lords, not the com-mon people. And the Dreamer adds ominously: unless Holy Church and these friars can hold together, the greatest mischief on earth is rapidly approaching. In these lines the poet seems to allude to the hostilities between friars and seculars made public in the sermons at Saint Paul's (1356–57). Yet, as we shall see, the friars are no more roughly handled than other representatives of church or state. Not until we come to the revision of the poem

[233]

will we find the friars singled out for special, and very unfriendly, attention.

There is little love for pardoners in fourteenth-century satirical literature: even Chaucer seems to regard his pardoner as the one unredeemable soul in the company on the road to Canterbury. Equally reprehensible is the one who appears among the folk of the field (A Prol. 65–72):

> There preached a pardoner, as he a priest were,
> Brought forth a bull with bishop's seals,
> And said that himself might absolve them all
> Of falseness of fasting and of vows broken.
> Lewed [Uneducated] men believed him well, and liked his speech,
> Came up kneeling to kiss his bull;
> He bunched them with his brevet [indulgence], and bleared their eye,
> And reached with his ragman [scroll] rings and broaches.

There is anger in this description, but it is also controlled, with a skillful play on words. The pardoner pokes the people in the face with his scroll, "blearing their eye" (which also means to deceive), and then uses the scroll like a croupier's stick to rake in the offerings. But our poet cannot long sustain this ironical detachment, and so he angrily addresses the poor victims of the pardoner's guile: Thus you give your gold to help gluttons, and leave it with lechers! If the bishop who allowed his seal to be used were truly blessed, the people might not be deceived; and the guilt must be shared by those parish priests who allow the pardoner to preach and then divide the offering with him. All of them are taking money that should go to the poor people of the parish.

Are the secular clergy any better than the others? Parsons and parish priests complain that the pestilence has reduced their income, and ask their bishop for permission to go to London "to sing there for simony, for silver is sweet." And what about lawyers (A Prol. 84–89)?

> There hovered a hundred in hoods of silk,
> Sergeants, it seemed, that served at the bar;
> They plead for pence and pounds the law,
> And not for love of our Lord unloose their lips once.
> Thou mightest better mete [measure] the mist on Malvern hills
> Than got a "hmmm" of their mouth ere money were shown.

The roll call continues with ecclesiastics of all ranks, from bishop

[234]

to deacon, going to London to take lucrative positions in the government as accountants or clerks of the king's bench. All ranks of society are represented in the field, from barons to bondmen, and many crafts: bakers, butchers, brewers, weavers, tailors, masons, miners, ditchers, and delvers. The prologue ends with the refrain of a popular song mingling with London street cries.

The prologue of *Piers the Plowman* has taught us to expect a balanced treatment of the various representatives of society. But we are not to demand impartiality, for, subtly but surely, the sheep are to be separated from the goats: those whose allegiance is to the tower are distinguished from those destined for the dungeon. Already we have seen hints that members of the establishment in London, both church and state, are corrupt, and that integrity is to be found, if anywhere, in the hinterlands among those who put themselves to the plow. In the words of Micah (1:5): *What is the transgression of Jacob? Is it not Samaria?*

From the tower on the hill comes a lovely lady to answer the Dreamer's questions and expound the basic Christian doctrines that are to guide his understanding throughout the poem, both *Visio* and *Vita*. In function she is reminiscent of Boethius's Lady Philosophy, but in fact she is Holy Church, and she begins by reviewing for the Dreamer certain fundamentals of Christian teaching. In the tower, she says, is Truth (God), who created you to worship him during your life on earth. He has given you clothing, food, and drink for your nourishment, and it is up to you not to use anything (such as drink) to excess (A I 33–35):

> Measure is medicine, though thou much yearn:
> All is not good to the ghost that the gut asketh,
> Nor liflode [sustenance] to the lykam [body] that lief is to the soul.

With such trenchant wisdom Holy Church warns the Dreamer against the dangers of the world, the flesh, and the devil. Believe not your body, she adds—in case her listener was foolish enough to think that the gut is always right—for a liar teaches your flesh in order to betray you if he can.

To whom does the money of this world belong? asks the Dreamer, and the lady replies (Mark 12:17): *Render to Caesar the things that are Caesar's, and to God the things that are God's.* Entrust your worldly treasure to reason and common sense. She then goes on to tell him that Wrong inhabits the dungeon in the dale, the "father of falsehood," that is the Devil, who incited Adam and

Eve to disobedience, counseled Cain to kill his brother, and deceived Judas with Jewish silver.

When the Dreamer wonderingly asks who she is, the lady responds with "Holy Church am I—you ought to know me: I received you first (at the baptismal font), and taught you your faith." Whereupon the Dreamer falls to his knees and asks her to tell him how to save his soul. "Truth is the best," says the lady, taking as her text *Deus caritas* (God is love, 1 John 4:8). For he who lives by truth, trustworthy in his speech, his deeds matching his words, with malice toward none, is called a god by the gospel (Luke 6:35; cf. Ps. 82:6 and John 10:34).

The reader acquainted with doctrinal literature of the period will have noticed that the teaching of Holy Church is remarkable for its simplicity. The stance of the poet is that of the prophets (Amos 5:15): *Hate the evil, and love the good, and establish judgment in the gate.* Do you want to avoid an eternity in the dungeon of Wrong? Then you must obey the teaching of the Bible (A I 119–22):

> But those that work the word that Holy Writ teaches,
> And end, as I ere said, in perfect works,
> May be siker [certain] that their soul shall wend to heaven,
> Where Truth is in Trinity and enthroneth them all.

In short, *Be ye therefore perfect* (Matt. 5:48). And the lady concludes her sermon with a curious exhortation (A I 125–25):

Lereth [Teach] it these lewed [uneducated] men, for lettered it knoweth
That Truth is treasure, truest on earth.

If we have not yet perceived the poet's viewpoint, we might jump to the conclusion that all is well with learned men, who know the gospel, and that it is the poor who stand in desperate need. But as we shall see, it is in fact the plowmen of this world who are destined for salvation, while the educated class, in both church and state, are sinking down into hell. This point is brought out in the conclusion to passus I by one of the author's favorite devices: he has the Dreamer ask a foolish question, which triggers an angry response from his teacher (A I 127–33):

> "Yet have I no kind knowing," quoth I, "ye must
>   kenne [teach] me better,
> By what craft in my corpse it cometh, and where."
> "Thou doted daffe," quoth she, "dull are thy wits!

> It is a kind knowing that kenneth in thine heart
> For to love thy Lord liefer than thyself;
> No deadly sin to do, die though thou shouldest."

The Dreamer here plays the role of the intellectual, intent on an understanding of psychological process, rather than simple acceptance of the divine imperative. After her initial angry explosion, Lady Holy Church patiently and movingly describes how the love of God was expressed by Christ's death on the cross. This love, she continues, was meant to be an example to us: the rich should help the poor, and priests should set an example of generosity to their parishioners (A I 149–73). These lines should be read aloud, with feeling, so that their tone can be appreciated. The poet is evenhanded in his criticism of all ranks, including laborers, but some feel the heat of his passion more than others. This is an angry passage, in which rich people and avaricious chaplains are rebuked by a poet who is alienated from them, and has little hope that they will respond to his criticisms. *And I will smite the winter house with the summer house; and the houses of ivory shall perish, and the great houses shall have an end, saith the Lord* (Amos 3:15). Holy Church is more careful than Amos to remind the listener of God's positive mandate (A I 180–81):

> Love is the liefest thing that our Lord asketh,
> And eke the graith [strait] gate that goeth into heaven.

But her message to the rich and powerful is just as severe.

Lady Meed at Westminster

Before Holy Church bids farewell to the Dreamer, she draws back a curtain (as it were) in one part of the field, to reveal a gathering of people around Lady Meed, who is to hold center stage in the first allegorical action. "Meed" means reward, or as it turns out bribery, and so it is not surprising that around this lady are gathered the various officers and practitioners who make up the government of the nation. These corrupt functionaries seek to bring about a marriage between Meed and Falsehood, and they end up at the seat of the English government in Westminster where the king is advised by Conscience and Reason to prohibit the marriage (A II–IV). After the cleansing of society in the confession scene (A V), the people turn to Piers, the humble plowman, to lead them to Truth (A VI–VIII). Thus we see that the *Visio* as

[237]

a whole is dominated by the two figures of Lady Meed and Piers, representatives on earth of the dungeon and the tower. We are clearly told which side we should choose, but the genius of the author shows in his ability to reveal the complexity of the social problems he addresses, even as he simultaneously deflates the pretensions of the worldly through irony and satire.

In obedience to Holy Church's command, the Dreamer looks to his left (A II 7–14):

> I looked on my left half, as the lady me taught
> And was aware of a woman, wonderly clothed,
> Purfled with a pelure [fur], the purest upon earth,
> Crowned with a crown, the king hath none better.
> All her five fingers were fretted with rings
> Of the pursest perrie [gems] that prince wore ever;
> In red scarlet robed, and ribboned with gold:
> There was no queen quainter that quick is alive.

Who is this woman? asks the Dreamer, and in her parting speech Holy Church leaves us in no doubt. She has often annoyed me, the lady says, and criticized my teaching to lords. In the pope's palace she is as familiar as I am—but she should not be so, for Wrong is her sire, while I come of a higher lineage (God). She then informs the Dreamer of the intended marriage of Meed and False. Stay away from all these if you wish to dwell with Truth! She then commends him to the Lord, and leaves him to interpret what he sees with no further help from her. Nevertheless, as we shall see, the Dreamer will not be without assistance from particular spokesmen for Truth such as Theology, Conscience, and Reason, all of whom speak out at critical moments in the drama.

The first to protest is Theology, when he hears the feoffment (in the form of a pact with the Devil) prepared by False for his marriage with Meed, and proclaimed publicly by Simony and Civil Law. In protesting this marriage Theology claims that Meed is actually a legitimate offspring of Amends (payment for services rendered), and that God intends to give Meed to Truth: *for the workman is worthy of his meat* (Matt. 10:10). After denouncing Simony and Civil for ruining Holy Church and harming the people, Theology tells them to take Meed to London and get a legal opinion on the proposed marriage.

The intervention of Theology triggers a grimly amusing scene in which all the machinery of bribery is set in motion to arrange the legalization of Meed's marriage to False in the court at West-minster. Favel (Flattery) fetches florins, ordering Guile to distrib-ute them to Simony, Civil, and Falsewitness, who in turn prom-ise False that they will make Meed his lawfully wedded wife. Amid all this hubbub there is a cry for horses, and Favel quickly fetches forth beasts of burden: Meed sits on a sheriff, False on a juryman, Simony and Civil on a pair of summoners, while bishops ride on deans and subdeans decked out like war-horses. A commissioner (bishop's deputy) is hitched to Civil's cart and ordered to fetch supplies from fornicators, while Liar pulls a large wagon carrying the remaining crowd of fools and deceivers. Behind this artful allegory we may detect not only a sense of humor but also moral outrage. The commissioner's use of a system of fines as a source of personal income is especially repugnant, and reminds us of Amos's angry denunciation of fines used by the Israelite priest-hood to maintain the Temple wine supply (Amos 2:8).

Word of this legal conspiracy reaches the king, who orders the arrest of the ringleaders, and specifically commands that Meed be brought before him. But Dread hears the king's instructions and hurries to warn the conspirators. Terrified, Falseness flies to the friars, Guile escapes and is hired as a merchant's apprentice, while Liar lurks through lanes, unwelcome and driven off be-cause of his many tales. We then follow the trail of this fugitive as he is taken in by pardoners, physicians, grocers, messengers, and friars. He helps the pardoners turn indulgences into mer-chandise; he is invited to conduct urinalyses for physicians; he shows grocers how to use additives to sell their decaying food; he hangs out with minstrels and messengers; and he is dressed as a friar and invited to stay with them as often as he wishes. When all the conspirators have fled, only lady Meed remains; and she trembles and weeps when she is arrested.

Despite the fact that Meed is technically in custody when she arrives in London, she is warmly received, for, as the poet re-marks, "They that woneth at Westminster worship her all" (A III 12). A delegation of justices calls on the lady and promises to help her gain the approval of the king, in spite of all that Con-science may do. Meed rewards them richly, and promises quick advancement to a group of clerks who offer to help her. A friar volunteers to be her confessor, assuring her that for a small con-sideration he will forgive her any and all sins, and that if she should finance the glazing of one of their windows, not only would her name be inscribed in the glass for all to see, but her soul would be assured of salvation. At this point the poet's restraint deserts him, and he speaks out angrily against such abuses. God strictly prohibited engraving of names when he said *Let not thy left hand know what thy right hand doeth* (Matt. 6:3). Those who thus proclaim their good deeds in public should beware lest worldly recognition be their only recompense, as our Savior said: *Verily I say unto you, they have their reward* (Matt. 6:2).

One other abuse that triggers the poet's wrath is Meed's attempt to bribe the Mayor of London. She intercedes on behalf of retailers, who are offering bribes so that the Mayor, as the one charged with enforcement, will not crack down when they inflate their prices. "For my love," says that lady, "love them each one, and suffer them to sell somewhat against reason" (A III 82–83). But as the author angrily points out, mayors and magistrates are appointed precisely to punish those who prey on poor people who must buy piecemeal. Instead they get rich through such bribes, with what the poor should be putting in their stomachs. You can be sure that if these officials were not corrupt, they would not build themselves such magnificent homes, nor would they own so many tenements. They had better remember what Scripture says about this (Job 15:34): *fire shall consume the tabernacles of bribery*. Although the poet is "merely" quoting the Bible here, the passage might well have caused corrupt officials to tremble. In less than twenty years, some of the great houses of London were destined to go up in flames.

The remainder of passus III is taken up with a debate before the king between Meed and Conscience. The king wants to forgive the lady and give her in marriage to Conscience, but the latter will not agree and launches into a denunciation of Meed: she is unreliable and a source of corruption; she killed your father (Edward II), poisoned popes (perhaps Benedict XI?), and has damaged Holy Church; she allows herself to be kept by all who can pay for her, and she frustrates the judicial process; like Chaucer's summoner she knows that "purse is the archdeacon's hell," and pays off the bishop's commissioner without fear of bell, book, or candle; she is a good friend of pope, bishop, and parson; the king's justices are ruined by her, and a faithful man can make no headway in court against the blizzard of her florins; lawyers defend only the wealthy, and poor men have no power to bring suit against injustice, so powerful is Meed!

The king is impressed by Conscience's indictment, but allows the lady to defend herself, and it is a tribute to the poet's artistry that she does so very skillfully. You know very well, Conscience, she says, that you yourself have depended on me many times. I did not kill any king, as you falsely accused me of doing, whereas you courted military disaster by making the king interpret the dark cloud and the cold weather in France as God's disapproval of the war, whereas I encouraged him to adhere to his military objectives. If it had not been for you, and if I'd had my way, the king would have become lord of all France, the richest of all realms! Besides, kings, emperors, and even popes must have meed to provide sustenance for those that serve them; all ranks of society, from priest to beggar, require meed as recompense for their services. In short, Meed makes the world go round.

To this persuasive presentation the king responds enthusiastically: "By Christ, as me thinketh, Meed is worthy the mastery to have!" (A III 221–22). But Conscience responds by distinguishing between "meed measureless," an unearned reward, and "measurable hire," just payment for services rendered. "Meed measureless" can be good, as when God graciously grants his servants on earth a heavenly reward, and it is bad when magistrates accept payment from evildoers; while "measureable hire" is as legitimate as barter, in which no money changes hands. In short, money is not in itself evil: everything depends on the use to which it is put. Once again the Bible is invoked: the good man is *He that putteth not out his money to usury, nor taketh reward against the innocent* (Ps. 15:5); it is corrupt officialdom *in whose hands is mischief, and their right hand is full of bribes* (Ps. 26:10).

Conscience concludes with a sermon based on 1 Samuel 15, which recounts the war between Israel and Amalek during the reign of Saul. The point of this story is that soldiers engaged in a holy war are not to take booty for themselves. Saul violated this rule when he allowed his troops to seize cattle and himself spared King Agag, perhaps with a view to collecting ransom. So it was meed that got the king in trouble: indeed God said to Samuel that Saul should die, and his hatred of this sin even extended to the king's descendants. I will not take the time, says Conscience, to point the moral (*culorum*) of this story: lest I get into trouble, I'll bring it to an end.

Whether the powers that be ever heard or read this sermon of Conscience is a matter of conjecture. But it seems altogether likely that some of the peasants did. Knighton reports that when the rebels were destroying John of Gaunt's palace, the Savoy, in June 1381 (Dobson, p. 184): "One of the criminals chose a fine piece of silver and hid it in his lap; when his fellows saw him carrying it, they threw him, together with his prize, into the fire, saying that they were lovers of truth and justice, not robbers and thieves." This incident is reminiscent of an earlier episode in the Bible involving holy war, when Achan son of Carmi was burned to death by Joshua for looting during the invasion of Canaan (Josh. 7). In any case it is noteworthy that the rebels sought to keep their forces under the discipline of holy war, thus showing that they understood very well the *culorum* of Conscience's sermon.

But we should be careful to distinguish between the future impact of the poem on others and the intention of the author at the time of writing. For an understanding of this we have only Conscience's dark prophecy (A III 266–71):

> I, Conscience, know this, for kind wit me taught,
> That reason shall reign, and realms govern;
> And right as Agag had, happen shall some;
> Samuel shall slay him, and Saul shall be blamed,
> And David shall be diademed and daunt them all,
> And one Christian king keep us each one.

We are still fifteen years away from the death of Edward III: does the poet envision some kind of disruption during the inevitable transfer of power? If so, he sees it as a hopeful event, leading to the establishment of a king who will walk in the ways of David. Like the prophets of old, the author of the A text is fundamentally optimistic, despite his dire warnings about the state of the nation. Thus he allows Conscience to end his sermon, not with gloom and doom, but with faith in the future of the country. No more shall Meed be master, but instead love, lowness, and integrity (leaute). If anyone goes against the truth, he shall receive strict justice, or even lose his life. No longer shall lawyers become wealthy, as they are now: they have become lordly, while real justice is poor and banished from society. Indeed, things are going to change (A III 281–82):

> But kind wit shall come yet, and conscience together,
> And make of law a laborer, such love shall arise.

Having heard both sides, the king now insists on a reconciliation, and orders Conscience to kiss Lady Meed. But Conscience refuses to do anything without the advice of Reason, who is then sent for and set on the bench in Westminster between the king and his son (the Black Prince). Is it possible to implement Conscience's brave new world, where reason governs? In passus IV we are given a test case, in which the integrity of the king is pitted against corruption, and integrity wins.

Peace comes into parliament and registers a complaint against Wrong. It is quickly evident that Peace is an ordinary citizen, and Wrong is an unscrupulous and powerful lord. Wrong has raped and stolen and cheated with impunity, and even maintains a small army of retainers by whose presence Peace and his neighbors are intimidated and, until now, reluctant to go to law. The poet confides that the king knew these charges were true, "for Conscience told him" (A IV 48), suggesting that this king can see beyond the surface of things, will judge the poor with righteousness, and will *reprove with equity for the meek of the earth* (Isa. 11:4).

Indeed the king's integrity is soon tested by a pair of shysters named Warren Wisdom and Witty, who advise Wrong to seek the help of Lady Meed. But when they approach the king with their bribes, the king orders Wrong to be put in irons, swearing, "He shall not these seven years see his feet once!" (A IV 73). Seeing that the king cannot be bought off, the two lawyers bring Meed to Peace and offer him compensation to settle out of court. Peace (the poor man) agrees with this, and appeals to the king to dismiss the charges against Wrong, but the latter refuses, declaring that such an action would encourage Wrong to break the law in future. Unless Reason has pity on him, says the king, he shall remain in the stocks.

When the king's rigorous decision is announced, some beseech Reason to allow Meed to provide bail for the prisoner. Whereupon Reason launches into an eloquent statement of the conditions under which he is willing to have mercy on breakers of the law (A IV 100–110):

> Reed [Advise] me not, quoth Reason, no ruth [pity] to have,
> Til lords and ladies love all truth
> And Purnel's purfle [lace] is put in her hutch [closet];
> Til children's cherishing be chastised with yards [rods]
> And harlots' holiness be holden for an hyne
>   [regarded as commonplace];
> Til clerks and knights be courteous of their mouths,

And hate to hear harlotry or mouth it;
Til priests their preaching prove it themselves,
And do it in deed to draw us to good;
Til St. James be sought where I shall assign,
That no man go to Galicia but if he go forever . . .

From this it is clear that when Reason is finally willing to show mercy, mercy will no longer be necessary. As we shall see, this kind of militant irony is a recurrent feature of the A text, and will reappear later in Truth's pardon for Piers.

For the present, Reason summarizes his doctrine in the proverb, "No evil unpunished, no good unrewarded." If you follow this rule, he says, I will guarantee (A IV 130–31):

That law shall be a laborer and lead afield dung,
And love shall lead thy land, as thee lief liketh.

When the court hears this verdict, Meed is laughed to scorn, Wisdom and Witty are for once left speechless, and the king asks Reason to stay with him as long as he lives. In the afterglow of this upbeat ending, we sense only a minor hint of hostility in the assignment of lawyers to the task of spreading manure in the fields. Twenty year later, however, the rebels marching on London were to kill every lawyer they encountered, just as a matter of principle. To what extent can "the power of the word" be invoked to link the poet's attitude toward lawyers with the deeds of the peasants? I do not favor any such connection, although for the author's own sake I trust that, by the time of the rising, death had dealt him a dint.

The Confession Scene

Next the Dreamer sees the folk of the field assembled to hear a sermon by Conscience designed to prepare them for confession. In view of what we have noted earlier about the impact of the plague in 1361–62, it is not surprising that Conscience uses this catastrophe to urge the people to turn unto him that smiteth them. He shows them that the pestilence resulted from sin, and that most recently it was pride that caused the great southwest wind on Saturday evening (January 15, 1362): fruit trees were blown down, ye men, to warn you to do better! Beeches and oaks were flattened, turning tail upward as if in fear of the destruction that is certain to come to sinners before Doomsday.

But this is not a sermon on the Apocalypse. Conscience calls attention to these warning signs because he wants to see justice roll down like waters, and righteousness as a mighty stream (Amos 5:24). Like all true prophets, he is not merely "against sin"; he spells out exactly what the people are to do. Wasters are to go to work and earn a living by some craft; Purnel is to put away her finery; Thomas is to take two sticks and teach his wife how to stay out of trouble; Wat is to restrain his wife's appetite for expensive headdress; merchants are to discipline their children and not indulge them simply because they can afford it. He urges prelate and priest to obey their own sermons and set an example for the people. And what about the religious, who live under a monastic rule? Hold strictly to your rule, says Conscience, lest the king and his council put a crimp in your income, and take custody of it until you reform. And all you pilgrims who seek Saint James and saints of Rome: seek instead Saint Truth, for he may save you all.

In response to this eloquent appeal, representative sinners step forth from the crowd to confess. The general purpose of this scene is to depict the cleansing of society in preparation for the pilgrimage to Saint Truth recommended by Conscience. But like so many of the devices used in the poem, this episode provides incidental satire on human weaknesses represented by the personified sins. In this connection it is interesting to observe that these sins are not given equal time: Purnel, representing Pride, vows to remove her fine clothing and substitute a hair shirt in order to humble her high heart; Lechery merely swears to eat only one meal on Saturdays and go on the wagon ("drink but with the duck"); Wrath does not appear at all in the A version, and one is tempted to conclude (barring accidental loss in copying) that the poet prefers not to denounce this sin, which might so easily be confused with righteous anger, an emotion that he clearly approves and has utilized in the writing of his poem. This leaves four sins that get most of the attention: Envy, Covetousness, Gluttony, and Sloth.

Envy comes dressed in a great coat, and his sleeves are like those of a friar. He bites his lips with suppressed anger, his clenched fist reveals vindictiveness, and this unhealthy emotional attitude has affected his digestion. He confesses the sin of back-biting against his neighbor; yet when he meets him in the marketplace, he greets him like a friend because he is afraid of him. "But had I mastery and might," he says, "I would murder him forever!" (A V 85). In church he asks Christ to bring sorrow on the thief who took his bowl and his torn sheet, and gazes enviously on the new clothes worn by a fortunate couple in the sanctuary. When they suffer losses, he laughs; when they prosper, he weeps and wails. Thus I live loveless, he confesses, like a wretched dog, my breast swelling from the bitterness of my gall. No patent medicine seems to do my system any good: if confession should help, it would be a miracle. His confessor, Repentance, seizes this opportunity to urge him to mend his ways: "Sorrow for sin saveth very many." Playing on two meanings of the word sorrow (remorse and enviousness), the wretched sinner concludes:

> I am sorry, quoth Envy, I am but seldom other[wise];
> And that maketh me so mad, for I ne may me avenge.

Next comes the gaunt figure of Covetousness, dressed in a threadbare coat, whose confession is an inventory of the practices of Guile in borough: as an apprentice he learned to lie and weigh falsely; when his master sent him to the fair with his merchandise, it would never have been sold in seven years, had not the "grace of guile" gone with him. Then I signed up with the drapers, he says, to learn my Donet (grammar): how to stretch out the cloth until ten or twelve yards measured thirteen. My wife used deceptive practices, both in weaving and in brewing: her name is Rose the retailer, and she has been a huckster these eleven years. But now I repent all this: my wife and I shall go on pilgrimage to Walsingham, and pray the true cross to bring me out of debt.

Gluttony is on his way to confession when he is hailed by Betty the brewster and invited into the tavern for a drink. Soon he is engaged in a drinking contest with a small army of disreputable companions, and ends up so drunk that he can scarcely make it home. Stumbling on the threshold, he passes out completely, leaving his wife and a serving girl with the unpleasant task of dragging him to his bed. After sleeping through the weekend, he wakes up, wipes his eyes and asks, "Where is the bowl?" But when his wife rebukes him for his wickedness, he is ashamed and vows to fast on Fridays.

Sloth is the final sin to step forward, unless we count Robert the robber as a separate member of the group. If we set aside the possibility of scribal error, it would appear to me that Sloth *is* Robert the robber, meaning that a life of thievery is the result of sloth—a perverse unwillingness to work hard in the normal way. This would explain Sloth's vow to restore his "wicked winnings." It is not the most common view of the sin, but, as we have noted, the poet often gives traditional concepts his own emphasis (Robert is put under Covetousness in the C version). The confession ends with Robert's prayer that Christ will forgive him as he did the penitent thief on the cross, and his tearful promise to reform his life. This repentance then merges with that of the folk in the field (A V 260–63):

> A thousand of men tho [then] thronged together,
> Weeping and wailing for their wicked deeds,
> Cried upward to Christ, and to his clean mother,
> To have grace to seek Truth, so God leave that they might.

Piers and the Plowing of the Half Acre

We have been shown what is wrong with society, and we have seen the repentance of the folk in the field. Now we are to meet the hero of the poem, Piers the plowman himself, who is the poet's answer to Lady Meed: a man of integrity. There are those among modern interpreters of the poem who would tell us that Piers is in some sense fallible, or that his way to Truth stands in need of improvement. Nothing could be farther from the truth: Piers is intended as a model for us all, even when he appears to be confessing himself a sinner, and the path to Truth which he offers is derived from basic Christian doctrine, sufficient in every way for salvation. If there is any hint to the contrary, it is to be found in the revisions which, as we have noted, are the work of another man, and not a part of the original poem.

Before introducing his hero, the poet cannot resist playing on our expectations of a pilgrimage by introducing a conventional pilgrim of the type already satirized in the prologue. He is dressed like a pagan—that is, in imitation of Near Eastern clothing to suggest that he has perhaps just come from Arabia. He has decorated himself with the emblems of famous shrines: ampules from Canterbury, signs of Sinai, shells of Galicia, and the cross keys and vernicle of Rome. When the folk ask him where he has been, he tells them he has seen Sinai, the Holy Sepulcher, Bethlehem, Babylon, Armenia, Alexandria, and many other places. But when they ask him how to find Truth, he confesses complete ignorance.

At this opportune moment, Piers the plowman puts forth his

head and offers to guide the pilgrims to Saint Truth. I know him well, says Piers, and I will show you the way. When they offer him money for his services, Piers angrily refuses it, and proceeds to describe the way to Truth by means of an allegorical map made up of the Ten Commandments, as well as humility, conscience, the great commandment (Matt. 22:37–40), and various requisite virtues. He who follows these directions will come finally to the celestial court of Truth, whose moat is of Mercy, walls of Wit to keep out Will (desire), battlements of faith, and the roof made of love and humility. Truth's tower rises to the sun. The gatekeeper is Grace and his assistant is Amend-you. When you get there, give him this password: I performed the penance enjoined by the priest, and am sorry for my sins. And if Grace permits you to enter, you shall see Truth sitting in your heart. Let no pride keep you from loving him and keeping his commandments. Remember, anyone who is kin to the seven sisters (seven virtues) who keep the posterns will be assured of admission; unless you are related to at least one of these seven, you may find it difficult to get in. At this news a cutpurse, an apeward, and a waferer disclaim any such kinship, and the latter vows that if he knew that to be a fact, he would not go one foot farther, "for no friar's preaching." But Piers hastens to reassure them that Mercy, along with her Son, always stands ready to admit them through grace.

The folk cry for a guide, and Piers agrees to lead them—except that he must first plow a half acre beside the highway. The women are set to work spinning, weaving, and sewing. When a knight offers to plow, Piers thanks him for proffering himself "so low," but says that he will work for them both and asks only that the knight defend the faith, keep law and order, and hunt down predators that break into his croft. As an afterthought Piers cautions the knight not to oppress tenants, mistreat bondmen, or waste time and money on bawdy entertainers. The knight agrees to all this, and Piers dresses for the pilgrimage, hanging a hopper (seed basket) at his neck instead of a scrip (traveler's wallet), suggesting that Piers' pilgrimage is not to be the conventional kind. I shall provide food for everyone who helps me, announces Piers, except for Jake the juggler, Janette of the stews, and Robin the ribald with his rusty words. He then makes his will (as if in preparation for a journey), and the plowing of the half acre begins.

At high prime (6 A.M.) Piers lets the plow stand, and finds that there are some sitting in the alehouse, helping him plow only with a "Hey, trolly-lolly!" (A VII 109). Enraged, Piers threatens to deny them his food, even if this means starvation, unless they get to work. In response to this outburst, some plead sickness or disability, and Waster and his Breton companion threaten to fight, warning Piers that they will eat his food whether he likes it or not. When the knight's official warning to Waster is ignored, Piers as a last resort sends after Hunger, who assaults Waster and the Breton so violently that the plowman has to intervene to save their lives. Seeing this, the ill and handicapped are suddenly cured (A VII 177–83):

> A heap of hermits henten [seized] them spades
> And delved dirt and dung to ditte [drive] out Hunger.
> Blind and bedridden were botned [cured] a thousand
> That lay as if blind and broken-legged by the highway.
> Hunger them healed with a hot cake,
> And lame men's limbs were lithed that time. . . .

But what about the morality of threatening starvation to get people to work? These men are my brothers, says Piers to Hunger, for whom Christ died, and Truth taught me to love them: what do you advise? Hunger responds: those that appear physically strong ("bold beggars and big") should be fed with beans, and if they complain, tell them to go to work and their diet will improve; but victims of genuine misfortune, the needy and naked, should be loved and supported with food or money. It is for this reason that the gospel says, *Make to yourselves friends of the mammon of unrighteousness* (Luke 16:9).

Piers wants to be sure that it is safe to follow Hunger's teaching, so he asks: "Might I sinless do as thou sayest?" (A VII 217). Hunger responds with a shower of biblical texts: *In the sweat of thy face shalt thou eat bread* (Gen. 3:19); *The sluggard will not plow by reason of the cold, therefore he shall beg in harvest, and have nothing* (Prov. 20:3); and the parable of the talents (Matt. 25:14–30). It is only natural, he adds, that everyone work at some job, such as teaching, tilling, or working with his hands. Christ himself commends both the active and the contemplative life (Luke 10:38–42), although the Psalter contains a special blessing for those who work with their hands (Ps. 128:2). For the record Hunger seems to concede obliquely that Christ commended the contemplative life (Mary) over the active life (Martha) while nevertheless leaving an impression that the Bible singles out the working man for particular praise.

In a final and unexpected request, Piers asks Hunger for medical advice: some of my servants are sick at times, he says, taking off from work as much as a week because of the stomachache. If you want to be healthy, advises Hunger, here are some rules: never drink until you have had some dinner; do not eat until Hunger sends you his sauce to savor your lips; save some until suppertime, and sit not too long at table, but rise up ere Appetite has eaten his fill. Let not Sir Surfeit sit at thy board. Follow these rules, and I dare say Physic shall sell his furred hood to buy food and learn to labor on the land. There are more liars than leeches—may the Lord amend them—they make men die prematurely with their prescriptions!

Piers receives Hunger's advice with enthusiastic approval, and grants him permission to leave. But Hunger will not go until he has been fed, and his appetite is so enormous that nothing satisfies him until harvest time when the new grain comes to market: then they feed him so full that he falls asleep. Whereupon Waster immediately quits work, and beggars eat only the best white bread and drink brown ale. Day laborers deign not to dine on day-old vegetables, and demand fresh meat or fried fish, cooked exactly to taste. Unless they have higher wages, they complain, blasting the time they became workmen, and cursing the king and his council for designing such laws as the Statute of Laborers. But while Hunger was their master, observes the poet, no one would chide or strive against the statute, so stern was his glance. Although it is clear that our author has a high regard for the role of the laboring man, he has no inclination whatever to give them preferential treatment. They have no right to take advantage of the special circumstances of the period following the plague to extort high wages from the landowners. The passus concludes with a threatening prophecy (A VII 306–11):

> I warn you workmen, win while you may,
> For Hunger hitherward hasteth him fast.
> He shall awake through water, wasters to chasten:
> Ere five years be fulfilled such famine shall arise,
> Through floods and through foul weathers, fruits shall fail,
> And so saith Saturn, and sendeth you to warn.

Truth's Pardon: The End of the Visio

The author of the A text seems to take a special delight in confounding our expectations. In the episode of Lady Meed we witness elaborate plans for a wedding that never takes place; at the appearance of the good plowman we are led to expect a literal pilgrimage that does not occur; and now, at the climactic moment of the entire *Visio*, we are presented with a pardon that is no pardon at all. The distinctive blend of irony and anger in this scene has left generations of interpreters puzzled, but once the reader is attuned to the poet's penchant for practical jokes, the meaning of his conclusion becomes painfully clear.

Because of the famine predicted by Saturn, Truth sends Piers a pardon, with a message instructing him to stay at home (that is, forget the proposed pilgrimage) and plow his land. The indulgence he sends is in the form of a pardon *a pena et a culpa* (from punishment and guilt), despite the fact that such certificates were not supposed to offer exemption from the guilt of sin. This generous pardon was offered to Piers and his heirs, and all who help him with his work, whatever their position in society. The poet then proceeds through the ranks, indicating how each group may or may not partake of the benefits of this pardon.

Kings and knights who defend Holy Church and govern the people are permitted to pass quickly through purgatory into paradise. Bishops who bless, and know both laws, observing the one and teaching men the other, who preach to their parsons the peril of sin, and how they are to save their flocks—such bishops have as full a pardon as the apostles, and will sit with them in a place of honor on Judgment Day. Merchants, in the margin (as an afterthought), were given many years remission of punishment, but the pope would not grant it them *a pena et a culpa*, because they failed to close down their shops on holy days and swore in God's name that their goods were of high quality when they knew better. But Truth sent them a special set of instructions, assuring them that they might buy and sell with a good conscience, as long as they used their profits to support hospitals, repair roads and bridges, provide dowries for maidens, subsidies for poor widows, scholarships for students or apprentices, and support for the religious orders. If they do these things, Truth promises to send Saint Michael himself to escort them to heaven when they die. As long as they avoid usury, avarice, false oaths, and guile in their transactions and follow a strict path, they have nothing to fear. Hearing this, merchants were merry and wept for joy, and gave Will expensive clothing as a reward for thus copying their clause.

Men of law had least share in the pardon of Truth, because they are all educated, and can't plead ignorance of the Psalter: *Lord, who shall abide in thy tabernacle? who shall dwell in thy holy hill? ... He that ... taketh (not) reward against the innocent* (Ps. 15:1, 5). Lawyers should receive their income from princes and prelates, and they should not take so much as one penny from poor people. But he who speaks for the poor and innocent without demanding money, and who gives him the benefit of his legal knowledge purely for love of the Lord, there is no devil that can harm him at all on his death day, for he shall be safely delivered unto the holy hill of the Lord as the Psalter promises. For there are three things that cannot be bought or sold: water, wind, and wit, all of them gifts of God, granted for our common good. The man who takes meed from a poor man for pleading his case in court will get very little pardon in purgatory, I believe, says Truth. You barristers and lawyers, you know whether I am lying or not! Since you know it is true, you'd do well to take my advice.

All true laborers who work with their hands, living with humble hearts in love and in law, have the same absolution that was sent to Piers. But beggars are not in the bull, unless there is a genuine reason for them to beg. False beggars defraud the truly needy, and beguile the giver against his will. They live loveless and lawless lives, scorning marriage and coupling with women like animals. Then they take their bastard child and break its back or some other bone in order to use it as an object of pity in their begging. That is why you see so many cripples in this miserable group. Those who live like this may well dread the time when they depart this life. But the old and helpless, women with child who cannot work, the blind and bedridden, with broken members, who take their mischief meekly, have as full a pardon as the plowman himself. For love of their humble hearts, our Lord has granted them their penance and their purgatory upon this pure earth.

It is hard to miss the deep emotion in the concluding lines of this pardon, but at the same time we should not lose sight of what has been accomplished. The wealthy and powerful have been reminded forcefully of their responsibilities, lawyers have been warned of the doom that awaits them if they do not change, while laborers, the poor, and the handicapped have been assured their salvation. Would it have been possible for anyone in the poet's audience to have seen an actual pardon containing such provisions? Certainly not. Those who obey the conditions of this "pardon" have also been obedient to the law of God, and therefore have no need of any pardon whatsoever. Indeed, they will have brought upon themselves *no punishment and no guilt,* and will thus receive in full what had seemed in the beginning a pardon that made excessive claims. Truth here employs the same kind of irony as that used earlier by Reason when he promised to show mercy at a time when mercy will no longer be needed (A IV 100–31).

At this dramatic moment a priest offers to read the pardon for Piers and translate it into English. The Dreamer, looking over their shoulder, could see that the text consisted of two lines only (A VIII 95a):

> *Et qui bona egerunt ibunt in vitam eternam;*
> *Qui vero mala, in ignem eternum.*

When the priest sees this, he exclaims, "Peter! I can find no pardon" (A VIII 95), and proceeds to give a translation: Those who do well will go into eternal life, but those who do evil will go into eternal fire. Of course the priest is correct: this is no pardon. It is in fact a deliberately chosen extract from the Athanasian Creed, which is binding on all Christians. Establish this clause in the minds and hearts of worshipers, and all the elaborate machinery of penance devised by the medieval church will become superfluous. The abuses that have grown up in connection with the employment of "real" pardons show that Lady Meed has found her way to the heart of the confessional. At one stroke, Truth cuts through the penitential red tape, and of course this confounds the literal-minded priest.

On the other hand, Piers completely understands Truth's message, and accepts it. But this message is not a "doctrine" to which one merely gives "assent"; it is a divine warning that ought to produce fear and trembling in the listener. And this is precisely the response that it elicits from the plowman. His anger with the priest, expressed in his tearing of the pretended pardon, quickly gives way to a penitential confession of faith (Ps. 23:4) and a vow to be less anxious for his bodily welfare (Matt. 6:25). In this brief confession, Piers both demonstrates the uselessness of indulgences and shows us the correct response to Truth's message. Isaiah called himself a man of unclean lips (Isa. 6:5); Job despised himself and repented in dust and ashes (Job 42:5); Piers confesses an excessive concern for his daily bread, and promises in future to show more faith in Christ's assurances in the Sermon on the Mount.

If Piers finds something in himself that needs reforming, the rest of us must surely search our hearts. But the priest who offered to interpret the pardon is apparently oblivious of the spiritual issues now vibrant in the air, and can only express a condescending surprise at the scriptural knowledge that Piers reveals in his confession. "By Peter!" he exclaims, "thou art lettered a little: who learned thee on book?" (A VIII 118). This precipitates a quarrel between the plowman and the priest, which causes the Dreamer to awaken and find himself alone on Malvern hills.

Traditionally in medieval vision literature, the poet disclaims responsibility for his dream and encourages the reader to draw his own conclusions about its significance. The author of the A text follows this convention, but leaves little doubt how we are to interpret his poem. I have thought about this dream many times, he says, wondering if it might be true. Cato says we should pay no attention to dreams, but the Bible, in stories of Joseph and Daniel, tells of dreams that came true. Many times at midnight, when men should be sleeping, I think about Piers the plowman, what kind of pardon he had, and how the priest impugned it, all by pure reason. And I concluded that doing well (Dowel) surpassed indulgences. Dowel will be honorably received on the Day of Judgment, and surpasses all the pardons of Saint Peter's church. He goes on to concede, lest anyone accuse him of heresy, that he does not doubt the pope's authority to distribute such indulgences, or his power to bind and loose (Matt. 16:19). But he insists that when the chips are down, it is safer to trust in Dowel than in pardons or masses said on behalf of your soul.

The conclusion to the *Visio* has a message that should be of considerable comfort to the poor and helpless, since it is only the rich and powerful who can afford the price of most indulgences and the singing of masses for the dead. To the latter group the poet addresses a final warning: I advise you rich who trust on such masses not to be any bolder to break the Ten Commandments! And especially you magistrates, mayors, and judges, who have the wealth of this world and are considered wise, and can afford pardons and papal bulls: beware of Doomsday, when you will be required to account for all your actions. A sackful of pardons will do you no good there; unless Dowel help you, I wouldn't give a crumb for your patent! Then, in a closing prayer, the poet asks God to give us all grace to lead such lives that on Doomsday Dowel will testify that we obeyed the commandments.

The *Visio* thus ends with a vindication of the Plowman and his way of life, measured against the sins and pretensions of church and state. In the process we have been introduced to a new concept, Dowel, embodying the good life as lived in accordance with Truth's pardon. And it is Dowel, as we shall see, that provides the point of departure for the *Vita*, the final section of the poem.

The Life of Dowel, Dobet, and Dobest

The ostensible purpose of the Dreamer is to set out in quest of the good life—the life lived in accordance with Truth. He does this by consulting various mental faculties and aids to his education: Thought, Wit, Study, Clergy (learning), and Scripture. Each of these is to give the Dreamer his or her definition of the kind of life that will lead to salvation, as implied in Truth's pardon. When he has completed his education, the Dreamer should finally be able to provide us with a reliable definition of the way of Truth. Such will be our expectation, that is, if we have forgotten about the poet's perverse inclination to play tricks, to let us cultivate a set of false expectations, as he did with the marriage of Meed, the pilgrimage of Piers, and the pardon of Truth.

In the first place, we quickly discover that there is no real progression from one spokesman to the next: no one definition is necessarily an improvement over another. Furthermore, the triad into which the concept of doing well is now divided refers, not to any single pattern of life more or less well imitated, but rather to three ranks of society that the poet wishes to examine: Dowel stands for the common people, Dobet the clergy (both secular and regular), and Dobest the episcopate. The standards applied to these ranks (good, better, best) merely reflect the escalating pressure for moral behavior in relation to positions of increasing responsibility. With this arrangement we can see that the commons, though much is demanded of them, are in a less vulnerable position than the other two groups. The clergy ought to lead more exemplary lives, and of course bishops ought to be better than priests.

Thus the quest of the Dreamer turns out to be not a search for something but an opportunity to expose the shortcomings of society when measured against the standards of Truth. This means that the Dreamer's questions are not those of a troubled author genuinely seeking answers but rather opening sallies in a debate designed to reveal sin, corruption, and hypocrisy. Interpreters of *Piers the Plowman* have long insisted that the *Vita* expresses the theological uncertainties of the poet—so long and so eloquently that it seems almost perverse to disagree. Yet I must insist, at least as far as the A version is concerned, that we will find it difficult if not impossible to understand the *Vita* unless we realize that it is filled with irony, satire, and even comedy, ingredients that are the opposite of what we should expect from an author who is unsure of himself. And it should not be surprising, to readers of the *Visio*, when we discover that most of the author's barbs are aimed at Dobet, the life of the clergy. It was a priest who sneered at the plowman's knowledge of Scripture, and we are not to be allowed to forget this. It is no exaggeration to say that a main purpose of the *Vita* is to prove that the path of learning is *not* the way to salvation.

The Dreamer roams in search of Dowel, asking repeatedly of folk that he meets who this man might be and where he might be found. At length he encounters a pair of friars, who insist that Dowel dwells with them, but the Dreamer does not seem convinced by their elaborate distinction between venial and deadly sin. Bidding them a polite farewell, he comes to a wood, leans against a linden tree, and falls asleep to the sound of the birds.

In his dream a large man approaches him, looking much like himself, and calls the Dreamer by name. "Who art thou," quoth I then, "that knowest my name?" (A IX 63). I am Thought, the man replies: I've been following you for seven years—haven't you seen me before? The Dreamer asks him where Dowel lives, and Thought responds by defining all three members of the triad as "three fair virtues." Dowel is meek and mild in speech, true of his tongue and his two hands, earns his living by labor—honest, sober, and upright. Dobet does thus, but in addition he is as low as a lamb, lovely of speech, and shares what he has with others. In some cases he joins the religious orders and makes himself a friend of the mammon of unrighteousness (Luke 16:9), glossing the Bible to show that what he is doing is right, and preaching on the text *Suffer fools gladly, seeing ye yourselves are wise* (2 Cor. 11:19). Dobest is above both, and bears a bishop's crosier, with a hook at one end to hold men in good life; it also has a point to strike down the wicked who may be intending to harm Dowel.

In this paraphrase I have tried to indicate that these opening definitions are quite simple, and yet the definition of Dobet already contains a hint of the hostility that is to emerge in later definitions of this group. The clergy are *supposed* to be humble and generous with what they have, but the glossing of the mammon verse from Luke by the religious orders is suspect, and the poet turns some of Saint Paul's irony in 2 Corinthians 11:19 against the condescending preachers who invoke him in their sermons. Many a definition in the *Vita* is this kind of two-edged sword. But Thought can also be perfectly serious, as he is in this often misunderstood description of the relationship of the three members of the triad (A IX 90–96):

> And as Dowel and Dobet did them to understand,
> They have crowned one king to keep them all,
> That if Dowel and Dobet did against Dobest,
> And were unbuxom at his bidding, and bold to do ill,
> Then should the king come and cast them in prison,
> And put them there in penance without pity or grace;
> But if [Unless] Dobest bid [intercede] for them, abide there forever.

This passage takes up one aspect of the relation of church and state in order to show that the royal power is to be used when necessary to give bishops a means of compelling discipline on both the commons and the clergy. In short, the king is the bishop's enforcer. He is to rule by the advice of his council, and with the assent of all ranks of society (A IX 97–100). When the Dreamer expresses dissatisfaction with this definition, Thought refers him to Wit, our next spokesman.

Wit is the resident psychologist of the *Vita*, and his initial response to the Dreamer's question is a classic description of the nature and destiny of man, cast in allegorical form. Dowel (mankind) dwells in a castle (the body), and is responsible, along with Dobet and Dobest, for defending Lady Anima (the soul) against the schemes of a proud chevalier of France, Prince of this World— the Devil (John 16:11). The constable of the castle is Inwit (conscience), who with his five sons (approximating the five senses) is charged with defending the Lady until Kind (God/Nature) sends for her and takes over the responsibility for her defense himself (that is, after the death of the body).

If we keep in mind the poet's prophetic stance, it should come as no surprise to discover that Wit's psychology is fundamentally optimistic. He points out to the Dreamer that God created man in his own image, and consequently provided him with all the means necessary to lead a good life. Thus man has been given Inwit (conscience) as a guide to both body and soul, and a restraint against excesses. The home of Inwit is the head, where he is in a firm position to govern, unless blood becomes stronger than brain (emotion overcomes reason). When this happens, then Inwit is bound or helpless, and the person runs wild. Such is the case with infants, fools (madmen), or drunkards who pour ale in their heads until Inwit is drowned. In the latter instance the result is that the Devil gains power over their souls. But in the case of infants or fools the Devil has no power because of anything that they do. As for infants, it is up to parents and friends to steer them away from wantonness while they are young; and if they are destitute, then Holy Church is responsible for keeping them from folly and providing subsistence until they grow wiser and are able to care for themselves.

Thus it should be evident that every person of understanding is given sovereignty over himself to protect his soul, and to clear himself of any charge, when he passes childhood, and save himself from sin: "For work he well or wrong, the wit is his own" (A X 75). When we look back at the friar's sermon near the beginning of the *Vita*, we can see that by comparison Wit's attitude toward sin is absolutely uncompromising: if the just man sinneth seven times in a day (Prov. 24:16), so much the worse for him. And it should be clear which side the author takes on this point: only Wit's psychology can prepare us to meet the absolute demands of Truth. If we follow his guidance, vices can be destroyed, and "sin hath no might" to strike root in our hearts.

Having presented his views on the mechanism of the soul and its relation to the body, Wit now launches into his own definition of the triad. Dowel is fear of God, Dobet is fear of the rod (of correction!), and Dobest is humility. Not surprisingly, Wit focuses on *attitude*, but it is clear that the groups in society are the same: commons, clergy, and episcopate. For each rank he has a biblical text. Dowel: *The fear of the Lord is the beginning of wisdom* (Ps. 111:10); Dobet: *Thy rod and thy staff they comfort me* (Ps. 23:4); and Dobest: *He that humbleth himself shall be exalted* (Luke 14:11). The rod of punishment and the staff of support belong to a venerable tradition of exegesis of the Twenty-third Psalm; but it is significant to note here that the assignment of a rod of punishment to the clergy is typical of what we may expect from this poet.

Was there any "upward mobility" in medieval society? Indeed there was, and it was made possible largely by the Church, which drew on all ranks, including the commons, in its quest for candidates for the priesthood. But our poet seems to have an aversion to this, or at least to the kind of person he saw striving for ecclesiastical preferment. This comes out in a digression following the definition of Dobet. If your conscience tells you that you are doing well, he says, do not ever seek to be better. As long as you live in accordance with God's word, do not become angry because of anything men say about you. Stay in your place, and do not seek to go higher: for if you do, your humility may give way to pride. A rolling stone gathers no moss (aimed at those who play the game of musical monasteries); and the jack of all trades is master of none (ambition in the marketplace). Paul warned us against "running about": *Let every man abide in the same calling wherein he was called* (1 Cor. 7:20). Whether you are a married man or a monk or a canon, live in such a way that you will be blessed for your steadfast life, even if you were a beggar. Do not complain against God, and be satisfied with your position.

In summarizing his definitions, Wit likens the flourishing of society to the growth of a flower. Just as a rose that is red and sweet, he says, grows out of a ragged root (the commons) and a rough briar (the clergy!), so Dobest (bishops) springs from Dobet and Dowel. The anticlerical nature of the image is clear, but we should also note that the commons are the root of society, and thus absolutely essential to its development. This is in sharp contrast to the viewpoint destined to appear in the B version, where the priesthood is the root, and the rest of society flower, leaf, and fruit (B XV 97–100).

Although it seems at times in the A text as if the common man is being readied for a messianic role, this never becomes explicit, because the poet is painfully aware of the shortcomings of the people. They are exploited, and this makes him angry; but a certain amount of their suffering is self-inflicted. This is made clear in the remainder of this passus by Wit's dissection of the institution of marriage. Dowel is made up of wedded folk, and "through wedlock the world stands" (A X 129). One is reminded of the Wife of Bath's triumphant observation (CT III 71–72):

> And certes, if there were no seed ysowe,
> Virginitee, thanne wherof sholde it growe?

But Wit is engaged in making a serious point: the flourishing of society is absolutely dependent on the soundness of the institution of marriage.

Wit traces the problems afflicting marriage in his time back to the Fall (Gen. 3:16), specifically to the birth of Cain (citing Ps. 7:14), and the subsequent intermarriage of the children of Seth and Cain despite God's warning against that. Indeed, God's purpose in sending the Flood was to wipe out that evil generation. But if we look around us, we can see that Cain's offspring are alive and well in the wretched marriages of today. Some marry for greed: a young girl is betrothed to an old man, or a wealthy widow is married for her money when she is of such an age that she will never bear a child unless it be in her arms. Since the pestilence many a joyless couple have jangled in bed, and the only offspring they have are foul words hurled at each other. You can be sure that none of them will win the side of bacon in Dunmow (a prize for the couple that has gone a whole year without quarreling).

In conclusion Wit urges all Christians to exclude covetousness from marriage. Let virgins marry virgins, widows wed widowers, and thank God for any incidental benefits that may come from the wedding. It goes without saying that fornication and adultery are to be strictly avoided. Such sins have practical consequences: their bastard offspring grow up to become loveless wanderers and wasters who, without God's grace, will end up going to hell. Summarizing the triad, Wit says that Dowel is to fear, Dobet is to suffer, and Dobest has a disciplinary function: to abase the proud.

The final passus of the *Vita* opens with the sudden appearance of Wit's wife, Dame Study, who launches into a brilliant monologue that provides both comic relief and satiric thrust. It is comic to discover that Wit, having just delivered an authoritative critique of marriage, has such an obstreperous wife; and it is her reckless assumption that the Dreamer is a quibbling intellectual that provides the basis for a sharp attack on learning.

Don't cast your pearls before swine, says Dame Study; they prefer slops to all the jewels that grow in paradise! I mean those who would rather have land and lordship than all the wisdom of Solomon. Indeed wisdom nowadays is not worth a straw unless it is brushed up with covetousness and used to frustrate justice. Those who can do this are called into council, and are treated as lords when in fact they are serving the devil. *Wherefore do the wicked live, become old, yea, are mighty in power?* (Job 21:7). Meanwhile he who has holy writ in his mouth is pushed aside to make room for professional entertainers. Minstrels know very well that if their stories are not mostly harlotry they will not receive so much as a groat, whether their audience includes king, knight, or canon of Saint Paul's! Lechery and loose tales, gluttony and great oaths, these are games nowadays!

But if these clerks or laymen do speak of Christ, during dinner, when minstrels are quiet, then they talk of the Trinity, how Two slew the Third, and offer a presumption to "prove" the truth. Thus they talk drivel on the daïs, and gnaw God in their gorge, when their guts are full. But the poor man may cry at the gate, trembling for hunger and cold, and no one takes him in; instead he is driven out like a dog and told to go elsewhere. He who shares thus with the poor has little love for the Lord who gave him all that he enjoys. If it were not for the fact that poor men are more merciful than the rich, many beggars would go to bed without food. God is much in the throats of these great masters, but among poor men are found his mercy and his works. To find the truly devout, you must go to the hinterlands (Ps. 132:6): *Lo, we heard of it at Ephratah: we found it in the fields of the wood.*

In the person of Dame Study, the poet has perhaps allowed himself to voice an extreme position, but there is a sincerity and an urgency in this speech that can scarcely be denied. Indeed the frequency with which the later versions refer back to this passage (in tones of anguish rather than anger, as in A) suggests that Study's fulminations had a profound impact on the reviser. In her rage, Dame Study speaks with utter seriousness and with profound disrespect for the high-ranking victims of her criticism. Deceiving friars have dreamed up questions, she continues, to please proud men and defile our faith when they sit at their feasts. Now every boy is bold, if he be rich, to talk about the Trinity to enhance his reputation, and to raise such questions as: why would God allow the serpent into Paradise? But Saint Augustine long ago had the answer to such quibblers, warning them not to be wiser than is fitting. Everything happens in accordance with God's will, whatever we may think!

At the height of her indignation, Dame Study now turns her attention back to the Dreamer. And now comes a miserable wretch (conyon), she says scornfully, who wants to pick my brains about a distinction between Dowel and Dobet—may he become deaf! Unless he first live to the minutest detail the life of Dowel, I dare say he will never Dobet, even if Dobest were to drag him by the heels! In response to this outburst, the Dreamer begs Wit to intercede, but the embarrassed and apparently henpecked husband can only laugh and bow and gesture to indicate that he will have to ask her for mercy himself.

When the Dreamer kneels obediently before her, asking only to be told what Dowel is, Dame Study suddenly turns gentle. I appreciate your meekness, man, she says, and so I shall direct you to my cousin Clergy (learning) and his wife Scripture. This she proceeds to do, using one of those allegorical maps of which the author is very fond (compare A VI 50–126). But before bidding him farewell, the Dame provides an inventory of subjects that go with a life of study, accompanied by her own colorful opinions. Concerning theology, for example, she confesses that it has often vexed her, because the more she looked into it, the more obscure it seemed. It is certainly not a science to be subtle about, and the only reason she tolerates it is that it exalts love above everything else. And when love is lord, grace will never be lacking.

With the blessing of Dame Study, the Dreamer now follows her directions to the house of Clergy and Scripture, where he is warmly welcomed. Wasting no time, the Dreamer asks about the triad. Scripture (Clergy in BC) replies with what is by now the conventional definition: Dowel is the life of laborers, Dobet the clergy (who lead a life of charitable aid to others and harmony among themselves!), and Dobest is prince over God's people, to preach and to chastise. There is no appreciable advance in this over earlier definitions, but the reason is not far to seek: the author is about to set off an argument by means of which the poem will be brought to its conclusion. In the *Visio*, we recall, the dream ends with an argument between Piers and the priest (A VIII 96–126); the *Vita* will end in a "dispute" between the Dreamer and Scripture. The difference is that whereas there was a profound disagreement between the plowman and the priest, the row between the Dreamer and Scripture is patently contrived to allow a final satirical thrust at the monastic orders, as well as at the wealthy and powerful. Throughout the dispute, the Dreamer is speaking tongue in cheek.

The opening for this argument is provided by Scripture, whose definition of Dobet turns into a tirade against the religious orders.

Dobet is endowed, she remarks, for the sake of poor men. I speak of true religious, not those who leap over the land to confess ladies (the friars). Gregory the Great truly said that a monk out of his cloister is like a fish out of water. But nowadays Religion has become a rider, a roamer of streets, a leader of lovedays, and a buyer of land. He trots on a palfrey from town to town, wears a dagger, and swears like a lord. This is the life of those that should live with Dobet, and even worse, if I were to tell all.

At this point the Dreamer interrupts: I thought that kings and knights represented the triad, since Christ himself said, *Princes sit in Moses' seat* (cf. Matt. 23:2). This misquoting of the gospel, where it is the scribes and the Pharisees, not princes, who sit in the seat of Moses, conveniently allows Scripture to point out that the rich and powerful have no special privileges in the eyes of God, and that indeed the poor have the promise of heaven while the wealthy do not. We are already quite aware that this is a sentiment with which the Dreamer strongly agrees, so that unless we are attuned to the poet's irony we will be surprised to discover that the Dreamer proceeds to attack Scripture's position in the manner of a disputatious clerk.

On the contrary, says the Dreamer to Scripture, I can prove that rich men *are* saved (Mark 16:16): *He that believeth and is baptized shall be saved.* Patiently Scripture responds that this verse refers to special circumstances, as in the baptism of converts from other faiths, whereas Christians have a common heritage of doctrine that must be obeyed before salvation can be assured. For example, continues Scripture, launching into her *finale*, there is the command to love God and your neighbor. This means that Christians should be kind to one another, and also help the heathen, in hope of improving them: certainly God never commanded us to kill them (as in the crusades), for he says himself in the Decalogue, *Thou shalt not kill*, and elsewhere, *Vengeance is mine; I will repay, saith the Lord* (Rom. 12:19). The *Vita* thus ends with a sharp thrust at one of the great causes adopted by the warrior class, and widely approved by medieval society. If God indeed opposes the crusades, a radical reassessment of what constitutes the good life is certainly in order. Having thus disrupted our conventional notions of piety, the author leaves us to ponder the meaning of his dream.

But as in the case of the *Visio*, we are given a closing meditation by the Dreamer designed to make clear what the poet wants us to learn from the *Vita*. And yet I am never the nearer, says the Dreamer, for all my walking, to a true knowledge of Dowel. For whatever I do in this life, I have been predestined either for salvation or damnation. Consider the cases of Solomon and Aristotle: who did better than they? Yet all Holy Church maintains that they are in hell! And this despite the fact that learned men now use their words to guide us to Dowel. But it may be unwise of me to follow their wisdom, considering what happened to them: I might end up in hell myself!

On Good Friday, he continues, a felon was saved who had lived as a thief all his life. Merely because he confessed to Christ on the cross, he had salvation sooner than Saint John the Baptist, Adam, Isaiah, or any of the prophets who had lain with Lucifer many long years. A *robber* had remission sooner than all of them! Who did worse than Mary Magdalene, David, slayer of Uriah, or Paul, who participated in the killing of Christians? Yet there is none so surely established in heaven as these, who lived such wicked lives when they were in the world.

The reader who has by this time become familiar with the author's tendency to tease us with false expectations will recognize, of course, that we are being treated to one more example of his perversity. As far as the Dreamer and the poet are concerned, these instances are not real problems, but ridiculous examples of theological impasse. They are what happens when, as Dame Study warned, you seek to be wiser than is fitting. Having treated us to this parade of absurdities, the Dreamer now makes the moral of the poem explicit.

And yet I have forgotten the teaching of my five wits, he says, namely that Christ never did commend learning. On the contrary he said: "When you are questioned by princes or *priests of the law*, have no fear to answer them, for I shall give you the grace of the Holy Ghost to answer them all" (cf. Mark 13:11, 13). This is a somewhat free paraphrase of the gospel, and it is worth noting that for "rulers and kings" the author has substituted "princes *and priests*," thus reminding us of that confrontation between Piers and the priest in the *Visio*, where the unlettered plowman is given the perhaps inspired ability to refute the legalistic priest from Scripture.

A final, clinching paraphrase of Saint Augustine caps the poet's denunciation of learning, and brings the *Vita* to an end (A XI 297–303):

Are none rather [sooner] ravished from the right belief
Than are those great clerks that conne [know] many books,
Nor none sooner saved, nor sadder [more sober] of conscience
Than poor people, as plowmen and pastors of beasts.
Souters [Cobblers] and sewers, such lewed jots [ignorant dolts]
Pierce with a *Paternoster* [Lord's prayer] the palace of heaven,
Without penance, at their parting, into the high bliss.

Learned commentators in modern times have been understandably reluctant to interpret the close of the A *Vita* as a decisive
denunciation of learning, and their reluctance may be due to more
than that personal commitment to the advancement of learning
we all share: for the reviser, as we shall see, does everything in
his power to refute this conclusion in the B and C versions of the
poem. But we are still more than twenty years away from the B
version, and it is well to remind ourselves that however hard it
may be for us to swallow the lesson of the *Vita*, John Ball and
his comrades had no such problem. Concerning the attitude of
the rebels toward literate members of society, the chronicler Walsingham had this to say (Dobson, p. 364): "It was dangerous
enough to be known as a clerk, but especially dangerous if an
ink-pot should be found at one's elbow: such men scarcely or
ever escaped from the hands of the rebels." Nowhere do I mean
to imply that the author of *Piers the Plowman* (A) would have sanc-
tioned the violence of the peasants in 1381. But in many respects
his attitude did pose a threat to the established order, and pointed
a dagger at the heart of the system governing both church and
state. His dream of a golden age proved very attractive to the
rebel leadership, and meant nothing but trouble for those who
stood in the way of its fulfillment.

The Peasants' Revolt of 1381

Following the death of Edward III in 1377, and during the mi-
nority of Richard II, the government of England suffered from a
lack of leadership as troublesome as that which had existed during the illness of the Black Prince and the last years of the old
king. Opposition to the interim rule of John of Gaunt was formidable, and his role in the surrender of English holdings on the
Continent did not enhance his popularity. Moreover, the action
taken by the good parliament of 1376 was arbitrarily repealed by
the duke's maneuvers in 1377, a very discouraging blow to re-
formers, and a sore point with Londoners, whose hatred of the
duke soon reached the boiling point.

[265]

The introduction of the poll tax in 1377 was designed both to force revenue from a sullen population and to pour money into faltering and unpopular enterprises. The resulting alienation of government and people was not unlike that experienced in modern times by the United States during the war in Vietnam. And when the hated poll tax was renewed in 1379 and again in 1381, the tide of resentment could no longer be contained. In the month of May in Essex the first sporadic resistance to the tax appeared, followed by riots in Kent, which soon became the focal point of discontent. When the rebels occupied Maidstone, they freed from prison the radical priest, John Ball, whose sermons provided ideological substance to the movement, and they chose as their military leader Wat Tyler, who seems to have been in charge by the time they entered Canterbury without opposition on June 10, 1381. When the young King Richard sent word to the rebels, asking for an explanation, they replied that they wanted "to save him from his treacherous advisers."

On June 12 the rebels assembled outside London at Blackheath, and were joined by a group marching in from Essex. It was here that John Ball preached his fiery sermon on the text "When Adam delved. . . ." The following day they entered the town via London Bridge, and joined with the poor of the city in the destruction of the Savoy, John of Gaunt's palace on the Strand. The duke was in Scotland, else he might have perished in the flames or at the hands of the rebels. While the Savoy was burning, other bands were searching the city for "enemies," who mainly consisted of lawyers and other functionaries associated with the judicial system. Those they found were killed on the spot, usually by beheading.

On Friday, June 14, the king was at last able to arrange a meeting with the rebels at Mile End, but while these negotiations were in progress, others of the mob entered the Tower and seized several government leaders hiding there, the most prominent of whom was the chancellor, Simon Sudbury, archbishop of Canterbury. According to Walsingham, it took eight strokes of the amateur assassin's sword to decapitate the archbishop. His body lay unburied on the ground, while his head was stuck on a pole, paraded through the city, and then placed above the gate of London Bridge.

A final attempt to negotiate with the rebel leadership occurred on Saturday, June 15, at Smithfield. At this face-to-face meeting between Wat Tyler and the boy king, the fate of a nation hung in the balance. A frustrated group of leaders, including William of Walworth, mayor of London, had to watch while Tyler stood insolently before the king, making his demands, and menacingly tossing a dagger from hand to hand. At this moment, it seems, an argument broke out, during which the mayor knocked the peasant leader to the ground. This seemed to waken the king's men, who immediately pounced on Tyler and killed him. Seeing this, the rebels lost courage, and when Richard dramatically called upon them to accept his leadership, their forces dispersed and the rebellion soon came to an end.

Considering that royal promises of amnesty had been given under duress, the king and his advisers lost no time in seeking out and executing the leaders of the revolt and reestablishing control over the population. This reaction was in some ways severe, and in other ways merciful: many were executed, but many were forgiven. There also was, inevitably, an effort to identify and deal with the sources of the trouble. John Ball was drawn and quartered, but determined men like William Courtenay, who replaced Sudbury as archbishop of Canterbury, were convinced that Ball was merely a John the Baptist, and that the real heart of the rebelliousness could be located in the radical teachings of John Wyclif, Oxford scholar and reformer, who thus far had escaped censure by the Church because of his association with John of Gaunt. When the council at Blackfriars met in May of 1382 under Courtenay's leadership, it condemned certain of Wyclif's teachings, although it refrained from mentioning the reformer by name. Wyclif had already retired from Oxford to Lutterworth, and so the action at Blackfriars was employed as an instrument for the "purification" of Oxford University, which took place during the summer of 1382, and was completed by Courtenay himself during a convocation at Oxford in November of that year. Thereafter the Lollard movement, with which Wyclif was associated, continued without benefit of intellectual leadership in Oxford.

Historians of the Peasants' Revolt have found it difficult to define precisely the relationship between that event and the poem *Piers the Plowman*. That there *is* a connection, of course, cannot be disputed. Correspondence between John Ball and some of his followers was recovered and preserved by some of the chroniclers, showing that the mad priest was not unfamiliar with the poem, as in this letter quoted by Walsingham (Dobson, p. 381):

[267]

John Sheep, sometime Saint Mary's priest of York, and now of Colchester, greeteth well John Nameless, and John the Miller, and John Carter, and biddeth them that they beware of Guile in borough [A II 187–90], and standeth together in God's name, and biddeth Piers Plowman go to his work, and chastise well Hobbe the Robber [A V 242–59], and take with you John Trueman, and all his fellows, and no more, and look shape you to one head, and no more [i.e., agree on a single leader].

John the Miller hath ground small, small, small. The King's son of heaven shall pay for all. Beware ere you be woe. Know your friend from your foe. Have enough and say "Whoa!" And do well and better [A *Vita*] and flee sin, and seek peace, and hold you therein. And so biddeth John Trueman and all his fellows.

Knighton preserves letters containing further allusions (Dobson, pp. 381–83). Thus Jack Carter prays "that ye make a good end of that ye have begun, and do well and aye better and better. . . . Let Piers the Plowman my brother dwell at home and dight us corn [A VIII 5], and I will go with you and help that I may to dight your meat and drink, that ye none fail; look that Hobbe the Robber be well chastised for losing of your grace, for you have great need to take God with you in all your deeds. For now is time to beware." Here Robert the robber is invoked to reinforce the ban on looting, which as we have seen was ruthlessly enforced in the destruction of the Savoy.

Jack Trueman sends a message without verbal echoes of the poem, but with an emphasis that could well be indebted to it (Dobson, p. 382): "Jack Trueman doth you to understand that Falseness and Guile have reigned too long, and Truth hath been set under a lock, and Falseness reigneth in every flock. No man may come to Truth but he sing *si dedero*. Speak, spend, and speed, quoth John of Bathon, and therefore sin fareth as a wild flood, true love is away, that was so good, and clerks for wealth work them woe. God do best, for now is time." John Ball himself urges all manner of man (Dobson, p. 383) "to stand manly together in Truth, and help Truth, and Truth shall help you." And he concludes: "Now reigneth Pride in price [reputation], and Covetousness is held wise, and Lechery without shame, and Gluttony without blame. Envy reigns with Treason, and Sloth is taken in great season. God do boot, for now is time amen." It is interesting that Ball mentions precisely the six sins of the A Version (V 45–259), omitting Wrath. Significantly, there are no verbal echoes in these letters that can be identified with anything peculiar to the B or C version.

Another contemporary witness, the writer responsible for that portion of the *Dieulacres Chronicle* covering the reign of Richard II, makes a curious mistake when he tells us that the peasants chose certain leaders among whom were "the abominable priest Johannes B [John Ball], Jack Straw, Piers Plowman and others bent on destroying the laws and customs of the kingdom . . ." (Gray's Inn MS. No. 9, f. 143^r). Although the parallel is inexact, one is reminded of a similar error by the Roman historian Suetonius, who blames Claudius's expulsion of the Jews from Rome (ca. A.D. 52) on disturbances in the Jewish community created by one *Chrestus* (*Vita Claudi*, xxv.4; cf. Acts 18:2), over two decades after the Crucifixion.

Historians would have much less trouble understanding how *Piers the Plowman* connects with the rising of 1381 if they had not been led by literary critics to view the poem as a single work by one author expressing one point of view. In fact, the peasants were inspired by the poem we know as the A version, and they knew nothing of its existence in any other form. Recent dialect studies by M. L. Samuels reveal that surviving manuscripts of A show a wide dialect distribution, while B and C manuscripts were mainly copied in a much more restricted area of the country from roughly Oxfordshire to the Severn estuary and Malvern hills. The first version reached a broad, popular audience; the B and C versions attracted a much more narrow (and intellectual) readership. Most important, as we shall see (to borrow a sentence from the description of the *Dieulacres Chronicle* by Clarke and Galbraith), *Piers the Plowman* "turns out to be the composite product of two writers of strongly opposed views" (p. 125).

In the present chapter I have given most attention to the A version of our poem, and this for two reasons. First, modern interpreters (with the important exception of Father Thomas P. Dunning) have tended to devote their attention to the revisions, and my aim has been to redress this balance. Second, the emphasis on A in this chapter truly reflects the impact of *Piers the Plowman* during the lifetime of its authors. It is the A text that made the headlines, the A text that expresses the ideology that provided the foundation for the revolt. Was its author then a heretic, a revolutionary? Not at all. As Father Dunning's study proves, his teaching is quite orthodox. The incendiary ingredient of the

A version is its sense of outrage at injustice, a feature that reminds us of the prophecies of Amos in the Old Testament. The prophet's anger over injustice led him to condemn those very features of Israel's religion that many of his contemporaries would have passionately defended. In *Piers the Plowman* the emotion of our anonymous A poet communicated itself effectively to men who shared his outrage at injustice but who had their own ideas on what to do about it. Unfortunately Holy Church's reminder that love is the dearest thing (A I 180) was drowned in the roar of the peasant army that stormed over London Bridge in 1381.

The B Version of Piers the Plowman (1383)

The man responsible for the revisions of *Piers the Plowman* may have conceived the idea for his poem and begun work on it as early as 1378, but internal evidence suggests that he did not complete it until perhaps the summer of 1383. In addition to the evidence in the text of his awareness of the Peasants' Revolt, to be considered later in this chapter, there are passages that seem to allude or refer (often in a very private way) to the council at Blackfriars that condemned the teachings of John Wyclif in May 1382 (B X 256–90), the repression of Wyclif's colleagues on the secular faculty at Oxford by Archbishop Courtenay in the summer and fall of that same year (B XX, especially 292–301), and the "crusade" of Henry Despenser, bishop of Norwich, in Flanders in the early summer of 1383 (B XIX 426–45). It may well be true that the general outline of the revision had already taken shape before the revolt, but it is also likely, as we shall see, that considerable portions of the poem were composed as an expression of the reviser's horrified reaction to the violence of 1381.

Since space limitations preclude a close reading of the B version, my aim here is to provide a few observations on its structure and some suggestions on how to understand it in relation to the original poem of 1362. To do this we must begin, not at the beginning, but in the middle, at the opening of the new poem, the B continuation (B XI–XX). Given world enough and time, we would then be in a good position to look back at the B revision of the A text, and more readily understand the rather complex intention behind those revisions. But for the present we must be satisfied with a panoramic view of the continuation only.

The B continuation is essentially biblical in structure. By that I mean that it begins with Genesis and ends with Revelation. Passus XI presents the world ("middle-earth") of Creation, and passus XX concludes with the coming of Antichrist and the threat of Doom. Between these extremes we find the familiar procession of the patriarchs, prophets, and of course the life, Passion, and Resurrection of Christ, followed by a depiction of the apostolic age. The Bible is thus the primary force in determining the shape of the poem. But readers of the present study will be aware, of course, that the Bible in the Middle Ages was part of a larger exegetical and literary tradition, and it is precisely this tradition that we must keep in mind in order to appreciate the various influences that converge to define the poem's biblical structure. Thus, in addition to the Bible itself we should be alert to the influence of paraphrases such as the *Cursor Mundi*, universal histories such as the *Polychronicon*, romances, and the medieval drama.

Given this biblical structure, we may now go to a step farther and say that what we have in the B continuation is a cosmological poem, composed as an adjunct to an existing work, the A version of *Piers the Plowman*. In this respect it resembles those continuations (*suites*) we find in the romance tradition, for example in the Arthurian cycle. Moreover, because it is dream-vision, and a vehicle for satire, it will not extend literally to Doomsday, but will conclude its biblical journey in the poet's own time, in the manner of Higden's *Polychronicon*. A comparison of the original poem with this new one is revealing: in the A text the field of folk (the world) is viewed *statically* against eternity (heaven and hell), while in B the field of folk is presented to us *dynamically*—that is, it appears in passus XIX–XX at the end of a mighty stream of divinely ordained historical events.

What motivated the B poet to undertake this formidable task of revision? In the most general terms he wished to countermand the challenge to the status quo contained in the original poem, and to reshape the potent figure of the plowman into a symbol more in harmony with his own very different solution to the world's problems. To be more specific, the B poet intended to modify, if not completely negate, the anti-intellectual and anti-clerical views expressed in the A version, but to this he adds a powerful indictment of his own, a passionate rebuke directed against the friars.

An important feature of the B version is the change in characterization of the Dreamer. Whereas in A the Dreamer either cooperates in enhancing the poet's own views or serves as a direct spokesman for him (as in A XI 250–303), in B the Dreamer's own views (as inherited from A) are attacked by various allegorical figures who are themselves now the spokesmen of the author. Part of B's admirable strategy for accomplishing this is to cast the Dreamer in the role of a fool, modeled on the Dummling motif in romances such as Chrétien's *Perceval*. Beginning in passus XI as Fortune's fool, Will is battered and instructed by his allegorical questioners until at the end of the poem (XX), as God's fool, he joins the defenders of Holy Church in Piers' barn of Unity. In the course of this journey we are shown (mainly in passus XI–XV) why certain views expressed in A are wrong, and what particular ideas should replace them.

Above all, the B poet sought to possess and redirect the figure of the plowman himself. To tamper in any obvious way with so charismatic and explosive a personage would certainly be self-defeating. What happens in the B continuation is that he is removed from center stage and turned into a symbol of the poet's ideal for the Christian life. The way in which he fades in and out of the action is reminiscent of the way the Grail functions in the Vulgate romances. The *Estoire del Graal*, for example, interlaces an essentially biblical narrative with occasional glimpses of the Grail made famous by Chrétien, using it to add luster to a familiar story, and to provide signs and portents of the Quest that is to take place in the time of Arthur. In an analogous way the B continuation is an *Estoire de Piers*, with a biblical structure containing intermittent glimpses of the plowman who serves as a landmark (Elizabeth Kirk's word) against a dark horizon, and who also points ahead to the plowing of the half acre that is presented allegorically near the end of the poem. Since Piers was already a popular figure (thanks to the A version), and since the humble plowman was so intimate and familiar a part of life in England in the fourteenth century, this employment by the poet of a kind of "you are there" device served admirably to present the biblical narrative of the B continuation in a new and exciting form.

Creation: The A Text Revisited (B XI–XV)

In his opening encounter with Clergy, the Dreamer is shown to be Fortune's fool (B XI 1–50), while at the same time he is allowed to articulate the author's indictment of the fraternal orders (B XI 51–102). But when he and Scripture discuss the meaning of

the text *Many are called but few are chosen* (Matt. 22:14), the Roman
Emperor Trajan suddenly appears to defend the salvation of the
righteous heathen (B XI 103–164; cp. A XI 250–70). Thereafter follows
a lengthy meditation in which the poet takes up issues treated in
the A version (B XI 165–310). (The points intended to correct the
A poet are here in italics). To begin with, love is more important
than learning, and we should follow Christ's teaching (Luke 14:12)
and invite the poor and helpless to dinner rather than our friends
(cp. A XI 38–50). *But we are all brothers, rich and poor alike. Therefore
let us love one another, and freely give, both of our possessions and of
our knowledge; and let us not blame anyone, though he may know more
Latin, nor foully rebuke him, for none is without fault* (B XI 191–209). Faith
and love, rather than learning, can overcome sin, and so we should
not rely *too heavily* (219) on learning. But the example of Christ's
poverty does *not* mean that poverty *itself* is a virtue. True, there
are many biblical examples of poverty; but poverty is a blessed
state *only if it is patient* (247–49); *and perfect poverty is voluntary* (261–
69).

Having thus prescribed faith in God as a remedy for poverty,
the author tries to forestall the counteraccusation that he is merely
defending the status quo, peddling quietistic medicine for the
masses. Perhaps you are thinking, he seems to imply, that I am
all in favor of poverty for the common people, but that I make
an exception in the case of priests. This is not true. Priests should
have the same faith in God's promise to provide that I have just
mentioned as characteristic of perfect poverty. They should certainly not take money for singing masses (B XI 274–88; cp. A III
237–39). Above all, there is no excuse for their ignorance (B XI 289–
308; not in A). But to conclude: poverty is better than riches *only if
it is patient* (B XI 309–10).

We have now reached the one passage in B XI–XV that actually
depicts God's Creation (B XI 311–59). Kynde (Nature) takes the
Dreamer to a mountain called Middle-Earth from which point he
is shown the Creation, a setting that exactly parallels what we
have already seen in Chaucer's *Parliament of Fowls*. But the closest
literary parallel, interestingly enough, is the Creation scene in the
Cornish *Origo Mundi* (123–34), where the list of animals and birds
coincides very closely to those described in the English poem.
The behavior of the animals and birds seems to the Dreamer quite
reasonable, hence he asks his next companion, Reason, why it is
that the animals follow reason while man does not. Reason re-

sponds by rebuking the Dreamer for lack of sufferance (B XI 367–94), thus turning one of the weapons of the A text against him (A X 85–116). The Dreamer's reaction to this is one of shame (B XI 395–402), thus putting himself in the proper frame of mind to receive instruction from his next tutor, Imaginatif (B XI 403–31). Fortune's fool has at last turned, and is now taking his first step on the long road that will lead him to God.

The main task of Imaginatif is to teach the Dreamer the value of learning. After some good-natured banter from his tutor (B XII 1–19), to which the now-receptive Dreamer responds with a gesture of humility (20–29), the real business of the passus begins with Imaginatif's definition of the triad (faith, hope, charity), which leads into a list of famous people who were encumbered by "catel and kynde wit" (57). The association of wealth (catel) with natural understanding (kynde wit) becomes a reasonable strategy on the part of the B poet when we remember that wealth was severely condemned in the A text, while "kind wit" was exalted. The reviser casts a shadow over the faculty that Holy Church praised above all others (A I 130) as a means of coming to Truth.

The remainder of passus XII is taken up with an impassioned defense of learning (clergye). First of all, says Imaginatif, Christ *did* make use of learning (cp. A XI 285–92): as when he wrote on the ground in defense of the woman taken in adultery (John 8:6, 8) (B XII 72–86). Furthermore, learning is necessary to make the Mass meaningful, and the education of the priesthood—gained through books—is necessary for salvation; whereas kynde wit is worldly wisdom, thus foolishness to God (B XII 87–114). You say that salvation is reserved for poor plowmen and shepherds (A XI 297–303), but you should not overlook the fact that at Bethlehem there were not only shepherds (kynde wit) but also the Magi (clergye) (B XII 141–59). There are good examples showing the superiority of learning over kynde wit (B XII 160–91). By the way, you seem to feel that the salvation of the penitent thief was an injustice (A XI 271–78), but you should know that although he was indeed saved, he does not have as exalted a position at the heavenly feast as those who lead holy lives (B XI 192–216). Imaginatif then criticizes the Dreamer for his tendency to be hot for certainty, warning him that Nature alone knows the answers to his questions, while learned men offer us interesting insights by interpreting the animals symbolically, as when Aristotle employs the peacock to expose the pride of rich men and the lark to praise the superiority

of the poor and humble. For this we should be grateful, and pray
for the souls of such learned men (B XI 217–74).

But the Dreamer interposes, reiterating his earlier objection (A
XI 257–70), to which his tutor responds by walking a theological
tightrope, concluding that God may well reward the just man who,
like Trajan, obeyed the best law he knew. Then Imaginatif vanishes, before the fool has a chance to ask him any more questions
(B XII 275–93).

In passus XIII–XIV the previous theoretical discussion of learning (clergye) and common sense (kynde wit) is given a new and
dramatic form. A banquet scene (XIII 21–214) enables the poet to
distinguish between true and corrupt learning, while incidentally
satirizing the shortcomings of the friars in the pompous figure of
the doctor. And the confession of Haukyn the active man (B XIII
220–XIV end) gives the author an opportunity to suggest that the
common sense (kynde wit) of the ordinary man has its limitations. Yet in making this comparison the value of learning continues to be affirmed by the presence at the banquet of Clergye
himself, who does his best to defend true learning, even though
he is obviously embarrassed by the behavior of the friar doctor.
In an amusing development, the Dreamer, chastened and now
under the control of his new companions, is given freedom to
unleash his natural hostility against the friar, until Conscience
signals Patience to urge him to be quiet.

In the other main episode, the confession scene, Haukyn's coat
is found to be stained with the seven sins, and he is brought to
the confessional, as it were, by the ministrations of Conscience
and Patience. One is immediately reminded of A passus V, but
there are significant differences. Here all the sins are concentrated
on the coat of a single individual who is identified as a minstrel,
a waferer, but who is clearly intended as a representative of the
common man, living the active life of a laborer. It dawns on us
only gradually, as we listen to Haukyn's confession and to the
teachings of his mentors, that this man represents the poor people who were so highly praised in A, while here he is being taught
that something more than the Lord's Prayer may be necessary
before he can be saved.

Patience is Haukyn's most important guide. It is Patience who
teaches him to take no thought for the morrow (B XIV 28–96), distinguishes between good and evil wealthy men (97–173), points
out that Christ's pardon is for poor *and* rich (174–200), and that the

sins are actually harder on wealthy men than on the poverty stricken (201–72). Patience concludes with a hymn in praise of poverty. This is a theme that we saw emerge near the beginning of the continuation, where the poet paid tribute to poverty, but only on condition that it be patient. Why is Patience so important?

It is not enough to say that patient poverty was a commonplace doctrine of the poet's day, or that he invokes it here out of a general concern for reform. For its use in *Piers the Plowman* is entirely restricted to the B and C texts, and it occurs only in passages containing direct or implicit criticism of ideas set forth in the A version. Hence I offer the following suggestion. If the B poet did not actually regard the A text as dangerous in itself, he may yet have feared that its angry denunciation of learning and riches might incite others to a dangerous course of action. If Haukyn had followed the advice of his spiritual teachers, the Peasants' Revolt would not have occurred. But in spite of all this criticism, we emerge from the episode with a much more positive feeling for Haukyn than we do for the friar doctor. The friar, pompous and learned, maintains his self-assurance throughout the banquet scene; but Haukyn, after his confession, weeps real tears, thus expressing his genuine penitence and a resolve to change his ways.

In the final passus on the theme of "the A text revisited" (B XV) the Dreamer meets Soul (*Anima*), his last and in some ways most important tutor, since what might be called his "brainwashing" is completed in this passus. Indeed the Dreamer-fool is so impressed by Patience's praise of poverty that he feels quite superior to people of rank and wealth: when he meets lords or ladies in the street, he refuses even to bow to them or wish them well, and in this folly he continues until Reason rocks him to sleep. In his dream he meets Soul, who defines himself and proceeds to rebuke the Dreamer for his lust for knowledge (B XV 12– 67). But the Dreamer is now quite ready to be taught, and the sermon of Soul is in reality aimed in a different direction. We have noted that the real audience addressed by Patience in passus XIV was the impatient poor of England in the time of the Peasants' Revolt. Now, in passus XV, the poet shifts direction and Soul addresses with considerable severity an audience of the wealthy and the powerful. In doing so he often employs ammunition from the A text, and he now has the cooperation of a Dreamer whose questions are invariably designed to be helpful.

Soul begins his homily by attacking the friars, recapitulating some of the charges made against them in A. To balance this, he also denounces corruption among the secular clergy, but in a way that reveals much more restraint, and even a concern lest he alienate colleagues in the audience who might look upon him as a traitor to the profession (e.g., B XV 89). He repeats the charges of the A poet (B XV 101–8; cp. A I 164–73, IV 105–8), but whereas in A, as we have seen, the clergy are the briar and the commons are the root of the rose of society (A X 119–24), in B it is the clergy who are the root of the tree of society (B XV 94–100), and the flourishing of the other estates is *contingent* on the integrity of the parish priest. The B poet believes firmly in the indispensability of the priesthood, whose role in the salvation of poor plowmen and shepherds is at least as important as the Lord's Prayer (A XI 302).

What is Charity? asks the Dreamer. To which Soul responds with *Except ye . . . become as little children, ye shall not enter into the kingdom of heaven* (Matt. 18:3), explaining that you must be childlike but not childish, and have a free liberal will (B XV 145–46). I have lived in the land, declares the Dreamer, my name is Long Will (=longsuffering, 1 Cor. 13:4), but I have never found full charity, before or behind! Clergymen teach me that Christ is everywhere, but I have never seen him (in the lives of others) except as *through a glass darkly* (1 Cor. 13:12). Here is a very profound statement indeed. Even Soul, with all his readiness to instruct, might well pause before attempting an answer. But the Dreamer makes this unnecessary by asking a few leading questions that allow his teacher to define charity further, leading to the dramatic moment when Will suddenly exclaims: "By Christ I would that I knew him (Charity)!" Soul's reply is, "Without the help of Piers Plowman you will never see him." And he goes on to hint that only Piers has the patience and perception to see through the masks that men wear to the true state of their wills. The plowman is thus the embodiment of the B poet's ideal (patient poverty), and the way has been paved for introducing him into the biblical drama which will resume in the next passus.

Charity, Soul continues, is not necessarily to be found among ascetics, some of whom make a display of their self-abasement; in fact it has no necessary connection with any station in life. It may appear in kings or beggars. It once appeared in a friar's frock, but that was long ago, in Saint Francis's time. It may appear in

[277]

the king's council, but not necessarily. Soul goes on to cite examples set by Christ and holy men of old (B XV 207–303). You wealthy men, both in and out of the church, should follow their example (B XV 304–39).

At this point in his sermon, Soul seems to be overcome by a feeling of melancholy at the discrepancy between the holiness of life in former times and the corruption and cupidity of leaders in his own time. In a somber passage he reviews the decay of society and the decline of learning (B XV 340–82). But with the words *sola fides sufficit* (faith alone suffices) he shakes off his depression and makes an appeal for a renewed effort to convert the heathen nations to Christianity. A strong missionary effort was an inseparable part of the vitality of the early Church: perhaps a renewal of this effort could cleanse the present generation of its cupidity. The teachers of Holy Church, after all, were meant to be *the salt of the earth* (Matt. 5:13). The Apostles converted the world, and there were only eleven of them; why is it that the veritable army of clerics today cannot do as much? (B XV 383–571). Soul's final summation is an eloquent call for the conversion of the heathen (B XV 572–601). This summary has something in common with Scripture's injunction in the A version to help the heathen (A XI 243–49). But in other respects the two passages are far apart. The God of the A text is Saint Truth; the God of the B continuation is Saint Charity.

Fall and Redemption (B XVI–XVIII)

Soul remains with the Dreamer long enough to call his attention to a garden, in which there stands a tree. This is of course the garden of Eden with its tree of the knowledge of good and evil, but very little space is devoted to the literal narrative. Instead Will swoons with joy at the mention of Piers' name, and in an inner dream the plowman explains the meaning of the vision by expounding the significance of the tree on the tropological, allegorical, and anagogical levels of biblical exegesis (B XVI 1–89). This is followed by a preliminary announcement of the coming Redemption (B XVI 90–166). The figure of Piers is a key element in these biblical passages. In the opening scene he is custodian of the "farm" of Eden; in the proclamation of the Redemption he becomes the traditional chivalric tutor of romance when he teaches Jesus the practice of medicine (lechecraft, B XVI 104). In this and other ways the plowman presides over the Old Testament narrative that we are tracing.

Awakening from the inner dream, Will now wanders "like an idiot" until he meets with Abraham (B XVI 167–275), Moses (B XVII 1–46), and the Good Samaritan (B XVII 47–350). This section of the poem represents the Old Testament period, with emphasis on how its teachers and leaders point the way to the New Testament, a function similar to that of the procession of prophets in the medieval drama. In this case Abraham stands for faith, Moses for hope, and the Good Samaritan for charity. The Samaritan, a transitional figure anticipating Christ himself, is given by far the most attention. By allegorizing the parable, he presents us with another foretaste of the Redemption (B XVII 83–123), and then, in response to a question from the Dreamer, he launches into an exposition of the doctrine of the Trinity (B XVII 124–350).

The Samaritan's emphasis on the Trinity cannot be accounted for simply as illustrative of the poet's interest in doctrinal matters. In the first place, he is here responding to what he must have considered a deficiency in the A version, where the doctrine of the Trinity receives little attention, and that little is not very positive (A XI 38–44). Much more important, the doctrine of the Trinity is an instrument in the poet's continuing emphasis on the necessity of grace. We have seen this emphasis almost from the beginning of the B continuation (esp. B XII 62ff.). Grace is the gift of the Holy Ghost which engenders humility, patience, and love. It abases the pride of the learned; it teaches patience to the poor; it redeems the wealthy who might otherwise be harsh and unkind to beggars who cry at the gate. Grace, with the help of free will, can withstand the combined assault of the world, the flesh, and the Devil. And it is of great importance in the Samaritan's teaching concerning the Trinity. The unforgivable sin, he says, is the sin against the Holy Ghost, which extinguishes grace. And when this flame dies, there is nothing left but the darkness of potential damnation. There is a special note of urgency here, for the darkness he warns against is about to descend on the field full of folk and envelop the ignorant armies of the Peasants' Revolt engaged in extinguishing the flame of human life.

After a brief waking interval, the Dreamer once again falls asleep and this time he dreams of the events of Palm Sunday, the trial of Christ, the Crucifixion, the debate of the four daughters of God, the Harrowing of Hell, and the Resurrection (B XVIII). Here the biblical narrative, strongly influenced by the medieval drama, reaches its climax in the Resurrection; the traditional Christ-knight theme, drawing on the poet's knowledge of romance, is elaborated with striking originality; and, not least, the Dreamer's spiritual progress culminates in the dramatic ceremony of creeping to the cross. On all this shines the light of Piers, the ideal representative of human nature. This passus is a triumph of the B poet's art, and I have long felt that behind its high emotion the author is making a strenuous effort to reconcile the warring factions of the summer of 1381.

The Apostolic Age and Apocalypse (B XIX–XX)

Up to this point I have ignored the rubrics in the manuscripts of the B version, which generally divide the poem (after the *Visio*) into three parts: Dowel (B VIII–XIV), Dobet (XV–XVIII), and Dobest (XIX–XX). For one thing, the manuscripts do not all agree in this matter. Moreover, although it is clear that the reviser understands how the triad is used in A, it is also clear that he himself is using it in a different and less precise way. As far as I can determine, the efforts of critics to harmonize the use of the triad in A with its use in BC have not been successful, for the very reason that the reviser's employment of it is so different. He is using these terms to express in a general way the momentum of the divine plan, the progress of sacred history from the Creation to the Last Judgment. But against this pattern of progress he shows us in passus XIX–XX mankind doing his worst. And so it is only with the profoundest sense of irony that the poet has given this section of his poem the title of "Dobest."

This last section extends from the Resurrection to the poet's own day. The most obvious features of the biblical structure are to be seen in passus XIX. First comes the Ascension (B XIX 1–193), then the sending of the Holy Ghost (B XIX 194–256), followed by the postbiblical history of the early Church (B XIX 257–330), and finally an anticipation of the apocalyptic Last Judgment (B XIX 331–478). Passus XX, of course, is a symphony of themes taken from virtually all that has gone before in the poem, and its setting is the field full of folk; but its structure and its driving momentum are attributable to our poet's use of apocalyptic tradition. Thus the last two passus provide impressive testimony to the fact that the B continuation is a poem not merely indebted to but actually based on the Bible.

The Dreamer attends Mass, during which he falls asleep and has a vision in which he sees the figure of Piers, covered with blood, and having the appearance of Jesus. In response to his question, Conscience explains that the figure is actually Christ, but he is wearing Piers' armor (human nature). The scene being depicted here is that of the Ascension, which in medieval tradition draws heavily for amplification on Psalm 24:7–10 and above all Isaiah 63:1–3. Its purpose in stressing the blood-stained figure of Christ ascending is to emphasize the exaltation of human nature that occurred at this moment in history. "A great dignity have we gotten," said Saint Leo, "when *our nature* is lifted up unto the right side of the Father." Christ descended to earth as God; he ascended to heaven as man. Our poet gives this traditional theme a new vividness by letting Piers represent the human nature that is exalted in the Ascension. In the sermon of Conscience that follows, Piers is given the power of the priesthood to bind and loose, and absolve men of their sins provided they first *pay what they owe*. The emphasis here seems to be on the power of the confessional to compel the reconciliation of a society torn by internal strife.

As the Dreamer moves through the feasts of the Church calendar, there unfolds for us a sequence of events that should by now be quite familiar. There is the sending of the Holy Ghost (Acts 2:1–4), followed by the granting of the gifts of the Holy Ghost adapted from 1 Corinthians 12:4ff. This leads into the poet's exposition of the history of the early Church (B XIX 257–330), which undergoes a process of allegorization reminiscent of the later romances, as when in Malory's *Morte Darthur* the Castle of Maidens episode becomes a form of the Harrowing of Hell. In like manner the B poet takes the "matter" of Piers' plowing of the half acre from the A version and gives as its "sense" the history of the Church. Piers has a team of four oxen (Matthew, Mark, Luke, and John), and four "stottis" (work horses) (Augustine, Ambrose, Gregory, and Jerome). He sows the seeds of the cardinal virtues, and harrows them with the Old Law and the New. He builds a barn called Unity, or Holy Church, in which to store the grain when it is harvested. Then Piers and Grace go into all the world (Mark 16:15) to till truth.

Meanwhile Pride comes with a great army of sins, boasting to

Conscience that he will destroy the seeds of the virtues sown by Piers and corrupt Unity, so that no one will know Christian from heathen. Conscience calls on all Christian people to come into Piers' barn, and Kynde Wit orders them to dig a moat, which is filled with tears of contrition. I care not, says Conscience, if Pride come now! But something goes wrong. The commons object to Conscience's insistence that they pay what they owe before receiving Communion. A brewer says that he does not intend to "hakke after holynesse." A vicar volunteers some remarks on the corruption of society, which he says is especially to be found among cardinals and the pope. A secular lord announces that he will employ the virtue of fortitude (i.e., brute force) to collect his rents, and a king remarks that he can justly take what he needs without asking anyone's permission—hence he can be houseled without making restitution. Conscience cautiously agrees, but adds that the king must rule his realm reasonably.

In this ominous conclusion to passus XIX the poet is making effective use of a feature from medieval drama, best seen in the Chester play of the Last Judgment. In its cast of characters are a pope, emperor, king, and queen, all saved; but also a pope, emperor, king, queen, justice, and merchant, all damned. In our poem, of course, the pope, cardinals, king, lord, and commons are not yet damned or saved. They are being weighed in the balances, but it is not yet too late. The storm clouds gather as the pope commands Christians to kill each other, the cardinals live in luxury, and king, lords, and commons cynically take what they can get. The lightning clenches for the stroke.

The final passus opens in what might be called the eye of the storm. In a deceptively quiet passage, the Dreamer, now wide awake, encounters a character called Need, who rebukes him for not associating himself with the philosophy of the king, lords, and commons expressed in the previous scene. After all, says Need, if you are governed by temperance, it is no sin for you to get your sustenance by sleight when you are hungry. Moreover Christ himself set an example of poverty which you should follow, hence you should not be ashamed to beg and be needy.

At the conclusion of Need's "sermon" the Dreamer falls asleep, and the final vision begins. Antichrist storms into the field full of folk and overturns the crop of truth, with the assistance of friars and the religious orders. The convent bells ring as everyone comes out to welcome Antichrist. Meanwhile, the poet tells us, there are a few "fools" who heed Conscience's advice to come into Unity and help defend it against the onslaught of Belial's children (B XX 50–78). Conscience cries out to Kynde for assistance, and thus begins the driving attack of the "Three Horsemen," Elde (old age), Kynde (nature), and Death (pestilence), against the army of Antichrist. The shattering impact of these democratic destroyers on the army of Antichrist is reported with grim humor (e.g., B XX 91–93). But the folk who survive the initial onslaught do not seem to have learned their lesson. Sinners abandon themselves to lechery and luxurious living. Indeed this was one of the consequences of the Black Death in the poet's own day; but it is also a phenomenon observed in Revelation (9:20–21). This theme the poet develops at considerable length in a passage containing some of his most effective satire (B XX 105–81).

From the alarms and excursions of the forces in the field the poet suddenly focuses attention on the final conversion of the Dreamer (B XX 182–212). Will finds himself in the path of the three horsemen, and one of them, Elde, actually overruns him and leaves his head bald. Elde's assault on the Dreamer is then amusingly described in a passage reminiscent of the famous description of old age, senility, and death in Ecclesiastes 12:1–7. When Elde has completed his work, the Dreamer looks up and sees Kynde passing by and Death drawing near. Now thoroughly frightened, he cries out to Kynde to avenge him, "for I would be hence" (B XX 202), an ambiguous wish, which could simply express a desire to escape danger, or more likely, I think, an offer to surrender the worldly values he has so long pursued. Kynde tells him to enter Piers' barn of Unity (Holy Church) and there learn some craft. And when the Dreamer asks what craft is best to learn, Kynde tells him to learn to love. Finally Will asks (B XX 208):

How shall I come to catel [possessions] so, to clothe me and to feed?

The fool! The whole poem has been designed to answer that question: God will provide. At last the Dreamer is prepared to accept the answer by coming into Unity, there to join those other "fools" who are still resisting the onslaught of Antichrist.

The poem concludes with a grim account of the storming of Holy Church. Worldly priests, siding with Covetousness in the army of Antichrist, begin the attack. Conscience cries for help from clergy (learning), and thus brings on the friars, the real villains of the narrative. Conscience is reluctant to admit them to Unity, and warns them to imitate Francis and Dominic in holiness and love. But the friars preach that all things should be in common, and corrupt the sacrament of penance with easy confession. Meanwhile, some of the defenders of Unity, wounded by Hypocrisy, are impatient with the painful plasters applied to their wounds by Contrition. They call for the friars. At first Conscience opposes this, but then he gives in and admits a friar, who proceeds to apply soothing plasters to the wounded. When the army of Antichrist renews its attack, Peace reports that the gatekeeper, Contrition, has fallen asleep, along with other defenders. Unity now lies helpless before the assault. Whereupon Conscience vows to go forth as a pilgrim in quest of Piers the plowman, who alone can destroy pride and restore Holy Church (B XX 378–84). Thus the poem's ending is not without hope, but in Conscience's cry for vengeance there remains the threat of Judgment.

The Eschatology of the B Version

Eschatology has to do with the last things that are to occur at the end of the world, the events of the "latter days," made known by revelation (apocalypse) in certain books of the Bible. We can see how influential this part of biblical tradition has been in omnibus works such as *Cursor Mundi* and the *Polychronicon*, to mention only two instances. But when we try to assess the influence of apocalypse in a literary work such as *Piers the Plowman*, we face a difficult question. The impact of this biblical tradition through the centuries has been enormous, and it is often not easy to distinguish in literature between a metaphorical use of apocalyptic concepts or images and a genuine belief on the part of an author that the world is indeed coming to an end in the near future. In a recent and most impressive study of the ending of the B version of *Piers*, Robert Adams eloquently states his conviction that the author "seems to have believed that he was seeing the end of the world in his lifetime" (p. 293), and I am persuaded that in this matter he is correct. In particular I would like to review his interpretation of Need, a character who appears at the beginning of the last passus, because this will offer us an opportunity to see in depth the poet's subtle and profound use of certain biblical verses that are important in apocalyptic tradition. At the same time, by such a review, we can come to appreciate Adams's assessment of the poet's eschatology, and also observe how this relates to the historical emphasis of the present chapter.

Critics have disagreed completely on how to read Need's speech (B XX 1–49), some arguing that his teaching expresses the poet's own views, others warning that Need is not to be trusted. I have inclined toward the latter opinion, largely convinced by the arguments of R. W. Frank, who long ago pointed out that Need's words echo the specious arguments of the friars in defense of their theoretical poverty. We have already had occasion to observe our poet's antimendicant point of view (e.g., B XI 59–102), and Need's speech prepares us for the poem's ending with a powerful indictment of the friars. Hence when Need encourages the Dreamer to beg, and even to obtain food by deception (sleighte), the reader should be on his guard.

Like many another personification in medieval allegory, Need comes to us from a biblical source, specifically a verse in the description of Leviathan in Job (41:13):

> In his neck will remain strength,
> And *want* will go before his face.

Modern translations are of no help in the part of this verse that concerns us (=AV 41:22). Thus the King James Bible reads: *and sorrow is turned into joy before him*; while the Revised Standard Version has: *and terror dances before him*. There seems to be a genuine crux here; other modern versions translate (sometimes by emending) to show "despair," "fear," "violence," or even "untiring energy" dancing or leaping before the face of Leviathan.

The medieval Latin Bible had "egestas," which the Early Version of the Wyclif Bible translates "need," and it is in this form that the verse came to be associated with the last days as described especially in Revelation, through the identification of Leviathan with *that old serpent, called the Devil, and Satan, which deceiveth the whole world* (Rev. 12:9). No doubt Need acquired some of his ominous magnetism from the third of the Four Horsemen who are forerunners of the serpent. This third rider is mounted on a black horse and carries scales, while a voice announces the high price of food that accompanies a famine (Rev. 6:5–6). Obviously "need" in this passage is quite literally a lack of food. But the Need who goes before the face of Leviathan in Job (41:13) represents a much more profound deficiency. For this insight we are indebted to the commentary on this verse by Gregory the Great in his *Morals on Job*.

In his exegesis of Job 41:13, Gregory distinguishes two kinds of need. First there is the want or need of the chosen, who, while in the exile of this life, long for the riches of the heavenly kingdom. Second, there is the want of the sinner, who, neglecting the object of his pilgrimage, thinks only of the visible things that he lacks in this world. The sinner in this state of mind is especially vulnerable to the cunning of the evil one, who steals upon him in a crafty manner without being detected and so makes void his virtues. The first half of the verse (*In his neck will remain strength*) expresses the power of Leviathan's violence; but the second (*And want will go before his face*) refers to the subtlety of his craft. Clearly Gregory's exposition here describes very accurately the technique that Need uses in his encounter with the Dreamer (B XX 1–49).

In a further comment on this verse Gregory alludes directly to the appearance of Antichrist in the latter days and, at the same time, stresses the desolated condition of the Church:

> For by the awful course of the secret dispensation, before this Leviathan appears in that accursed man whom he assumes, signs of power are withdrawn from Holy Church. For prophecy is hidden, the grace of healings is taken away, the power of longer abstinence is weakened, the words of doctrine are silent, the prodigies of miracles are removed. . . . For though signs will not be wanting to the faithful in their contest with him, yet his [following] will be so great, that those of our people will seem to be rather few or none at all.

Thus we see that a lack of spirituality will strike the Church itself, leaving it in precisely that weakened and defenseless position that the poet goes on to describe in his account of the coming of Antichrist (B XX 57–60):

> Friars followed that fiend, for he gave them copes,
> And the religious reverenced him and rang their bells,
> And all the convent came forth to welcome that tyrant
> And all his, as well as him, save only fools. . . .

And even these fools, the last defenders of Piers' barn, are compromised by the soporific medications of the friar-physician.

If our poet was armed with a biblical concordance, it would have been easy for him to identify other passages in which the word "egestas" (need) is used. Thus in Proverbs the sluggard is warned of the coming of need as a way-goer (AV traveller), and poverty (AV want) as an armed man (Prov. 6:9–11). In another passage, Agur son of Jakeh prays that the Lord give him only what is necessary for life: if he has too much, he may deny the Lord; but if he has too little, he may steal and forswear the name of God (Prov. 30:8–9). These verses were particularly embarrassing to the friars, and were consequently used to good effect by Archbishop FitzRalph in his sermons against them.

In addition to these key verses having to do directly with Need, Adams suggests that the context for our understanding of him is affected by the traditional division of the history of the Church into four stages, based in part on Psalm 91:5–6: *Thou shalt not be afraid for the Terror by night; nor for the arrow that flieth by day; nor for the pestilence* (V negotio) *that walketh in darkness; nor for the destruction* (V daemonio) *that wasteth at noonday.* Equally important is the description of the opening of the seven seals in Revelation (6:1–8:5), a passage used by commentators to characterize the flow of Church history. By the twelfth century, the four dangers enumerated in Psalm 91 were understood to be associated with those threatening the Church from its foundation to the end of the world. The first age was one of violent opposition; the second, that of seditious teaching (heresy); the third, hypocrisy; and the fourth age, that of the noonday demon, was to be the period of deception by Antichrist. In a general way the defections represented by king, lord, vicar, and commoner (B XIX 389–478) could be associated with the initial three dangers; in which case the fourth danger, the noonday demon, is represented by Need, who meets the Dreamer when it is "nearly noon" (B XX 4).

From all this Adams draws the conclusion, with which I agree, that the poet is here foreseeing the literal end of things, and that Antichrist is himself, not merely a term of opprobrium directed against some individual whom the poet wishes to attack (B XX 50–72). It is this conviction that leads to the extremism, for instance, of Patience's advice to Haukyn that he care not for food even to the extent of dying (sooner than allowing his patience to desert him), since he who loves Christ does not love this world (B XIV 53–59). Possibly the author even believes that the "son of perdition" has already been born and is walking to and fro on the earth. At the very least, "Need is a frighteningly active evangelist, an inverted John the Baptist preparing the way for his false master, Antichrist" (Adams, p. 295).

Such apocalyptic fervor, Adams points out, is not a feature of the mendicant debate that was taking place at the time (for example in the sermons of FitzRalph), and so he tentatively suggests that the poet's eschatology may have come from the antifraternal writings of the Parisian seculars of the thirteenth century (e.g., William of St. Amour). The parallels he cites, notably in the *Liber de Antichristo*, do indeed suggest that our author may have known and used such works, but I would also suggest that apocalyptic fervor is not likely to have been acquired from reading about battles of the preceding century. If the poet is anticipating the literal end of the world, and I believe he is, then that desperate expectation must come from an event that had a direct impact on him personally. And it is entirely possible that the most shattering event of this poet's life was the peasant rising of 1381, when peace was taken from the earth, and Christians in England were engaged in killing one another (Rev. 6:4). This event, along with the council at Blackfriars and Archbishop Courtenay's inquisition at Oxford the following year, convinced the author that the latter days were at hand.

The Peasants' Revolt in the B Version

No doubt to Geoffrey Chaucer the London riots were alarming at the time, but once order was restored he seems to have given no more serious thought to the matter, and his clearest reference to these events occurs in a comic context: in "The Nun's Priest's Tale" the sound of the mob is compared to the noise of barnyard animals at the sight of the fox (*CT* VII 3394–97):

> Certes, he Jakke Straw and his meynee [company]
> Ne made nevere shoutes half so shrille,
> Whan that they wolden any Flemyng kille,
> As thilke day was maad upon the fox.

But no such attitude was possible for the author of the B version of *Piers the Plowman*, to whom the events were too shocking to become the subject of explicit reference or discussion.

The nearest thing to an overt allusion to the events of June 1381 occurs in the midst of a passage devoted to bishops (B XV 535–67), yet even this reference is given to us in code. While calling attention to the need for a renewal of the evangelical fervor of the early Church, Soul suggests that those bishops who have honorary appointments in heathen lands should actually go there and seek to convert the heathen population. There is something sardonic in this recommendation, since the individuals he singles out for such a mission are notorious favorites of the papal curia with what we would call phony appointments, whose only contribution to the Church takes the form of self-aggrandizing busywork (B XV 538, 557–58):

> That bear bishops' names of Bethlehem and Babylon,
> That hippe about in England to hallow men's altars,
> And creep among curates and confess against the law.

This is one of several passages in which bishops are seriously criticized (e.g., B X 256–90), but it differs from the others in that it was revised by the insertion of an addition passage (B XV 539–56) preserved only in MSS. R and F, in which Soul reminds us that the Church used to be blessed with self-sacrificing bishops. Christ himself performed baptisms and made bishops with the blood of his heart, and many a saint afterward suffered death for the faith in heathen lands. Saint Thomas à Becket, archbishop of Canterbury, was martyred among unkind (unnatural) Christians for the right of this and all Christian realms. Holy Church was highly honored by his death. He is an example to all bishops, and a bright mirror (B XV 556):

> And sovereignly to such that of Surrye beareth the name.

In the nineteenth century Walter W. Skeat, editor of the poem, sensed that this line contained a "pointed personal allusion," but it has not been easy to break the poet's code, to understand who it is that "bears the name of Syria." And it is only by chance that recently, while rereading the Chester plays, I noticed a stanza spoken by Annas in "The Irenmongers Playe" (16A) which begins as follows:

> Come hither, Symon of Surrey,
> And take this crosse anon in hye.

Annas is addressing the *hominem Cyrenaeum nomine Simonem* (Matt. 27:32, Vulgate) who carries the cross of Christ. This identification of the home of Simon of Cyrene (AV) offers a solution to the encoded reference: we may infer that the bishop who followed the bright example of Saint Thomas (martyred in 1170) would be a man whose first name is "Simon," and the only person who fits this description is Simon Sudbury, archbishop of Canterbury, assassinated by the mob on June 14, 1381.

Our poet was not the only one to draw this parallel between Becket and Sudbury. In his *Vox Clamantis* (I, 14) John Gower provides a detailed comparison of the martyrdom of the two arch-bishops. Four men plotted Thomas's murder, while a hundred thousand killed Simon; the one was felled by the wrath of a king, the other by the madness of the masses; both prelates were righteous and suffered undeservedly; Thomas's executioner was a knight, while Simon's was a peasant. Later on in this same chapter Gower speaks further of the mob's participation in the violence: "One man helped in what another man did, and another agreed that they would be bad, worse, and worst." Surely in this inversion of the triad adapted by John Ball from the A version we see Gower's awareness of the impact of *Piers the Plowman* on the peasant movement.

Apart from this one encoded reference to Simon Sudbury in B XV 556, the effect of the rising on the poem must be read between the lines. Such is the case, for example, with the Samaritan's definition of the Trinity (B XVII 124–350). This passage begins with the analogy of the hand: the fist represents the might of the Father, the fingers the wisdom of the Son, and the palm the power of the Holy Spirit. This analysis is traditional enough, and it is only necessary to call attention to the particular reason for its use here. It is introduced in order to show why the sin against the Holy Ghost (Matt. 12:31–32) cannot be forgiven: when the palm is injured, the hand is entirely incapacitated, incapable of making a fist or using the fingers; just so the sin against the Holy Ghost inhibits God's grace and prevents the granting of mercy.

The Samaritan's other analogy is the torch or taper, and the purpose here is the same: from the wax (Father) and the wick (Son) comes forth the flame of the Holy Spirit. But if this flame is extinguished, there is nothing left to melt the might of the Father into mercy. The snuffing out of this light is the sin against the Holy Ghost. This might at first seem to be merely a repetition of the idea presented in the hand image, but a closer look shows that the extinguishing of the light of the Spirit has more than one meaning. Just as when the flame of a wick is extinguished (B XVII 214–16):

> So is the Holy Ghost, God, and grace without mercy
> To all unkind creatures that covet to destroy
> Leal [Loyal] love or life that our Lord shaped.

The extinguishing of the flame is the taking of a human life. Note especially that murder is an unnatural ("unkind") act, as the poet indicated earlier in his reference to the martyrdom of Saint Thomas "among unkind Christians." Use of the word "unkind" in this passage invariably has this meaning.

What if I was caught up in the excitement of events, filled with a sense of the rightness of the peasants' cause, and participated in the destruction of property and the "execution" of lawyers and corrupt officialdom? And what if now I stand in awe of my own actions, and am ready to repent? Then, says the Samaritan, the Father will forgive you, and anyone else who sorrowfully repents *and makes restitution* (B XVII 235).

But what if I do not have any means of repaying the full amount of damage I have done? Above all, how could I restore to life the human being for whose death I am responsible? To which the Samaritan responds (B XVII 237–38):

> And if it suffice not for assets, that in such a will dieth,
> Mercy for his meekness will make good the remnant.

The poet next turns to the question of who was responsible for the uprising. Rich men are denounced because of their covetousness and their consequent failure to be generous and thus close the gap between the rich and the poor which lies behind the violence (B XXII 258–68); churchmen (meaning the friars especially) who encouraged the rioters by taking Acts 2:44 as their text in sermons and misinterpreting it (cf. B XX 273–74) are warned that they are guilty of murder by mouth if not by hand (B XVII 269–75); those who actually committed murder are said to have committed the sin against the Holy Ghost (B XVII 276–92); and the Samaritan here comes within an ace of saying that these latter will *never* be forgiven. The passage is full of anguish (B XVII 284–88):

> How might he ask mercy, or any mercy him help,
> That wickedly and willfully would mercy anynte [destroy]?
> Innocence is next God, and night and day it crieth,
> "Vengeance, vengeance, forgiven be it never,
> That shent [destroyed] us and shed our blood, forshaped
> [unmade] us as it were.

From the Latin that follows line 288 we learn that in the call for vengeance our poet is alluding to the cries of the souls that were slain for the word of God in Revelation 6:10, *How long, O Lord, holy and true, dost thou not judge and avenge our blood on them that dwell on the earth?*

This seems to leave little room for the redemption of anyone involved in the violence, and the Dreamer, deeply disturbed, raises the question (B XVIII 392):

> "I pose I had sinned so, and should now die,
> And now am sorry, that so the Saint Spirit agulte [sinned against],
> Confess me, and cry his grace, God, that all made,
> And mildly his mercy ask, might I not be saved?

Somewhat reluctantly the Samaritan concedes that *his mercy is above all his works* (Ps. 145:9), but that before his mercy can be shown, restitution will be necessary, except that genuine contrition will suffice if the guilty party cannot pay. Why is God so severe in this matter? Because "unkindness" (code word for the violence) is contrary to all reason. For there is no one *unable* to love, if he so chooses, and to offer from his heart good will and a good word to all men, granting them mercy and forgiveness, loving them as himself, and amending his own life (B XVII 343-48). Having made this pronouncement, the Samaritan rides off like the wind.

The full severity of the poet's response to the destruction and bloodshed of 1381 is allocated to the Samaritan. In the following passus, devoted to the Passion and Resurrection of Christ, the poet interweaves a positive appeal to the warring factions of English society. Students of *Piers the Plowman* have had nothing but praise for B passus XVIII, as the emotional and artistic high point of the continuation. With this I am in complete agreement, and merely wish to call attention to a source for the poet's emotion beyond the subject itself. Below the surface of the gospel narrative, I believe, we can sense the author's effort to effect a reconciliation of the hostile forces in England through his treatment of the Passion.

It is possible, for example, to see something of the poet's concern for reconciliation in his treatment of Longinus, the soldier who pierced Christ's side with a spear (John 19:34). According to apocryphal tradition, Longinus was blind, and is miraculously healed when blood runs down the spear shaft to his eyes. When he sees what he has done to Jesus he falls to his knees (B XVIII 88-91):

> "Against my will it was, Lord, to wound you so sore!"
> He sighed and said, "sorely it me athinketh [repents];
> For the deed that I have done I do me in your grace;
> Have on me ruth [pity], rightful Jesus," and right with that he wept.

It is true that tradition may have determined the inclusion of this story. Yet it seems to be used here for more than tradition's sake: namely, as an example of true repentance for an act of violence, a model confession for any who may be guilty of extinguishing the flame of human life.

Later on, in the Harrowing of Hell episode, the poet's concern comes closer to the surface, particularly in Christ's speech to Satan. In his opening remarks the Lord articulates the conventional theme of the guiler beguiled (B XVIII 324-72). But in the remainder of his speech Jesus expresses his intention to show mercy on the Day of Judgment. My nature requires, he says, that I show mercy to mankind, for I am related by blood to all men. And certainly I shall not damn to death those brethren who are even more closely related to me, by baptism as well as blood! Just as a king may pardon a condemned felon, so I may decide on forgiveness at the last. And even though holy writ says that no evil should be unpunished, I can show mercy—on condition that some effort toward atonement for sin has been made (B XVIII 373-88). After they have been cleansed in the prison of purgatory, *many* of my brethren shall see my mercy. Why not all of them? Jesus continues (B XVIII 392-93):

> For blood may suffer blood [to go] both hungry and cold,
> But blood may not see blood bleed, but him rue [have pity].

Thus Jesus imposes the same conditions as did the Samaritan, but in muted form. These lines are followed by a quotation from Saint Paul (2 Cor. 12:4): *I heard unspeakable words, which it is not lawful for a man to utter.* The use of this verse in the context seems abrupt, but I understand it to express (following Derek Pearsall) the poet's awareness of "the limits to which his vision of Christ's promise of mercy can be taken." In the remainder of the speech, Jesus again speaks reassuringly of his intention to show mercy to all those who loved him and believed in his coming.

Lucifer is bound with chains, and the passus moves rapidly to its close. Many hundreds of angels harp and sing, and Peace pipes a note of poetry (B XVIII 409–15):

> "After sharp showers," quoth Peace, "most sheen is the sun;
> Is no weather warmer than after watery clouds.
> Nor no love liefer, nor liefer friends,
> Than after war and woe, when Love and Peace be masters.
> Was never war in this world, nor wickedness so keen,

[293]

That Love, an him list, to laughing ne brought,
And Peace through patience all perils stopped."

Then Mercy and Truth embrace, and Righteousness and Peace
kiss each other (Ps. 85:10). The scene then ends with music and the
singing of the *Te Deum*.

The reconciliation of Truth and Love first of all represents the
resolution of the paradox of justice and mercy through the redemption. As such it is the rightful climax of this section of the
poem. But this reconciliation also has an urgent application in the
poet's own time. The song of Peace is both a benediction and a
prayer: let there be no more war and woe, let perils cease, and
let love and peace turn wickedness to friendship and smiling. Occurring as they do in the context of the Resurrection, these lines
constitute a powerful appeal to the hostile forces in contemporary
England.

As we now see, readers of *Piers the Plowman* who expect the
poet to refer to "Jakke Straw and his meynee" will be disap-
pointed. There are no such direct references even in the C version, which most agree was written no earlier than 1387. But those
who look carefully will find much that relates to the Peasants'
Revolt, written in anguish between the lines.

Prophecy and Apocalypse: The A and B Versions Compared

Students of the Bible will be familiar with the usual distinction
made by commentators between prophecy and apocalypse, that
is, between the pre-Exile prophets and books like Daniel and Revelation. The prophet is concerned with the here and now, the
issues facing his nation and people. His aim is to establish justice
in the gate. On the other hand, the post-Exile writer of apocalypse despairs of doing anything about the present situation, and
instead announces an imminent divine intervention in human af-
fairs. His subject is the consummation of history, the end of the
world. For this reason it is often said that the prophets are fundamentally optimistic, since despite their threatening prognosti-
cations, they do seem to be acting as if they thought that the
behavior of the people could be changed and the nation saved.
Similarly the writer of apocalypse is said to be pessimistic in that
he holds out no hope of correcting a bad situation, and simply
calls for endurance in the face of world cataclysm.

Without insisting on an exact parallelism, I would like to suggest that of the two poems that comprise the work we know as *Piers the Plowman*, the original (A) version is prophetic, and the revision (BC) is apocalyptic. Of course, after more than a millennium of biblical tradition we should not expect to find the kind of pure distinction observable when, for instance, the prophecies of Amos are compared with the visions of Daniel. When the A poet sees the trees uprooted by the southwest wind in 1362 and is reminded of one of the fifteen signs of Doomsday (A V 18–20), this does not turn his poem into an apocalypse. Nor is the revision converted into prophecy by the presence of passages calling for the establishment of justice in the nation. The reviser's intention, after all, was to make two poems into one, and even in the continuation he was often influenced (e.g., in B XV 68–144) by the original poet.

Nevertheless, our review of the A version and the B continuation in this chapter reveals, I think, that the two works offer an interesting contrast in biblical style and substance. The A poet offers us a merciless exposure of corruption in high places, and, like Micah in the Old Testament, he seems to suggest that only through humble plowmen and shepherds will it be possible to restore the integrity of the nation. Learning corrupts, and learning accompanied by power corrupts absolutely. Let the king rule, but let him rule with the advice and counsel of Reason and Conscience. If he does so, then there will be no need for the learned, predatory officialdom that now is; all these functions will wither away, and lawyers will be given the task of spreading manure. The A poet would not have approved the deeds of the rebels in 1381, but we ought to acknowledge that his poem contained the seeds of a substantial cultural revolution.

In the B continuation we have seen a complex effort on the part of the author, both to defuse the explosive ideology of the A version and to present an alternative response to the crisis as he sees it. The sharp thrust of the original poem is blunted by subjecting the Dreamer (as spokesman for the views of A) to a relentless inquisition, until Will becomes malleable and is ready to adopt a new attitude (B XI–XV). Then, with the gathering momentum of biblical history behind him, the B poet returns to the field full of folk, now seen as the stormy landscape of apocalypse (B XVI–XX). At the very end of the poem the defenses of Holy Church crumble, and Conscience is forced to abandon the barn and go in search of Piers the plowman. The end is not yet, but who can suppose that it is very far away? The pessimism of the B poet does not frequently reach the surface (as in B XV 340–82), but neither is it often far away, and one senses it above all in the poet's conclusion. The one hope that he holds out is the possibility of salvation for the individual: in the midst of apocalyptic confusion, the Dreamer takes the simple steps necessary to save himself from the tribulation to come (B XX 182–212).

Both the A and B texts are, of course, profoundly religious in outlook, and both contain incisive criticisms of English society in the fourteenth century. But here the resemblance ends. The A version, with its praise of the essential spirituality of the commons and its angry condemnation of learning and wealth, gives aid and comfort to those desirous of revolutionary action against the social order, as John Ball perceived. The B version, however, calls for a revolution, not of society, but within the individual. And while these two classic views of man and society are perhaps not ultimately irreconcilable, they nevertheless stand in significant opposition in the A and B versions of *Piers the Plowman*.

CHAPTER ONE. *Medieval Drama*

A full list of texts and studies may be found in Carl J. Stratman, *Bibliography of Medieval Drama*, rev. ed., 2 vols. (New York: F. Unger, 1972). Editions of the major English cycles appeared mostly in the Early English Text Society series beginning in the late nineteenth century, but new editions are needed, and are beginning to appear. A useful review of the present state of editing of dramatic texts is the essay by Ian Lancashire, "Medieval Drama," in A. G. Rigg (ed.), *Editing Medieval Texts: English, French, and Latin Written in England* (New York and London: Garland, 1977), pp. 58–85. On page 76 Lancashire mentions the founding of the editorial project known as Records of Early English Drama (REED for short), which will coordinate efforts to publish all known regional records related to the drama in England down to the closing of the theaters in 1642. Several volumes have already appeared; when this work is finished no doubt the history of the medieval drama will have to be completely rewritten.

There are nevertheless important studies that will continue to be influential for years to come. In addition to the monumental works of E. K. Chambers, *The Medieval Stage*, 2 vols. (Oxford: Clarendon Press, 1903), Karl Young, *The Drama of the Medieval Church*, 2 vols. (Oxford: Clarendon Press, 1944), and Hardin Craig, *English Religious Drama of the Middle Ages* (Oxford: Clarendon Press, 1955), there are two more recent studies that are already recognized as landmarks: O. B. Hardison, Jr., *Christian Rite and Christian Drama in the Middle Ages* (Baltimore: Johns Hopkins Press, 1965), and V. A. Kolve, *The Play Called Corpus Christi* (Stanford: Stanford

University Press, 1966). Moreover, in the preparation of this chapter I also made use of a veritable shelf of recent volumes on various aspects of the drama by Richard Axton (1974), David Bevington (1975), Stanley J. Kahrl (1974), Alan Nelson (1974), Robert Potter (1975), Eleanor Prosser (1961), Richard Southern (*The Medieval Theatre in the Round*, 2d ed., New York, Theatre Arts Books, 1975), Glynne Wickham (*Early English Stages: 1300 to 1660*, 2 vols., London: Routledge & Paul, 1959–72), and, last but by no means least, Rosemary Woolf, *The English Mystery Plays* (Berkeley: University of California Press, 1972). A most impressive and inclusive study of recent date is William Tydeman, *The Theatre in the Middle Ages: Western European Stage Conditions, c. 800–1576* (Cambridge: Cambridge University Press, 1978).

The Cornish drama, very important but unfortunately much neglected, bears witness to the popularity of regional drama in the late medieval period. *The Creation of the World* or *Gwreans an Bys* (ed. Whitley Stokes) was a postmedieval revision of the most important Cornish text, the *Ordinalia*, a three-part fourteenth-century cycle edited and translated by Edwin Norris, *The Ancient Cornish Drama*, 2 vols. (Oxford, 1859). The other major text is a rare type of drama, otherwise not preserved in England—the saint's life: edited and translated by Whitley Stokes, *The Life of St. Meriasek, Bishop and Confessor: A Cornish Drama* (London, 1872). More accessible and more recent are the translations of these two primary texts by Markham Harris: *The Cornish Ordinalia* (Washington, D.C.: Catholic University of America Press 1969) and *The Life of Meriasek* (Washington, D.C.: Catholic University of America Press, 1977). My effort to date the *Ordinalia* some years ago is recorded in *Mediaeval Studies*, 23 (1961): 91–125. There have been two excellent studies of the cycle as a whole: Robert Longsworth, *The Cornish Ordinalia: Religion and Dramaturgy* (Cambridge, Mass.: Harvard University Press, 1967), and Jane A. Bakere, *The Cornish Ordinalia: A Critical Study* (Cardiff: University of Wales Press, 1980).

The best recent anthology is David Bevington (ed.), *Medieval Drama* (Boston: Houghton Mifflin, 1975), which includes a substantial selection of liturgical texts as well as cycle plays, saints' lives, moralities, and humanist drama of the sixteenth century. Among the collections of essays published in recent years I particularly recommend Jerome Taylor and Alan H. Nelson (eds.), *Medieval English Drama: Essays Critical and Contextual* (Chicago: University of Chicago Press, 1972). Of the dozen and a half essays in this volume I am especially indebted to E. Catherine Dunn, "Voice Structure in the Liturgical Drama: Sepet Reconsidered" (pp. 44–63), V. H. Kolve, "*Everyman* and the Parable of the Talents" (pp. 316–40), and David J. Leigh, "The Doomsday Mystery Play: An Eschatological Morality" (pp. 260–78). For the connections between medieval drama and iconography I am obliged to the various studies of M. D. Anderson (Lady

Trenchard Cox), notably her *Drama and Imagery in English Medieval Churches* (Cambridge: Cambridge University Press, 1963); and for the history of the cardinal sins I thank Morton W. Bloomfield, author of *The Seven Deadly Sins* (East Lansing: Michigan State College Press, 1952). References to *Piers the Plowman* are to the parallel text edition by Walter W. Skeat, 2 vols. (Oxford: Clarendon Press, 1886). For archaeological information on the Cornish rounds I recommend R. Morton Nance, "The Plen an Gwary or Cornish Playing Place," *Journal of the Royal Institution of Cornwall*, 24 (1935): 190–211, and for recent work at Castilly, Charles Thomas, "The Society's 1962 Excavations: The Henge at Castilly, Lanivet," *Cornish Archaeology*, 3 (1964): 3–14, esp. p. 11. For a full and sensitive discussion of the Second Shepherds' Play see the excellent essay by Míceál Vaughan, "The Three Advents in the *Secunda Pastorum*," *Speculum*, 55 (1980): 484–504. Many fascinating issues in the study of the medieval drama had to be left out of this chapter. For recent articles that break new ground in different ways, see D. W. Robertson, Jr., "The Question of 'Typology' and The Wakefield *Mactacio Abel*," *American Benedictine Review*, 25 (1974): 157–73; David L. Jeffrey, "Franciscan Spirituality and the Rise of Early English Drama," *Mosaic*, 8 (1975): 17–46; and Gail McMurray Gibson, "Bury St. Edmunds, Lydgate, and the *N-Town Cycle*," *Speculum*, 56 (1981): 56–90.

Finally, as an example of the intense current interest in the field of medieval drama, I subjoin a list of important publications devoted entirely to the Chester plays that have appeared in the last decade: *The Chester Mystery Cycle: A Facsimile of MS Bodley 175*, with an introduction by R. M. Lumiansky and David Mills (Leeds: University of Leeds School of English, Scolar Press, 1973); *The Chester Mystery Cycle*, ed. R. M. Lumiansky and David Mills (London: Oxford University Press, 1974; Early English Text Society, Supp. Ser. 3); Lawrence M. Clopper, "The History and Development of the Chester Cycle," *Modern Philology*, 75 (1978): 219–46; *Chester*, ed. Lawrence M. Clopper (Toronto: University of Toronto Press, 1979; Records of Early English Drama); *A Complete Concordance to the Chester Mystery Plays*, ed. Jean D. Pfleiderer and Michael J. Preston (New York and London: Garland, 1981); Peter W. Travis, *Dramatic Design in the Chester Cycle* (Chicago and London: University of Chicago Press, 1982); R. M. Lumiansky and David Mills, *The Chester Mystery Cycle: Essays and Documents*, with an essay, "Music in the Cycle," by Richard Rastall (Chapel Hill and London: University of North Carolina Press, 1983).

CHAPTER TWO. *Medieval Lyrics and the Church Calendar*

The lyrics, ballads, and songs quoted in this chapter come from so many sources that it will be most convenient to list them below alphabetically by the abbreviations used throughout to identify them.

XIII   Carleton Brown, *English Lyrics of the XIIIth Century*
          (Oxford: Clarendon Press, 1932).
XIV   Carleton Brown, *Religious Lyrics of the XIVth Century*
          (Oxford: Clarendon Press, 1957).
XV   Carleton Brown, *Religious Lyrics of the XVth Century*
          (Oxford: Clarendon Press, 1939).
Aubrey   John Aubrey, *Three Prose Works*, ed. John Buchanan-
          Brown (Carbondale, Ill.: Southern Illinois University
          Press, 1972), "Remaines of Gentilisme and Judaisme,"
          pp. 176–78.
Child   Francis J. Child, *The English and Scottish Popular Ballads*, 5
          vols. (Boston: Houghton Mifflin, 1882–98, reprinted by
          Dover, 1965).
EEC   Richard L. Greene, *The Early English Carols* (Oxford:
          Clarendon Press, 1977, 2d ed).
EETS ES   *Early English Text Society.* Extra Series.
EETS OS   *Early English Text Society.* Original Series.
Evans   R. H. Evans, *Old Ballads*, 4 vols. (London, 1810).
Kinsley   James Kinsley, *The Poems of William Dunbar* (Oxford:
          Clarendon Press, 1979).
N   *A Norton Critical Edition: Middle English Lyrics*, selected
          and edited by Maxwell S. Luria and Richard L.
          Hoffman (New York, 1974).
OBC   *The Oxford Book of Carols* (London: Oxford University
          Press, 1928).
Padelford Frederic M. Padelford, "The Songs in Manuscript
          Rawlinson C.813," *Anglia*, 31 (1908): 309–97.
Stevick   Robert D. Stevick, *One Hundred Middle English Lyrics*
          (New York: Bobbs-Merrill, 1964).

In sketching the popular traditions concerning Mary Magdalene I have used the Temple Classics edition of *The Golden Legend*, and David Bevington's anthology *Medieval Drama* (Boston: Houghton Mifflin, 1975). For general background see Helen M. Garth, *Saint Mary Magdalene in Medieval Literature* (Baltimore: Johns Hopkins Press, 1950), Marjorie M. Malvern, *Venus in Sackcloth: The Magdalen's Origins and Metamorphoses* (Carbondale, Ill.: Southern Illinois University Press, 1975), and Joseph Szövérffy, " 'Peccatrix Quondam Femina': A Survey of the Mary Magdalen Hymns," *Traditio*, 19 (1963): 79–146. Clifford Davidson treats the play against this background in "The Digby *Mary Magdalene* and the Magdalene Cult of the Middle Ages," *Annuale Mediaevale*, 13 (1972): 70–87. F. C. Gardiner, in *The Pilgrimage of Desire* (Leiden: Brill, 1971), provides a thorough and sensitive tracing of the development of the Christ as Pilgrim theme from Luke 24:13–35. I am especially indebted to Joseph Harris, " 'Maiden in the Mor Lay' and the Medieval Magdalene Tradition," *Journal of Medieval and Renaissance Studies*, 1 (1971): 59–87, for this magisterial treatment of a controversial subject. Not everyone accepts his interpretation, however, as can be seen in Siegfried Wenzel, "The Moor Maiden—A Contemporary View," *Speculum*, 49 (1974): 69–74, and E. J. Dobson and F. L. Harrison, *Medieval English Songs* (New York: Cambridge University Press, 1979), pp. 188–93. The latter volume provides an excellent basis for study of the music of Middle English lyrics, and is intended for use with "Medieval English Lyrics," a recording produced by Harrison and Dobson and published by Decca as Argo ZRG 5443 (stereo). For the newly discovered Scottish version of "The Maid and the Palmer" (Child 21), see David Buchan, "The Maid, the Palmer, and the Cruel Mother," *Malahat Review*, 3 (1967): 98–107.

The last twenty years have seen a remarkable increase of interest in the medieval lyric, beginning with three excellent studies: Stephen Manning, *Wisdom and Number* (Lincoln: University of Nebraska Press, 1962); Rosemary Woolf, *The English Religious Lyric in the Middle Ages* (Oxford: Clarendon Press, 1968), and Peter Dronke, *The Medieval Lyric* (London: Hutchinson, 1968; 2d ed., 1978). At the end of the decade appeared books by Sarah A. Weber, *Theology and Poetry in the Middle English Lyric* (Columbus: Ohio State University Press, 1969), and Raymond Oliver, *Poems Without Names* (Berkeley: University of California Press, 1970). Three more studies have appeared in the seventies: Douglas Gray, *Themes and Images in the Medieval English Lyric* (London: Routledge & Paul, 1972), Edmund Reiss, *The Art of the Middle English Lyric* (Athens: University of Georgia Press, 1974), and David L. Jeffrey, *The Early English Lyric and Franciscan Spirituality* (Lincoln: University of Nebraska Press, 1975). A valuable tool for further study of the lyric is now available in Michael J. Preston, *A Concordance to the Middle English Shorter Poem*, 2 vols. (Leeds: W. S. Maney & Son, 1975).

CHAPTER THREE. *Chaucer's* Parliament of Fowls
and the Hexameral Tradition

For direct quotations of Chaucer, I have used *The Works of Geoffrey Chaucer* (2d ed.), ed. F. N. Robinson (Boston: Houghton Mifflin, 1957), but for background and commentary I am also indebted to *Geoffrey Chaucer, The Parlement of Foulys*, ed. D. S. Brewer (Manchester: Manchester University Press, 1973). The Latin text of Saint Ambrose's *Hexameron* was edited by C. Schenkl, and appears in the series *Corpus Scriptorum Ecclesiasticorum Latinorum*, vol. 32, pt. 1 (Vienna, 1896), pp. 3–261, and a translation of this is included in vol. 42 of the Fathers of the Church series, entitled *Saint Ambrose: Hexameron, Paradise, and Cain and Abel*, trans. John J. Savage (New York: Fathers of the Church, Inc., 1961). Saint Basil's *Hexameron* is in Migne, *Patrologia Graeca* 29.3–208, and is translated by Agnes

C. Way in the Fathers of the Church series, vol. 46 (New York, 1963). A convenient summary of the biblical background is in Frank Egleston Robbins, *The Hexaemeral Literature: A Study of the Greek and Latin Commentaries on Genesis* (Chicago: University of Chicago Press, 1912).

Studies of Chaucer are so numerous that I shall make no attempt to point the way to them all. For the uninitiated I would recommend *A Companion to Chaucer Studies*, rev. ed., ed. Beryl B. Rowland (Toronto: Oxford University Press, 1979), which has a chapter on the *Parliament of Fowls* by Donald C. Baker, pp. 428–45. Undoubtedly the most substantial study of our poem is the book by J. A. W. Bennett, *The Parlement of Foules: An Interpretation* (Oxford: Clarendon Press, 1957), which is widely available and has as its frontispiece a black and white reproduction of "The Creator with His Creatures" from the *Holkham Bible Picture Book* f.2ᵛ (British Library MS. Add. 47680). One side of Chaucer's poem I have neglected is the possibility of contemporary allusion in it to perhaps a royal marriage, and for this I can do no better than recommend Haldeen Braddy, *Chaucer's Parlement of Foules in Relation to Contemporary Events*, first published in 1932, but reprinted in an expanded edition (New York: Octagon, 1969).

By way of conclusion let me list a few articles that I found especially useful. R. W. Frank, Jr., "Structure and Meaning in the *Parliament of Fowls*," *Publications of the Modern Language Association*, 71 (1956): 530–39, provided a voice of common sense at a time when it was urgently needed. Beryl B. Rowland, "Chaucer's 'Throstel Old' and Other Birds," *Mediaeval Studies*, 24 (1962): 381–84, first called my attention to the possibility of personal observation in Chaucer's description of the birds. B. F. Huppé and D. W. Robertson, Jr., in the chapter on the *Parliament* in their book, *Fruyt and Chaf* (Princeton, N.J.: Princeton University Press, 1963), were revolutionary in their philosophical and religious emphasis at the time of publication, and to some extent they are still well ahead of the rest of us in their understanding of the poem. In the collection of essays edited by A. C. Cawley, *Chaucer's Mind and Art* (Edinburgh: Oliver and Boyd, 1969), Cawley himself has written a most readable essay, "Chaucer's Valentine: *The Parlement of Foules*," pp. 125–39. John P. McCall, "The Harmony of Chaucer's *Parliament*," *Chaucer Review*, 5 (1970): 22–31, seeks to explain the "current despair" of critics in their efforts to understand the poem, arguing that the reconciliation they seek is not to be found in poetry "in this world here." David Chamberlain, "The Music of the Spheres and *The Parlement of Foules*," *Chaucer Review*, 5 (1970): 32–56, has produced one of the finest articles on this poem that we have. I am convinced he is right in suggesting a correction to the form of the roundel of the birds, which makes the *Parliament* exactly 700 lines long, and that Boethius's musical theory is important for an understanding of the poem. H. M. Leicester, Jr., "The Harmony of Chaucer's *Parlement:* A

Dissenting Voice," *Chaucer Review*, 9 (1974): 15–34, may stand as a recent example of what McCall terms the "current despair" over the poem. Members of this Hardyesque school love Chaucer, but are unable to award him full artistic merit except in those works where they can prove to their own satisfaction that he shares their pessimistic view. Hence the *Parliament*, for them, is a peculiarly difficult poem. Finally, let me recommend the entertaining essay by Emerson Brown, Jr., "Priapus and the *Parlement of Foulys*," *Studies in Philology*, 72 (1975): 258–74. In a mock serious analysis, Professor Brown seeks to read Priapus *in malo* and *in bono*, scattering much wisdom along the way. The whole is written in a spirit of high comedy which I am confident Chaucer would approve. This is perhaps the best solution to the problem of a modernist reading of Chaucer's poetry.

Among some very good articles on the *Parliament of Fowls* that have appeared since this chapter was written, let me call attention to one by Michael R. Kelley, "Antithesis as the Principle of Design in the *Parlement of Foules*," *Chaucer Review*, 14 (1979): 61–73, in which the author offers an interesting insight that may help explain why critics seem to differ so profoundly over the poem. Kelley sees a greater focus on unity of *design* in Chaucer's poem than on surface unity, and with this I must agree. See especially pp. 70–72. For an excellent discussion of the origin of the valentine tradition in relation to Chaucer, see Jack B. Oruch, "St. Valentine, Chaucer, and Spring in February," *Speculum*, 56 (1981): 534–65. The case for associating the *Parliament* with the marriage of Richard II to Anne of Bohemia has been re-opened by Larry Benson, "The Occasion of the *Parliament of Fowls*," in *The Wisdom of Poetry: Essays in Early English Literature in Honor of Morton W. Bloomfield*, ed. Larry D. Benson and Siegfried Wenzel (Kalamazoo, Mich.: Medieval Institute Publications, 1982), pp. 123–44.

CHAPTER FOUR. *The* Pearl *Poet*

Interest in these poems has always been high, but the recent record of publication is especially impressive. Two complete editions have appeared in just the last few years: *The Works of the Gawain-Poet*, ed. Charles Moorman (Jackson: University Press of Mississippi, 1977), and *The Poems of the Pearl Manuscript: Pearl, Cleanness, Patience, Sir Gawain and the Green Knight*, ed. Malcolm Andrew and Ronald Waldron (Berkeley: University of California Press, 1979). It will be noticed that scholars continue to disagree on whether to call the author the Pearl- or Gawain-poet, which means that publications on the topic should be sought under both headings. Fortunately we now have a thorough bibliography that will save much time and effort: Malcolm Andrew, *The Gawain-Poet: An Annotated Bibliography, 1839–1977* (New York: Garland, 1979). The best edition of *Saint Erkenwald* is that of Clifford Peterson (Philadelphia: University of Pennsylvania Press, 1977), and its bibliography (pp. 143–47) lists everything of direct relevance to the poem, including translations and earlier editions.

In quoting from these poems in the chapter, I have tried to retain as much of the original language as possible by simply modernizing the spelling and putting glosses in brackets. In these texts the inevitable loss from translation is especially great, and it is better to try to read the original if possible. For this purpose I would recommend using A. C. Cawley and J. J. Anderson (eds.), *Pearl, Cleanness, Patience, Sir Gawain and the Green Knight* (New York: E. P. Dutton, 1976, paper). The book is inexpensive and the extensive glosses are very reliable. If you must resort to a translation, Malcolm Andrew's *Bibliography* will point the way. Among the complete translations listed, those of John Gardner and Margaret Williams include *Saint Erkenwald*, and the latter also appears separately in translations by Loomis and Willard, and Brian Stone (see Peterson, p. 143).

To go beyond the impressionistic in study of this group one should have at his elbow *A Concordance to Five Middle English Poems*, compiled by Barnet Kottler and Alan M. Markman (Pittsburgh: University of Pittsburgh Press, 1966), and make use of standard editions such as that of E. V. Gordon for the *Pearl* (Oxford: Clarendon Press, 1953). Libraries that do not have large holdings may yet have collections of criticism such as R. J. Blanch (ed.), *Sir Gawain and Pearl: Critical Essays* (Bloomington: Indiana University Press, 1966), and John Conley (ed.), *The Middle English Pearl: Critical Essays* (Notre Dame, Ind.: University of Notre Dame Press, 1980). Of recent books on the subject I might suggest especially A. C. Spearing, *The Gawain-Poet: A Critical Study* (Cambridge University Press, 1980), Edward Wilson, *The Gawain-Poet* (Leiden; Brill, 1976), Barbara Nolan, *The Gothic Visionary Perspective* (Princeton, N.J.: Princeton University Press, 1977), chapter 5 on *Pearl*, Thorlac Turville-Petre, *The Alliterative Revival* (Cambridge: D. S. Brewer, 1977) (good for general background, with a particularly valuable discussion of *Cleanness*), and William A. Davenport, *The Art of the Gawain-Poet* (London: Athlone Press, 1978). For a good introduction to numerology (apropos of the use of the number 12 in the *Pearl*), see David L. Jeffrey (ed.), *By Things Seen: Reference and Recognition in Medieval Thought* (Ottawa: University of Ottawa Press, 1979), essay by Russell H. Peck, "Number as Cosmic Language," pp. 47–80. This volume has a variety of valuable essays on backgrounds of medieval culture. A recent article by A. C. Spearing "Purity and Danger," *Essays in Criticism*, 30 (1980): 283–310, employs insights from anthropology to illuminate the *Pearl* poet's concern with purity, especially in *Cleanness*.

CHAPTER FIVE. *Piers the Plowman as History*

The status of *Piers the Plowman* studies is perhaps unique in that although we have come a long way in our understanding of the poem during the last century, we still have a long way to go. In no other poem to my knowledge are there so many lines and even long passages where interpreters either are at a loss as to the meaning or else disagree absolutely on what the meaning is. "Langland" has accordingly been praised, blamed, or (worst of all) treated with condescension. The unspoken agreement entered into by most present-day students of the poem to treat the authorship question as settled bids fair to paralyze the efforts of the current generation of scholars to achieve a new breakthrough in understanding. For those of us who know how precarious is the position of those who argue for single authorship, the present "treaty" is no problem; but for those on the outside (and I am thinking here particularly of historians), it is an effective barrier to progress; at a time when we particularly need the help of specialists outside the field of English literature, that help is not forthcoming precisely because of the authorship assumption. A case in point is the excellent research on the background of the Peasants' Revolt by Rodney Hilton, whose book *Bond Men Made Free* (London: Temple Smith, 1973) was of great help to me in the writing of this chapter. Hilton in this and other studies shows that he is a historian who likes to investigate historical movements in relation to literature—see especially his work on Robin Hood in chapters 10–14 of *Peasants, Knights and Heretics* (Cambridge: Cambridge University Press, 1976). And yet Hilton in *Bond Men Made Free* approaches the text of *Piers the Plowman* very gingerly (pp. 159–60, 178, 211, 215, 221–23); whereas given any encouragement to read the A version by itself he might have seen there the "ideological content" of the 1381 uprising as distinct from the "traditional social criticisms by orthodox preachers" that the poem seems to offer when it is read in its revised forms (*Bond Men Made Free*, p. 21). Indeed, the comments of most recent historians are accompanied by a certain puzzlement that *Piers the Plowman* should have any appeal at all to John Ball and his ilk. The separation of A from BC is all that is required to solve that problem.

C. S. Lewis once teasingly referred (in conversation) to the *Piers Plowman* "factory," and it is true that studies of the poem have been cranked out at an alarming rate in recent years. Indeed the quantity of these publications constitutes a kind of barrier in itself. My hope is to encourage a renewed interest in the poem in relation to its social, cultural, and especially historical background. In the pages that follow I set forth a compact summary of scholarship and desiderata in order to provide an overview for interested readers who are not specialists in the field. My summary is divided in a manner designed to highlight the various areas of specialization that I think are important for future research— areas represented by the headings for each of the subsections. I apologize in advance to those in the English field if it seems to them that I have neglected their work: I am making a special effort to point the way to issues outside the area of traditional literary criticism.

Whenever the text is cited by version, passus, and line number, I am referring to the edition of Walter W. Skeat, *Piers the Plowman in Three Parallel Texts*, 2 vols. (Oxford: Clarendon Press, 1886; frequently reprinted). I use this old edition partly because it is probably still the most widely available in libraries, and also because the dust has not yet settled in the controversies surrounding the appearance of new editions in recent decades (see below, TEXTUAL CRITICISM). I would like to urge anyone not at all familiar with the poem to begin by reading the A version, preferably in a form other than Skeat's parallel text edition, where one's eye is always tempted to stray across the page to see what the other versions have done to the text you are reading. The least expensive edition of the A version is the one edited by Thomas A. Knott and David C. Fowler, *Piers the Plowman: A Critical Edition of the A-Version* (Baltimore: The Johns Hopkins Press, 1952; reprinted in paperback). There is a need for an edition of A in modernized form, but right now none is available. After completing the A version, I would recommend reading the B continuation (B XI–XX). There are numerous modernizations of the B text that would be satisfactory, but the most accessible (and inexpensive) is the paperback edition in modern prose by J. F. Goodridge, Penguin Books, 1959, revised 1966 and frequently reprinted.

For a full listing of studies and versions see A. J. Colaianne, *PIERS PLOWMAN: An Annotated Bibliography of Editions and Criticism, 1550–1977* (New York: Garland, 1978 [Garland Reference Library of the Humanities, vol. 121]). In citing references below I shall generally use the symbol # followed by the item number(s) in Colaianne. Thus the translation by Goodridge mentioned above is identified as #162 (item 162, p. 41, of Colaianne's *Bibliography*).

ALLEGORY

What is the rationale of medieval allegory? This is not easy to answer under the best of circumstances, and the use of allegory in *Piers the Plowman* is particularly hard to define. Frank's distinction (#336) between "symbol allegory" (found in Dante) and "personification allegory" (in *Piers*) has been challenged by Gradon (#351), and a new, though not infallible, approach to the subject has been confidently set forth by Aers (#181). Three critics have independently spoken of "Langland's incarnational language" (#267, 292, 419), while in different ways Howard (#390), Muscatine (#480, 482), and Delany (#301) emphasize the political or social significance of allegory. A recent intriguing study by Priscilla Martin, *Piers Plowman: The Field and the Tower* (London, Macmillan, 1979) (cf. also #397), probes very deeply indeed into the function of allegory in the poem. The handicap represented by her assumption of single authorship (which leads her to postulate a poet who wavers or is not sure of himself) is counterpoised by new and valuable insights into the operation of the allegory. Other studies of interest on the subject of allegory are: #196, 242, 250, 258–61, 271, 274, 364, 429, 431, 436, 452, 470, 478, 495, 503, 504, 527, 539, 542, 550, 559, 583, 585, 592, 595, 614, 619.

BIBLE
What is the nature and extent of biblical influence on *Piers the Plowman?* There are numerous valuable studies of particular passages that draw on the Bible or biblical exegesis, notably by Kaske, whose discussion of the speech of "Book" is an outstanding example (#414, 416; see also #309, 386). Book-length studies are those by Robertson and Huppé (#528), Fowler (#335), Bloomfield (#219), and Ames (#190). Other studies on this topic are: #1, 177, 183, 186, 197, 217, 218, 225, 310, 342, 349, 350, 378, 380, 412, 414, 422, 423, 424, 444, 448, 449, 526, 539, 561, 572, 573, 588, 589–91.

COMPUTER
The authorship question (see #1–73 and pp. 173–74) has been dealt with by David V. Erdman and Ephim G. Fogel, *Evidence for Authorship: Essays on Problems of Attribution* (Ithaca: Cornell University Press, 1966); their adjudication of the *Piers the Plowman* controversy appears on pp. 408–19. But for an objective assessment of the question we need a computer study of the type published recently by Yehuda T. Radday, *The Unity of Isaiah in the Light of Statistical Linguistics* (Hildesheim: Gerstenberg, 1973). The only thing on *Piers the Plowman* that comes close to this in objectivity is the study (done without benefit of computer) by Sister Frances A. Covella (#21), a part of which has since been published separately in *Language and Style*, 9 (1976): 3–16. Will a computer expert in the field of the humanities please come forward? See also below, TEXTUAL STUDIES.

DANTE
Since the studies of Paulo Belleza (#200, 201), J. J. Jusserand (#405), and W. J. Courthope (#285) at the turn of the century, scholars have occasionally found it intriguing to compare Dante and Langland (#263, 301, 336, 481). There is one book-length study by Cali (#249) and also a recent dissertation by Mussetter (DAI 36:8035A). Further consideration of Langland by Dante scholars would be welcome.

FRIARS
The place of the friars in *Piers the Plowman* has been touched on in passing by students of the fraternal orders (#332, 355, 530), but aside from a few other notices (#374, 528), the only substantial progress has been achieved by R. W. Frank, Jr. (#337, 340). More study, especially by his-

torians, is badly needed, in particular having to do with the role of friars in the history of Oxford University during the seventies and eighties of the fourteenth century (#30).

HISTORY

For the historical background in this chapter I am indebted to May McKisack, *The Fourteenth Century, 1307–1399* (Oxford: Clarendon Press, 1959; Oxford History of England, vol. V), W. A. Pantin, *The English Church in the Fourteenth Century* (Cambridge: Cambridge University Press, 1955), Rodney Hilton, *Bond Men Made Free: Medieval Peasant Movements and the English Rising of 1381* (London: Temple Smith, 1973), and R. B. Dobson, *The Peasants' Revolt of 1381* (London: Macmillan, 1970), whose translations of documents dealing with the revolt are used in this chapter (especially Knighton and Walsingham). The chronicle of Dieulacres Abbey is excerpted by M. V. Clarke and V. H. Galbraith in "The Deposition of Richard II," *John Rylands Library Bulletin* 14 (1930): 164–81.

A good example of the kind of problem requiring the expertise of historians is the criticism of bishops that we find in the revisions (B X 256–90; C X 255–81). In B they are criticized for presuming to correct others; in C for failing to act. No doubt these passages would become clearer if we knew what bishop(s) the author might be addressing, but in order to do this we need to resolve the question of dating the B text (#90, 117, 121, 122, 139, 335), which most scholars put no later than 1377, while as my chapter shows I am inclined to believe that it was not completed before the summer of 1383. For my identification of the reference to Archbishop Sudbury (B XV 554–56) see "A Pointed Personal Allusion in *Piers the Plowman*," *Modern Philology*, 77 (1979): 158–59, and to references there add W. L. Warren, "A Reappraisal of Simon Sudbury . . .," *Journal of Ecclesiastical History*, 10 (1959): 139–52. In looking for a bishop who might be the object of the poet's wrath in the C version, I have settled on William Courtenay as a likely possibility. See Joseph Dahmus, *William Courtenay, Archbishop of Canterbury, 1381–1396* (University Park: Pennsylvania State University Press, 1966). Courtenay was named archbishop following the assassination of Sudbury on June 14, 1381. What is the meaning of those references to "prince's letters" (C X 281, XXII 309)?

During the last decade I have appealed to historians for help with *Piers the Plowman*, once in a survey of scholarship (#334), and again at the close of a review article devoted to Kirk's book (#431). Most historians with an interest in *Piers* wrote many years ago (#251, 262, 284, 294, 405), although historical studies did continue beyond midcentury (#211, 382, 531, 543) and into the seventies (#286, 301, 438).

LATIN

Important work has been done on identification and explication of the Latin quotations in the poem (#186, 187, 448, 572). But especially intriguing is the use of Latin rules of grammar to explicate certain passages (#189, 408, 467, 548, 552, 558). See also M. N. K. Mander, "Grammatical Analogy in Langland and Alan of Lille," *Notes and Queries*, 26 (1979): 501–4. For a new translation of Alan of Lille, see *The Plaint of Nature*, translation and commentary by James J. Sheridan (Toronto: Pontifical Institute of Medieval Studies, 1980).

LAW

Use of the law and legal metaphors in *Piers* is a wide-open field. One has the feeling that the author (of BC) has seen the inside of a law office (B XI 296–99). Some good work has been done (#184, 212, 213, 320, 432, 531), but much more needs doing. Of interest to some may be the possibility that the poem itself influenced the establishment of a law of foundations (#473, 474).

LITURGY

The most thorough studies of the liturgy in the poem are dissertations by DiPasquale (#307) and Vaughan (#599). Further development of Vaughan's views may be found in "The Liturgical Perspectives of Piers Plowman, B, XVI–XIX," *Studies in Medieval and Renaissance History*, n.s. 3 (1980): 87–155. That Langland used the liturgy to any extent is doubted by Adams (#180), and affirmed by Kaske (#409). Particular cases are discussed by Alford (#184), Hill (#379), and St. Jacques (#538). The latter has also published on Langland and the liturgy in *Revue de l'Université d'Ottawa*, 37 (1967): 146–58, and in *English Studies in Canada* (Toronto), 3 (1977): 129–35. His general review of recent research and desiderata appears in *Mosaic*, 12, ii (1979): 1–10. The problem here is well expressed by Robert Longsworth, speaking of a similar issue in his study *The Cornish Ordinalia: Religion and Dramaturgy* (Cambridge, Mass.: Harvard University Press, 1967), p. 117: "To what extent, therefore, is the vernacular drama a simple product of its liturgical origins and to what extent does it seek self-consciously to be liturgically instructive?" For "vernacular drama" substitute "*Piers the Plowman*" and you have the very question that needs to be addressed.

METER, DICTION, AND STYLE

Skeat's views of the meter of *Piers* are still important, and can be found in his revision of Edwin Guest, *The History of English Rhythms* (#352); in his introduction to vol. 3 of *Bishop Percy's Folio Manuscript*, ed. J. W. Hales and F. J. Furnivall (London, 1868), pp. xi–xxxix; and in the section on meter in his introduction to the parallel-text edition of *Piers* (#71), vol. 2, pp. lviii–lxi. The fullest treatment occurs in J. P. Oakden (#651), supplemented by articles on the alliterative revival (#635, 650, 660–61), its meter (#665, 667), and the possible division of *Piers* into quatrains (#629,

636). The most perceptive student of Langland's style is John Burrow
(#243, 244). For recent studies see Eby's dissertation (#630) and the Speculum Anniversary Monograph by Robert William Sapora, Jr., *A Theory
of Middle English Alliterative Meter with Critical Applications* (Boston: Medieval Academy of America, 1977). Luckily Sapora applies his theory to
the A text only, which is available in modern editions that do not tamper
with the meter. Unfortunately the new Kane-Donaldson B text (#78)
emends extensively to "correct" the meter, thus producing a crisis for
metrical studies. Should we take the new B text to be representative of
the poet's practice, and base our analyses on it? It is no good to say that
we will exclude emended lines from consideration, because it is precisely
those lines that may be evidence of irregularity in the poet's metrical
practice. Much will depend on the confidence of scholars in the relia-
bility of the new edition of the B version. See below, TEXTUAL CRIT-
ICISM. For a good assessment of recent views on the scansion of *Piers
Plowman*, see the article by Marc Beckwith, "The Alliterative Meter of
Piers Plowman," *Comitatus*, 12 (1981): 31–39.　·

MONASTICISM

Langland's attitude toward monasticism has long been a matter of dispute. Was he a prophet of the reformation? "And then shall the abbot
of Abingdon, and all his issue forever, Have a knock of a king, and
incurable the wound" (B X 326–27). Some earlier critics tended to affirm
that he was (#71, 284), but more often the criticism has stressed Langland's orthodoxy (#345, 346), even to the extent of suggesting that he
may have been a Benedictine (#4, 219) or a Cistercian (#453). Only recently have the poet's monastic leanings been called into question (#177).
For some time it has seemed to me that the bias of the author is that of
the secular clergy at Oxford (#30). If he had to choose sides in an argument between Uthred de Boldon (monk) and William Jordan (friar),
he sided with Uthred (#456, 502, 532), but he did not hesitate to denounce
bequests (B XV 304–39) and he had a low opinion of the donation of Con-
stantine (B XV 519–29). Although he harbored a special hostility toward
the friars (B and C texts only), he did have good things to say about
monks from time to time (e.g., B V 169–81; B X 300–305).

RHETORIC

The importance of preaching in the style and content of *Piers* has frequently been recognized (#497, 498, 502, 540, 562, 628, 668). More recent
studies range from analyses of particular figures or passages (#625, 637,
642, 657, 664) to large-scale studies of the poem or related rhetorical traditions (#426, 454, 615–17). The results of rhetorical approaches are thus
far inconclusive. Perhaps a prerequisite to further rhetorical analysis is
a clearer understanding of the literal level, the historical meaning of the

text (see above, HISTORY). When we have learned to "walk from the text out into history," this could then pave the way for the rhetoricians.

SATIRE

Critics have traced the classical and medieval sources of satire in the poem (#182, 621), analyzed the nature of the satire itself (#232, 363, 433, 518, 618), and compared it with the closely related genre of Complaint (#322, 323, 430, 512). Especially interesting is the fact that some discover inner contradictions, or forces in the poem working against the satirical purpose (#245, 457, 594, 609). If critics were willing to respect the integrity of versions of the poem (at least keep A separate from BC), most of these "contradictions" would quickly evaporate (see comment on Priscilla Martin's excellent new book above under ALLEGORY). Also, few seem aware of the irony that runs through the A version: for an approach that might work well here see Edmund Reiss, "Medieval Irony," *Journal of the History of Ideas*, 42 (1981): 209–26.

SOURCES

The subject index to Colaianne's *Bibliography* (pp. 185–95) lists some three score authorities that have been suggested as sources for *Piers the Plowman*. These include Alanus de Insulis, Boethius, Chrysostom, Duns Scotus, Higden, Hilton, Joachim de Fiore, Ockham, Richard of St. Victor, and Geoffrey of Vinsauf. The poem has also been placed in the tradition of Penance (#484), the "guide" convention (#500), and the Quest (#575). Many see the poem as Augustinian (#210, 312, 324, 389, 422, 424, 444, 492, 526, 544–548), and a few see it as scholastic (#501, 516, 517). The assumption that the author was not well educated is on the decline at last, but has endured long enough to retard identification of Langland's sources. More work needs to be done by scholars able to set aside nineteenth-century assumptions about the range of the author's reading (as Bloomfield does in postulating the influence of Joachim of Fiore, #219).

TEXTUAL CRITICISM

Colaianne's *Bibliography* lists editions (#74–86) and textual studies (#87–138). But a new phase in textual criticism of *Piers the Plowman* was inaugurated with the publication in 1975 of the Kane-Donaldson edition of the B text (#78). Their inclination toward radical emendation has been matched independently by A. V. C. Schmidt in his edition of the B text (Everyman, 1978), whereas a more conservative edition of the C text has been provided by Derek Pearsall (Edward Arnold, 1978). My own concern over these developments has been expressed in a review of Kane-Donaldson (*Yearbook of English Studies*, 7 [1977]: 23–42) and of Schmidt and Pearsall (*Review*, 2 [1980]: 211–69). Most of us had hoped, I am sure, that the publication of the Athlone edition (London, 1960–) of *Piers the Plowman*

[311]

would solve the editing problem and allow us to concentrate on "the poem." The result is, alas, just the opposite. Much textual work remains to be done, especially in the application of theory to the textual problems that abound. Once more (as in the area of historical meaning), outsiders are needed to step in and adjudicate.

Above all, objective (scientific) studies are needed, and it may be that the computer (see above), important for the authorship question, can also be of service in resolving textual problems (#132).

THEOLOGY

General studies of the theological background have been provided by Hort (#389) and Erzgräber (#324, 325), and much has been done on the treatment of the sins, notably by Bloomfield (#221), but also recently by Bowers (#226). More specific studies have been done on Wrath (#222), Patience (#492, 568), Envy (#223), Sloth (#568, 607), and the righteous heathen (#263, 315, 532). General treatment of theological themes can be found in Coleman (#277), Howard (#390), and Orsten (#493), and the influence of the mystics is discussed in several studies (#314, 317, 597, 605, 623). There are dissertations tracing in the poem the problem of evil (#254), ways of knowing (#365–71), an anti-Ockhamist neoplatonic world view (#446), the ways of Providence (#469), and the image of God (#480, 520). Daniel M. Murtaugh's book, *Piers Plowman and the Image of God* (Gainesville: University Presses of Florida, 1978), grows out of his dissertation (#480). All these studies contribute in various ways to our understanding of ideas expressed in the poem. What we particularly lack in this area is exploration of the interaction of theology and history, or in other words a study of the way in which actual events (like the Peasants' Revolt) impinge on theological discussion, expecially at Oxford in the 1370s and 1380s (see WYCLIF below).

WYCLIF

Most early critics of the poem, including historians, were convinced that it expressed a Wycliffite point of view (#234, 262, 455, 576) or at least that this was the way it was read in the sixteenth century (#358, 610). There was early dissent from this view (#280), but real opposition tends to be recent (#330) and latent, the latter because most modern (literary) critics assume or deny without argument that Langland was influenced by Wyclif (see Derek Pearsall, C text [1978], V 2n and XVII 220n). We are indebted to commentators from behind the Iron Curtain for continuing to affirm the Wycliffite cast of the poem against mounting opposition in the West. Such is the view expressed in the introduction to D. M. Petrushevsky's Russian translation, *Videnie Uill'iama o Petre Pakhare* (Moscow: Akademiia Nauk SSSR, 1941), and more recently in various studies by Ladislav Cejp (#258–61). A single affirmation, by an American student, of similarities in the thought of Langland and Wycliff may be found in Palmer's dissertation (#501). Recently a new phase in the argument has been launched by Pamela Gradon, "Langland and the Ideology of Dissent," in the *Proceedings of the British Academy, London*, 66 (1980): 179–205 (Sir Israel Gollancz Memorial Lecture; London: Oxford University Press, 1982). Future analysis of the problem will have to take into account the conclusions of this important lecture.

At present the most substantial work on Wycliffite/Lollard materials is being done by Anne Hudson (Lady Margaret Hall, Oxford), whose *Selections from English Wycliffite Writings* (Cambridge: Cambridge University Press, 1978) provides a foretaste of what will soon be available in her four-volume edition of a cycle of Wycliffite sermons, of which volume I (Oxford: Clarendon Press, 1983) has appeared. Recently the New Wycliff Society was formed, and the first issue of the NWS Newsletter appeared in the fall of 1979. Here are some of the aims of the NWS as expressed in its newsletter: "What is needed is a greater sense of Wyclif's context: who was at Oxford with him? who was lecturing? what did they have to say? what was the immediate reaction to Wyclif's work?" If these questions are seriously pursued in NWS monographs, their intersection with historical study of *Piers the Plowman* will be inevitable.

RECENT STUDIES

In view of the scarcity of studies of the A text, it is indeed fortunate that we now have a (posthumous) revision of the late Father T. P. Dunning's *Piers Plowman: An Interpretation of the A Text* (2d ed.), revised and edited by T. P. Dolan (Oxford: Clarendon Press, 1980). Historians would do well to have this book at their elbow while reading the A version, and to ponder the paradox that its message invites: the poem is at once orthodox in its teaching (as Dunning shows), and revolutionary in its implications (as this chapter argues). Is it possible for a literary work to be both orthodox and revolutionary? Indeed it is.

A healthy reaction to the current dilemma of textual studies might take the form of close studies of individual manuscripts. A valuable start in this direction has been made by A. G. Rigg, in his examination of manuscript collections. See "Medieval Latin Poetic Anthologies (II)," *Mediaeval Studies*, 40 (1978): 387–407, in which Rigg carefully describes the Oxford MS Bodley 851, containing (among other things) an A text followed by a C version where A leaves off. This is a manuscript possibly made by or for John Welles, a monk of Ramsey Abbey and scholar of Gloucester College, Oxford, who spoke against Wyclif in the council at Blackfriars (1382). An edition of this manuscript (A-text portion only), together with their theories concerning it, has been published by A. G. Rigg and Charlotte Brewer, *Piers Plowman: The Z Version* (Toronto: Pontifical Institute of Medieval Studies, 1983).

Important developments are occurring in the investigation of eschatology in *Piers the Plowman*, as indicated in this chapter. The article by Robert Adams is "The Nature of Need in *Piers Plowman* XX," *Traditio* 34 (1978): 273–301. A general book on backgrounds that also discusses *Piers* in its final chapter, and has many points of contact with Adams, is *Antichrist in the Middle Ages: A Study of Medieval Apocalypticism, Art, and Literature*, by Richard K. Emmerson (Seattle: University of Washington Press, 1981). Since this volume went to press there has appeared Vincent DiMarco's *Piers Plowman: A Reference Guide* (Boston: G. K. Hall, 1982). This is a remarkably useful tool which I have reviewed in *Analytical and Enumerative Bibliography*.

Index

[315]